THE MILLENNIAL KINGDOM

THE BOOKS OF DR. WALVOORD . . .

THE
MILLENNIAL KINGDOM

by

JOHN F. WALVOORD

ZONDERVAN
PUBLISHING HOUSE OF THE ZONDERVAN CORPORATION
GRAND RAPIDS, MICHIGAN 49506

ISBN 0-310-34091-8

Printed in the United States of America

83 84 85 86 87 88 — 20 19 18 17

PREFACE

The Apostle Paul, in expressing the Biblical hope of resurrection, delivered the dramatic pronouncement: "If we have only hoped in Christ in this life we are of all men most pitiable" (1 Cor. 15:19). What is true of the hope of resurrection is true of Christian hope in general. Faith without hope is just as dead as faith without works. The study of prophecy embracing as it does the totality of God's purpose and plan as revealed in the Scriptures is therefore neither trivial nor unimportant but the vital heart of all that is included in Christian faith. Though it is to be expected that the interpretation of prophecy should encounter difficulties, it is nevertheless the supreme goal of Biblical theology to determine what is the ordered and detailed program of future events prophesied in the Word of God.

The interpretation of the prophetic Scriptures require certain essential presuppositions without which the study of prophecy becomes empty speculation. It must be assumed, first, that the Bible speaks with the same inspiration, accuracy, and authority in matters of prophecy as can be observed in its historical and theological sections. The study of prophecy is an impossibility for an intelligent liberal who denies the inspiration of the Bible for to him there can be no certain prophetic Word. Though liberals have attempted to debate subjects relating to prophetic truth, their writings are usually only learned statements of unbelief and incredulity and reveal an essential agnosticism as far as revelation of the future is concerned.

Even among those who accept the inspiration of the Bible and do not question its verbal accuracy, serious division has arisen on the proper method of interpreting prophecy. The question is whether prophecy should be interpreted literally or not. This issue was raised in the writings of the early church fathers and was brought to a head in the third century in the Alexandrian school of theology which attempted to give to all Scripture an

v

68640

allegorical or nonliteral meaning. Among the orthodox fathers Augustine countered the Alexandrian heresy by suggesting a two-fold principle of interpretation of Scripture, namely, a literal interpretation of Scripture as a whole, but a spiritual or nonliteral interpretation of prophetic Scripture. With this presupposition he was able to deny a future millennium, and he became the principal source of amillennialism as it is taught today. The viewpoint of Augustine that most prophecy cannot be interpreted literally was unfortunately accepted without much debate by the Roman Catholic Church and was largely embraced by the Protestant Reformers. Though there was tenacious retention of such doctrines as eternal punishment for the wicked and eternal heaven for the blessed and reaffirmation of the doctrine of final judgment, the more detailed scheme of prophecy fell by the wayside.

The premillennial system of interpretation of Scripture interprets prophecy in the same way as other Scripture. It denies the Augustinian separation of prophecy from other Scripture as if it required a separate principle of interpretation. Though recognizing that some Scriptures are contextually indicated as containing figures of speech and not intended for literal interpretation, premillennial interpretation finds no need for spiritualizing prophecy any more than any other portion of Scripture. It is this literal interpretation of Scripture which is the crux of the whole argument between the amillenarian who denies a future millennial reign of Christ and the premillenarian who affirms it.

The ultimate dissolution of the contention between amillenarians and premillenarians cannot be achieved simply in the realm of hermeneutics or debate on how we should interpret the Scriptures. It rather depends on whether it is possible under either scheme to erect a system of Biblical interpretation which does justice to the entire Scripture, and especially its prophetic portions. On this subject scholars to this day have disagreed though it is usually admitted that the literal interpretation of prophecy leads inevitably to a premillennial system which affirms a future millennial reign of Christ on earth.

There is a growing consciousness within the church that premillennialism is more than a dispute on the twentieth chapter of Revelation and that instead it involves a system of interpretation of the entire Scripture from Genesis to Revelation. The doctrine of a future millennium on earth affects the interpretation of the Abrahamic covenant with its promise to Israel of inheriting the land promised to Abraham their forefather. It is by careful distinction of the promises made to Abraham, the promises made to Abraham's physical seed, and the promises made to Abraham's spiritual seed as contained in both the Old and New Testaments, that a full premillennial explanation is given of the Abrahamic covenant.

Even more specific in its relation to premillennialism is God's covenant with David in which David is promised that his descendants would rule over the house of Israel forever. This covenant is reiterated several times in the Old Testament and is specifically repeated to Mary in connection with the birth of Christ. If interpreted literally it leads inevitably to the doctrine of a future reign of Christ on earth to fulfill these promises.

Premillennialism is also related to the literal fulfillment of the new covenant revealed in Jeremiah and Ezekiel. This covenant pictures a period in human history when God would replace the Mosaic covenant with a new covenant which He would write upon their hearts. It would be fulfilled in the period when Israel would no longer need to teach every man his neighbor and proclaim the truth of Jehovah, for as the prophet wrote: "They shall all know me, from the least of them unto the greatest of them, saith Jehovah." (Jer. 31:34). The promises to Abraham, the promises to David, the promises to Israel of future possession of the land, and the promises to Jeremiah that Israel would continue as long as the sun and moon endure (Jer. 31:35-36) combine to provide a symphony of prophetic truth which is the grand prelude to the millennial reign of Christ.

To the Old Testament picture the New Testament adds its continuing revelation of future things. Of prime importance to the premillennial interpretation of Scripture is the distinction provided in the New Testament between God's present purpose for the church and His purpose for the nation Israel. Individuals who are descendants of Jacob in this present age have equal privilege with Gentiles in putting their trust in Christ and forming the body of Christ the church. The New Testament as well as the Old, however, makes clear that the nation Israel as such has its promises fulfilled ultimately in the future reign of Christ over them. At that time Israel will be His people and God will be their God. The New Testament makes plain according to the premillennial interpretation that God's present purpose is not the fulfillment of the prophecies of the Old Testament of the kingdom reign on earth during which Satan will be bound and all the nations will come to worship at the feet of the King of kings. The present age, according to premillennial interpretation, is the fulfillment of God's plan and purpose, revealed in the New Testament, to call out a people from Jew and Gentile alike to form a new body of saints. It is only when this purpose is completed that God can bring to pass the tragic judgments which precede the millennial reign of Christ and inaugurate the righteousness and peace which characterize the millennial kingdom.

The grand finale of prophecy is the book of Revelation, compared by Lewis Sperry Chafer to a union station in which all lines of prophecy have their destination. Here the church is addressed in the opening chapters. Here is gathered the consummation of the times of the Gentiles. Here is fulfilled the tribulation which is promised Israel as a purging preparation for their entrance into the millennium. The climax of the book of Revelation is the glorious second coming of Christ in which His enemies are destroyed; the millennial kingdom is set up, and Satan is bound. As the book of Revelation reaches its denouement in the closing chapter, the eternal state with its prophetic picture of New Jerusalem is revealed, reflecting the eternal glory of Christ. The consummation of Scripture as well as the consummation of God's divine plan is the revelation of Jesus Christ. To these doctrines premillennial interpretation gives its accent, its detail, and its grand scheme of moving events.

Whether one accepts premillennial interpretation or not, it

behooves any intelligent student of Scripture to make some effort to understand what the premillennial interpretation of Scripture really is and to weigh the supreme theological question as to whether the present age is the millennium or whether Scripture demands a future fulfillment of the hundreds of prophecies that pertain to the kingdom on earth. This is the task attempted in this volume.

Though some attention is given to postmillennialism, and an extended treatment of amillennialism is provided, the major purpose of the discussion is to present the positive arguments for the premillennial interpretation of Scripture. The author does not presume that all will agree, but it is his hope that to some extent he has captured the testimony of Scripture on this central theme of the millennial reign of Christ with its important bearing on our understanding and interpretation of the present task of the church.

A word of appreciation is due *Bibliotheca Sacra* for gracious permission to reproduce in revised form much of the material appearing in the series of articles on millennial theology. Throughout the volume the American Standard Version of 1901 is used except as otherwise indicated.

This study is commended to God and to students of the Word in the hope that its pages will extend the understanding of the prophetic Scriptures.

ACKNOWLEDGMENTS

The author gratefully acknowledges the kindness of authors and publishers in giving permission to reproduce material in this volume as follows:

The Abingdon Press—*Contemporary Religious Thought,* by Thomas S. Kepler.

Allis, Oswald T.—*Prophecy and the Church,* by Oswald T. Allis.

Baker Book House—*Millennial Studies,* by G. L. Murray.

Broadman Press—*A Grammar of the Greek New Testament,* by A. T. Robertson; *Word Pictures in the New Testament,* by A. T. Robertson.

Christian Education Press—*I Believe,* by Nevin C. Harner.

Dallas Theological Seminary—*Systematic Theology,* by Lewis Sperry Chafer.

Dunham Publishing Company—*Things to Come,* by J. Dwight Pentecost.

William B. Eerdmans Publishing Company—*The Second Coming of Christ,* by Louis Berkhof; *Systematic Theology,* by Louis Berkhof; *The Basis of Millennial Faith,* by F. E. Hamilton; *Millennium in the Church,* by D. H. Kromminga; *Crucial Questions about the Kingdom of God,* by George E. Ladd; *The International Standard Bible Encyclopaedia,* 1939, edited by James Orr; *The Seed of Abraham,* by Albertus Pieters.

Emeth Publications, Inc.—*God Remembers,* by Charles L. Feinberg.

Hospers, Gerrit H.—*The Principle of Spiritualization in Hermeneutics,* by Gerrit H. Hospers.

The Judson Press—*Systematic Theology,* by A. H. Strong.

Landis, Ira D.—*The Faith of Our Fathers on Eschatology,* by Ira D. Landis.

Moody Press—*The Book of Revelation,* by William R. Newell.

Thomas Nelson and Sons—American Standard Version of the Holy Bible. Used by permission of the copyright owners, The National Council of the Churches of Christ in the U.S.A.

Oxford University Press—*Biblical Doctrines,* by B. B. Warfield.

Presbyterian and Reformed Publishing Company—*The Millennium,* by Loraine Boettner.

Fleming H. Revell Company—*Daniel and the Latter Days,* by Robert Culver; *Christian Workers' Commentary,* by James M. Gray.

Charles Scribner's Sons—*Personal Religion,* by Douglas C. MacIntosh.

TABLE OF CONTENTS

THE MILLENNIAL KINGDOM

CHAPTER I

CONTEMPORARY MILLENNIALISM

The Biblical teaching on the subject of the millennium is an important part of the study of prophecy. It has been an area of controversy ever since the third century. In the last two hundred years it has especially been studied. Today more than ever questions are being raised concerning what the Bible teaches about a millennium on earth. Are we in the millennium now? Or, can we expect such an age in the future? The answer to these questions forms the burden of the inquiry that is here being undertaken.

The events of the last quarter of a century or more have had a tremendous impact on the thinking of the scholarly world. In philosophy there has been a trend toward realism and increasing interest in ultimate values and ethics. In science the moral significance of scientific knowledge and the growing realization that physical science is a part of world life and meaning have emerged. In theology there has been what amounts to a similar revolution, particularly in the study of prophecy.

One of the significant facts of the theology of the last century is its emphasis on eschatological or prophetic questions. Even the works of liberal theologians frequently discuss the Christian outlook. Millar Burrows, for instance, in his work, *An Outline of Biblical Theology*, rightly gives a long chapter to the subject, and current liberal theological anthologies such as Thomas Kepler's *Contemporary Thinking about Jesus* and his *Contemporary Religious Thought* both have considerable sections on eschatology from recent writings of liberal theological scholars.

For the most part, writing in eschatology among the liberals is limited to the search for ultimate ethical values rather than a statement of a prophetic program. Illustrating this point of view is the volume *Jesus and His Coming* by J. A. T. Robinson appearing in 1957 which attempts to show that the prophecies

3

of the second coming of Christ were actually fulfilled in connection with His first coming and that Jesus Himself never predicted a literal second coming. The view of the early church, including that expressed by Paul and the apostles in the Scriptures themselves, according to liberal interpretation is an error.

Neo-orthodox theologians have not contributed significantly to eschatology though they have not been entirely silent. Emil Brunner's *Eternal Hope* is a sample of this kind of literature. Generally speaking, the subject of eschatology is being re-examined in all branches of theology. Ray C. Petry, for instance, has contributed a large work on *Christian Eschatology and Social Thought.* John Bright has written a prize-winning volume, *The Kingdom of God,* related to the eschatological field. H. H. Rowley has written *The Relevance of the Apocalyptic,* and Paul A. Minear has published *Christian Hope and the Second Coming.* Alongside of these writings from those who are not premillenarian and who do not accept the inspiration of Scripture are a host of competent and scholarly works written by thorough students of the prophetic Word of which the most comprehensive recent volume is *Things to Come* by J. Dwight Pentecost. The twentieth century may well go down in history as the century which gave birth to neo-orthodoxy on the one hand and renewed study of eschatology on the other.

I. Definition of the Millennium

The word *millennium* means *thousand years.* While the word itself never occurs in the Bible, it refers to the thousand years mentioned six times in Revelation 20. By both Jews and Christians this period of one thousand years is often identified with the many promises of the Old Testament of a coming kingdom of righteousness and peace on the earth in which the Jews would be leaders and in which all the nations would have great blessing both spiritual and economic. A study of the millennium involves an understanding of this large volume of prophetic Scriptures. Since the third century there has been an increasing difference of opinion concerning the practical meaning of this subject, which has resolved into the question of whether we can take all these passages about this coming kingdom literally. Some take it we are in the millennium now; others expect it to come to pass in the future before Christ comes; still others expect that Christ must return first before this kingdom can come. These views are respectively called amillennialism, postmillennialism, and premillennialism. It is necessary to have these modern viewpoints on the millennium clearly in mind before one can understand the meaning of arguments for and against each view.

Premillennialism. Practically all students of the early church agree that premillennialism, or, as it is also called, chiliasm, was the view held by many in the apostolic age. It is the oldest of the various millennial views. Chiliasm, from the Greek work *chilias* meaning *one thousand,* is the teaching that Christ will reign on earth for one thousand years following His second advent. Premillennialism as a term derives its meaning from the belief that the second coming of Christ will be before this millennium and therefore premillennial. Both terms refer to the same doctrine.

As a system of doctrine premillennialism is necessarily more literal in its interpretation of prophecy than the other viewpoints. It views the end of the present age as sudden and catastrophic, with great judgment upon the wicked and the rescue of the righteous. It is characteristic of premillennialism both ancient and modern to distinguish the dealings of God with Israel and with the church. As Van Oosterzee (1817-1882), a Dutch theologian who was premillennial, brings out, premillennialism distinguishes the church which Christ founded as separate from the saints of the Old Testament: "It is, however, more exact, not to fix the date of the beginning of the *Christian* Church before the appearing of the historical Christ. . . . From the outpouring of the Spirit on the first Christian Pentecost the Church was really brought to life."[1]

Premillennialism generally holds to a revival of the Jewish nation and their repossession of their ancient land when Christ returns. Satan will be bound (Rev. 20:2) and a theocratic kingdom of righteousness, peace, and tranquillity will ensue. The

---

[1]Jan Jacob Van Oosterzee, *Christian Dogmatics* (New York: Charles Scribner's Sons), II, 701.

righteous are raised from the dead before the millennium and participate in its blessings. The wicked dead are not raised until after the millennium. The eternal state will follow the judgment of the wicked. Premillennialism is obviously a viewpoint quite removed from either amillennialism or postmillennialism. It attempts to find a literal fulfillment for the prophecies in the Old and New Testament concerning a righteous kingdom of God on earth. Premillennialism assumes the authority and accuracy of the Scriptures and the hermeneutical principle of a literal interpretation wherever this is possible.

Amillennialism. This, the most popular modern view of the millennium, is traced by its own adherents as far back as Augustine and Origen (third and fourth centuries), and it subsequent rise continued in the Roman Catholic Church.[2] Its most general character is that of denial of a *literal* reign of Christ upon the earth. Satan is conceived as bound at the first coming of Christ. The present age between the first and second comings is the fulfillment of the millennium. Its adherents are divided on whether the millennium is being fulfilled now on the earth (Augustine) or whether it is being fulfilled by the saints in heaven (Kliefoth). It may be summed up in the idea that there will be no more millennium than there is now, and that the eternal state immediately follows the second coming of Christ. As they freely recognize that their concept of the millennium is quite foreign to the premillennial view they have been given the title *amillennial* by most writers.

It should be observed that two radically different concepts are embraced in the two major divisions of amillennialism. If the millennium is on earth now, and the kingdom prophecies being fulfilled, this determines the meaning of a large volume of Scripture and leads to important conclusions relative to the present age. If the millennium is to be fulfilled only in heaven in a

---

[2]Cf. the summary by Oswald T. Allis of amillennialism, *Prophecy and the Church*, pp. 2-6 (Philadelphia: The Presbyterian and Reformed Publishing Co., 1945). The subtitle of his book is "An examination of the claim of dispensationalists that the Christian Church is a mystery parenthesis which interrupts the fulfillment to Israel of the kingdom prophecies of the Old Testament."

very spiritualized sense, then these same prophecies do not apply to us at all, but only to the saints in glory. There is in fact very little unity between these views. The only points of agreement are that a millennium after the second advent of Christ is denied and that the prophecies about the millennium should be spiritualized and not taken literally. Aside from this agreement, the major divisions of amillennialism are at opposite poles.

Most amillenarians consider the second advent of Christ a distinct future event just as do the premillenarians. Some modern amillenarians, however, spiritualize not only the millennium but also the second advent. This modern view of the Lord's return identifies the coming of Christ as a perpetual advance of Christ in the church that includes many particular events.

William Newton Clarke, for instance, held that the promises of the second coming are fulfilled by "his spiritual presence with his people," which is introduced by the coming of the Holy Spirit at Pentecost, accompanied by the overthrow of Jerusalem, and ultimately fulfilled by continual spiritual advance in the church.[3] In other words, it is not an event, but it includes all the events of the Christian era which are the work of Christ. Such a viewpoint not only fails to provide for all the attendant events related to the second coming of Christ but eliminates the millennium completely. Essentially it is amillennial, though not the historic type. This viewpoint—held by many liberals of our day--contributes practically nothing to the millennial issue.

Postmillennialism. Originating in the writings of Daniel Whitby (1638-1726), a Unitarian controversialist of England, postmillennialism holds that the present age will end with a period of great spiritual blessing corresponding to the millennial promises accomplished through preaching the gospel. The whole world will be Christianized and brought to submission to the gospel *before* the return of Christ. The name is derived from the fact that in this theory Christ returns *after* the millennium (hence, *post* millennium). A great many variations exist which are comprehended in this general title, and some forms of amillennialism

---

[3]William N. Clarke, *An Outline of Christian Theology*, fifth edition, pp. 443-46.

are closely akin to postmillennialism. Kromminga traces post-millennialism to the middle ages, citing Joachim (d. 1226) of Floris, celebrated as an interpreter of the book of Revelation.[4] Augustine (354-430) also believed in the coming of Christ after the millennium and could for this reason be classified as post-millennial. His view of the millennium, however, was so removed from a literal kingdom on earth that it is virtually a denial of it, and he is better considered as an amillennialist.

In general the limits of postmillennialism include those who find a rather literal fulfillment of Old Testament promises of a kingdom on earth of righteousness and peace as illustrated in Charles Hodge, as well as those who are imbued with a general spirit of optimism regarding the ultimate success of Christianity in the world. While some of Whitby's writings were publicly burned as heresy, particularly his views on the Trinity, many conservative theologians rapidly embraced and propagated his viewpoint on the millennium. Postmillennialism today is not commonly held, and the controversy that continues is principally between amillennialism and premillennialism.

II. The Modern Trend Toward Amillennialism

The decline of postmillennialism. Before the first World War, the combined onslaught of higher criticism and modern humanism had wrought havoc in the theological world. Liberals were outdoing each other in the race to see who could disbelieve the most. Postmillennialism was at its peak and homilies poured out glowing accounts of the triumphant progress of Christianity, recognition of the universal brotherhood among men, and the power of the church in world affairs. The first World War brought these trends to an abrupt halt. After all, man was not adequate within himself as humanism had contended, and the day of a golden age in which Christian principles should dominate the world after the postmillennial pattern seemed indefinitely postponed. It was time for an inventory to discover what real assets remained.

After the shock of World War I, two trends became evident.

[4]D. H. Kromminga, *Millennium in the Church* (Grand Rapids: Wm. B. Eerdmans Publishing Co., 1945). p. 20.

The liberals began a movement back to the Bible. A comparison of writings of liberal theologians in the twenty years before the World War and the twenty years after it makes this plain enough.[5] In eschatology the trend away from postmillennialism became almost a rout with the advent of World War II. It was deemed clear to the scholarly theological world that any earthly millennium of righteousness was indefinitely postponed, and there were grave doubts if any progress whatever had been achieved.

Douglas Clyde MacIntosh of Yale wrote during World War II, "The recent crisis is not the first in the life of the Church, but it is undoubtedly one of the worst, perhaps the very worst in all Protestant history. . . . On the whole, evangelical Christianity has been an ebbing tide in this twentieth century."[6] With a realistic appraisal of the decline of the church in its power and influence, it was comparatively easy to retire behind the less ambitious program of amillennialism which claimed little for the present and does not attempt to solve the future course of human history.

The lines of millennial discussion were defined somewhat as for and against an earthly millennium. This seemed to be the significance of the trend of world events. Historic amillennialism was against the idea of a literal kingdom of Christ on earth and all signs seemed to point to no progress in this direction. The ground was provided for abandonment of postmillennial optimism and leaving to heavenly realms any idealistic system of peace and righteousness.

The resurgence of amillennialism. In the last two decades there has been an evident resurgence in amillennialism. The converts have come from many sources. Those who had become skeptical about a millennium on earth to be achieved through Christian influence and the church found it a natural conclusion that their error lay in taking too seriously the glowing prophecies of the Old Testament of a kingdom of righteousness and peace on earth. There were no signs of such an era on the horizon, and both

---

[5] A book like *An Outline of Biblical Theology* by the liberal scholar Millar Burrows of Yale University, with 10,000 Scripture citations, would never have seen the light of day under the liberalism of thirty years ago.
[6] Douglas C. MacIntosh, *Personal Religion* (New York: Charles Scribner's Sons, 1942) pp. 232, 234.

Christians and non-Christians were talking darkly of the end of civilization and a third and final world war in which man would destroy himself. It seemed in the spirit of the times to conclude that there would be no millennium on earth and that freedom from sin and war was to be found only in heaven. While the downward course of the modern world was no embarrassment to premillenarians who had been preaching about such a trend for years, the church as a whole was unwilling to admit any accuracy in the premillennial view. Instead the tendency was to return to the conservatism of the Reformation which made no pretense of being specific about the millennium.

Three main streams of theology have converged in our day to make amillennialism without question the majority view of the church. First, the old conservatism which had abandoned the hope of Daniel Whitby for a millennium on earth found refuge in the ancient creeds, which for the most part say nothing about the millennium. Their position was. that the real issue was faith in the Bible and in the person and work of Christ. Why argue about prophecy when the very foundations are threatened? While there is some force to this argument, Christianity will not survive on an undefined loyalty to Scripture. The hope of future events is inseparable from Christian faith and any vagueness weakens and limits the whole perspective.

A second influence in the resurgence of amillennialism is the growth in power of the Roman Catholic Church. Since the day of Augustine this body has been almost entirely amillennial. Their very structure of church government and their program of works depend on use of the Old Testament promises about the coming kingdom as fulfilled in the church. In a day when liberalism has weakened Protestantism, the solid influence of tradition and continuity of the Roman Church has had a profound appeal. Nothing could be more antithetical than the Roman Church and premillennialism, and its influence is definitely amillennial.

A third influence in the present power of amillennialism is found in liberal Protestant theology. With low views of the inspiration of Scripture and with no concern for any consistent interpretation of Scripture, the tendency toward skepticism in eschatology is marked. If postmillennialism could no longer be held, why not be skeptical of any millennium at all? Without availing themselves of historical arguments except when convenient to their purpose, liberals have united in almost one voice in their denunciation of premillennialism and the doctrine of an earthly reign of Christ.

Trend toward amillennialism in liberal theology. In the liberal theological tendency toward amillennialism there appears an element which has not been evaluated properly in current arguments on the millennial issue. It is evident that premillennialism constitutes a large segment of conservative Christianity of our day. It was soon discovered by liberal theologians that it was a most effective device in combatting the old conservatism in theology to attack premillennialism. Any attack or discrediting of premillennialism redounded to the benefit of liberal theology without exposing them to embarrassing questions concerning their own belief in the Scriptures. Premillennialists could be attacked with impunity. Liberals who did so could pose as defenders of the Reformed faith, as those seeking the purity and unity of the church, as those who wanted to reclaim the Bible from a false and misleading form of interpretation. Liberals who could not stand examination on any essential of conservative Christian theology were found in the strange role of champions of Reformed theology because they denounced premillennialism. No doubt some of them were sincere in their error, but their zeal betrayed the hidden and sometimes unconscious motive.

Growing attack on premillennialism. In the last decade a further tendency to exploit this argument has appeared in the device to divide premillennialists into the old school of interpretation which often contented itself with a theology which was premillennial only in its eschatology, and the more recent type which makes premillennialism a system of theology. Conceding that premillennialism was ancient and to that extent honored, they denounced what they termed *dispensationalism* as a new and modern error.[7] Scholars who had no interest whatever in premillennialism wrote on fine points of dispute among premillen-

---

[7]Cf. Allis, *op. cit.*

nialists as if the existence of unsolved problems and disagreements proved beyond doubt that the principles on which the interpretation was based were hopelessly involved. Conservative scholars were influenced into playing right into the hands of the desire of liberals to divide the remaining strength of conservative theology.

One of the curious aspects of the current literature on the millennial issue is the singling out of the *Scofield Reference Bible* for attack. This edition of the Bible which has had unprecedented circulation has popularized premillennial teachings and provided ready helps of interpretation. It has probably done more to extend premillennialism in the last half century than any other volume. This accounts for the many attempts to discredit this work. The recent book of Oswald T. Allis, *Prophecy and the Church,* a product of a lifelong study and a special year of research, directs most of its attack to refuting the Scofield Bible. *Millennial Studies* by George L. Murray, published in 1948, the result of twelve years of study on the millennial problem, mentions the Scofield Bible more than any other work. The refutation of the Scofield Bible is curious because each succeeding writer apparently believes his predecessors have not succeeded in disposing of this work once for all. This belief apparently is well founded for the Scofield Bible continues to be issued year after year in greater numbers than any of its refuters.

The current millennial debate is singular for its negative quality. While premillennialism has had poor handling by many of its own adherents, it has at least aimed at being constructive, offering a definite system of interpretation and providing a positive voice. While amillennialism has attracted many scholars and has produced many works on the millennial issue in the last two decades, for the most part their approach has been one of ridicule and attack on premillennialism rather than an ordered presentation of their own system of beliefs. This direction of published studies has been born of the nature of the amillennial theory—a denial of the millennium. Amillennialists have also rightly argued that if they successfully disposed of their opponents who were premillennial they would have no effective opposition to their own viewpoint. The negative attitude was also one of necessity, as amillennialists are by no means agreed on the essentials of their own system of eschatology and millenarianism.

One of the most unfortunate and harmful aspects of the trend toward amillennialism is the desperation evidenced in the nature of their attempts to discredit other viewpoints. In particular, in their refutation of premillennialism every aberration which has been held by any premillenarian has been upheld as typical of the movement. Even honored scholars such as Allis and Kromminga are guilty in numerous instances of flagrant *ad hominem* argument. Their obvious purpose is to prove that dispensational premillennialism has a tendency to heresy in all fields of theology. Kromminga, though a premillenarian, in his first reference to the Scofield Bible, attempts to prove that Scofield was guilty of "heretical aberration" in the doctrine of the Trinity. His proof for this is a rather obscure reference to Israel as the wife of Jehovah and the church as the wife of Christ.[8]

Allis tries to link premillennialism with Russellism because both believe the Abrahamic covenant is unconditional.[9] Again, Allis in discussing the offer of the kingdom by Christ asserts that the issue is that if Christ offered the Jews a millennial kingdom He was by so much saying that the cross was unnecessary. He says the argument "amounts to this, Could men have been saved without the Cross?"[10] As Allis would be the first to admit, no group of millennialists have been more faithful in preaching the necessity of the cross than premillennialists, and to say that their view requires declaring the cross unnecessary is a conclusion which no premillenarian would reach. Allis has forgotten that he is a Calvinist and that God can make a bona fide offer of something which in His sovereignty and foreknowledge He knows will not and cannot eventuate—a principle which has many illustrations in the Bible, as, for instance, the dealings of God with Moses (Ex. 32:9-14; Num. 14:11-20). This unfortunate tendency to raise

---

[8]Kromminga, *op. cit.*, pp. 23-24.
[9]Allis, *op. cit.*, p. 48.
[10]*Ibid.*, p. 75.

false issues in the attack on premillennialism only confuses the issue, and makes partisans of those who should be in Christian fellowship however they may differ in the millennial doctrine. While objectivity has been lacking in all viewpoints of the millennium, on the scholarly level amillennialism has probably sinned the most.

While not directly related to millennial literature, there has been a significant current trend in institutions of learning in America respecting the doctrine of the millennium. In theological institutions the common viewpoint is that of amillennialism. The most notable change has been in liberal seminaries, which were predominantly postmillennial before World War I. While there is still much talk of a "better world" and "bringing in the Kingdom," it is quite divorced from millennial discussions. Most theological seminaries view the millennium as an unfruitful area for study and tend to suspend judgment on any detailed exegesis of related Scriptural passages.

A significant exception and contrast to the trend toward amillennialism is found in Bible institutes which are definitely more Biblical in their curriculum than the great majority of theological seminaries. The Bible institute movement in America has not only been predominantly premillennial from the start, but there has been no noticeable trend away from this position. The way in which premillennialism is held by Bible institutes is also significant. The viewpoint is in part unconscious, that is, their curriculum is not designed to propagate premillennialism in itself. The acceptance of premillennialism is rather as a means of interpreting the entire Bible and acquainting students with a consistent form of interpretation. The thousands of institute graduates being poured forth each year constitute one of the bright spots for premillennialism in the current trend. On a popular level Bible institutes or related organizations publish a large amount of literature which follows the premillennial interpretation of Scripture.

Taken as a whole, the current trend in millennial literature indicates a mounting attack on premillennialists by those who hold the amillennial position, a forsaking of postmillennialism as outmoded, and an increasingly significant use of the millennial issue by liberals to divide and conquer those remaining in conservative theological circles. The qualities of the respective arguments remain for detailed study.

III. THE IMPORTANCE OF MILLENNIAL DOCTRINE

The question has been raised whether the discussion of the millennial doctrine is in itself important and worthy of the consideration of the scholarly world. There remains today a tendency to dismiss the whole subject as belonging to another age and as being foreign to intellectual studies of our day. D. C. MacIntosh refers to premillennialism as obsolete: "the whole obsolete idea of a literal, visible return of Jesus to this earth."[11] On the other hand, the continued production of books on the subject points to a growing realization that the issue is more important than appears on the surface. If premillennialism is only a dispute about what will happen in a future age which is quite removed from present issues, that is one thing. If, however, premillennialism is a system of interpretation which involves the meaning and significance of the entire Bible, defines the meaning and course of the present age, determines the present purpose of God, and gives both material and method to theology, that is something else. It is the growing realization that premillennialism is more than a dispute about Revelation 20 that has precipitated the extended arguments on the issue in our day. For the first time it seems to be commonly recognized that premillennial theology has become a *system* of theology, not an alternate view of eschatology which is unrelated to theology as a whole.

It has already been noted that premillennialism is a stubborn obstacle to liberal theology as well as being utterly opposed to the principles governing Roman Catholic Theology. The reason for this is that premillennialism uses a literal interpretation of the prophetic Word which is the backbone of comprehensive Bible study. Premillennialism not only takes the Bible as authoritative in opposition to liberalism, but believes that an ordinary believer

---

[11]MacIntosh, *op. cit.*, p. 203.

can understand the main import of the Scriptures including the prophetic Word. This is contrary to the Roman conception. The present Bible-study movement in this country as illustrated in Bible and prophetic conferences and the Bible institutes is almost entirely premillennial in its background. In fact, it is considered a common charge against premillenarians that they are guilty of bibliolatry or worship of the Bible. Opposition to premillennialism particularly by the liberals is largely against regarding the Bible as the only final authority. MacIntosh states flatly that "the explanation" for "the long-expected and theoretically hoped-for second coming of Christ . . . is to be found in the doctrine of the miraculous inspiration and consequent literal infallibility of the Bible."[12] This to him is "incredible."[13] It is inevitable that defense of premillennialism becomes a defense of the Bible itself and its sole authority in speaking of future events and programs of God.

The millennial doctrine determines also large areas of Biblical interpretation which are not in themselves prophetic in character. The distinctions in dispensational dealings of God, the contrasts between the Mosaic period, the Abrahamic promises, the present age of grace, and the unfulfilled prophecies about the coming kingdom are of major importance in Biblical interpretation and systematic theology. Many of these issues are largely determined by the millennial doctrine. Distinctions in particular which pertain to the character of the present age in its purpose and program are involved. If the present purpose of God is to bring in a millennium through Christian influence and preaching, that is one thing; if there is no millenium at all, that is another; if the millennium is yet to be fulfilled on the earth through the second coming of Christ, that is still another. The concept of the present age is therefore vitally affected by the doctrine of the millennium. It is not too much to say that millennialism is a determining factor in Biblical interpretation of comparable importance to the doctrines of verbal inspiration, the deity of Christ, substitutionary atonement, and bodily resurrection. These doctrines are held by both premillenarians and conservative amillenarians. It is of course

---

[12]*Ibid.*, pp. 192-93.
[13]*Ibid.*, p. 193.

true that to an individual a denial of the deity of Christ is more momentous and far-reaching than denial of premillennialism, but, as far as a system of interpretation is concerned, both are vital. The growing recognition of the importance of the millennial doctrine is one of the principal causes of resurgence of interest in this field.

IV. CONCLUSION

The modern viewpoint on the millennium presents a distinct theological challenge. With the decline of postmillennialism, the lines are drawn between premillennialism and amillennialism. The question is whether there will be a literal reign of Christ on the earth following His second advent, as the premillenarians believe, or whether the prophecies of the millennium are being fulfilled now, as the amillenarians hold. It is to this latter question that the discussion will be directed. Is the church on earth in the present age in the millennial kingdom of which the Scriptures speak? Is Augustine essentially right that the present interadvent period between the first and second comings of Christ will fulfill all the millennial promises? Are the more modern amillenarians right who reject the Augustinian thesis and refer these millennial pictures to heaven itself? Does amillennialism have the answer to the millennial question? The answers to these and related questions will be the object of this study.

CHAPTER II

THE ANSWER OF POSTMILLENNIALISM

While postmillennialism is the most recent of millennial theories, a number of reasons prompt the study of this aspect of millenarianism before other viewpoints. The millennial issue as a whole tends to become complicated and burdened with detail until the principles are often forgotten. The postmillennial view because of its relative simplicity affords a typical study in millennialism which throws significant light on the problems presented by other views. The beginnings, rise, and present decline of postmillennialism afford a test case for millennial doctrine. The Cartesian principle of solving the more simple problems first justifies the present order of consideration.

One of the outstanding facts about postmillennialism is that it was, until the present generation, one of the most important and influential millennial theories. It was probably the dominant Protestant eschatology of the nineteenth century and was embraced by Unitarian, Arminian, and Calvinist alike. It influenced as well the prevailing concept of amillennialism during this period. In the twentieth century the course of history, progress in Biblical studies, and the changing attitude of philosophy arrested its progress and brought about its apparent discard by all schools of theology. Postmillennialism is not a current issue in millenarianism, but the principles that brought it into being and resulted in its downfall are highly significant.

As previously defined, postmillennialism is the doctrinal belief that Christ will return after (*post*) the millennium and usher in the eternal state with the final judgment of men and angels. It is opposed to premillennialism, which holds that Christ will return before (*pre*) the millennium. Many variations exist within postmillennialism in the concept of the nature of the second advent of Christ and of the nature of the millennium itself. Postmillennialism sometimes almost merges with amillennialism, and yet in other forms is quite distinct. James Snowden, for instance, consistently classifies amillenarians as included in postmillennialism.

I. THE RISE OF POSTMILLENNIALISM

Postmillennialism not apostolic. While Daniel Whitby (1638-1725) is commonly given the credit for the rise of postmillennialism as a division of millenarianism, the roots which brought his theory to life extend back to the early centuries of the church. All seem to agree that postmillennialism is quite foreign to the apostolic church. There is no trace of anything in the church which could be classified as postmillennialism in the first two or three centuries. The millenarianism of the early church was premillennial, that is, it expected the return of Christ before a millennium on earth.

Rise of figurative interpretation. The first notable denial of this premillennial viewpoint was made by Origen (185-253). His allegorical method of interpretation resulted in the destruction of not only the millennial doctrine but most other important aspects of Christian belief including the doctrine of resurrection. Origen, however, was clearly not a postmillenarian, and his contribution is his method of allegorical and figurative interpretation which became later a component of postmillennialism.

Rise of millennial interadvent theory. The eschatology of Augustine was an important milestone in the history of millennialism. He held that the age between the first and second advents is the millennium of which the Scriptures speak and that the second advent would occur at the end of the millennium. This is definitely a postmillennial viewpoint as it places the second advent *after* the millennium. For various reasons, however, Augustine is better classified as an amillenarian inasmuch as his view amounts to a denial that there will be any literal millennium on earth. His important contribution to postmillennialism is obvious, however, especially as his amillennial views became the dominant belief of both the Roman Church and the Reformers.

Failure of Augustinian millennialism. While Augustine was not a postmillenarian in the modern sense of the word, it is highly significant that postmillennialism arose partly from the success and partly from the failure of the Augustinian view. Augustine, with his denial of a millennium after the second advent, succeeded in displacing premillenarianism as the prevailing belief of the church. His most significant contribution, however, lay in the fact that history has proved the details of his system to be wrong and the resulting readjustment made postmillennialism seem plausible. Allis, an ardent Augustinian, sums up Augustine's contribution in these words:

"He taught that the millennium is to be interpreted spiritually as fulfilled in the Christian Church. He held that the binding of Satan took place during the earthly ministry of our Lord (Lk. x. 18), that the first resurrection is the new birth of the believer (Jn. v. 25), and that the millennium must correspond, therefore, to the inter-adventual period or Church age. This involved the interpreting of Rev. xx. 1-6 as a 'recapitulation' of the preceding chapter instead of as describing a new age following chronologically on the events set forth in chap. xix. Living in the first half of the first millennium of the Church's history, Augustine naturally took the 1000 years of Rev. xx. literally; and he expected the second advent to take place at the end of that period. But since he somewhat inconsistently identified the millennium with what remained of the sixth chiliad of human history, he believed that this period might end about A. D. 650 with a great outburst of evil, the revolt of Gog, which would be followed by the coming of Christ in judgment."[1]

As Allis goes on to admit, Augustine's prophecy of the return of Christ did not materialize at about A. D. 650,[2] nor did the hopeful adjustment of this date to 1000 A.D. by his followers meet with any more success. Obviously there was something wrong with Augustine's interpretation. Even the expedient of the Reformers who held that they were in the "little season" (Rev. 20:3)

---

[1]Oswald T. Allis, *Prophecy and the Church*, p. 3.

[2]Augustine nowhere states that the second advent would take place at A.D. 650. This is a rather hasty induction that Allis makes based upon Augustine's general chronology which brought the sixth millennium to a close at A.D. 650. Augustine himself leaves the *terminos ad quem* of the present interadvent age indefinite, perhaps as long as one thousand years after the incarnation.

has now with the passing years become untenable. It was the easiest way out to conclude that Augustine was wrong in dating the binding of Satan with the earthly ministry of Christ (Luke 10:13). The millennium, then, began sometime during the centuries following. Another view was that the millennium itself was of indefinite duration, not one thousand years. Either interpretation paved the way for postmillennialism with its concept of a millennium at the close of the present age preceded by a time of conflict and trouble. Thus while the theory of Augustine was proved untrue in its main elements, it nevertheless opened the way for both a continued amillennialism and for the rise of postmillennialism.

Joachim of Floris. The first genuine postmillennialist according to Kromminga[3] was Joachim of Floris, a twelfth-century Roman Catholic writer, founder and abbot of the monastery of Giovanni del Fiore (or Floris) in Calabria. His exposition of Revelation is a classic of the period. His view of the millennium is that it begins and continues as a rule of the Holy Spirit.[4] He had in view three dispensations, the first from Adam to John the Baptist; the second began with John; and the third with St. Benedict (480-543), founder of his monasteries. The three dispensations were respectively of the Father, of the Son, and of the Spirit. Joachim predicted that about 1260 the final development would take place and righteousness would triumph.[5] While Kromminga is probably right in classifying Joachim as a postmillenarian, it is clear that he differs from the modern type, though it is still common to designate the millennium as a reign of the Holy Spirit.[6]

Postmillennialism before 1700. In the interval between Joachim and Daniel Whitby, no doubt others qualified as postmillennial. Berkhof cites a number of Reformed theologians in the Netherlands during the sixteenth and seventeenth centuries who were

---

[3]D. H. Kromminga, *The Millennium in the Church*, p. 20.
[4]Cf Benz, *Zeitschrift fuer Kirchengeschichte* (1931), p. 86 f., cited by D. H. Kromminga, *op. cit.*, p. 20.
[5]Cf. *The New Schaff-Herzog Encyclopedia of Religious Knowledge*, VI, 184, *s. v.* "Joachim of Fiore."
[6]Cf. A. H. Strong, *Systematic Theology*, p. 1013, "a period . . . under special influence of the Holy Ghost."

postmillennial: "Coccejus, Alting, the two Vitringas, d'Outrein, Witsius, Hoornbeek, Koelman, and Brakel" of which the majority expected the millennium to be future.[7] Strangely, in his discussion of postmillennialism Berkhof does not so much as mention Daniel Whitby who popularized postmillennialism in the eighteenth century. A. H. Strong, however, makes no apology for being a follower of Whitby, stating, "Our own interpretation of Rev. 20:1-10, was first given, for substance, by Whitby."[8]

Daniel Whitby. Modern postmillennialism is usually considered the child of Daniel Whitby. His major contribution was his reversal of the prevailing amillennial viewpoint of Revelation 20. Augustine, it will be remembered, held that Revelation 20 was a recapitulation of the previous chapters of Revelation. Whitby advanced the idea that Revelation 20 followed chronologically the events of Revelation 19, and that the millennium, while in the interadvent period, was still future, possibly remotely future. This at once provided a way of escape from the incompatibility of the events of history of his day with millennial prophecies and allowed a more literal interpretation of the glowing promises of a golden age of righteousness and peace on earth to be fulfilled in the future.

Postmillennialism becomes an influential system of theology. It can hardly be said that the view of Whitby was a result of a movement to return to literal interpretation of prophecy. Whitby himself was a Unitarian. His writings bearing on the Godhead were publicly burned and he was denounced as a heretic. He was a liberal and a freethinker, untrammelled by traditions or previous conceptions of the church. His views on the millennium would probably have never been perpetuated if they had not been so well keyed to the thinking of the times. The rising tide of intellectual freedom, science, and philosophy, coupled with humanism, had enlarged the concept of human progress and painted a bright picture of the future. Whitby's view of a coming golden age for the church was just what people wanted to hear. It fitted the thinking of the times. It is not strange that theologians

---

[7]Louis Berkhof, *Systematic Theology*, p. 716.
[8]Strong, *op. cit.*, p. 1014.

scrambling for readjustment in a changing world should find in Whitby just the key they needed. It was attractive to all kinds of theology. It provided for the conservative a seemingly more workable principle of interpreting Scripture. After all, the prophets of the Old Testament knew what they were talking about when they predicted an age of peace and righteousness. Man's increasing knowledge of the world and scientific improvements which were coming could fit into this picture. On the other hand, the concept was pleasing to the liberal and skeptic. If they did not believe the prophets, at least they believed that man was now able to improve himself and his environment. They, too, believed a golden age was ahead.

Two principal types of postmillennialism. Stemming from Whitby, these groups provided two types of postmillennialism which have persisted to the twentieth century: (1) a Biblical type of postmillennialism, finding its material in the Scriptures and its power in God; (2) the evolutionary or liberal theological type which bases its proof on confidence in man to achieve progress through natural means. These two widely separated systems of belief have one thing in common, the idea of ultimate progress and solution of present difficulties. Postmillennialism in itself does not have the principle or method to attain a system of theology, yet its main elements constitute a distinct branch of theology. The influence and contribution of postmillennialism to theology is at least worthy of consideration.

II. Postmillennialism as a Theological System

The diverse elements which have united in agreement on postmillennialism make it difficult to make fair general statements of the position of postmillennialism. Included in postmillennialism are Unitarians who deny the deity of Christ and inspiration of Scriptures as well as Calvinists who affirm both. From the vantage point of the observed history of postmillennialism over several centuries, it is possible, however, to speak in at least general terms of this answer to the millennial question and draw some significant conclusions.

The postmillennial attitude toward the Scriptures. Within the ranks of postmillenarians there are all types of attitudes toward the Scriptures. Charles Hodge, an ardent postmillennialist, without doubt accepted the Scriptures as the infallible Word of God. On the other hand, Walter Rauschenbusch and Shirley Jackson Case, who are classified by some as postmillennialists, felt free to deal with the Scriptures with a light hand. The basic fault of postmillennialism is its method of interpretation of Scripture rather than its doctrine of inspiration. In order to find fulfillment of millennial promises in the present age, it is necessary for them to follow an allegorical or figurative system of interpretation in great areas of Biblical prophecy. This method has historically subverted not only prophecy but every important doctrine. Without question the real issue in the millennial controversy is right here. Practically all scholars agree that a strictly literal interpretation of prophecy leads to the premillennial concept of the millennium, while if the figurative method be employed Scripture may be interpreted in favor of other views. Postmillennialists quite frankly accept the figurative method as necessary to their interpretation.

James H. Snowden in a determined effort to establish postmillennialism as against premillennialism nevertheless writes: "It is true that many of these prophecies when so applied must be taken poetically and not literally. . . . It is further true that many of these prophecies are as yet only partially and often only very faintly realized. . . ."[9] Snowden, while admitting that premillenarians prevailed in early centuries, traces the introduction of the figurative and allegorical method of interpretation to Origen: "Origen in the first half of the third century was the first to raise an influential voice against the premillenarian view. He interpreted the millennial imagery of the Bible in a figurative sense and thus adopted a principle of interpretation which has been followed ever since, though he also introduced a method of 'allegorizing' Scripture which has long since been discarded."[10] It should be noted that Snowden admits that the figurative method became widely used in the third century and was therefore not

[9]James H. Snowden, *The Coming of the Lord* (New York: Macmillan Company, 1919), pp. 237-38.
[10]*Ibid.*, pp. 18-19.

apostolic or in common use before; that he distinguishes the allegorical and figurative methods of interpretation in an attempt to escape the excesses of Origen; and that he claims that the result of the adoption of this new method was the abandonment of premillenarianism. Snowden presents the usual arguments in favor of the figurative method of interpretation: that the Bible is an Oriental book and abounds in figurative language; that literal interpretations are often "absurd"; that all viewpoints find some allegorical passages; that apocalyptic literature is especially symbolic.[11] Without discussing further the relative merits of the figurative method, it is at least clear that postmillennialism necessarily adopts this method of interpreting millennial prophecy—a method which is admittedly not apostolic in its historic origin. Postmillennialism depends upon a system of interpretation which does not find literal fulfillment of the millennial passages. The dangers of this system are well illustrated in the history of the church since Origen, its founder, and infiltrate the systems of interpretation of both the Roman Church and modern liberalism. Making Scripture figurative which should be taken literally subverts its meaning and evades its authority. The result is the denial of the plain intent of the Scriptures.

The postmillennial doctrine of the millennium. Generally speaking, postmillennialism finds the millennium in this present interadvent period. If millennial prophecy is taken more literally, the millennium is usually pushed to the remote future, as Loraine Boettner does in his book *The Millennium;* if more liberties are taken in explaining millennial Scriptures, the entire present age is considered the millennium, differing from the amillennial concept only in the idea of a growing triumph and final victory before the second advent. James Snowden takes this latter view and finds the kingdom of God in the present age the only earthly millennium which will ever exist.

Snowden's contribution may be divided into two aspects—his concept of the kingdom of God and his interpretation of Revelation 20. Snowden's interpretation of Revelation 20 amounts to an endorsement of the amillennial position. His lengthy

---

[11]*Ibid.*, pp. 35-39.

chapter on the interpretation of Revelation 20 is principally one of ridicule of the premillennial interpretation. He is quite sure that the premillennialists are wrong. When he faces the problem of a positive interpretation, he finds it difficult to offer more than two possible interpretations. He frankly is not sure of his interpretation: "We may be sure what a passage of Scripture does not mean, and yet not be sure what it does mean."[12] In general he offers two views: (1) that the events mentioned in Revelation 20:4-6 are already past—"The souls whom John saw in the vision are the souls of the martyrs and confessors reappearing in the faithful and brave Christians in the days of the Roman persecution";[13] (2) that the millennium mentioned here is a picture of the souls in heaven—following the interpretation of Warfield.[14] According to Allis, this viewpoint originated in the amillenarians Duesterdieck (1859) and Kliefoth (1874).[15] Snowden finds the second viewpoint preferable: "This seems to us to give a clear and practical meaning to this passage."[16] In effect Snowden rules out Revelation 20 as casting any light on the form of the millennium which will eventuate in the earth. Snowden's doctrine of the millennium is reduced to his concept of the kingdom of God in its course in the world before the second advent. If it were not for the evident idea of progress and triumph in the earth of the kingdom of God Snowden would be classified as an amillennialist. His concept of the kingdom of God is definitely postmillennial in its details and deserves a careful study.

The kingdom of God to Snowden is a rule of God in the hearts of believers in Christ. He defines it: "The sense, however, in which it is commonly used is the rule of God in the hearts of obedient souls. It is a general designation for all those in all ages who turn to God in faith and constitute the total society of the redeemed."[17] The present age is the process of growth of this kingdom in human hearts, and the millennium on earth is

---

[12]*Ibid.*, p. 177.
[13]*Ibid.*, pp. 178-79.
[14]*Ibid.*, p. 181.
[15]Allis, *op. cit.*, p. 5.
[16]Snowden, *op. cit.*, p. 184.
[17]*Ibid.*, p. 51.

achieved through the advance of this kingdom of God. He finds that the kingdom is not materialistic, political, or of the earth, but it is rather spiritual and within the heart. Snowden's exposition of the spirituality of the kingdom is typical of postmillennialism:

"In the New Testament the material trappings of the kingdom, as prefigured in the Old Testament in forms adapted to the religious development of that day, are stripped off and it appears in its pure spirituality. It is now clearly brought out that the kingdom has its seat in the heart and consists in the rule of God in the soul or in moral and spiritual dispositions and habits. Jesus expressly set forth this inward spiritual nature of the kingdom in contrast with the outward materialistic form of the Jewish expectation of this day: 'And being asked by the Pharisees, when the kingdom of God cometh, he answered them and said, The kingdom cometh not with observation: neither shall they say, Lo, here! or, There! for lo, the kingdom of God is within you' (Luke 17:20-21). Paul expresses the same truth when he declares that 'the kingdom of God is not eating and drinking, but righteousness and peace and joy in the Holy Spirit' (Rom. 14:17). It begins in repentance and faith and goes on to purify and pervade the whole personality in mind and heart, soul and body, character and conduct and life. It sets up the throne of God in the heart, 'casting down imaginations, and every high thing that is exalted against the knowledge of God, and brings every thought into captivity to the obedience of Christ' (II Cor. 10:5). The beatitudes of Jesus describe its inner spirit and substance as humility, meekness, righteousness, mercy, purity and peacefulness. Paul, describing the same inner kingdom, says 'the fruit of the light is in all goodness and righteousness and truth' (Eph. 5:9), and 'the fruit of the Spirit is love, joy, peace, longsuffering, kindness, goodness, faithfulness, meekness, self-control' (Gal. 5:22-23)."[18]

Snowden then accommodates other aspects of truth to this central idea of the kingdom of God within the individual. The church is only a means of expression of this kingdom, not the

---

[18]*Ibid.*, pp. 55-56.

kingdom itself. This accounts for the failures of the church. Snowden labors to justify the paradoxical term "democratic kingdom"
in an attempt to link postmillennialism with the political trend
toward democracy immediately following the first world War.[19]
He finds further that Jesus did not accept the prevailing Jewish opinions of the first century of a literal kingdom on earth: He
merely "adopted this mode of expression and accommodated his
teaching to it. . . ."[20]

In general, therefore, the postmillennial concept of the millennium is a rule of the Spirit of God in the heart, beginning in
the past and continuing in the future in ever increasing power.
Christ is now on the throne in heaven and will never have an
earthly throne. The righteousness and peace of the kingdom
refer to the kingdom of God, not the whole earth. The appeal is
to the individual to let the Spirit reign in the heart and achieve
millennial spiritual blessings as a result.

The postmillennial idea of progress. The postmillennial viewpoint is definitely optimistic in regard to the future, that is, they
believe there will be definite progress toward the goal of the
triumph of the gospel and the power of God in the world. In
this they are opposed to premillenarians who believe that the
millennium will be brought about by the sudden return of
Christ and the accompanying catastrophic events. The parables
of Matthew 13 are interpreted by postmillenarians as presenting the progress of the gospel and the triumph of the power of
God over evil. The mustard seed becomes a great tree, speaking
of the growth of the kingdom of God. The leaven, which postmillennialism regards as the triumph of the gospel, leavens the
whole lump—converts the whole world.

David Brown, a leading nineteenth-century postmillenarian,
promotes this viewpoint: "The *growing* character of the kingdom,
taught by the 'mustard seed,' and the *penetrating* and *assimilating*
character, taught by 'the leaven,' go on till 'the whole (earth)
is leavened,' and all the world have been brought to lodge in the

---

[19]*Ibid.*, pp. 61-68.
[20]*Ibid.*, p. 68.

branches of the mighty tree of life."[21] Snowden, who agrees with this interpretation, quotes Trench with approbation on the same point: "Nor can we consider these words, 'till the whole is leavened,' as less than a prophecy of a final complete triumph of the gospel in that it will diffuse itself through all nations, and purify and ennoble all life."[22]

Snowden goes on to emphasize the character of this develop- ment of the kingdom. It is not only progressive but is slow and not without periodic crises. Snowden cites the conclusions of geolo- gists that the age of the earth is 100,000,000 years and quotes Professor Nathanael S. Shaler of Harvard that "man will probably continue for another hundred million years."[23] It is clear that Snowden embraces fully the conclusions of evolutionists regarding progress in the earth, and that with this theory as a guiding light the second advent is projected into the future by 100,000,000 years.

Snowden continues, "This scientific view of the age of the earth is the background against which we must now read and interpret Scripture teaching; and we may expect to find that it will revo- lutionize our view of Scripture at points, just as had been done by astronomy and geology. For when we come to look at it, we find in the Scriptures clear intimations and indications that the second coming of Christ with the end of the world is yet a long way off. . . . The world is only in the morning of its day and humanity is only in its infancy. Vast vistas of time stretch out before it in which our world will develop its resources and man will grow into maturity. All our achievements, industry and invention, science and art, education and social progress, liberty and brotherhood, ethics and religion, are only in their bud and will put forth their full bloom and ripened fruit. Even now [1919] world unity is looming up on the horizon and will be achieved tomorrow; and then the path will just be cleared for unified and speeded-up hu- man progress. . . . We have good grounds, then, for believing that the end of the world, with its attendant events of the second coming of Christ, the general resurrection and the final judg-

---

[21]David Brown, *Christ's Second Coming: Will It Be Pre-Millennial?* (New York: Robert Carter & Brothers, 1851), p. 333.
[22]Cited by Snowden, *op. cit.*, p. 77.
[23]Snowden, *ibid.*, p. 79. Cf. Nathanael S. Shaler, *Man and the Earth*, p. 215.

ment, is yet a very remote event."[24] One wonders whether if Snowden were living today he would care to make the same statement.

The progress of the kingdom is attended however, by periodic crises. Snowden finds this in accord with nature in which a flower after long growth suddenly bursts into bloom. He finds parallels in Scripture—the crises of the Exodus, the death and resurrection of Christ, Pentecost, the destruction of Jerusalem, the World War. He concludes: "The kingdom of God has followed and will follow this general law of gradual yet catastrophic growth from its first inception in this world to its climax in the final events that will issue in the eternal state."[25]

One of the few modern exponents of postmillennialism is Loraine Boettner who has expressed his doctrine in his book *The Millennium* published in 1958. In many respects his interpretation is similar to that of Charles Hodge rather than Snowden. He believes that the millennium is "a golden age of spiritual prosperity during this present dispensation, that is, during the Church age, and is to be brought about through forces now active in the world. It is an indefinitely long period of time, perhaps much longer than the literal one thousand years. . . . Postmillennialism further holds that the universal proclamation of the Gospel and the ultimate conversion of the large majority of men in all nations during the present dispensation" is to be realized.[26] Boettner follows normal postmillennialism in beginning the millennium at the end of the age rather than making it coterminous with the entire interadvent period as does amillennialism.

Method of consummating the kingdom. At no point does the premillennial and postmillennial viewpoints clash more abruptly than on the method of consummating the kingdom. The postmillennarian believes that the millennium will be brought on the earth by a long process of preaching of the gospel with subsequent transformation of society. The kingdom of God reaches its consummation principally by the work of the Holy Spirit, but it includes many other factors. A. A. Hodge, a postmillenarian,

[24]*Ibid.,* pp. 80-81.
[25]*Ibid.,* p. 84.
[26]Lorraine Boettner, *The Millennium,* (Philadelphia: Presbyterian Reformed Publishing Company, 1958) pp. 14-15.

writes: "The process by which this kingdom grows through its successive stages towards its ultimate completion can of course be very inadequately understood by us. It implies the ceaseless operation of the mighty power of God working through all the forces and laws of nature and culminating in the supernatural manifestations of grace and of miracle. The Holy Ghost is everywhere present, and he works directly alike in the ways we distinguish as natural and as supernatural—alike through appointed instruments and agencies, and immediately by his direct personal power."[27] Hodge goes on to enumerate the church, civilization, science, political and ecclesiastical societies, Christian missions, Christian workers as means to the end. He finds the kingdom coming "in all the growing of the seeds and all the blowing of the winds; in every event, even the least significant, which has advanced the interests of the human family. . . ."[28] It is clear that postmillennialism as to its method of bringing in the kingdom of God is quite removed from the premillennial doctrine that the kingdom will be consummated by the second advent.

The postmillennial doctrine of the second advent. Not all postmillenarians will agree on the doctrine of the second advent. In general, their viewpoints fall into two classifications. The more Biblical type of postmillennialism conceives of the millennium as a thousand years or at least an extended time yet future in which the gospel will triumph, at the close of which Christ will return to the earth in a bodily second advent which is a distinct and important event.

Charles Hodge may be taken as representative of this Biblical type of postmillennialism. He sums up his doctrine on the second advent as follows: "The common Church doctrine is, first, that there is to be a second personal, visible, and glorious advent of the Son of God. Secondly, that the events which are to precede that advent are (1) The universal diffusion of the Gospel; or, as our Lord expresses it, the ingathering of the elect; this is the

---

[27]A. A. Hodge, *Popular Lectures on Theological Themes* (Philadelphia: Presbyterian Board of Publication, 1887), pp. 295-96.
[28]*Ibid.*, pp. 296-97.

vocation of the Christian Church. (2) The conversion of the
Jews, which is to be national. As their casting away was national,
although a remnant was saved; so their conversion may be national,
although some may remain obdurate. (3) The coming of Anti-
christ. Thirdly, that the events which are to attend the second
advent are:— (1) The resurrection of the dead, of the just and of
the unjust. (2) The general judgment. (3) The end of the
world. And, (4) the consummation of Christ's kingdom."[29]

Hodge recognizes a second view in that other theologians conceive of the coming of Christ as repeated and spiritual rather
than bodily.[30] Snowden finds that Christ "comes" at various
critical points in history—in the Old Testament against Babylon
and Assyria, to the Ephesian Church in the New Testament (Rev.
2:5), to the churches in Sardis and Philadelphia (Rev. 3:3, 11-
12).[31] Snowden finds the conversion of Constantine, the Reformation, the Civil War in the United States, and the first World War
as illustrations of the coming of the Lord. Snowden concludes:
"Every act of judgment and justice and every new manifestation
of sympathy and service is a coming of God and of Christ."[32] He
goes on to cite the "Battle Hymn of the Republic" as evidence:
"Mine eyes have seen the glory of the coming of the Lord." In
particular he finds the coming of the Lord in the destruction of
Jerusalem which he treats at length, the coming of the Lord in
His resurrection, and the coming of the Lord on the Day of
Pentecost.[33] In addition to these "comings" of Christ, Snowden
speaks of a "final coming of Christ"[34] which is at "the end of
the world in a remote future."[35] In this final coming of Christ,
Snowden places the general resurrection and final judgment, both
of which he hastens to qualify as spiritual rather than physical.

It is clear from this brief survey of the postmillennial doctrine
of the second coming that the "blessed hope" of an imminent

---

[29]Charles Hodge, *Systematic Theology* (New York: Charles Scribner's
Sons, 1887), III, 792.
[30]Charles Hodge, *ibid.*, III, 792-800.
[31]Snowden, *op. cit.*, pp. 124-28.
[32]*Ibid.*, p. 128.
[33]*Ibid.*, pp. 128-40.
[34]*Ibid.*, p. 141.
[35]*Ibid.*, p. 143.

return of Christ is entirely lost in the postmillennial viewpoint. While Hodge is literal in his interpretation of Scripture to the point of recognizing the conversion of the Jews, in his view the coming of the Lord is no more imminent than in Snowden's. Further, the doctrine of the second coming itself is slurred and obscured by including in the doctrine every providential work of God in the history of the world.

Summary of postmillennial theology. The general features of postmillennialism are not difficult to summarize. Postmillennialism is based on the figurative interpretation of prophecy which permits wide freedom in finding the meaning of difficult passages—a latitude which is reflected in the lack of uniformity in postmillennial exegesis. The prophecies of the Old Testament relative to a righteous kingdom on earth are to be fulfilled in the kingdom of God in the interadvent period. The kingdom is spiritual and unseen rather than material and political. The divine power of the kingdom is the Holy Spirit. The throne which Christ is predicted to occupy is the Father's throne in heaven. The kingdom of God in the world will grow rapidly but with times of crisis. All means are used in advancing the kingdom of God—it is the center of God's providence. In particular the preaching of the gospel and spread of Christian principles signal its progress. The coming of the Lord is regarded as a series of events. Any providential dealing of God in the human situation is a coming of the Lord. The final coming of the Lord is climactic and is in the very remote future. There is no hope of the Lord's return in the foreseeable future, certainly not within this generation. Postmillennialism, like amillennialism, believes that all the final judgments of men and angels are essentially one event and will occur after a general resurrection of all men and before the eternal state. Postmillennialism is distinguished from premillennialism which regards the millennium as future and after the second advent. Postmillennialism is distinguished from amillennialism by its optimism, assurance of the ultimate triumph of the kingdom of God in the world, and its relative fulfillment of the millennial idea on the earth. Theologians like Hodge find rather literal fulfillment, including the conversion and restoration of Israel as a nation. Others like Snowden regard the millennium of which Revelation 20 speaks as referring to heaven.

III. PRESENT DECLINE OF POSTMILLENNIALISM

The difficulties of the postmillennial system of theology. In general it is fair to say that postmillennialism is not a current issue in theology. While it is not the purpose of this discussion to refute postmillennialism, the system can be analyzed with a view to determining the cause of its collapse in our generation. Of necessity, the discussion will be brief on each cause. The important fact is that postmillennialism has declined and its reasons are significant.

The inherent weakness of postmillennialism as a system. As a system of theology based upon a subjective spiritualizing of Scripture, postmillennialism lacks the central principles necessary for coherence. Each postmillennialist is left more or less to his own ingenuity in solving the problem of what to do with prophecies of a millennium on earth. Even a random survey of their interpretations of such a key passage as Revelation 20, as previously discussed, demonstrates this lack of uniformity. The result is that postmillennialism has no unified front to protect itself from the inroads of other interpretations. At best postmillennialism is superimposed upon systems of theology which were developed without its aid. When an interpretation is equally acceptable to the Calvinist, Arminian, and Unitarian, it ceases to be a determinative principle.

Trend toward liberalism. During the last century postmillennialism has found it impossible to resist a trend toward liberalism. While premillennialism, for instance, is unchanged in its attitude toward the inspiration and authority of Scripture and all major doctrines, there has been a most noticeable trend toward liberalism in institutions and groups which have embraced postmillennialism. The contrast of Charles Hodge and

James Snowden in succeeding generations of postmillennialists is most illuminating. The significant fact is that postmillennialism lends itself to liberalism with only minor adjustments. If millennial prophecies could be spiritualized, why not the doctrine of inspiration, the deity of Christ, the substitutional atonement, the doctrine of resurrection, and the final judgment? The principle of spiritualizing Scripture and avoiding its literal exegesis, if applied to prophecy, could as well be applied to other fields. In any event, the old conservative, Biblical postmillennialism has long since passed from the contemporary scene. Boettner stands almost alone among modern scholars still defending conservative Biblical postmillennialism.

Failure to fit facts of current history. Probably the immediate cause of the decline of postmillennialism was the events of the first half of the twentieth century involving two great world wars. While Snowden and others continued to proclaim their postmillennialism after the first world War, their millennium was far removed from the contemporary scene. No longer was it possible to preach that the promised millennium was at hand. The cold facts of world affairs brought a chill to postmillenarians. In any case, their cause was lost and they rapidly lost adherents. The second World War with its brutality and world tension which followed stilled apparently forever the idea of anything comparable to a millennium on earth. As postmillennialism had risen in an atmosphere of scientific and educational progress, so it declined in an atmosphere of war and world chaos.

Trend toward realism in theology and philosophy. The first half of the twentieth century witnessed also a change in the attitude of liberal theology and philosophy. In theology, the humanistic liberalism of the first twenty-five years of the century began to disappear. Liberals found that their philosophy and theology was impractical. It did not produce converts and inspire benevolence. There was need for a return to Biblical ground and more realism in dealing with human sin. The trend in philosophy kept pace. It too began to adjust itself to a world of real sin and strife. The second World War had a terrific impact on both liberalism and philosophy. A survey of their writings during this period will demonstrate a new appreciation of sin, of divine sovereignty, of human weakness, and the recognition of a possible catastrophic end of the world and ultimate judgment of God. Such a theological and philosophical atmosphere did not generate new converts to postmillennialism. Institutions which had formerly taught this viewpoint moved over into the less specific camp of amillennialism. The facts of the contemporary scene seem to point to no millennium on earth and no definable progress in making the world a Christian community. Postmillennialism was out of step and outmoded.

Trend toward amillennialism. Having lost hope of a golden age and having real doubts whether the world as such will be brought under the sway of Christian principles, it remained to find a new millennial theory. Amillennialism seemed to be the answer for many. This viewpoint gave some freedom. They could believe the coming of the Lord indefinitely postponed, or they could believe it was imminent. They could believe the present age was a millennium if they chose, or they could relegate it to heaven. They would be in the comfortable fellowship of most of the Reformers, the Roman Church, and modern liberal theologians. They could at least unite on a negative—they did not believe in a literal millennium or kingdom on the earth.

The remaining millennial issue. The decline of postmillennialism brought into sharper focus the clash between amillennialism and premillennialism. This, at least, is the present area of debate. Some central problems of postmillennialism remain: the principle of spiritualizing Scripture or giving it a figurative meaning, the subjective approach by which each expositor is given wide liberty in determining the meaning of a passage, and the search for principles of interpretation which will provide a unified system of theology. The decline of postmillennialism is a significant failure of the spiritualizing principle of interpretation and the failure of Biblical expositors following this method to arrive at an interpretation of prophecy that fits historic fulfillment. The problem is large and deserving of the attention of all really interested in arriving at a true interpretation of the Scriptures.

CHAPTER III

AMILLENNIALISM IN THE ANCIENT CHURCH

In recent years interest has been revived in the *origin* of millennial theology. This has been caused, first, by the decadence of postmillennialism which seemed to demand a new search for perspective in this field; second, by the popularity of premillennialism with its claim that the early church was premillennial; and, third, by the trend toward more serious Biblical studies—a result of the decline of extreme liberalism. The reduction of millennial theories to only two principal viewpoints—amillennial and premillennial—has tended to simplify the issue and make the millennial argument largely one for or against a literal millennium.

The nature of the arguments bearing on the millennium has also been significant. These have been characterized by: (1) a fresh study of literature of the fathers to see if it is necessary to concede that the ancient church was premillennial, as had previously been almost universally allowed by all parties; (2) a fresh study of the Scriptures by the amillennialists to defend themselves from the obvious Biblical approach of premillennialists; (3) a more vigorous attack on premillennialism, attempting to prove its doctrines dangerous and heretical to orthodox theology as a whole. Many of the significant books in the controversy have come from the pens of amillennialists, and these books in turn are refutations of earlier books of the premillennialists. Of particular interest is the recent restudy of millennialism in the ancient church with the objective of destroying or at least weakening the weighty argument of premillennialists that the ancient church was in sympathy with their viewpoints.

I. AMILLENNIALISM IN THE FIRST CENTURY

For most sober students of the Scriptures, the basic question in regard to the millennium is whether the Bible itself teaches decisively one view or the other. For the present discussion we can disregard that form of modern liberalism which might admit that the New Testament taught essentially the principal doctrines of premillennialism but pushes it aside as an error on the part of the apostles. It is assumed here that the New Testament is correct and the problem is not one of inspiration. In other words, is the New Testament as well as the Old premillennial or amillennial?

No Biblical record of millennial controversy. The New Testament bears no record whatever of a millennial dispute. Though the early church was concerned over many doctrinal questions, no disputes on this issue are recorded. The question of the disciples, "Lord, wilt thou at this time restore again the kingdom to Israel?" (Acts 1:6), occasioned no denial from the Lord Jesus, but merely the reminder that it was not for them to know the "time." The request of the mother of James and John for preferment of her sons in the kingdom was not refused on the ground that no future earthly kingdom was in prospect, but that the places of honor were reserved for those chosen by the Father (Matt. 20:20-23). While the argument from silence is never decisive, Christ also told His disciples, "If it were not so, I would have told you" (John 14:2). If no earthly kingdom was in prospect, it seems strange also in view of the prevailing Jewish concept of an earthly kingdom that Christ should tell His disciples, "I appoint unto you a kingdom, as my Father hath appointed unto me; that ye may eat and drink at my table in my kingdom, and sit on thrones judging the twelve tribes of Israel" (Luke 22:29-30). The positive testimony of Revelation 20 with its six references to a reign of Christ on earth for one thousand years, while hotly disputed and denied significance by the amillennialists, is nevertheless their stubborn foe. These references to the millennial doctrine are at least more than straws in the wind. If the amillennial viewpoint as held in modern times is correct, it would have called for extensive correction of the prevailing idea among the Jews that an earthly kingdom was their Messianic prospect.

Lack of evidence for amillennialism in first century. Leaving for later discussion the basic problem of Scriptural interpretation, the question remains as to what positive evidence there is for amillennialism in the first century. The question assumes considerable proportions inasmuch as George N. H. Peters lists fifteen advocates of premillennialism for the first century indicated as such outside the Scriptures themselves.[1] While some of these no doubt would be disputed by amillennialists, all concede that Papias (80-163), who seems to have been intimate with John the Apostle and Polycarp, was premillennial if we may believe Irenaeus who was a pupil of Polycarp. What can the amillennialists offer in support of the antiquity of amillennialism?

It is not difficult to find claims from amillennialists on the antiquity of their view. Ira D. Landis states flatly, "Jesus and the apostles were Amillennial in their eschatology."[2] His proof for this in his chapter on the history of millennialism is limited to one paragraph which states that Christ opposed Pharisees and that Pharisees were premillennialists; therefore Christ was an amillennialist. Landis ignores the opposition of Christ to Sadducees who probably denied a literal millennium. In his discussion which follows, in which he depreciates everyone claimed to be premillennial, the only extra-Biblical proof is that he cites Barnabas as not being premillennial among first-century writers.

Is Barnabas amillennial? The classification of Barnabas is at present disputed though he has long been considered premillennial. Landis decides the argument in one sentence: "The epistle ascribed to Barnabas is not Premillennial as is claimed, but decidedly anti-Judaistic."[3] Other amillennial writers who are more objective in their scholarship seem to have nothing more to suggest than that the testimony of Barnabas is not conclusive in its support of the premillennial viewpoint. Louis Berkhof while claiming that half the church fathers were amillen-

---

[1]George N. H. Peters, *The Theocratic Kingdom*, I, 494-95.
[2]Ira D. Landis, *The Faith of Our Fathers on Eschatology*, p. 369.
[3]*Ibid.*, p. 370.

nial during the second and third centuries (without offering
any proof) does not even suggest that this was true in the first
century.[4] According to the amillenarians themselves, then, evidence for amillennialism in the first century is reduced to the
disputed testimony of Barnabas. Over against this is the undisputed fact that Papias and others were definitely premillennial
in this same period. As the case of Barnabas is the only available
evidence for amillennialism according to the amillennialists themselves, a brief examination of his testimony will be made.

Kromminga who gives the testimony of Barnabas lengthy
consideration points out that Barnabas in chapter IV of his
Epistle subscribes to the interpretation that the Roman Empire
is the fourth of the empires of Daniel.[5] This seems to imply that
Barnabas thought the coming of the Lord was near for he refers
to the fact that "the final stumbling-block approaches. . . ."[6]
Kromminga further cites chapter XV of the *Epistle of Barnabas*
as being the main passage in point: "Attend, my children, to
the meaning of this expression: 'He finished in six days.' This implies, that the Lord will finish all things in six thousand years,
for a day is with Him a thousand years. And He Himself testifieth,
saying: 'Behold, today will be a thousand years.' Therefore, my
children, in six days, that is, in six thousand years, all things
will be finished. 'And He rested on the seventh day.' This meaneth:
when His Son, coming shall destroy the time (of wicked man)
and judge the ungodly and change the sun and the moon and
the stars, then shall He truly rest on the seventh day."[7]

Barnabas seems to teach from this passage that the present
age, starting from creation, will be completed in six thousand
years—a common if unwarranted teaching. Of importance is his
statement that "His Son" will come at the end of six thousand
years, destroy the wicked, judge the ungodly, change the sun,
moon, and stars, and then rest on the seventh day, i.e., for a thousand years. The plain implication that Christ will come before
the final one thousand years has been taken almost universally

---

[4]Louis Berkhof, *Systematic Theology*, p. 708.
[5]D. H. Kromminga, *The Millennium in the Church*, pp. 30-31.
[6]Cited by Kromminga, *ibid.*, p. 31.
[7]Kromminga, *loc. cit.*

to be a representation of a premillennial advent. Gibbon who was infidel and totally impartial toward the millennial controversy interprets Barnabas (apparently) as follows: "The ancient and popular doctrine of the millennium was intimately connected with the Second Coming of Christ. As the works of creation had been finished in six days their duration in the present state, according to tradition, was fixed to six thousand years. By the same analogy it was inferred that this long period of labor and contention, which was now almost elapsed, would be succeeded by a joyful Sabbath of a thousand years, and that Christ with His triumphant band of the saints and the elect who had escaped death, or who had been miraculously revived, would reign upon the earth till the time appointed for the last and general resurrection . . . the reigning sentiment of the orthodox believers."[8]

Not only impartial historians but also many amillennialists concede that this passage indicates Barnabas is properly classed as a premillenialist. Albertus Pieters, a long-time foe of premillennialism, in his series of articles in the *Calvin Forum* (August-September, 1938) agrees that both Papias and Barnabas are premillennial. W. H. Rutgers who attacks premillennialism without reserve nevertheless finds Barnabas merely doubtful and not clear.[9] Landis, as we have seen, dismissed Barnabas as a premillenarian, but made no claim that he was amillennial. Only Kromminga of all authors consulted seems to believe that Barnabas is an amillenarian.

The contribution of the late D. H. Kromminga to the millennial controversy is one of the curious aspects of the current argument. Kromminga classifies himself as a premillenarian, believing it necessary to interpret millennial passages literally. It is evident from his writings, however, that he is more concerned in maintaining the tenets of covenant theology than of premillennialism, and his denominational and associational relationships were predominantly amillennial. His works on the millennium are so obviously catering to amillennial arguments that apart from the

---

[8]Edward Gibbon, *The Decline and Fall of the Roman Empire*, I, 532.
[9]W. H. Rutgers, *Premillennialism in America* (Oosterbaan & Le Cointre. Goes, Holland, 1930), p. 55.

facts he presents the value of his argument is often stultified. In his discussion of Barnabas he labors for many pages to classify Barnabas as amillennial, and his entire chapter on the "Extent of Ancient Chiliasm" is devoted to it. His argument concedes that Barnabas is not a postmillenarian. Kromminga finds, however, in the spiritual interpretation and application which Barnabas makes of Exodus 33:3, Ezekiel 47:12 and Zephaniah 3:19, that his method is figurative interpretation, which he thinks is typical amillennialism.[10] This is at best an argument that Barnabas is not a consistent premillenarian, but it certainly does nothing to negative his positive statements. Certainly modern premillenarians make a similar use of the Old Testament in typology and spiritual applications without denying the basic method of literal interpretation which is the basis for premillennialism.

About the only notable contribution of Kromminga in his entire discussion of Barnabas is his reference to the fact that Barnabas evidently believed in the judgment of the wicked at the second, premillennial advent rather than at the end of the millennium. Kromminga infers this contradicts the usual premillennial view.[11] What Kromminga himself overlooks is that Barnabas does not say that the wicked are raised from the dead. Judging from the context, Barnabas is stating merely that the living wicked are judged "when His Son, coming, shall destroy the time (of the wicked man) and judge the ungodly. . . ."[12] Barnabas merely leaves out any statement about how the millennium will end. Even if Kromminga is right, however, it again would indicate only a variation rather than a denial of premillennialism. As far as making a positive contribution in favor of amillennialism, Barnabas has nothing to offer. The overwhelming testimony of reputable scholars has been for many years that Barnabas is properly a premillenarian, and it should be borne in mind that the literary evidence is entirely unchanged. The current attack on Barnabas is of recent origin and arises from the desire to shrink the historical basis of premillennialism.

---

[10]Kromminga, *op. cit.*, pp. 36-38.
[11]*Ibid.*, p. 32.
[12]*Ibid.*, p. 31.

Conclusion. It may be concluded, therefore, that the first century is barren of any real support to the amillennial viewpoint. While, indeed, the evidence is not altogether clear and not abundant for this century, it is significant that amillennial protagonists have contented themselves with minimizing premillennial claims with no real attempt to support their view by historical evidence. The first century is a lost cause for amillennialism.

II. AMILLENNIALISM IN THE SECOND AND THIRD CENTURIES

The second century without evidence for amillennialism. The second century, like the first, is devoid of any testimony whatever for amillennialism except at its close. To be sure, Rutgers states with enthusiasm: "Chiliasm found no favor with the best of the Apostolic Fathers, nor does it find support in the unknown writer of the Epistle to Diognetus. . . . We find no trace of the teaching in Athenagoras, Theophilus, Tatian, Hegesippus, Dionysius of Corinth, Melito of Sardis or in Apollinaris of Hierapolis."[13] This bold assertion is an astounding confession. Rutgers' evidence that chiliasm found no favor is that a whole century rolled by with no voice lifted against it. He concludes that chiliasm found no favor! If Peters is right, there were many premillennialists in their era, including some whom Rutgers believes have no trace of millennial teaching. Peters lists Pothinus, Justin Martyr, Melito, Hegesippus, Tatian, Irenaeus, Tertullian, Hippolytus, and Apollinaris as second-century premillennialists.[14] Rutgers' statement is merely wishful thinking with no positive evidence.

The best that the most ardent amillennialist can do in the first two centuries, then, is to claim the disputed Barnabas and hide behind the silence of many of the fathers. If amillennialism was the prevailing view of the church during this period, we are left without sources or evidence.

The acknowledged lack of evidence for amillennialism in the second century is all the more remarkable because amillennialists are making so much in our day of the comparatively few evidences

---

[13] W. H. Rutgers, *op. cit.*, p. 57.
[14] G. N. H. Peters, *op. cit.*, I, 495-96.

for premillennialism. If premillennialists are wrong for building upon such evidence as has been discovered—much of it almost beyond dispute—in support of early belief in the millennial reign of Christ, what is the case for amillennialism which has no evidence at all which is undisputed? For 150 years after the crucifixion of Christ, the amillenarians have only one disputed exponent—Barnabas—who is commonly conceded by many amillennialists and most neutral scholars to be premillennial. Such is the void that faces those seeking evidence for amillennialism.

Beginnings of amillennialism in the third century. At the very close of the second century and the beginning of the third we come upon the first bona fide amillenarians, Gaius (or Caius) who wrote early in the third century; Clement of Alexandria, a teacher at the school there from 193 to 220; his pupil, Origen (185-254); and Dionysius (190-265). It was from these men that premillennialism suffered its first vocal and effective opposition. The nature of this opposition, its exegetical grounds, and the effect upon premillennialism are all significant.

Most of what is known about Gaius comes from other sources which are very much opposed to premillennialism. It is probable that he is properly classed as an amillenarian. The nature of the teachings of Clement and Origen are, however, well established and their ground for opposition to premillennialism is very significant.

The use of the allegorical method and Platonic philosophy. The allegorizing method of interpreting Scripture which Kromminga attempted to find in Barnabas is clearly evident in Clement. Rutgers in his refutation of premillennialism, however, shows little enthusiasm for the basis of Clement's argument: "Clement, engrossed and charmed by Greek philosophy, applied this erroneous allegorical method to Holy Writ. It was a one-sided emphasis: opposed to the real, the visible, phenomenal, spacial and temporal. A Platonic idealistic philosophy could not countenance carnalistic, sensualistic conceptions of the future as that advanced by chiliasm. It shook the very foundation of which chiliasm rested. Robertson observed that 'it loosed its [chiliasm's] sheet-anchor—naive literalism in the interpretation of Scripture.' "[15]

Heresies of Origen advance amillennialism. The work of Origen, if anything, was worse than Clement who was his teacher. No doctrine was safe from his use of the allegorical method, even the doctrine of resurrection. His method subverted the plain meaning of Scripture by a principle of interpretation so subjective that the interpreter could make what he willed from the written revelation. It was natural that one who opposed literal interpretation of Scripture in other realms should do the same in regard to the millennium. The influence and place of Origen is well-known and beyond question, and his hermeneutical method is repudiated at least in part by all modern scholars.

Beginning of decline of premillennialism. Dionysius, who was Bishop of Alexandria in the latter part of the third century, is noted for his controversy resulting from the teachings of Nepos, an ardent premillennialist, who as bishop had taught and written with such effectiveness that whole churches were withdrawing in protest against the spiritualization of Origen. Eusebius who gives the account (Chapter 24 of his *Church History*) describes a three-day conference held by Dionysius in which the matter was thoroughly discussed with the result that the schism was healed.[16] Nepos had died sometime previous to the conference.

With the close of the third century, the evidence indicates a distinct increase in power in amillennialism and a corresponding loss of power for the premillennialists. It is clear that the rising tide of amillennialism comes almost entirely from the Alexandrian school—in particular, from Clement, Origen, and Dionysius, all of this locality. Accompanying this change in the church was the corresponding political change under Constantine which became effective in the fourth century. With the coming of Augustine a new day and a new chapter in the history of millennialism was written.

Testimony of first three centuries to amillennialism. Before considering the great influence of Augustine, which seems to

---

[15]W. H. Rutgers, *op. cit.*, p. 64.
[16]Cf. D. H. Kromminga, *op. cit.*, pp. 61-63.

have dominated the church for centuries afterward, it is necessary to recapitulate and evaluate the sources of amillennialism thus far discovered. In the first two centuries only the disputed testimony of Barnabas can be cited. With the close of the second century and continuing through the third a new foe to premillennialism arose in the Alexandrian school of interpretation. Its roots were in Platonic philosophy and in keeping with it the literal and plain meaning of Scripture was sacrificed for allegorical interpretations, often of a most fanciful kind. Premillennialism was attacked then, not as a teaching unwarranted by the Word of God, but rather because it was a literal interpretation of it. The method used against premillennialism was unfortunately used against other major doctrines of Christianity with devastating effect. In their doctrines of the person of Christ, of sin, of salvation, and of eschatology the evil results of the allegorical method are easily traced. It was to this foe of proper interpretation of Scripture that premillennialism owed its decline. It may be concluded, then, that amillennialism in the first three centuries rests for the most part on silence, on one disputed representative in the first century, none in the second, and a fallacious and destructive principle of interpretation in the third century.

CHAPTER IV

AMILLENNIALISM FROM AUGUSTINE TO MODERN TIMES

I. IMPORTANCE OF AUGUSTINE

It is difficult to overestimate the importance of Augustine in the history of theology. Not only did his thinking crystallize the theology which preceded him, but to a large extent he laid the foundations for both Roman Catholic and Protestant doctrine. B. B. Warfield, quoting Harnack, refers to Augustine as "incomparably the greatest man whom, 'between Paul the Apostle and Luther the Reformer, the Christian Church has possessed.' "[1] While the contribution of Augustine is principally noted in the areas of the doctrine of the church, hamartiology, the doctrine of grace, and predestination, he is also the greatest landmark in the early history of amillennialism.

The importance of Augustine to the history of amillennialism is derived from two reasons. First, there are no acceptable exponents of amillennialism before Augustine. Prior to Augustine, amillennialism was associated with the heresies produced by the allegorizing and spiritualizing school of theology at Alexandria which not only opposed premillennialism but subverted any literal exegesis of Scripture whatever. Few modern theologians even of liberal schools of thought would care to build upon the theology of such men as Clement of Alexandria, Origen, or Dionysius. Augustine is, then, the first theologian of solid influence who adopted amillennialism.

The second reason for the importance of Augustinian amillennialism is that his viewpoint became the prevailing doctrine of the Roman Church, and it was adopted with variations by most of the Protestant Reformers along with many other teachings of Augustine. The writings of Augustine, in fact, occasioned

---

[1]B. B. Warfield, *Studies in Tertullian and Augustine*, p. 114. citing in part Harnack, *Monasticism and the Confessions of St. Augustine*, p. 123.

the shelving of premillennialism by most of the organized church. The study of Augustine on the millennial question is a necessary introduction to the doctrine as a whole.

In this discussion of the millennial question a restudy of Augustine is especially apropos. Here we have one of the first great theologians of the Roman Church recognized by both Catholic and Protestant as an original thinker and solid contributor to the doctrine of Christendom. The fact that Augustine was amillennial in his viewpoint is noted with pride by modern amillenarians to show that their position is historic and a part of the central teaching of the church. Allis, for instance, loses no time in his attack on premillennialism to point out in the second page of his volume that Augustinian amillennialism was the norm for the church of the middle ages.[2] While the significance of much of the material relating to the millennium in writers before Augustine is debated, Augustine is clear in this position—the general facts of his position are not disputed. We have, then, concrete teaching which can be treated objectively.

In the previous study in postmillennialism, the current decline of postmillennialism was traced to certain specific factors: (1) its principle of spiritualizing the meaning of Scripture; (2) its trend toward liberalism; (3) its failure to fit the facts of history; (4) a trend toward realism in philosophy; (5) the present trend toward amillennialism. As postmillennialism is suitable for a test case for the principles of the millennial issue as a whole, so Augustinian amillennialism is suitable as a test case for amillennialism. In other words, does the viewpoint of Augustine demonstrate a proper method of interpreting Scripture? Does it provide a basis for liberalism? Does it fit the facts of history? Does it fit the trend of modern thought? While all of these questions are not decisive, it is clear that the question of method of interpreting Scripture, relation to liberalism and fulfillment in history are important bases for judgment of Augustine's views on the millennium.

---

[2]Oswald T. Allis, *Prophecy and the Church*, pp. 2-5.

II. AUGUSTINE ON THE MILLENNIUM

The present age the millennium. Augustine's concept of the millennium is not difficult to grasp nor are the major facts subject to dispute. Augustine conceived of the present age as a conflict between the City of God and the City of Satan, or the conflict between the church and the world. This was viewed as moving on to the ultimate triumph of the church to be climaxed by a tremendous struggle in which the church would be apparently defeated, only to consummate in a tremendous triumph in the second coming of Christ to the earth. Augustine held that the present age of conflict is the millennium. Following as he did the chronology of the Septuagint which is somewhat longer than Ussher's chronology in the Old Testament, he found that the Christian era is the sixth millennium from creation. This age apparently began somewhat before Christ, according to chronology, but Satan in any case was bound, an event described as taking place during the lifetime of Christ on earth in Luke 10:18.

Allis states, "He held that the binding of Satan took place during the earthly ministry of our Lord (Lk. x. 18) ."[3] Augustine himself expressed it, "This binding of Satan began when the church began to spread from Judea into other regions, and lasts yet, and shall do until this time be expired."[4] Augustine considered the progress of the millennium in his day (400 A.D.) well advanced.[5] He, however, qualified this expectation: "In vain therefore do we try to reckon the remainder of the world's years. . . . Some say that, it shall last four hundred, some five hundred, some a thousand years after the ascension. Everyone has his view, it were vain to try to show on what grounds."[6]

Trivial grounds for rejecting premillennialism. Augustine's interpretation of Revelation 20 is not very specific. As in his entire discussion of this doctrine, the treatment is cursory and brief. He discusses Revelation 20 in three or four pages and dis-

---

[3]Allis, *ibid.*, p. 3.
[4]Augustine, *City of God*, XX, 8.
[5]Cf. Allis, *op. cit.*, p. 3. Allis states Augustine dated the second advent as occurring A.D. 650, but Augustine himself avoids date setting.
[6]Augustine, *op. cit.*, XVIII, 53.

misses without any real argument the literal view. In fact, Augustine, like many others, does not seem to grasp the principles involved.

He has only one reason for avoiding the literal view—some had made the millennium a time of carnal enjoyment, a view which Augustine rightly opposed. As Augustine himself put it: "This opinion [a future literal millennium after the resurrection] might be allowed, if it proposed only spiritual delight unto the saints during this space (and we were once of the same opinion ourselves); but seeing the avouchers hereof affirm that the saints after this resurrection shall do nothing but revel in fleshly banquets, where the cheer shall exceed both modesty and measure, this is gross and fit for none but carnal men to believe. But they that are really and truly spiritual do call those of this opinion Chiliasts."[7] Thus on trivial grounds Augustine abandons the literal interpretation of Revelation 20. Somehow, for all his genius, he did not see that he could abandon this false teaching without abandoning the doctrine of a literal millennium.

In spite of adopting a spiritualized interpretation of Revelation 20, Augustine seems to accept a literal interpretation of the time element—it would be a thousand years. Instead of a future millennium however, he considered it already present. Revelation 20 was, then, a recapitulation of the present age which Augustine held was portrayed in the earlier chapters of Revelation. The present age, for Augustine, is the millennium promised in Revelation 20. Augustine, however, also held to a future millennium, to round out the seven millenniums from Adam which he held comprised the history of man. This future millennium, he held, was not literal but is synonymous with eternity—a use of the number in a symbolic sense only.

Summary of Augustinian amillennialism. In Augustine, therefore, we have specific and concrete teaching on the millennium.[8] There is no future millennium in the ordinary meaning of the term. The present age is the millennium; Satan is bound now;

[7]*Ibid.,* XX, 7.
[8]Cf. *ibid.,* XX: Allis, *op. cit.,* pp. 3-5; D. H. Kromminga, *The Millennium in the Church,* pp. 108-13.

when Christ returns the present millennium will close, the future millennium or eternity will begin. It remains, now, to test this teaching in its principles, implications, and fulfillment.

III. THE PRINCIPLE OF SPIRITUALIZED INTERPRETATION

In arriving at his conclusion regarding the millennium Augustine used the principle of spiritualizing Scripture freely. While he did not use this principle in interpreting Scripture relating to predestination, hamartiology, salvation, or grace, he found it suitable for interpreting prophecy. A candid study of his interpretation leaves the examiner with the impression that Augustine did not give a reasonable exegesis of Scripture involved. Augustine's doctrine that Satan is bound in this age—an essential of his system of interpretation—is a notable illustration of spiritualized and strained exegesis (cf. Luke 10:18 with Rev. 12:7-9; 20:2-3). Nothing is clearer from Scripture, the history of the church, and Christian experience than that Satan is exceedingly active in this present age against both Christians and unbelievers. Ananias is declared to have had his heart filled with Satan (Acts 5:3). The one to be disciplined in the Corinthian church is delivered unto Satan (1 Cor. 5:5; cf. 1 Tim. 1:20). The Christian is constantly warned against Satan's temptations (1 Cor. 7:5; 2 Cor. 2:11; 11:14; etc.). Paul declares that he is sorely tried by the buffeting of the messenger of Satan (2 Cor. 12:7). While the Christian can have victory over Satan, there is no evidence whatever that Satan is inactive or bound. It is no wonder that Warfield, though a disciple of Augustine, completely abandons this idea of Augustine as far as earth is concerned and limits it to the idea that "saints described are removed from the sphere of Satan's assaults,"[9] i.e., Satan is bound in respect to heaven only. While Warfield's explanation is no more sensible than Augustine's as far as an exegesis of the Scriptures is concerned, it at least accords with the facts of church history. It can be stated flatly that Augustine's exegesis is an outright error as far as the binding of Satan is concerned.

---

[9]B. B. Warfield, *Biblical Doctrines*, p. 651.

The exegesis of Augustine on Revelation 20 as a whole fares no better. After concluding that the binding of Satan is synonymous with the victory of Christ in His first advent, he draws the strained conclusion that the "first resurrection" of Revelation 20:5 is the spiritual birth of believers. The context in Revelation 20:4 makes it clear that as far as this passage goes those who are "raised" are those who "were beheaded for the witness of Jesus, and for the word of God, and which had not worshipped the beast, neither his image, neither had received his mark upon their foreheads." The subject of the passage is not the living but the dead; not the church as a whole, but the martyrs only. To spiritualize this portion of Scripture to make it conform to the course of the present age is to destroy all its plain literary meaning. Augustine's view required also, of course, the spiritualization of many Old Testament passages bearing on the future righteous kingdom on earth, and this he does in his treatment of the Old Testament.

IV. AUGUSTINE'S CONCEPT OF THE PRESENT AGE

It is central to Augustine's theology that he regards the church as ultimately triumphant. While his viewpoint varies somewhat from postmillennial theology, the similarities are so marked that some have taken Augustine to be postmillennial. Like the postmillennialist, Augustine regarded the present age as a progressive triumph culminating in the second advent and the final judgment of men. He differed from the postmillennialists only in the matter of the degree of that triumph. As Augustine held that the millennium was already well advanced when he lived, he found it necessary to account for the widespread evidence of sin in his day and the comparative inadequacy of the church to bring in a golden age of righteousness. He accordingly did not claim that the present age was a literal fulfillment of the promised age of righteousness, but was rather a time of conflict in which evil often seemed to have the upper hand. Like the postmillenarians, however, he did not doubt that ultimately righteousness would triumph.

While Augustine's predictions of continued struggle and conflict have been abundantly fulfilled to the present day, there is little evidence that there has been any progress toward the ultimate goal. It is significant that many present-day amillenarians have further retreated from the predictions of triumph and are content to leave a golden age to eternity future or limited to heaven. Premillenarians will not necessarily disagree with Augustine's basic idea of conflict in the present age nor with the idea that the second advent will signal the coming of righteousness to the earth, but they attach a different meaning to both the present age and the second advent.

V. The Failure of Fulfillment of Augustinian Amillennialism

The test of any system of interpretation is its correspondence to the facts of history. This is especially true in interpretation of prophecy. The question may fairly be asked whether the history of the church and the world since Augustine has given any confirmation of the essentials of his interpretation.

The Augustinian concept of the binding of Satan has already been shown to be without Scriptural or historical warrant. Certainly there has been no real change in the working of Satan in the world and plainly no lack of activity of Satanic forces. The concept of progress and a triumphant church, while not stressed by Augustine in the postmillennial way, falls far short of fulfillment or even significant attainment. The Christian era has been no golden age of righteousness nor has the church conquered the world. It is more accurate to recognize that the world has to a large degree possessed the church.

One feature of Augustinian millennialism has notably failed. Augustine, as has been previously brought out, considered the coming of Christ within one thousand years after the ascension an essential to his system. So impressed was Augustine with the necessity of interpreting literally the six references to the one thousand years in Revelation 20 that he departed from his spiritualization of the passage to assert it. Because of his involvement with the theory that the entire history of man would be finished within seven millenniums, he considered it entirely possible that the sixth millennium, the last in ordinary world history, had already begun when Christ was born. Based on calculations from chronology of the Septuagint, Augustine concluded, according to Allis, that the second advent might occur in the year A.D. 650.[10] This would seem the most flagrant date-setting one could imagine. In fairness to Augustine, however, it should be said that he does not mention any date and recognized the possibility of error in the system of chronology which he followed. Allis reaches his conclusion from Augustine's general chronology. Augustine was positive that in any case the millennium was started no later than the ascension and would last·no longer than one thousand years.[11]

The year 650 came and went with no notable events to fulfill the promise in Augustine's teaching. Attention was soon fastened on the year A.D. 1000. The belief was widespread that the second advent would occur on this date. As Kromminga points out, not only at the year 1000 but also in the year 1044, and again in 1065, there was hope that the second advent would occur on Good Friday when Good Friday happened to coincide with the Day of Annunciation (March 25, the day accepted as the time Gabriel made the announcement to Mary).[12] The expectation of the church based on Augustinian eschatology was not fulfilled, and it became evident that by no stretch of the imagination was the Augustinian teaching to be considered fulfilled. For a time they could hope they were in the "little season" (Rev. 20:3), but as the years wore away this became increasingly untenable. Both of Augustine's suggestions—the year 650 and the year 1000 or thereafter—were obsolete.

VI. Resulting Revision of Amillennialism

Two major viewpoints eventuated out of the welter of speculation which continued to regard the coming of Christ as an imminent event.

The millennium the end of interadvent period. The postmillennial idea that the millennium was literal, but would begin someday after the time of Christ, had many adherents. All sorts

---

[10]Cf. Allis, *op. cit.*, p. 3.
[11]Augustine, *op. cit.*, XVIII, 53.
[12]Kromminga, *op. cit.*, p. 117, citing Glaber, Erdmann, etc.

of starting points were suggested. Even to modern times post-millennialists were wont to start the millennium at such time as to bring its consummation in their lifetime. Hengstenberg, for instance, began the millennium in the ninth century, which would bring the second advent in his lifetime. Others began the millennium in more recent times. Allis cites Durham as dating its beginning in 1560.[13] Normal postmillennialism follows Whitby, however, in finding the entire millennium or golden age still future. Both Roman Catholic and Reformed scholars were in total confusion as far as arriving at an agreed teaching on this matter.

The millennium indefinite in length. A popular and more tenable position was adopted by some who spiritualized the time element of the millennium along with the teachings which relate to it. Undoubtedly this is a more consistent position even if it leaves the passage indefinite. In any case the outstanding feature of Augustinian amillennialism which captured the church and caused the eclipse of premillennialism proved to be a total failure in the history of the church. There was absolutely nothing to confirm the Augustinian view of the millennium in the centuries which followed him. If the law of fulfillment is essential to establish an interpretation, the Augustinian view is tried and found wanting.

VII. THE AMILLENNIALISM OF THE PROTESTANT REFORMATION

Reformers adopt Roman amillennialism. The Roman Church did not make any significant advance in the doctrine after Augustine, and Protestant teachings did not fare much better. Without attempting within the limited discussion possible here an analysis of the whole Protestant Reformation, it is safe to conclude that the early years of Protestantism saw little if any advance over the Augustinian view. It is clear that the great Protestant leaders such as Calvin, Luther, and Melanchthon are properly classed as amillennial. As far as millennial teaching was concerned, they were content to follow the Roman Church in a weakened Augustinian viewpoint.

---

[13]Allis, *op. cit.,* p. 4.

Premillennialism superficially considered. Calvin's discussion of the millennium is a fair sample of the attitude of the Reformers. They treated the doctrine superficially and arbitrarily, making the view ridiculous by misrepresentation. Calvin, for instance, has this to say: ". . . not long after arose the Millenarians, who limited the reign of Christ to a thousand years. Their fiction is too puerile to require or deserve refutation. Nor does the Revelation, which they quote in favour of their error, afford them any support; for the term of a thousand years, there mentioned, refers not to the eternal blessedness of the Church, but to the various agitations which awaited the Church in its militant state upon earth. But the whole Scripture proclaims that there will be no end of the happiness of the elect, or the punishment of the reprobate. . . . Those who assign the children of God a thousand years to enjoy the inheritance of the future life, little think what dishonour they cast on Christ and his kingdom."[14]

While Augustine discarded premillennialism because he took a carnal interpretation of the millennium as essential to the view, Calvin commits a greater error in assigning to the premillennial view a limited eternity of one millennium. Neither view would be claimed by any thinking premillenarian of our day.

VIII. MODERN AMILLENNIALISM

Amillennialism continues to follow Augustine. Because of the analytic treatment of amillennialism from a modern viewpoint, which will follow, it will be sufficient here to observe the broad trend of amillennialism in modern times. For the most part amillenarians of today, such as Allis and Berkhof, claim to follow in the hallowed tradition of Augustine while admitting the need for adjustment of his view to the actual modern situation.

Rise of the heavenly millennium view. A new type of amillennialism has arisen, however. Allis traces this view to Duesterdieck (1859) and Kliefoth (1874) [15] and analyzes it as a reversal of the fundamental Augustinian theory that Revelation 20 was a re-

---

[14]John Calvin, *Institutes of the Christian Religion* (Philadelphia: Presbyterian Board of Christian Education, 1936), II, 250-51 (Book III, 25).
[15]Allis, *op. cit.*, p. 5.

capitulation of the church age. The new view, instead, follows the line of teaching that the millennium is distinct from the church age though it precedes the second advent. To solve the problem of correlation of this interpretation with the hard facts of a world of unbelief and sin, they interpreted the millennium as a picture not of a time-period but of a state of blessedness of the saints in heaven.[16]

Warfield, with the acknowledged help of Kliefoth,[17] defines the millennium in these words: "The vision, in one word, is a vision of the peace of those who have died in the Lord; and its message to us is embodied in the words of XIV. 13: 'Blessed are the dead which die in the Lord, from henceforth'—of which passage the present is indeed only an expansion. The picture that is brought before us here is, in fine, the picture of the 'intermediate state'—of the saints of God gathered in heaven away from the confused noise and garments bathed in blood that characterize the war upon earth, in order that they may securely await the end."[18]

Summary of modern amillennialism. Among amillennialists who are classified as conservative, there are, then, two principal viewpoints: one which finds fulfillment in the present age on earth in the church; another finding fulfillment in heaven in the saints. The second more than the first requires spiritualization not only of Revelation 20 but of all the many Old Testament passages dealing with a golden age of a righteous kingdom on earth.

Such are the antecedents of modern amillennialism. It remains, now, to analyze this historic doctrine in its modern setting in the light of the Holy Scriptures. Both premillennialism and amillennialism have many honored and historic exponents. The question remains which view provides the best interpretation of the entire Word of God. Obviously the Scriptures do not teach both viewpoints, and this is not a trivial matter. The contemporary serious trend of studies in this direction, while

---

[16]Allis, *loc. cit.*
[17]Warfield, *Biblical Doctrines*, pp. 643-44.
[18]*Ibid.*, p. 649.

not always pure in motive, finds justification in the significance of the question. What, after all, is the answer of amillennialism to the main issues of Christian doctrine? This is the question which is now to be considered.

Chapter V

AMILLENNIALISM AS A METHOD OF INTERPRETATION

I. The Issue

There is a growing realization in the theological world that the crux of the millennial issue is the question of *method* of interpreting Scripture. Premillenarians follow the so-called 'grammatical-historical' literal interpretation while amillenarians use a spiritualizing method. As Albertus Pieters, an avowed amillennialist, writes concerning the problem as a whole: "The question whether the Old Testament prophecies concerning the people of God must be interpreted in their ordinary sense, as other Scriptures are interpreted, or can properly be applied to the Christian Church, is called the question of spiritualization of prophecy. This is one of the major problems in biblical interpretation, and confronts everyone who makes a serious study of the Word of God. It is one of the chief keys to the difference of opinion between premillenarians and the mass of Christian scholars. The former reject such spiritualization, the latter employ it; and as long as there is no agreement on this point the debate is interminable and fruitless."[1] The issue, then, between amillennialism and premillennialism is their respective methods of interpretation, and little progress can be made in the study of the millennial issue until this aspect is analyzed and understood.

II. The Popularity of the Amillennial Method

It is quite apparent that the amillennial method of interpretation of Scripture which involves spiritualization has

---

[1] Albertus Pieters, *The Leader*, September 5, 1934, as cited by Gerrit H. Hospers, *The Principle of Spiritualization in Hermeneutics*, p. 5.

achieved a considerable popularity. It is not too difficult to account for the widespread approval of the spiritualizing method adopted by many conservative theologians as well as liberal and Roman Catholic expositors. Fundamentally its charm lies in its flexibility. The interpreter can change the literal and grammatical sense of Scripture to make it coincide with his own system of interpretation. The conservative and liberal and Roman Catholic can each claim that the Bible does not contradict his concept of theology. It is this very factor, however, which raises grave doubts concerning the legitimacy of a method which produces such diverse systems of interpretation. One of the major difficulties of amillennialism both as a system of theology and as a method of interpretation is that it has never achieved unity on the very essentials of Biblical truth. In the material which follows this will have many illustrations.

It is significant that the first successful opposition to premillennialism came from the adoption of a spiritualizing principle of interpretation. The Alexandrian school of theology which came into prominence in the third century followed a principle of interpretation which regarded all Scripture as an allegory. They succeeded in arousing considerable opposition to the premillenarians of their day even if it was at the price of subverting not only the millennial doctrine but all other Christian doctrine as well. It remained for Augustine to give a more moderate application of this principle of interpretation. In general, he held that only prophecy should be spiritualized and that in the historical and doctrinal sections of Scripture the 'historical-grammatical' literal method should be used. This was a decided improvement as far as theology as a whole was concerned, even if it left the millennial issue unsolved and at the mercy of the allegorical school. Because of the weight of Augustine in other major issues of theology where he was in the main correct, Augustine became the model of the Protestant Reformers who accepted his amillennialism along with his other teachings.

It is quite clear from the literature of the Reformation that the millennial issue was never handled fairly or given any considered study. The basic issues of the Reformation involved the right of private interpretation of the Scriptures, the individual priesthood of all believers, the doctrine of justification by faith, and similar truths. It was natural for the emphasis to rest in this area, and for eschatology as found in the Roman Church to be corrected only in denial of purgatory and other teachings which were regarded as inventions. It was customary to accept Roman teachings where the error was not patent. Premillennialism at the time of the Reformation unfortunately was expounded chiefly by small groups of somewhat fanatical enthusiasts who were often discredited by extreme doctrines.

Because amillennialism was adopted by the Reformers, it achieved a quality of orthodoxy to which its modern adherents can point with pride. They can rightly claim many worthy scholars in the succession from the Reformation to modern times such as Calvin, Luther, Melanchthon, and, in modern times, Warfield, Vos, Kuyper, Machen, and Berkhof. If one follows traditional Reformed theology in many other respects, it is natural to accept its amillennialism. The weight of organized Christianity has largely been on the side of amillennialism.

Many other factors increase the prestige of amillennialism. As a system of doctrine it enhances the church as an institution, a continuance of God's administrative government. This strengthens the power of ecclesiasticism. The simplicity of the amillennial eschatology has a strong appeal as a way of unifying the many elements indicated in a literal interpretation of Scripture. It tends also to concentrate attention upon present problems and practical truth. Amillenarians do not need to hold prophetic conferences and preach often on prophetic themes. It is comparatively easy to grasp a simple formula of final resurrection, final judgment, and eternal state, and not to attempt to harmonize hundreds of verses in Scripture which give details of the future.

Amillenarians can also claim, with some ambiguity, that they are aiming at a spiritual interpretation of Scripture—meaning by this its ultimate practical meaning rather than its literal sense. On the whole, it is not difficult to explain the charm of amillennialism which has appealed to scholar and lay-man alike. One can understand the psychological reasons which dismiss premillennialism as an impractical and contradictory amassing of details of prophecy and the study of prophecy it-self as fruitless and confusing.

While the popularity of amillennialism is therefore easily accounted for, the very nature of this popularity raises some serious questions. It is quite apparent in the literature of amil-lennialism that both in its historic origin and its modern discus-sion amillenarians are quite unwilling to face squarely the prob-lems of their own system. Only under the goading of scholarly premillennial works and the tremendous acclaim of premillen-nialism in the Bible study movements of recent centuries have amillenarians been willing to back up and to consider formally, as for instance M. J. Wyngaarden does,[2] the reasons behind pre-millennial theology. It is still the fashion to resort to ridicule rather than to objective study of the conflicting viewpoints.

A proper study of the millennial issue demands, first, an analysis of the methods of interpretation which have produced amillennialism and premillennialism. This lays bare the prob-lem and opens the way to see the issue in its true light.

III. ANALYSIS OF THE AMILLENNIAL METHOD OF INTERPRETATION

Amillennial use of the literal method. The amillennial method of interpreting Scripture is correctly defined as the spiritualizing method. It is clear, however, that conservative amillennialists limit the use of this method, and in fact adopt the literal method of interpreting most of the Scriptures. The methods followed by the allegorizing school of Alexandria which characterized the early amillennialists are now repudiated by all modern scholars. As Pieters states: "No one defends or em-ploys the allegorizing method of exegesis. Calvin and the other great Bible students of the Reformation saw clearly that the method was wrong and taught the now generally accepted 'gram-matical-historical' literal interpretation, so far as the Scriptures

---

[2]*The Future of the Kingdom in Prophecy and Fulfillment.*

in general are concerned. That they retain the spiritualizing method in expounding many of the prophecies was because they found themselves forced to do so in order to be faithful to the New Testament."[3]

Not only Pieters but all conservative amillenarians recognize the need for literal interpretation. In addition to Pieters, Payne[4] cites Hamilton,[5] Allis,[6] Calvin,[7] Luther,[8] and others as supporting the principle of literal interpretation as the only proper grammatical-historical method. Amillenarians use two methods of interpretation, the spiritualizing method for prophecy and the literal method for other Scriptures. They differ from early amillenarians who regarded all Scripture as an allegory. The extent of application of one method or the other is determined by their rules for use of the spiritualizing method.

It is obvious at the beginning that, if the interpreter has a choice of method in interpreting Scripture, a large door for difference of opinion is opened. The general designation of prophecy as the field of spiritualization is by no mean definite. In fact, amillenarians who are conservative interpret many prophecies literally and, on the other hand, use the spiritualizing method in some instances where prophecy as such is only remotely involved. The modern liberal scholar, who is also an amillenarian, feels free to use the spiritualizing method rather freely in areas other than prophecy whenever it suits his fancy, and being bound by no law of infallible inspiration need not be concerned if the result is not consistent. The spiritualizing method once admitted is not easy to regulate and tends to destroy the literal method. While the amillennial use of the literal method is general among the conservatives, among liberal groups it has less standing and use.

---

[3]Pieters, "Darbyism vs. The Historic Christian Faith," *Calvin Forum*, II, 225-28, May, 1936.
[4]Payne "Amillennialism as a System" (unpublished Doctor's dissertation), pp. 82 ff. It is regrettable that this work including the long chapter on "The Spiritualizing Principal of Interpretation," has not been published.
[5]F. E. Hamilton, *The Basis of Millennial Faith*, pp. 38, 40, 58.
[6]Oswald T. Allis, *Prophecy and the Church*, p. 238.
[7]F. W. Farrar, *History of Interpretation*, pp. 193-94.
[8]*Ibid.*, p. 327 f.

Amillennial use of the spiritualizing method. Conservative amillenarians, as we have seen, are somewhat embarrassed by the early allegorical school of amillennialists and with one voice deny the allegorical method as proper in interpreting Scripture. As Pieters stated above, "No one defends or employs the allegorizing method of exegesis."[9] In regard to the allegorical method, Farrar writes: "Allegory by no means sprang from spontaneous piety, but was the child of Rationalism which owed its birth to the heathen theories of Plato. It deserved its name, for it made Scripture say something else than it really meant. . . . Origen borrows from heathen Platonists and from Jewish philosophers a method which converts the whole Scripture, alike the New and the Old Testament, into a series of clumsy, varying, and incredible enigmas. Allegory helped him to get rid of Chiliasm and superstitious literalism and the 'antitheses' of the Gnostics, but opened the door for deadlier evils.[10]

Now just what is the spiritualizing method and how does it differ from the allegorical? An allegory is commonly considered to be an extended metaphor. As Hospers puts it: "To exemplify: 'Israel is like a vine,'—that is a simile. 'Israel is a vine,' —that is a metaphor. And Psalm 80 gives an extended description of this idea, and that is an allegory."[11] Spiritualization of the same word *Israel* would involve in Webster's definition of spiritualization: "to take in a spiritual sense,—opposed to literalize."[12] In other words, if Israel should mean something else than Israel, e.g., the church in the New Testament composed largely of Gentiles, this would be spiritualization. Actually the church is not Israel at all, but has certain similarities to Israel (as well as many contrasts) just as the vine used in Psalm 80 is similar in its properties to Israel.

It can be seen that spiritualized and allegorized interpretations are not children of different races, but one family of thought separated only by degree of application. In both methods the ordinary literal meaning is denied. Actually, Israel is

---

[9]Pieters, *loc. cit.*
[10]Farrar, *loc. cit.*, cited by Payne, *op. cit.*, p. 81.
[11]Hospers, *op. cit.*, p. 10.
[12]*Webster's New International Dictionary*, Second Edition. *s.v.* "spiritualize."

no more a vine than Israel is the church. The difference in allegorizing and spiritualizing is for practical purposes nominal rather than essential. It is one of degree rather than one of principle.

It is clear, however, that the amillennial doctrine of spiritualization is far more restrained and less destructive to doctrine in general than the old allegorizing method which knew no rules and respected no boundaries. Conservative amillenarians have made a determined effort to formulate principles and rules governing the use of spiritualization in Scripture.

Hamilton summarizes these principles in his attack on interpreting Old Testament Scriptures literally: "But if we reject the literal method of interpretation as the universal rule for the interpretation of all prophecies, how are we to interpret them? Well, of course, there are many passages in prophecy that were meant to be taken literally. In fact a good working rule to follow is that the literal interpretation of the prophecy is to be accepted unless (a) the passages contain obviously figurative language, or (b) unless the New Testament gives authority for interpreting them in other than a literal sense, or (c) unless a literal interpretation would produce a contradiction with truths, principles or factual statements contained in non-symbolic books of the New Testament. Another obvious rule to be followed is that the clearest New Testament passages in non-symbolic books are to be the norm for the interpretation of prophecy, rather than obscure or partial revelations contained in the Old Testament. In other words we should accept the clear and plain parts of Scripture as a basis for getting the true meaning of the more difficult parts of Scripture."[13]

Most premillenarians would agree with Hamilton that obvious figurative language or instances where the New Testament gives authority for interpreting the Old Testament in other than a literal sense would be just grounds for use of the spiritualizing method. Obviously, some Scriptures of the Old Testament and a few passages of the New Testament have a figurative meaning. The difficulty arises in the third rule and its application.

---

[13]Hamilton, *op. cit.*, pp. 53-54.

The spiritualizing of passages other than those that are plainly not to be taken literally is justified to avoid contradiction or conflict with doctrinal portions of Scripture which are not symbolic. This is just the question. Amillenarians believe that a future literal earthly millennial kingdom of Christ would be such a contradiction; premillenarians hold that it is not. If every problem of Scriptural interpretation is to be solved by spiritualization, there are left no boundaries for proper doctrine, no certain basis for erecting a theology. The so-called rules of amillennialism turn out to be no help at all because their basis is the extremely subjective judgment of what is a contradiction.

The controversy between the spiritualizing and the literal schools of interpretation can for this reason hardly be settled in the field of abstractions. It is necessary to examine the teachings of each school of thought in detail and to sustain or refute the exegesis of related Scripture and to erect a coherent and self-consistent system of theology. In such an effort certain facts would stand out in the amillennial system of spiritualization.

IV. Dangers of the Amillennial Method of Interpretation

It is admitted by amillenarians: (1) that when they use the method of spiritualization of Scripture they are interpreting Scripture by a method which would be utterly destructive to Christian doctrine, if not limited largely to eschatology. (2) They do not follow the spiritualizing method of interpretation in relation to prophecy in general, but only where it is necessary to deny premillennialism. (3) They justify the spiritualizing method as a means of eliminating problems of fulfillment of prophecy—it is born of a supposed necessity rather than a natural product of exegesis. (4) They do not hesitate to use spiritualization in areas other than prophecy if it is necessary to sustain their system of doctrine. (5) As illustrated in current modernism which is almost entirely amillennial, it has been proved by history that the principle of spiritualization spreads easily into all basic areas of theological truth. If the earthly reign of Christ can be spiritualized, so can His resurrection, His miracles, His second coming. Modern liberals can justify their denial of literal resurrection by use of the same hermeneutical rules that Hamilton uses for denial of an earthly millennial kingdom. (6) The amillennial method does not provide a solid basis for a consistent system of theology. The hermeneutical method of amillennialism has justified conservative Calvinism, liberal modernism, and Roman theology alike. Even conservative amillenarians are in almost total confusion, as will be shown later, in their spiritualized interpretation of passages taken literally by the premillenarians and in such basic and elementary problems as the fulfillment of the millennial kingdom idea. (7) Amillennialism has not arisen historically from a study of prophetic Scripture, but rather through its neglect. The inherent difficulties of the amillennial method of interpretation are discovered principally by study of their interpretation of Scripture. It becomes apparent early in such a study that amillennialists have no real guiding principle in spiritualization and that they come to widely different conclusions. In fact, as will be shown, the principal unifying factor which dominates amillennial interpretation is its negative note, its denial of an earthly reign of Christ. The expedients that are used and the interpretations of kingdom passages of Scripture that are reached to achieve this negative conclusion are often mutually destructive of each other. Having analyzed the method of amillennial interpretation, it now follows that an analysis of their interpretation of Scripture itself must be undertaken.

CHAPTER VI

AMILLENNIALISM AS A SYSTEM OF THEOLOGY

I. THE GROWING IMPORTANCE OF MILLENNIALISM

While the millennial controversy is nothing new, it has come to be recognized only recently that it plays such an important part in determining the form of theology as a whole. Instead of being simply a way of interpreting prophecy, millennialism now is seen to be a determining factor in any system of theology. Premillennialism, amillennialism, and postmillennialism each influence the system of theology of which each is a part. The controversy between amillennialism and premillennialism, for this reason, has taken on a new and sharper antagonism and its outcome is now seen to assume significant proportions.

There is a growing tendency to recognize the importance of the millennial issue as a factor in determining various theological systems. Recent attacks on premillennialism by Allis, Landis, Mauro, Rutgers, Murray, and Boettner are based on the theory that the controversy is much more than a dispute on eschatology. Hence the premillenarian is linked with Russellism by Allis[1] and accused of denying the necessity of the death of Christ by both Allis and Mauro.[2] Landis spares no epithets to denounce premillennialism as utter heresy.[3] The opening sentence of Chapter I of this book classifies premillenarians as one with the "false prophets" predicted by Christ in Matthew 24:4.[4] He begins Chapter II by declaring, "Chiliasm is a crafty device of leftwing modernism. . . . Premillennialism is a fungus growth of first-century Pharisaic rabbinism."[5] Even Kromminga, a pre-

---

[1]Oswald T. Allis, *Prophecy and the Church*, p. 43.
[2]*Ibid.*, p. 75.
[3]Ira D. Landis, *The Faith of Our Fathers on Eschatology.*
[4]*Ibid.*, p. 3.
[5]*Ibid.*, p. 31.

millenarian, tries to prove that dispensational premillennialism has a tendency to "heretical aberration" in the doctrine of the Trinity as illustrated in the Scofield Reference Bible.[6]

Boettner quotes with approval the definition by J. G. Vos of dispensational premillennialism which labels it "the false system of Bible interpretation represented by the writings of J. N. Darby and the Scofield Reference Bible. . . ."[7] Boettner himself charges "that premillennialism lends itself more to an emotional type of preaching and teaching. . . . Premillennialism has little sympathy with the detailed, scientific, painstaking study of Scripture, and is apt to be quite impatient with a scholar or theologian who spends hours trying to arrive at the correct exegesis of a text."[8]

While these attacks are mostly unjustified, they point to a growing realization that premillennialism is more than an eschatology, that it involves a system of interpretation. Premillenarians are slower to recognize this fact than amillenarians. Robert T. Culver, an able premillenarian scholar writes: "I insist that the question of the millennium in both the Bible and history of interpretation is essentially a question of eschatology, and that it ought to be permitted to remain so."[9] He goes on to object to the idea of a " 'Premillennial system of theology,' " as well as "a distinctive 'Amillennial system of theology.' "[10] He argues: "When Amillennialism has been championed by large sections of such theologically diverse bodies as the Roman Catholic Church, branches of the Lutheran Church, sections of Presbyterian and Reformed Churches, Methodist, Southern Baptists, and notably by the Church of God (Winebrennarian group) it is sheer folly to create the fiction of a distinctive 'Amillennial system of theology.' "[11]

In speaking of "amillennial theology," the writer does not contend that the amillennial issue determines every theologi-

---

[6]D. H. Kromminga, *Millennium in the Church*, p. 23-24.
[7]Loraine Boettner, *The Millennium*, p. 5.
[8]*Ibid.*, p. 7.
[9]Robert D. Culver, *Daniel and the Latter Days*, p. 20.
[10]*Ibid.*, p. 21.
[11]*Loc. cit.*

cal judgment, neither does Calvinism or Arminianism, which is often in substantial agreement on such important subjects as the deity of Christ, inspiration of the Scriptures, doctrine of the Trinity, etc. It is simply that there are certain obvious characteristics of amillennialism that permeate with varying degrees of importance all areas of theology. The discussion to follow attempts to state the extent of amillennial influence on theology as well as its limits. It is certainly true that there are large areas of agreement between conservative amillenarians and premillenarians. It is not true that premillennialism is confined to eschatology. The writer is acquainted with a hundred or more sets of systematic theology, many of which have been examined in some detail. In all of them the influence of the millennial position of the particular author is discernible throughout the volume to one who is looking for this factor. While amillennialism, being a negative affirmation, does not have the power to create a complete system, the principles which lead to that negation are influential in many areas.

It is the purpose of the present discussion to trace some of the influences of amillennialism upon theological systems. In the nature of the case, it will be necessary to survey a large field rather than analyze its parts, and to form general rather than particular conclusions. While it is not always easy to determine *causal* factors in doctrine, it can be shown at least that the amillennial approach is in harmony with certain theological ideas and is conductive to certain trends. The important fact which stands out in this field of investigation is that amillennialism is more than a denial of premillennial eschatology; it is an approach to theological interpretation which has its own characteristics and trends.

II. AMILLENNIAL INFLUENCE ON BIBLIOLOGY

While the influence of the amillennial theory upon bibliology has seldom been recognized by its own adherents, it is, in fact, one of the important results which accrue from its relation to Biblical interpretation. In the previous discussion of amillennialism as a method of interpretation, the use of figurative or spiritualizing interpretation of the Bible by the amillenarians was found to be the basic concept of their system and that which distinguished it from premillennialism. While amillenarians reject the figurative method of interpreting the Bible as a general method, it is used extensively not only in the interpretation of prophecy but in other areas of theology as well. It was shown that the only possible rule which could be followed by the amillenarian was hopelessly subjective—the figurative method was used whenever the amillenarian found it necessary to change the literal meaning of Scripture to conform to his ideas.

The dangers of this type of figurative interpretation should be apparent to anyone who respects the inspiration of Scripture. By it, any passage of the Bible can be construed to mean something other than its plain, literal meaning. The danger is well recognized by the amillenarians themselves as is witnessed by their rejection of the allegorical method and their earnest attempts to safeguard their method by various rules and guiding principles. It has already been shown how impossible it is to form any safe boundaries for the use of the spiritualizing method. The modernist who spiritualizes the resurrection of Christ does so by almost the same techniques as are used by B. B. Warfield[12] who finds heaven described in Revelation 20:1-10. Further, the history of modern liberalism has demonstrated that its adherents are drawn almost entirely from ʹamillennial ranks.

What, then, is the amillennial influence on bibliology as a whole? The answer is already apparent when the diverse theological systems of Roman Catholic, modern liberal, and modern conservative writers are found to be all using essentially the same method. To be sure, the modern liberals who no longer hold to verbal inspiration do not need to spiritualize the Scriptures to arrive at their interpretation. They can simply declare the Scriptures in error and go on. But the first inroad

---

[12]*Biblical Doctrines*, pp. 643-64. Warfield is variously classified as postmillenarian and amillenarian. His theology has some characteristics of both millennial interpretations.

of liberalism in the church historically in Origen, and in modern times as well, has been by subverting the meaning by spiritualizing the words. While no doubt other errors are found in these three widely differing theological positions, their respective theologies could not have the variance that exists if each interpreted the Scriptures literally. The one factor which would correct everything would be a return to the literal meaning of the Bible. The introduction of the spiritualizing method in bibliology has opened the door for every variety of false doctrine according to the whims of the interpreter.

Amillennialism clearly, then, offers no defense against modern liberalism. While this conclusion may be disputed by amillenarians, the widespread defection of amillenarians to liberalism is an obvious fact in modern theology. It becomes all the more significant when it is realized that there has been practically no defection to modernism from those who were consistently premillennial. In fact, it is almost a byword in modern theology that a premillenarian is identified with Bible-believing conservatives who have resisted the modern trend of theology. Premillennialism has gone hand in hand with conservative belief in the inspired Word of God, while amillennialism has no consistent testimony in this regard.

One of the obvious problems of amillennialism in the field of bibliology is that their method of interpretation leaves large areas, particularly of the Old Testament, without any generally accepted meaning. As the spiritualizing method is by its nature almost entirely subjective, it is impossible to find any considerable measure of agreement on the spiritualized interpretation of great Old Testament prophecies which are taken literally by the premillenarian. When approaching the more difficult task of interpreting a New Testament book like Revelation, the utter bankruptcy of the common historical interpretation of this book becomes evident. There are literally scores of interpretation of the book of Revelation by the amillenarians who have attempted to interpret this book by the historical setting which was contemporary to them. The history of interpretation is strewed with the wreckage of multiplied schemes of interpretation which are every one contradictory of all the others. The writer has personally examined some fifty historical interpretations of Revelation, all of which would be rejected by any intelligent person today. The literal method which regards the bulk of Revelation as future is the only consistent approach possible. The spiritualizing method of interpretation is a blight upon the understanding of the Scriptures and constitutes an important hindrance to Bible study.

Amillennial bibliology by its use of the spiritualizing method has departed from the proper objective interpretation of the Scriptures, according to the ordinary grammatical sense of the terms, and has adopted a subjective method in which the meaning is to some extent at the mercy of the interpreter. Its subjective character has undermined amillennial theology as a whole. To the extent the spiritualizing method is used, to that very extent their theology loses all uniformity and self-consistency. In fact, as far as amillennialism itself is concerned, there is neither principle nor method to erect a self-consistent system of theology. The only consistent amillennial theologies which exist today are those which have most resisted the spiritualized method of interpretation and have to the greatest extent isolated its use. The ranks of modern amillenarians are largely dominated by the liberals in theology. While amillennialism can hardly be blamed for destructive higher criticism which has undermined faith in the Bible, it can be said that it had no defense against it as far as its method and attitude are concerned. After all, if Scripture which teaches something contrary to a preconceived theory can be altered by spiritualizing it, of what importance is the concept of inerrancy? If amillennialism did not furnish the material of modern liberalism, it at least provided the atmosphere. While there have been a number of outstanding conservative theologians who were amillennial, the institutions in which they taught and the denominations of which they were a part have for the most part left the fold of conservatives. The spiritualizing method of interpretation has proved the Achilles' heel of amillennial conservatism. The amillenarian who wants to forsake conservatism for liberalism needs no change in method and the transition is not difficult. On the other hand, a premillenarian if enamored of modern liberalism would have to forsake all he had formerly stood for in order to adopt liberalism.

III. AMILLENNIAL INFLUENCE ON THEOLOGY PROPER

Amillennialism as such does not profoundly influence the area of theology proper except indirectly by giving comfort to modern liberalism. Conservative amillenarians have differed little from premillenarians on essential doctrines relating to God. The major differences in doctrine in regard to the Godhead continue to be controversies between Calvinists, Arminians, and Socinians and their modern representatives.

A comparison between amillennial and premillennial theologies will reveal an important difference, however, in their respective views of the meaning of the incarnation. While the amillennial view confines itself to the limited perspective of fulfillment of the soteriological purposes of God, the premillenarian notes the frequent reminders in the Gospels that Christ came also to fulfill the Davidic covenant, promising a king and a throne forever and the fulfillment of the strictly Jewish Messianic hope. Likewise the concepts of the second advent of Christ as well as the significance of the present advocacy of Christ are somewhat different. The amillenarian tends to put less stress on the present ministry of Christ in heaven and to simplify the significance of prophecies regarding the second advent. Among some amillenarians the spiritualizing method of interpretation has robbed the second advent of its prophetic significance as a single future event. It has become only a process or symbol of divine providence in daily Christian experience. The historic creeds have resisted this tendency.

While agreeing on the person of the Holy Spirit, disagreement exists on the nature of the ministry of the Third Person in the various dispensations. The tendency of amillennial theology is to treat the work of the Holy Spirit as essentially the same in all ages. For this reason, amillenarians usually reject the dispensational distinctions in the work of the Holy Spirit ordinarily held by premillenarians. Amillenarians usually hold that the Spirit indwelt saints in the Old Testament, regenerated them, and empowered them in much the same manner as in the New Testament. By contrast, premillenarians normally view the present work of the Holy Spirit in the church as distinct from all other ages, and the baptism of the Holy Spirit as unique.

The influence of amillennialism on theology proper can be said, then, to be relatively unimportant as compared to other fields. The major difficulty here, as elsewhere, arises when the spiritualizing method of interpretation is applied, and to the extent this is resisted the difficulties subside.

IV. AMILLENNIAL INFLUENCE ON ANGELOLOGY

While conservative amillenarians and premillenarians agree in general on the doctrine of angels including the area of Satanology and demonology, only premillenarians present a united front in interpreting the Scriptures in this division of theology. The fact that amillennialism includes the diverse elements of conservative and liberal theology results in sharp differences in their teaching concerning angels. Liberal amillenarians tend to deny the existence of angels and relegate it all to pagan mythology, thereby denying also the Scriptural revelation.

An examination of conservative theologies dealing with angelology will, however, demonstrate that in general they minimize the importance and significance of angels in theology while premillenarians magnify the doctrine. The important point of departure is the disagreement regarding the binding of Satan during the millennium. On this point amillenarians are at variance with themselves. Augustine held that Satan was bound at the first coming of Christ. This, of course, is a flagrant spiritualization both of Revelation 20 and of all other passages dealing with the power of Satan in the world. It is characteristic of modern amillenarians to have a low view of the present power and activity of Satan. The obvious disagreement of Augustine's view with the facts of the history of the world and the church have in recent centuries helped to spark the new type of amillennialism which finds the millennium in heaven and limits the binding of Satan to inactivity in heaven itself rather than on earth. Amillenarians to this day have no united testimony on the real meaning of the binding of Satan and usually ignore it, except when attacking premillennialism.

The attitude of amillenarians to the binding of Satan is another illustration of how the spiritualizing method in regard to prophecy affects other areas. The amillenarian concept of the present binding of Satan, which is a future event to the premillenarian, results in a definite underestimating of the present power of Satan. Modern amillenarians such as Allis and Berkhof still embrace fundamentally the view of Augustine that Satan was bound at the first advent. But how can the Scriptures be harmonized with such a view? The answer is that they can be harmonized only by spiritualizing plain and factual statements of the Bible which obviously were not intended to be spiritualized. A survey of important Scripture references makes this clear.

Acts 5:3 records the words of Peter to Ananias: "Ananias, why hath Satan filled thy heart to lie to the Holy Spirit, and to keep back part of the price of the land?" Again in 1 Corinthians 7:5 Satan is spoken of as "tempting" Christians. In 2 Corinthians 4:3-4, Satan is revealed as one blinding the minds of all unbelievers. According to 2 Corinthians 11:14, Satan is often fashioned as an angel of light. Paul speaks of a messenger of Satan which buffeted him (2 Cor. 12:7). Satan hindered Paul in coming to the Thessalonians (1 Thess. 2:18). The future lawless one is said to come "according to the working of Satan with all power and lying wonders" (2 Thess. 2:9). Hymenaeus and Alexander are delivered to Satan (1 Tim. 1:20). 1 John 3:8 declares as a present truth, "He that doeth sin is of the devil." Children of God are contrasted to children of the devil (1 John 3:10). In 1 Peter 5:8, the direct statement and exhortation is made: "Be sober, be watchful: your adversary the devil, as a roaring lion, walketh about, seeking whom he may devour." How can anyone hold to the impossible theory that Satan is bound now when the Scriptures expressly state that Satan tempts, deceives, blinds, hinders, works lying wonders, and that he is walking about seeking whom he may devour? Such a theory is possible only when the spiritualizing method is used in interpreting the plain and literal statements of Scripture.

Amillenarians have escaped some of the force of the difficulty by minimizing and limiting the meaning of the binding of Satan itself. Calvin and Luther, for instance, while amillenarians, gave due recognition to the power of Satan with the idea that God is sovereign and that Satan has only a restricted area in which he is free to work. Berkhof who carefully avoids the issue of the binding of Satan in his chapter on angelology, seizes upon the explanation of Calvin that fallen angels "drag their chains with them wherever they go."[13] By this means a middle position is taken which on the one hand recognizes the binding of Satan and on the other escapes the difficulty of contradicting the plain meaning of Scripture on the present power of Satan. In general, the fact remains that the amillennial view of angelology tends to have a doctrine of sin and Satan which is less realistic than that of the premillenarians.

V. AMILLENNIAL INFLUENCE ON ANTHROPOLOGY

Amillennial anthropology, including as it does conservative, liberal and Roman Catholic viewpoints, has more variance within itself than with premillennial anthropology. This area of theology is probably less affected by the millennial controversy than any other. The differences that do exist do not seem to connect directly with the millennial issue. Certain tendencies, however caused, can be noted.

Amillennial theology of the conservative Protestant kind has become identified in the last two centuries with the covenant theory of theology as contained in the covenant of works, covenant of redemption, and covenant of grace.[14] While some premillenarians attempt to combine the covenant theory with premillenarianism, it has been more common for premillenarians to follow a dispensational emphasis founded upon recognition of the Biblical covenants. The covenant theory has affected anthropology to the extent that the covenant of works becomes

---

[13] L. Berkhof, *Systematic Theology*, p. 149.
[14] See L. Berkhof, *ibid.*, pp. 211 ff.

related to the fall. As usually explained, the covenant of works postulates a covenant between God and Adam in which Adam is promised eternal life for being obedient in the test of the forbidden fruit. While recognizing the reality of the test involved for Adam and Eva, premillenarians have tended to confine their view to the more explicit statement of Scripture, questioning the promise of eternal life for obedience, which is nowhere mentioned in the Bible, and weakening the force of the covenant idea.

In place of the covenant of works as such, premillenarians often offer the Edenic covenant. This covenant though not expressly called a covenant in Scripture includes all the aspects of man's responsibility before the fall, including the prohibition of the forbidden fruit. As understood by the premillenarians, this covenant ceased to exist when the fall occurred and was succeeded by the Adamic covenant providing the basic conditions for man's life on the earth after the fall, some of which conditions continue until the end of the present world order. While the issue is not to be minimized, it can be traced only indirectly to the millennial controversy. Many amillenarians also question the covenant of works. It introduces, however, the covenant theory as principally an amillennial influence and as opposed to the dispensational viewpoint of Scripture which is more normal to premillenarianism.

In regard to the depravity of man, premillenarianism embraces the concept of total depravity, taking a serious view of the sinful state of man and finding him totally unable to commend himself to God or effect his own salvation. In this regard, amillennialism again has no certain voice, the conservatives generally accepting the doctrine of total depravity as expressed in Calvinism, but the Roman Catholic and modern liberal amillenarians having different views. While this can be related to the method of spiritualizing the Scriptures, other factors seem to outweigh the millennial influences. Taken as a whole, anthropology is not directly related to the millennial issue.

VI. AMILLENNIAL INFLUENCE ON SOTERIOLOGY

The question of millennial influence on the doctrine of soteriology has been raised in recent years by the amillenarians themselves, and they have attempted to distinguish the soteriology of premillenarians from that held by amillenarians. In this area of theology, as in previous ones, amillenarians would do well to unify their own theology. The concepts of Roman theology and modern liberal theology, both amillennial, are in striking contrast to the views held by the Protestant Reformers. In both the Roman and modern liberal view, human works play a large part in salvation. In both, the work of Christ on the cross is not considered a final dealing with sins or "finished" in the Reformed understanding of the term. In the conservative amillennial as well as the premillennial view, eternal security, assurance of salvation, complete justification, and regeneration issue from simple faith in Jesus Christ. It follows that there is more difference between various schools of amillennial thought than there is between conservative Reformed amillennialism and premillennialism.

The present controversy between amillenarians and premillenarians is not on the factors mentioned, however. Instead, the difference of opinion has arisen from the conflicting system of theology resulting from covenant theology as opposed to dispensational theology. The respective merits of these opposing schools of interpretation will be given attention in a later discussion which will take up the controversy in detail.

For the purpose of the present survey the two approaches to theology may be distinguished in general terms. Covenant theology is the view that all the dispensations from Adam to the end of human history are aspects of God's soteriological program. In other words, the dispensations are different presentations of the way of salvation in a gradually unfolding progression. The tendency of this viewpoint is to regard God's general purpose as essentially that of saving the elect, to blend the various Biblical revelations regarding Israel, the Gentiles, and the church into one stream, and to minimize the differences between the various dispensations. In contrast, the dispensational theology, while not disputing the view of the unity of God's plan of salvation, finds in the various dispensations periods of stewardship which are not directly related to salvation. In a word, the dispensationalist does not consider the program of God for salvation as the sole purpose of God, and in fact denies that some of the dispensations are basically soteriological. The Mosaic law under the dispensational approach, while a way of life, is not considered a way of salvation. Heaven was not among its rewards nor was hell among its punishments.

The amillenarian who follows covenant theology will accordingly have a decidedly different viewpoint of the meaning of Scripture than the dispensationalist. There is difference of opinion on the essential meaning of some of the dispensations. While agreeing on the ground and in general on the terms of salvation, there is conflict on the relation of God's plan of salvation to the revealed character of the Biblical dispensations. The importance of this issue is obvious, and deserves a more extended treatment which will follow later.

VII. Amillennial Influence on Ecclesiology

Next to the field of eschatology itself, ecclesiology offers the greatest contrast between the amillennial and premillennial views. Here exist some basic conflicts which arise in the nature of the case from the differing views of the character of the present age. As this will be given attention later in a special treatment, it will be sufficient to outline the problem.

In ecclesiology, several aspects of amillennialism converge to produce a distinctive doctrine of the church. From the covenant theology usually embraced by amillenarians comes the concept of the essential unity of the elect of all dispensations. The fact that all the saints of all dispensations are saved on the basis of the death of Christ is interpreted as a just ground for concluding that the term *church* is properly used of saints in both the Old and New Testaments. Hence Jews and Gentiles who were saved in the Old Testament period are considered as included in the Old Testament church on much the same basis as saints in the New Testament are included in the New Testament church. In fact, the usual tendency is to deny any essential difference in the nature of their salvation.

As amillenarians deny any future dispensation after the present age, they also deny any future to Israel as a nation. The many promises made to Israel are given one of two treatments. By the traditional Augustinian amillennialism, these promises are transferred by spiritualized interpretation to the church. The church today is the true Israel and inherits the promises which Israel lost in rejecting Christ. The other, more modern type of amillennialism holds that the promises of righteousness, peace, and security are poetic pictures of heaven and fulfilled in heaven, not on earth. This view does not necessarily identify Israel and the church. Some combine both viewpoints. It is obvious that the Augustinian view, in particular, has a tremendous influence upon ecclesiology. The Roman Church builds much of its claim for sovereignty on the inheritance from Israel of the combined political and religious authority revealed in the Old Testament. The concept of the church as an institution is enhanced, and ecclesiastical organization and authority given Scriptural sanction. By so much, also, the New Testament revelation of the church as essentially a spiritual organism rather than an organization is often slighted and in effect denied. The great contrast between legalism as found in the Mosaic dispensation and grace as revealed in the present age is usually ignored. The effect is often a repetition of the Galatian error.

As contrasted to dispensational premillennialism, amillennialism tends to slight the doctrine of the body of Christ in ecclesiology as well as the distinctive basis of grace as the ground for the believer's walk before God in this age. Even a casual survey of amillennial theologies will reveal the tendency to limit discussion to the matters of church organization, church ordinances, and the means of grace. By contrast, premillennial treatments of ecclesiology tend to enlarge the concept of the church as the body of Christ—an organism rather than an organization —and give extended treatment to the spiritual life of the believer. Ecclesiology offers one of the principal areas of disagreement in relation to the millennial issue. Amillenarians are fully aware of this and, like the recent work of Allis—*Prophecy and the Church*—are relating the millennial issue to the doctrine of the church. All seem to agree that it is important to analyze the amillennial doctrine of the church and attention will be given to this aspect of the doctrine later.

VIII. AMILLENNIAL INFLUENCE ON ESCHATOLOGY

In the field of eschatology, the principal differences occasioned by the millennial issue are found. Here again amillennialism does not present a united front and includes almost every variation not specifically classified as postmillennial or premillennial. The modern liberal rules out any specific scheme of eschatology according to his own ideas, denying usually the ordinary doctrines of the second advent, resurrection, and final judgment as held by the historic church. The Roman Church, of course, has its own complicated doctrine of future things which is quite foreign to that of Protestantism. The present analysis will need to be limited to the essential features of conservative Reformed millennialism.

The doctrines of Reformed amillennialism in regard to eschatology are quite clear. They usually include as the essentials the doctrine of the second advent of Christ, the resurrection of the dead, the final judgment of all, and the eternal state. A period of trouble corresponding to the predicted time of tribulation is usually assigned to the period just before the second advent, but in general terms. Under the amillennial viewpoint, the portions of Scripture dealing with the rapture and the judgment of the church, the resurrection of the righteous dead, the resurrection of the wicked dead, the judgment of the Gentiles, the judgment of Israel, and the judgment of Satan and angels are all combined in a closely knit sequence of events attending the second advent itself. The premillennial objection of this form of doctrine consists fundamentally in rejection of the spiritualizing of the many passages involved in order to make them conform to the pattern desired by the amillenarian. For instance, the amillennial view that the judgment of the Gentiles in Matthew 25:31-46 as the final general judgment is rejected by the premillenarian on the ground that the passage deals only with the living Gentiles, not any resurrected peoples, nor the church. Without doubt, the millennial controversy is largely settled by answering the question of validity of the interpretation of these events in Scripture. The amillennial doctrine in this area demands a careful analysis and special attention will be given later to the major items of study.

IX. CONCLUSION

In this general survey of the influence of the amillennial view on theology as a whole, it was shown that the principal areas of influence in order of importance are eschatology, ecclesiology, and soteriology. In these three areas, particular attention must be paid to the nature of amillennial influence, and the discussion to follow will take up these areas in turn, beginning in Chapter VII with soteriology.

CHAPTER VII

AMILLENNIAL SOTERIOLOGY

Recent discussions of the millennial issue in theology have crystallized the problem of the relation of millennialism to the doctrine of salvation. The growing realization that premillennial doctrine affects theology as a whole has inspired an attempt to prove that premillennialism teaches or implies a heretical view of salvation. Allis writes, for instance: "The Dispensational interpretation of prophecy minimizes the Cross! The traditional interpretation magnifies it."[1] Philip Mauro goes a step further in his pamphlet, "Dispensationalism Justifies the Crucifixion." Having made their accusation with one broad statement, they sometimes withdraw it with another, as in the case of Allis, "Dispensationalists do not reject the Cross or minimize its importance: they glory in it."[2] The impression is left, however, by the space that separates the accusation from the retraction that premillenarians are either inconsistent or heretical. The idea that the millennial controversy affects the doctrine of salvation is, however, not held by all. Rutgers finds the doctrine of salvation as held by conservative amillenarians and premillenarians a point of agreement rather than disagreement.[3]

It is the purpose of this discussion to evaluate the influence of amillennialism on the soteriology of its adherents. Such an approach will serve as a background for consideration of the influence of premillennialism on its soteriology. While there is a large measure of agreement between them, certain important differences can be noted.

---

[1]Oswald T. Allis, *Prophecy and the Church*, p. 121.
[2]*Ibid.*, p. 234.
[3]*Premillennialism in America*, p. 289.

I. Historical Development

Without attempting a detailed historical analysis, it is possible to trace the broad movement of amillennialism in relation to soteriology. Beginning with Augustine, amillennialism became identified with a theology which was continued in Protestantism. Augustine had a profound sense of the unity of the divine purpose and program. His form of amillennialism identified the millennium with the present age. He viewed Christianity as being engaged in a vital struggle, the City of God versus the City of Satan. The outcome will be victory at the second advent of Christ. As a part of this program, Augustine developed a doctrine of sin which involved man's total depravity, and a doctrine of grace which provided for man's inability through the sacraments as ministered by the church. Salvation was mediated through the church and its sacraments and, though it was by faith, it was attainable only through unceasing effort. While the precise relation of Augustine's amillennialism to his soteriology is debatable, it is clear that his amillennial view of the present age and the role of the Roman Church in it was an essential part of his theology. The subsequent history of Roman doctrine evinces clearly the trend toward more emphasis on the place of the sacraments as the means of grace, less emphasis on man's inability, and more delineation of works as the basic ground of salvation in the Roman system. The Augustinian denial of a future to Israel or of a future kingdom of righteousness and peace on earth in literal fulfillment of the Old Testament prophets tended to enhance legalism and human effort and to subtract from divine grace immediately bestowed apart from sacraments by a work of the Holy Spirit. Augustinian soteriology, whether or not a fruit of amillennialism, went hand in hand with a system of salvation by religious works which has continued in Roman theology to the present day. The spiritualizing method of interpretation of Scripture fostered by Augustine was helpless to counter this trend in the Roman Church.

Modern liberal Protestantism has continued the amillennial tradition of Augustine, but has abandoned his soteriology.

While it is difficult to generalize on the doctrine of salvation in modern liberal Christianity, it may be observed that it usually denies the efficacy of the death of Christ, as well as the necessity of it as the ground of salvation, and transfers the work of salvation from God to man. Again, salvation is largely a matter of human works, following ethical ideals, achieving a mystic union with God through religious experiences. While modern liberalism is amillennial in relation to the millennial issue, it is really lacking in any vital soteriology. Man does not need to be saved because man is not lost. All he needs is education, religious experience, and resolution. It is reformation rather than regeneration. The influence of amillennialism in modern liberal theology is more remote than in Roman theology. The main difficulty is not one of interpretation of the Scripture, but the denial of its authoritative revelation. In general, it may be concluded that the amillennial influence on soteriology in Roman theology and in modern liberalism is of only secondary importance.

The amillennialism question comes more immediately to the fore when comparing conservative amillennialism with premillennialism. Here the essential theological positions are similar. Both hold the Scriptures as inspired and authoritative. Both hold to essentially the same concept of the death of Christ as the work of God which is the ground of salvation. Because of this unity, it is possible to note significant variations in their soteriology in relation to the millennial issue.

II. Relation of Amillennialism to Covenant Theology

The major source of difference lies in the so-called covenant theology of the amillennialists in contrast to the dispensational theology of the premillenarians. While all amillenarians are not covenant theologians, and all premillenarians do not observe the same dispensational distinctions, in general the distinction between them is covenant theology versus dispensationalism. This distinction is not always evident, however, as some modern premillenarians attempt to follow a form of covenant theology as opposed to dispensationalism of the type espoused by the Scofield Reference Bible. This generally carries with it a weakened and limited premillennialism.

The idea of a covenant relation between God and man is, of course, as old as the Scriptures. God frequently dealt with man in the Old Testament on obvious covenant grounds. In the New Testament, a gracious covenant is contained in the very gospel message itself—the promise of grace and salvation to those who believe. While there is considerable difference in approach in the definition and use of covenants in the Bible, both premillenarians and amillenarians are in agreement on the existence of the covenant of grace which is proclaimed in the Scriptures.

Upon closer examination, however, a sharp cleavage is found in the concept of the covenant idea. Covenant theologians such as Charles Hodge conceive of the covenant of grace as originating in eternity past in a covenant agreement between the persons of the Trinity. This is sometimes called the covenant of redemption as a covenant within the Godhead, sometimes a covenant of grace as between God and man as represented in Christ, and by a number of other terms, such as covenant of mercy, evangelical covenant, national-ecclesiastical covenant, and covenant of life.[4] As none of these terms is found as such in the Bible, their definition is largely what theologians have made them. The basic idea, however, is that the central purpose of God is salvation of the elect, and that this from eternity past has been the determining principle of divine providence.

Along with the idea of an eternal covenant of grace is the covenant of works which God is supposed to have made with Adam before the fall. While including the Biblical material embracing the Edenic arrangement, it makes the important addition, without Scriptural warrant, of promising life to Adam and Eve if they proved obedient. Under this arrangement the harshness of predestination and the theology of the decree of God seemed to be softened by making it to some extent conditional upon man's decision.

---

[4] Cf. C. F. Lincoln, "The Covenants" (unpublished Doctor's dissertation), pp. 79-80.

A number of features appear in covenant theology which can be mentioned only in abbreviated form in this discussion.[5] Covenant theology is of comparatively recent origin.   There seems to be no reference to a covenant of works as defined by covenant theologians until after 1600.[6] It was stated in extended form by Cocceius about 1645. While the covenant of grace as a general offer of grace in the gospel was commonly held, the idea of an eternal covenant within the Godhead as the covenant of grace seems to have originated about the same time. In any case, covenant theology as such is not in the historic creeds of the church, was not taught explicitly by Calvin or the other Reformers, and even in the Westminster Confession was recognized only indirectly. In the Westminster Confession the covenant with Adam is regarded as the "first" and the covenant of grace as the "second," thereby making it clear that the latter is not considered in its eternal character.

Covenant theology is definitely a product of theological theory rather than Biblical exposition. While covenant theologians such as Berkhof labor over many Scriptural proofs, the specific formulas of the covenants are inductions from Calvinistic theology which go beyond the Scriptures. Charles Hodge, a covenant theologian, states plainly: "God entered into covenant with Adam. This statement does not rest upon any express declaration of the Scriptures."[7]

The situation with the covenant of grace is somewhat different. The purpose of extending grace to man is obviously an eternal purpose of God.   The aspect which is theoretical rather than Biblical is the creation of a covenant arrangement in regard to grace in the Godhead in which a "bargain" is struck in the eternal counsels of God, with the Father promising to extend grace, the Son to procure it by His death, and the Spirit to apply it. The original idea of the covenant of grace regarded it as an event subsequent to the fall of man, that is, an offer of grace with attendant promises to fallen

---

[5]For a statement of covenant theology by one of its able adherents, cf. L. Berkhof, *Systematic Theology*, pp. 262-300.
[6]C. F. Lincoln, *op. cit.*, p. 101.
[7]Charles Hodge, *Systematic Theology*, II, 117.

man. This was the view of Cocceius, and the Consensus Helveti-cus and the Westminster Confession so regarded it. Witsius (1636-1708) in his *Economy of the Covenants* seems to be the first advocate of the idea of a covenant of grace from eternity past. Charles Hodge followed Witsius and other Calvinists found the covenant of grace in eternity past an important ingredient in the decree of God. The point of distinction in covenant theology, then, is not simply an assertion of a covenant of grace in the broad sense of the offer of grace to man, but the doctrine that the covenant of grace is an important and determinative aspect of the eternal decree and is in fact the central purpose of God.

Covenant theology as held today is confined largely to amillennial Reformed theologians who are essentially conservative and following closely in the theology derived from the Reformation. Modern Arminians and Unitarians, while usually amillennial, do not accept covenant theology. Modern Baptists, while often essentially Calvinistic, are not followers of the covenant idea. Covenant theology is therefore confined to a minority of contemporary amillennialists. On the other hand, it is not uncommon to find some premillenarians who embrace in part the covenant idea. It is therefore not only difficult to generalize, but the very relation of amillennialism to covenant soteriology might be questioned. In spite of these facts, a definite relation exists between amillennial covenant theology in the field of soteriology and the concept of the same field by the premillenarian. This is not only supported by obvious facts, but explains some of the antagonism between the soteriology of amillenarians and premillenarians.

III. Covenant Theology in Conflict with Dispensationalism

The major conflict of covenant theology is with dispensationalism. Covenant theology regards all dispensations as phases of the one purpose of God expressed in the covenant of grace. Dispensations are different and progressive applications of the same essential principles of grace. Berkhof's summary of the covenant view may be taken as representative: "On the basis of all that has been said it is preferable to follow the traditional lines by distinguishing just two dispensations or administrations, namely, that of the Old, and that of the New Testament; and to subdivide the former into several periods or stages in the revelation of the covenant of grace."[8] The entire Old Testament constitutes under covenant theology a progressive revelation of one covenant, the covenant of grace, and all the Biblical covenants are phases or developments of it. The final revelation is given in the New Testament. This in effect declares that God has one central purpose, the salvation of the elect, and that all the dispensations are essentially the fulfillment of this purpose. By contrast, the premillennial and dispensational interpretation of Scripture builds upon the successive Biblical covenants which are expressly revealed in the Bible, interprets them literally, and conditions the form and responsibility of life in successive dispensations according to the covenants which apply.

It is not possible in limited space to undertake the refutation of covenant theology and the defense of a dispensational view. The major objections to the covenant view can only be stated. Covenant theology is built upon a spiritualizing method of interpreting the Scriptures. In order to make the various covenants of the Old Testament conform to the pattern of the covenant of grace, it is necessary to interpret them in other than their literal sense. This is illustrated in the promises given to Abraham and to Israel which are interpreted as promises to the New Testament church. Berkhof states, in regard to the covenant of grace: "The main promise of God, which includes all other promises, is contained in the oft-repeated words, 'I will be a God unto thee, and to thy seed after thee.' Gen. 17:7."[9] The promise was intended to be applied to Abraham's physical seed and Abraham himself. It is characteristic of covenant theology to appropriate these promises as belonging to all who receive grace under the covenant of grace. The covenant theory allows no place for literal fulfill-

---

[8]Berkhof, *op. cit.*, p. 293.
[9]*Ibid.*, p. 277.

ment of Israel's national and racial promises and either cancels them on the ground that Israel failed to meet the necessary conditions or transfers them to the saints in general. From the dispensational and literal standpoint, this is misappropriation of Scriptural promises.

As previously stated, a serious objection to the covenant of grace is that it is nowhere directly stated in Scripture in the form claimed by the amillenarian covenant theologians. The concept of an eternal covenant of grace was never seriously advanced until the post-Reformation period when it was proposed by Witsius. It is not contained in the historic creeds of the church as an eternal covenant.

One of the serious errors of the covenant theologians is their disregard of the essentially legal and nongracious rule provided by the Mosaic covenant. The New Testament in no uncertain terms describes it as a ministry of death and condemnation, and it is never described as a way of salvation. Allis, however, plainly states, "The law is a declaration of the will of God for man's *salvation*."[10] He further states, "The reward of obedience is life; the penalty for disobedience is death."[11] Again, "The priest and the altar make it possible for sinful man to obtain mercy from a righteous God. In this respect the law is an impressive declaration of the covenant of grace."[12] It is hard to reconcile such a theory to the direct statement of Scripture that "the law was given by Moses, but grace and truth come by Jesus Christ" (John 1:17). According to Galatians 2:16, justification is impossible by the law. Paul denounced this concept as a perversion of the gospel (Gal. 1:7-9) which deserved the severest condemnation. If the Mosaic law could provide salvation, then it was a salvation by religious works and not of faith. Such a viewpoint does violence to the pure grace of God provided in Christ.

---

[10]Oswald T. Allis, *op. cit.*, p. 39.
[11]*Loc. cit.*
[12]*Ibid.*, pp. 39-40.

IV. THE REDUCTIVE ERROR OF COVENANT THEOLOGY

Covenant theology is another illustration of overstatement of that which is true in its right perspective. All Reformed theologians would agree that God has a complete and comprehensive purpose as stated in the theological doctrine of the decree of God. Under this concept, all events of every classification have been determined by God from eternity past, but with full respect to the manner of their execution. Thus the necessary element of freedom is preserved and man acts according to his will while at the same time fulfilling the decree of God. Under a proper concept of this decree of God, it must be held that the decree of God is holy, wise, and good, in keeping with the attributes of God. All the events of the created world are designed to manifest the glory of God. The error of covenant theologians is that they combine all the many facets of divine purpose in the one objective of fulfillment of the covenant of grace. From a logical standpoint, this is the reductive error--the use of one aspect of the whole as the determining element.

The dispensational view of Scripture taken as a whole is far more satisfactory as it allows for the literal and natural interpretation of the great covenants of Scripture, in particular those with Abraham, Moses, David, and with Israel as a whole, and explains them in the light of their own historical and prophetical context without attempting to conform them to a theological concept to which they are mostly unsuited. This explanation fully sustains the fundamental thesis of Calvinism, that God is sovereign and all will in the end manifest His glory. The various purposes of God for Israel, for the church which is His body, for the Gentile nations, for the unsaved, for Satan and the wicked angels, for the earth and for the heavens have each their contribution. How impossible it is to compress all of these factors into the mold of the covenant of grace!

The amillennial viewpoint in soteriology as contained in the covenant theory limits the saving purpose of God to the salvation of the individual soul. The dispensational interpretation of Scripture, on the other hand, magnifies the death of

Christ as providing not only the ground of salvation of all saints in all ages—essentially one way of salvation for all—but also the ground for the peculiar and unique features of grace revealed to the church, the body of Christ, the saints of this present dispensation. It secures for them not only the riches of grace in Christ, but the ground for victory over present sin. The death of Christ under the dispensational viewpoint also constitutes the basis for the fulfillment of the new covenant to Israel, the promises of grace to the nation Israel in the prophesied kingdom on earth when the Son of David will reign. Properly understood, the dispensational viewpoint magnifies and enriches the meaning of the death of Christ and frees it from the limiting restrictions of covenant theology.

V. Conclusion

By way of general conclusion, it may be stated that amillennial soteriology has its own peculiar characteristics. Amillennialism provides the spiritualizing method of interpretation of the Old Testament necessary to covenant theology. It permits the Roman Catholic as well as the modern liberal soteriology. While amillennialism cannot be charged with being the causal factor of all the variations of soteriology held by amillenarians, its material and method permit them. On the other hand, a genuine premillennial and dispensational interpretation rules out at once the Roman Catholic, the modern liberal and, if applied consistently, the covenant theology view as well. The millennial issue does provide, then, an influence in the field of soteriology which demands more recognition than has been given to it in the history of doctrine.

Chapter VIII

AMILLENNIAL ECCLESIOLOGY

Few doctrines are more central in the Christian faith than the doctrine of the church. The teachings concerning its nature, form of government, its sacraments, the priesthood of the church, its essential duties, it rights, and its relation to the world and to the state combine to form an important segment of Christian truth. Given the doctrine of the church, the rest of a theological system can almost be deduced.

It is the purpose of this aspect of the study to trace the influence of amillennialism in the field of ecclesiology and to form some estimate of its importance and results. There has been growing realization that some relation exists and that those who differ on the millennial issue usually hold differing concepts of the church itself.

I. The Influence of Amillennialism on Roman Ecclesiology

As amillennialism had its rise historically in the Roman Church and developed as an integral part of the Roman system, significant facts appear in the history of the period from Augustine in the fourth century to the Reformation. The Roman Church, first of all, regarded itself as the continuation of Israel as a spiritual entity. The political or theocratic character of Israel as well as its religious life was considered as continuing in new form in the Roman Church. Like Israel, the Roman Church was a combined political and spiritual society. Just as Israel had power under God to legislate, to govern itself politically and religiously, so the Roman Church claimed for itself similar power. As the spiritual is higher and more important than the political, so the church claimed authority over the secular state.

The amillennial interpretation of Scripture was, of course, essential to this Roman viewpoint. Only by denying fulfillment of the promises of God to Israel and by spiritualized interpretation transferring them to the Roman Church could any vital connection between Judaism and Christianity be established. The church had to be the successor and inheritor of Israel's promises. This is characteristic of the amillennial system of interpretation. The premillennial interpretation, for instance, would never have issued into the Roman system if consistently applied. The amillennial approach was indispensable to the Roman system of doctrine. Apart from it, the Roman system would have been without authorization in its use of truth committed to Israel only.

In the period before the Reformation, the Roman Church tended to emphasize the external nature of the church. Its organization, authority, sacraments, and religious rites were for the most part external, and adherence and submission to the external Roman Church were the indispensable prerequisites for salvation and fellowship in Roman Christianity. The Roman Church did not deny that there existed the so-called invisible church, but they defined this as a fellowship of believers derived from being a part of the visible, that is, the Roman Church. They held that there is no church invisible which is not a part of the visible Roman Church, and the important question was whether one was a part of this visible church. As Berkhof summarizes the Roman position: "From the day of Cyprian down to the Reformation the essence of the Church was sought ever increasingly in its external visible organization. The Church Fathers conceived of the catholic Church as comprehending all true branches of the Church of Christ, and as bound together in an external and visible unity, which had its unifying bond in the college of bishops. The conception of the Church as an external organization became more important as time went on."[1]

---

[1] L. Berkhof, *Systematic Theology*, p. 562. The modern Roman Church also identifies the mystical with the visible church. Pope Pius XII in an encyclical letter issued in August, 1950, denounced those in the Roman Church who hold "they are not bound by the doctrine . . . which

The tendency of ecclesiology in the Roman Church before the Reformation and to a large extent ever since has been an emphasis on the external character of the church. This had its rise in the idea that the church is essentially theocratic, a continuation of God's purpose toward Israel. This in turn was built on the spiritualizing system of interpretation fostered by Augustinian amillennialism. While amillennialism does not lead necessarily to the conclusions drawn by the Roman Church, the conclusions that were reached would have been impossible without the amillennial viewpoint.

Some of the more particular conclusions of the Roman Church are traced to appropriation of the Jewish promises in the Old Testament. The sacramental idea received much of its impetus from the Levitical rites and the Aaronic priesthood. From the Protestant point of view, of course, much of Romanism is derived unabashed from paganism, and for this amillennialism is not responsible. On the other hand, a literal interpretation of the prophetic Word would have ruled out paganism as well as the ritualism. The complicated religious rites and ceremonies for the most part did not come into the church until amillennialism had become the dominant viewpoint.

II. The Ecclesiology of the Reformation

The Protestant movement begun in the Reformation was in large measure corrective of the abuses which had become prevalent in the Roman system. The sacraments were overhauled and reduced to New Testament Biblical formulas. The priesthood was restored to all believers. The hierarchical system was changed in most of Protestantism to Biblical patterns. Justification became a work of God in true believers instead of a work mediated through the church. The Protestant movement, however, was not able to extricate itself completely from Roman influence. This is evidenced in eschatology, in the long disputes

teaches that the mystical body of Christ and the Roman Catholic Church are one and the same things . . . and reduce to a meaningless formula the necessity of belonging to the true church in order to gain salvation." Cf. *Time*, Sept. 4, 1950, pp. 68, 71.

over transubstantiation, and more particularly in continuing to a large extent the emphasis on the external church. While most of the Reformers did not limit the church to its external form and recognized the true body of believers as such, the tendency to organization and attempts to enter the political arena early were in evidence.

The Reformation did not change essentially the concept of the church. For most Reformers it was still largely a visible entity with its roots in Judaism and its boundaries including all the saints. The church was thought of as the logical successor of Israel, the inheritor of its spiritual promises. Indeed, the church was considered to have begun in the Old Testament, by some with Adam, and by others with Abraham. Calvin refers to the saints of the Old and New Testament under the one title of the "Church."[2] Calvin further states explicitly: "The covenant of all the fathers is so far from differing substantially from ours, that it is the very same; it only varies in the administration. . . . Moreover, the apostle makes the Israelites equal to us, not only in the grace of the covenant, but also in the signification of the sacraments. . . . Wherefore it is certainly and clearly proved, that the same promises of an eternal and heavenly life, with which the Lord now favours us, were not only communicated to the Jews, but even sealed and confirmed by sacraments truly spiritual."[3] Calvin held that the New Testament church differed from saints in the Old Testament principally in degree of revelation. In the Old Testament they had the shadows, but the realities were revealed in the New Testament. Essentially Calvin along with many of the Reformers continued the basic Roman conception that the saints of the Old and New Testaments belong to the same entity, the church. In order to achieve this end, however, the Reformers had to deny to the Jews all their distinctive promises and had to nullify the hope of Israel for an earthly kingdom of righteousness. Calvin, for instance, refers to "the folly of the whole nation of the Jews in the present age, in expecting any earthly

---

[2]John Calvin, *Institutes of the Christian Religion*, I, 503
[3]*Ibid.*, I, 466, 468, 470.

kingdom of the Messiah. . . ."[4] His conclusions were an outgrowth of amillennial theology and its method of interpretation. It is quite clear that the leaders of the Reformation continued in the main the basic Roman idea of the church as the successor of Israel as well as being one with Israel. The church, in their viewpoint, varies in details and in administration, but is essentially the same in both Testaments.

III. THE CONCEPT OF THE KINGDOM OF GOD

An important phase of amillennial ecclesiology is its teaching on the concept of the kingdom of God. The kingdom of God is an important Scriptural theme, and its understanding opens the door to a great body of truth. According to the premillennial view, while there is a form of the kingdom of God in the present age, the fulfillment of the promises of a kingdom of God as given to Israel will be fulfilled in a future millennial age, following the second advent.

While all premillenarians do not agree on a precise definition of the concept of the kingdom of God, they all must, in order to be premillenarian, hold to a future kingdom on earth following the second advent. George E. Ladd, for instance, makes the kingdom "primarily a soteriological concept"[5] and identifies the kingdom as more or less "a single concept . . . *God's saving will in action.*"[6] While this is essentially Augustinian amillennialism in definition of the kingdom, Ladd as a premillenarian definitely supports the idea of a future kingdom following the second advent of Christ, even though he falters on the literal interpretation of the millennium as a thousand years.[7] Augustine in the fifth century introduced what was then a new idea, that the kingdom of God predicted by the prophets is a present reality in the interadvent period,

---

[4]*Ibid.*, I, 488.
[5]George E. Ladd, *Crucial Questions About the Kingdom of God*, p. 83.
[6]*Ibid.*, p. 97.
[7]*Ibid.*, p. 147-48, "The 1000 years may well be a symbol for a long period of time, the extent of which is unknown." Ladd does Augustine, the amillenarian, one better. Augustine, though amillennial, held to a literal thousand years.

and that this is to be identified with the church. The church, then, as defined by amillenarians, is the kingdom of God, and its progress is the advance of divine salvation and the establishment of righteousness in the earth.

The Roman Church took up the idea of Augustine and identified the church with the kingdom of God, but it also went a step farther in identifying the kingdom of God with its own ecclesiastical organization. As Berkhof states: "Augustine viewed the kingdom as a present reality and identified it with the Church. For him it was primarily identical with the pious and holy, that is, with the Church as a community of believers; but he used some expressions which seem to indicate that he also saw it embodied in the episcopally organized Church. The Roman Catholic Church frankly identified the Kingdom of God with their hierarchical institution."[8] Under amillennial influence, then, the kingdom of God was divorced from its connection with the millennial reign of Christ following the second advent, separated from the nation Israel, and made identical to the church in the present age, and specifically identified with the Roman Church. The process by which this was accomplished involved the spiritualization of the Old Testament's promises to Israel, denying some, translating others into the Roman Church. The stark contrast of what the Roman Church is as compared to the millennial kingdom illustrates the extremes to which spiritualization of Scripture can go.

In the Reformation the Reformers seem to have returned somewhat to the position of Augustine. This is defined by Berkhof as a denial of the Roman position that the kingdom of God is identical to the *visible* church, i.e., the whole company of believers.[9] This is essentially the position of amillennial conservatives today. Liberal theologians following the lead of Ritschl have regarded the kingdom of God not as a congregation of believers but a system of ethical ideals. The advance of the kingdom for them is the advance of ethical principles. Augustine, Rome, the Reformers, and the modern liberal agree,

[8]Berkhof, *op. cit.*, p. 569.
[9]*Loc. cit.*

however, in denouncing the concept that the kingdom of God is essentially Messianic, the rule of Jesus Christ as the Son of David following the second advent. They emphasize that the kingdom of God is on earth now, and its advance and ultimate triumph is the advance and triumph of the church.

IV. AMILLENNIAL ECCLESIOLOGY IN RELATION TO ISRAEL

The most obvious fact of amillennial ecclesiology is that it denies any millennial period following the church age in which righteousness and peace will flourish on earth. All the prophetic anticipations of such a period are either considered conditional and therefore uncertain, or are to be fulfilled in the church in the present age. The denial of a future millennium is based on the method of giving a spiritualized interpretation to Old Testament kingdom prophecies. While all amillenarians are not agreed on the details of the interpretation of the Old Testament kingdom promises, the same general principles are usually recognized by all of them.

No future for Israel as a nation. Amillennial ecclesiology denies to Israel any future as a nation. Israel is never to be a political entity in the world in fulfillment of the promises of a glorious kingdom period. Promises in the Old Testament, such as Jeremiah 31:35-37, which assure Israel's continuance as "a nation before me for ever," are interpreted merely in the racial concept or as fulfilled spiritually in the sense that the *church* shall continue forever. While Allis does not seem to expound the passage directly, he links it with the new covenant with the teaching simply that "the prophet is picturing the ultimate and final state of God's people."[10] The interpretation stultifies any hope of Israel for a national future. Their only hope is spiritual, by entering into faith in Christ in the present interadvent age.

Israel's promises spiritualized. Two forms of interpretation seem to prevail among the amillenarians in regard to the way in which Israel's promises shall be fulfilled. The traditional

---

[10]Oswald T. Allis, *Prophecy and the Church*, p. 238.

Reformed position as illustrated in Calvin is that the church takes Israel's place as its spiritual successor. Calvin regarded Israel's hope of a future kingdom as without warrant—in fact, he held that this hope was a result of their spiritual blindness imposed as a judgment because of their rejection of Christ. Calvin stated: "And the folly of the whole nation of the Jews in the present age, in expecting an earthly kingdom of the Messiah, would be equally extraordinary, had not the Scriptures long before predicted that they would thus be punished for their rejection of the gospel."[11] Calvin's interpretation is based partially on the idea that Israel had erroneously interpreted the promises of a future kingdom on earth literally, and partially on the thought that Israel had forfeited these promises by disobedience. He seems to put most of his argument on the former point, however. Calvin wrote: "The point of controversy between us and these persons, is this: they maintain that the possession of the land of Canaan was accounted by the Israelites their supreme and ultimate blessedness, but that to us, since the revelation of Christ, it is a figure of the heavenly inheritance. We, on the contrary, contend, that in the earthly possession which they enjoyed, they contemplated, as in a mirror, the future inheritance which they believed to be prepared for them in heaven."[12] Calvin held, then, in the main, that the literal interpretation of Israel's promises was wrong in the first place. They were intended to teach Israelites their prospect in heaven rather than in earth.

Alternative view: Israel's promises literal but conditional. While an ardent Calvinist, Allis places most of his argument on the point that the promises were conditional, and not fulfilled because of Israel's disobedience and rejection of Christ. The fulfillment of the Abrahamic covenant according to Allis is conditioned upon obedience. Allis states: "It is true that, in the express terms of the covenant with Abraham, obedience is not stated as a condition. But that obedience was presupposed is clearly indicated by two facts. The one is that obedience is

---

[11]Calvin, *op. cit.,* I, 488.
[12]*Ibid.,* I, 490.

the precondition of blessing under all circumstances. . . . The second fact is that in the case of Abraham the duty of obedience is particularly stressed."[13]

Allis agrees with Calvin, however, in regarding the New Testament church as the true Israel, the organic continuance of the church of the Old Testament. He denounces in unsparing terms those who hold that Israel must mean Israel: "Carrying to an almost unprecedented extreme that literalism which is characteristic of Millenarianism, they [the Brethren Movement] insisted that Israel must mean Israel, and that the kingdom promises in the Old Testament concern Israel and are to be fulfilled to Israel."[14]

Allis is guilty, in this instance, of a serious misrepresentation. It so happens that there is considerable opposition to Calvin's view not only among premillenarians but among postmillenarians and even amillenarians. Charles Hodge, for instance, a representative postmillenarian, regards practically all the New Testament references to Israel as referring to those of that race, i.e., not the church as such. Hodge states in regard to Romans 11:26, which Allis takes for granted is allusion to the church: "Israel, here, from the context, must mean the Jewish people, and *all Israel,* the whole nation."[15]

William Hendriksen, formerly Professor of New Testament Literature at Calvin Seminary, a well-known amillenarian, in expounding Romans 11:25-26 also holds that Israel means Israel —the elect of Israel as he puts it.[16] Allis' "unprecedented extreme" turns out to be somewhat normal even among fellow amillenarians. The Roman Catholic idea that the church is the true Israel in fact is fading from contemporary amillenarians. The essentially postmillennial idea that Israel will be incorporated in the church and her promises fulfilled to her in a spiritualized sense seems to be gaining popularity.

The amillennial dilemma. The two forms of interpretation of the Old Testament promises to Israel as illustrated in Calvin

---

[13]Allis, *op. cit.,* p. 33.
[14]*Ibid.,* p. 218.
[15]Charles Hodge, *Commentary on Romans,* p. 589.
[16]William Hendriksen, *And So All Israel Shall Be Saved,* p. 33.

and Allis are contradictory in principle and tend to destroy each other. If the Old Testament promises were never intended to teach a future for Israel as a nation, as Calvin teaches, then there is no need to account for their lack of literal fulfillment by postulating that the promises were conditioned to Israel as a nation. If the promises are conditional, by so much it is granted that they were intended to be understood literally and as promising an earthly kingdom of righteousness and peace. Allis, in combining these two principles, is guilty of combining two arguments which are mutually destructive, based as they are on vitally different principles of interpretation. In doing so, he is probably moved by the hope of refuting premillennial arguments that the promises are unconditional and rest in the sovereignty of God for fulfillment—a future millennial kingdom whether Israel is obedient or disobedient. The position of Calvin, spiritualizing Israel's promises and referring them to the church, is nearer the normal amillennial position and serves to clarify the difference between the premillennial and amillennial positions.

While considerable difference of opinion exists among amillenarians regarding the best method of disposing of the mass of Old Testament prophecies which seem to indicate a future earthly kingdom for Israel, they agree in the main principle, that is, that these promises will not be fulfilled to Israel in a kingdom age to follow the present dispensation. Whether cancelled because of rejection of Christ as Messiah or spiritualized according to Calvin's formula, amillennialism with one voice condemns any literal fulfillment of these promises.

V. AMILLENNIAL ECCLESIOLOGY IN RELATION TO DISPENSATIONAL DISTINCTIONS

In addition to nullifying most of the meaning of Israel's promises, amillennialism does not seem to grasp many of the distinctive New Testament revelations concerning the church. While amillenarians do not deny the concept of the church as an organism in contrast to the church as an institution, they do not find much distinctive in this form of revelation. It is simply the contrast between reality and profession, or between the church visible and invisible. It is not something new, distinct, and unique.

Dispensational distinctions such as the mystery character of the entire present age are definitely denied by amillenarians. For them the present age is clearly anticipated in the kingdom prophecies of the Old Testament. Premillenarians, especially dispensationalists, on the other hand, usually regard the present age as hid from Old Testament prophets, and constituting a new and unrevealed development in the plan of God. All along the line in treating important doctrines relating to the church the amillenarians ignore or minimize the distinctive truth relating to the church. The fact of the new creation in which the church is related to the resurrection of Christ, the doctrine of the baptism of the Holy Spirit as forming the church into the body of Christ, the unique ground of justification based on being "in Christ," the universal indwelling of the Holy Spirit in every believer in this age, and the distinctive prophetic hope of the church are qualified or denied by amillennial ecclesiology. Many precious truths are lost in the broad generalizations which characterize the amillennial treatment of ecclesiology.

VI. CONCLUSION

Taken as a whole, it is clear that amillennialism does not yield the same type of ecclesiology as either premillennialism or postmillennialism. The millennial issue is far more pointed in ecclesiology than is generally recognized. In fact, it is not too much to state that many of the millennial issues such as the question of fulfillment of promises to Israel are the touchstones of theology as a whole as well as of ecclesiology. Outside of eschatology itself, no area is more vitally related to millennialism than ecclesiology.

CHAPTER IX

AMILLENNIAL ESCHATOLOGY

While amillennialism has its influence in all areas of theology, it is natural that it should affect eschatology more than any other. As a form of denial of a future millennial kingdom on earth, it stands in sharp contrast to premillennial eschatology.

In previous discussion of amillennialism, it has been brought out that amillennialism is by no means a unified theology, including within its bounds such diverse systems as modern liberal theology, Roman Catholic theology, and conservative Reformed theology. It is therefore impossible to generalize on amillennial eschatology without dividing it into these major divisions. Aside from various small sects who include within their tenets the premillennial concept, premillennialism for the most part presents a united front on eschatology in all major areas. Amillennialism, however, disagrees within itself on major issues.

I. MODERN LIBERAL ESCHATOLOGY

Modern liberal eschatology almost without exception follows the amillennial idea. Modern liberalism usually disregards postmillennialism, or the idea of a golden age of righteousness on earth, as well as premillennialism which advances such an age after the second advent. For them, all promises of ultimate righteousness are relegated to the life after death.

Homrighausen has called the idea of a millennium on earth "a lot of sentimental heavenism."[1] He goes on to denounce both millennial otherworldliness and the idea that this world is heaven as well: "Millennialists are right in their basic discoveries that this world is fragmentary and needs re-creation.

---

[1] Elmer G. Homrighausen, "One World at a Time," *Contemporary Religious Thought,* Thomas S. Kepler, editor, p. 372.

They are right in their insistence that this is an 'end' world; things here come to an end and have a limit. They are right in their insistence upon the other world, and in their emphasis upon the pull of God's power of resurrection. But their abnormal interest in the other world, their reading of eschatology in mathematical terms of time, their otherworldliness and consequent passivity as regards this world, is wrong. But Christians need to be saved, too, from that modern dynamic materialism which romantically sentimentalizes this world into the ultimate. This identifies the time world with the eternal world. This paganism is a hybrid attempt on the part of man to make the creature into the creator. In Christian circles it makes the Kingdom of God a blueprint for a world order. We admire this vehement realism, but we absolutely reject its presumptions that this world is a self-contained and a divine heaven. We live on earth! One world at a time."[2] In other words, there will be no millennium of righteousness on earth either before or after the second advent.

In some terms of modern liberalism, there remains an element of postmillennialism which believes that the kingdom of God in the world is advancing and will be ultimately triumphant. In one sense this can be regarded as amillennial in that it denies any real fulfillment to millennial promises. It is dyed in bright hues of optimism and visionary idealism. Its doctrinal background is postmillennialism rather than amillennialism even though amillennialism often has an optimistic note as well. Usually in modern liberal eschatology, however, the idea of progress and improvement is treated with some skepticism even as it is in modern philosophy. The trend is that indicated by Homrighausen—"one world at a time."

In modern liberal amillennialism there is much more than mere denial of a millennium. The same spiritualizing tendency manifest in the interpretation of millennial passages in the Bible is applied to most other aspects of eschatology. In particular the ideas of resurrection and of final judgment are relegated to the realm of obsolete ideas.

---

[2]*Loc. cit.*

Typical of modern liberal approaches to the doctrine of resurrection is that of Reinhold Niebuhr. Presenting the idea that the phrase in the Apostles' Creed, "I believe in the forgiveness of sins, the resurrection of the body and the life everlasting," is the genius of the Christian faith, in particular that the resurrection of the body is, he nevertheless states, "The idea of the resurrection of the body can of course not be literally true."[3] Niebuhr goes on to refer to the "myth of the resurrection."[4] His definition of the resurrection of the body is reduced to "the idea of social fulfillment."[5] That is, man will have a life after death as an individual, but without necessarily a bodily resurrection. The key to this interpretation is that he does not take literally the prophecies of Scripture regarding resurrection.

Modern liberal amillennialism also denies a literal judgment for sin. If there is no literal resurrection, how can there be literal judgment for sin? Nevin C. Harner writes: "Many people probably don't think any longer of a heaven of golden streets and pearly gates up above the sky, or a hell of fire and brimstone down below the earth. For one thing, now that we know our earth is a planet spinning around on its axis, there is no longer any 'up' or 'down.' Furthermore, such a heaven is designed to please bodies, and such a hell is made to punish bodies. But if in the future life we don't have bodies, or at least bodies like the ones we now live in, there will be little satisfaction in golden streets and little point in endless fire. You can't very well burn a spirit. There is something to be said for picturing the life beyond in spiritual terms, rather than in bodily terms. This is not to say that there will be no judgment, and no rewards or punishments awaiting us. Indeed, we are being judged all the while, and the rewards and punishments can be seen even now. Every day is Judgment Day."[6] In other words, Harner believes there will be no future judgment and no fu-

---

[3] Reinhold, Niebuhr, *Beyond Tragedy*, as reprinted in *Contemporary Religious Thought*, Thomas S. Kepler, editor, p. 373.
[4] *Ibid.*, p. 380.
[5] *Ibid.*, p. 377.
[6] Nevin C. Harner, *I Believe*, p. 83.

ture resurrection of the body. The principle of spiritualizing Scripture is carried by the modern liberal to its ultimate extreme unencumbered with any idea of inspiration of Scripture and need for literal interpretation. Such is the legacy of spiritualization and unbelief as they combine in modern liberal amillennialism.

II. Roman Catholic Eschatology

It is not within the scope of this discussion to treat the large area involved in Roman Catholic eschatology. The objections of Protestant theology to Roman eschatology have been the subject of voluminous writings ever since the Reformation. In general, however, it may be said that Roman eschatology tends to take Scripture more literally than modern liberal amillennialism. A vivid doctrine of judgment for sin after death, of resurrection of the body, and ultimate bliss for the saints are central aspects. Protestant objection has been principally to the doctrine of purgatory with all its kindred teachings and to the denial of the efficacy of the work of Christ on the cross, making unnecessary any purgatory or any human works whatever to qualify the believer in Christ for immediate possession of salvation, and security, and immediate entrance into heaven upon death. As in modern liberal amillennialism, however, Roman theology would be impossible if a literal method of interpretation of Scripture was followed. Roman theology concurs with amillennialism in denying any future kingdom of righteousness on earth after the second advent, and in its essential method follows the same type of spiritualization as modern liberalism.

III. Reformed Eschatology

Many of the excesses in eschatology which characterize modern liberalism and Roman Catholicism are not found in Reformed eschatology. Reformed eschatology for the most part intends to honor the Scriptures as the Word of God and accepts the central doctrines of the bodily resurrection of all men, a final judgment before God, and an eternal state of bliss or punishment. Reformed eschatology has been predominantly amillennial. Most if not all of the leaders of the Protestant Reformation were amillennial in their eschatology, following the teachings of Augustine.

The Reformed doctrine of the second advent of Christ has some similarity to the premillennial view. Both believe that the second advent will be the personal and bodily return of Jesus Christ to the earth. Both deny spiritualization of the second advent such as characterizes the liberal school of theology. Both believe that the second advent as taught in the Scriptures must be interpreted literally. Their disagreement lies in the interpretation of events which precede and follow the second advent. Reformed theologians who follow the amillennial interpretation usually minimize and spiritualize the time of tribulation preceding the second advent, particularly in such passages as Revelation 6-19. Amillenarians often find the tribulation being fulfilled in contemporary events, and interpret Revelation 6-19 as history. While interpreting the second advent literally, they to some extent spiritualize the tribulation. Likewise there is difference in viewpoint on the significance of the second advent itself. The amillenarian holds that it is the event beginning the eternal state while the premillenarian holds it begins the millennial kingdom on earth.

Greater divergence exists in the interpretation of the final judgments. It is characteristic of both the postmillennial and amillennial interpretations to merge all the Scriptural judgments connected with the second advent into one general judgment. The premillenarian separates many of these judgments both as to time and subjects. Amillenarians group together the judgment of the nations (Matt. 25:31-46), the judgment of the church (2 Cor. 5:9-11), the judgment of Israel (Ezek. 20:33-38), the judgment of the martyrs (Rev. 20:4-6), the judgment of the wicked dead (Rev. 20:11-15), and the judgment of the angels (2 Pet. 2:4; Rev. 20:10). It is not the purpose of the present discussion to refute the amillennial position on the judgments nor to sustain the premillennial, but the wide divergence of the two viewpoints is evident.

Of major importance in arriving at the respective doctrines characterizing the amillennial and premillennial concept of the judgments is the determining factor of spiritualizing versus literal interpretation. The amillenarian can deal lightly with the various Scripture passages involved, and with no attempt to explain them literally. The difference in character between the church being judged in heaven and the living nations being judged on earth as in Matthew 25 is glossed over and made the same event, even though there is no mention whatever of either the church or of resurrection in Matthew 25. The judgment of martyrs before the millennium and the judgment of the wicked dead after the millennium as outlined in Revelation 20 are brought together by the expedient of denying the existence of the millennium after the second advent.

It is obvious that the amillennial viewpoint is a combination of spiritualizing and literal interpretation. While they believe in a literal second advent and a literal judgment of all men, they do not apply the form of literal interpretation to the details of the many passages involved. It is because the premillenarians insist on literal interpretation of the details as well as the event that they find the various judgments differing as to time, place, and subjects.

The extent of spiritualization being used by amillenarians in eschatology is highly significant, as has been noted in previous discussions. The spiritualizing principle has been excluded as far as robbing eschatology of any specific events such as the second advent or a literal resurrection of the dead. On the other hand, the spiritualizing method has been used whenever the literal method would lead to the premillennial viewpoint. It is precisely on the points at issue between them that the spiritualizing method is used by the amillenarians. The premillennial interpretation is thus waved aside as inadequate, confused, or contradictory not by sound exegetical methods but by denial that the passages in question mean what they seem to mean if taken literally. It is for this reason that the controversy between the millennial views often has more sound and fury than facts, and in the minds of many scholars the matter is settled before it is fairly examined.

Even Louis Berkhof who is notably lucid and factual in his treatment of theological disputes writes concerning premillennialism: "In reading their description of God's dealings with men one is lost in a bewildering maze of covenants and dispensations, without an Ariadne thread to give safe guidance. Their divisive tendency also reveals itself in their eschatological program. There will be two second comings, two or three (if not four) resurrections, and also three judgments. Moreover, there will also be two peoples of God, which according to some will be eternally separate, Israel dwelling on earth, and the Church in heaven."[7]

We can hardly expect those who admittedly are bewildered and confused to be able to debate the issues, though Berkhof does much better than most amillenarians. The attitude of Berkhof, however, is significant. To him it is transparent that any doctrine other than the amillennial interpretation is simply impossible. But should amillennialism be taken for granted? Why should there not be three or four resurrections instead of one? What is wrong with there being two peoples on earth? Why on the face of it should we dispute the distinction between the rapture and the second coming? The answer is simply that it contradicts amillennialism, but it does not contradict the Bible literally interpreted. Certainly if one is to reject a doctrine because it is complicated, no theologian could for a moment accept the doctrine of the Trinity or debate the fine points of the relation of the two natures in Jesus Christ.

The doctrine of the eternal state, however, is for the most part one of agreement rather than disagreement. Those who distinguish the program of God for Israel and the church find them fulfilled in the eternal state. While this is rejected by the amillenarians who merge all the saints of all ages into one mass of redeemed humanity, it is not of the same importance theologically as other points of divergence. Reformed amillenarians and premillenarians unite on the important point of a

---

[7]Louis Berkhof, *Systematic Theology*, p. 710.

literal eternity, in which both heaven and hell will be peopled.

The millennial controversy can only be dissolved by a careful analysis of the details of premillennialism. The amillennial contention is, in brief, that premillenarians do not have a case, that their interpretations are confused, contradictory, and impossible. The answer to these charges has, of course, already been made in the abundant premillennial literature available today. It is the purpose of the discussion which will follow, however, to take up the mainsprings of the premillennial interpretation of Scripture and to establish the important and determining interpretations of Scripture which underlie premillennialism as a system of theology. Amillennialism has failed to present any unified system of theology or eschatology. Within its ranks, consistent with its main principles, are the widest divergences on every important doctrine. The purpose of the further discussion of premillennialism is to show that a consistent premillennialism can be erected with principles embedded in its system of interpretation. These at once are determining and corrective so that a premillenarian is always properly a conservative and Protestant theologian. The issues raised briefly in the survey of amillennial theology which is here concluded will be considered again seriatim as they come in conflict with tenets of premillennialism.

Chapter X

THE HISTORICAL CONTEXT OF PREMILLENNIALISM

I. Importance of the Evidence of History

While modern premillennialism depends upon Scriptural foundations for its apologetic and theological statement, it has nevertheless a significant historical context. It is regrettable that some historians have held low views of premillennialism, with the result that premillennialism has seldom had fair consideration in historical treatments of Christian doctrine. Liberals and skeptics surveying the evidence with theological indifference have often arrived at a fairer view of the evidence for premillennialism in history than those endeavoring to defend another millennial position.

It is hardly within the province of a theological study of premillennialism to include an adequate history of the doctrine. An exhaustive modern study of the subject remains for someone to undertake. Fortunately, the main issues are clear in even a casual study, and the significant evidence in relation to premillennialism can hardly be disputed by any scholarly sources produced to date. The evidence for premillennialism in the Old and New Testaments and in the literature and theology of the early church at least in its main elements is commonly recognized. It needs here only to be restated as forming the historical context of modern premillennialism.

The testimony of history unites in one river of evidence that the theology of the Old and New Testament and the theology of the early church was not only premillennial, but that its premillennialism was practically undisputed except by heretics and skeptics until the time of Augustine. The coming of Christ as the prelude for the establishment of a kingdom of righteousness on earth in fulfillment of the Old Testament kingdom prophecies was the almost uniform expectation both of the Jews at the time of the incarnation and of the early church. This is essential premillennialism however it may differ in its details from its modern counterpart.

II. Premillennialism in the Old Testament

Premillennialism is founded principally on interpretation of the Old Testament. If interpreted literally, the Old Testament gives a clear picture of the prophetic expectation of Israel. They confidently anticipated the coming of a Savior and Deliverer, a Messiah who would be Prophet, Priest, and King. They expected that He would deliver them from their enemies and usher in a kingdom of righteousness, peace, and prosperity upon a redeemed earth. It is hardly subject to dispute that the Old Testament presents such a picture, not in isolated texts, but in the constantly repeated declaration of most of the prophets. All the major prophets and practically all the minor prophets have Messianic sections picturing the restoration and glory of Israel in this future kingdom. This is so clear to competent students of the Old Testament that it is conceded by practically all parties that the Old Testament presents premillennial doctrine if interpreted literally. The premillennial interpretation offers the only possible literal fulfillment for the hundreds of verses of prophetic testimony.

These facts are usually admitted by opponents of premillennialism. Allis, a determined foe of premillennialism, states: "The Old Testament prophecies if literally interpreted cannot be regarded as having been fulfilled or as being capable of fulfillment in this present age."[1] In other words, a literal fulfillment would demand a millennial kingdom on earth after the second advent, i.e., the premillennial interpretation. Floyd Hamilton, who attacks premillennialism, concedes, "Now we must frankly admit that a literal interpretation of the Old Testament prophecies gives us just such a picture of an earthly

---

[1]Oswald Allis, *Prophecy and the Church*, p. 238.

reign of the Messiah as the premillennialist pictures. That was the kind of a Messianic kingdom that the Jews of the time of Christ were looking for, on the basis of a literal interpretation of the Old Testament."[2] It is agreed, then, that a literal interpretation of the Old Testament supports the premillennial viewpoint and that the Jews at the time of Christ held just such views of the Old Testament.

Amillenarians have followed two main routes to escape the logical result of this admission. The first has been to hold that a literal interpretation of the Old Testament was wrong. This is essentially the position of Hamilton quoted above. While he admits, "In fact, the Jews were looking for just such a kingdom to be set up by the Messiah in Jerusalem,"[3] he continues, "Jesus Himself, in speaking of that whole idea said, 'The kingdom of God is within (or, in the midst of) you' (Luke 17:21), thus contradicting the idea that it was to be an earthly, literal Jewish kingdom."[4] As he goes on to explain, the error in the premillennial interpretation is that they interpret the prophecies literally just as the Jews did.

The other route followed by amillenarians is another expedient for disposing of the prophecies of the Old Testament without literal fulfilment. This line of thought is to admit that the Old Testament prophecies rightly promise the Jews a kingdom on earth as usually presented by premillenarians, but to cancel this promise on the ground that it was conditioned on faith and obedience. In other words, the promise will never be fulfilled because Israel failed. As Allis puts it, ". . . obedience is the precondition of blessing under all circumstances."[5] He goes on to argue that obedience is the condition for fulfillment of all God's covenant relations, specifically the Abrahamic covenant, the Davidic covenant, and the Gospel of grace.[6]

These two lines of amillennial argument, are, of course, contradictory. One assumes that a literal interpretation is right

[2]Floyd Hamilton, *The Basis of the Millennial Faith*, p. 38.
[3]*Ibid.*, p. 39.
[4]*Loc. cit.*
[5]Allis, *op. cit.*, p. 33.
[6]*Ibid.*, pp. 32-48.

but fulfillment is forfeited for disobedience. The other assumes that literal interpretation is wrong and therefore only spiritual fulfillment is to be expected. Amillenarians like Allis use both principles even though their respective premises nullify each other. It is plain that they are determined at all costs to dispose of these kingdom promises without being too particular as to what method is followed. Premillenarians hold, of course, that the promises are unconditional and to be interpreted literally, and that premillennialism as found in the New Testament confirms the premillennialism of the Old Testament in no uncertain terms.

III. PREMILLENNIALISM IN THE NEW TESTAMENT

Two forms of evidence. The answer to the amillennial objection to premillennial interpretation of the Old Testament is found in the New Testament in two principal forms. First, the expectation of the Jews for literal fulfillment of the kingdom promises is confirmed. Second, this confirmation proves that the Old Testament promises are unconditional as to ultimate literal fulfillment.

It has been noted that rightly or wrongly it was the universal expectation of the Jews that the kingdom promises would be literally fulfilled. What does the New Testament have to say about this expectation?

Confirmation to Mary. In Luke 1:32-33, Mary is told by the angel, in relation to the child Jesus, "He shall be great, and shall be called the Son of the Most High: and the Lord God shall give unto him the throne of his father David: and he shall reign over the house of Jacob for ever; and of his kingdom there shall be no end." In view of the common Jewish expectation, how would Mary interpret such a prophecy?

It should certainly be clear that Mary would consider this revelation a confirmation of the literal interpretation and literal fulfillment of the Davidic covenant. She would naturally expect that her child Jesus would sit on an earthly Davidic throne. In spite of the disobedience of Israel in the Old Testament, and the long years in which no one sat on the throne of David, here was confirmation of the precise expectation common among the Jews.

Did Mary for one moment hold the amillenarian view? Would she spiritualize this passage—the throne of David is God's throne in heaven; the kingdom is a spiritual kingdom; Israel is synonymous with the church? Certainly not! It was totally foreign to her thinking. If the amillenarians are right, Mary was sadly deceived. The prophecy of the angel could hardly have been better worded to confirm the ordinary Jewish hope as well as the exact essentials of the premillennial position—the literal and earthly fulfillment of the Davidic covenant.

Confirmation by the teaching of Christ. It is, of course, true that Christ taught much concerning the spiritual aspects of God's kingdom. The Messianic kingdom on earth following the second advent by no means exhausts kingdom truth. The important point is, however, that whenever the precise kingdom promises of the Old Testament are introduced, these promises and their literal fulfillment are never denied, corrected, or altered, but are instead confirmed.

There is much positive evidence in the New Testament for premillennial teachings. It is clear that the Jews rejected Jesus Christ as their King and Messiah, and also as their Savior, and in so doing fulfilled literally those prophecies dealing with His rejection and death. His rejection did not alter the kingdom promises, however.

When the mother of James and John sought special privilege for her sons in the kingdom (Matt. 20:20-23), her request was not denied on the ground that she had a mistaken idea of the kingdom, but rather that the privilege she requested was to be given to those chosen by the Father. Again Christ the night before His rejection and crucifixion told His disciples that they would sit on thrones, judging the twelve tribes of Israel in the kingdom (Luke 22:29-30).

In Acts 1:6, when the disciples wanted to know when the kingdom was going to be restored to Israel, they were not told that they were in error, that the kingdom would never be restored to Israel, but only that it was not for them to know the "times or seasons, which the Father hath set within his own authority" (Acts 1:7).

Confirmation by the teaching of Paul. When Paul raises the question concerning the future of Israel, in Romans 9-11, and considers the possibility of God rescinding His promises to them as a nation and casting them off forever, he exclaims, "God forbid" (Rom. 11:1). The whole tenor of Romans 9-11 is to the point that while Israel for the present is cut off the olive tree of blessing, Israel is scheduled to be restored at the second advent, when the Deliverer will come out of Zion. It is expressly stated in this regard that "the gifts and the calling of God are not repented of" (Rom. 11:29), i.e., that God will fulfill His purpose regarding the nation Israel.

Confirmation by John. The book of Revelation is, of course, the classic passage on premillennialism. Revelation, while subject to all types of scholarly abuse and divergent interpretation, if taken in its plain intent yields a simple outline of premillennial truth—first a time of great tribulation, then the second advent, the binding of Satan, the deliverance and blessing of the saints, a righteous government on earth for 1000 years, followed by the final judgments, and the new heaven and new earth. The only method of interpretation of Revelation which has ever yielded a consistent answer to the question of its meaning is that which interprets the book, however symbolic, as having its general revelation plain, one to be fulfilled literally, and therefore subject to future fulfillment.

Absence of controversy. One of the most eloquent testimonies to premillennial truth is found in the absolute silence of the New Testament, and for that matter the early centuries of the church, on any controversy over premillennial teaching. It is admitted that it was universally held by the Jews. It is often admitted that the early church was predominantly premillennial. Yet there is no record of any kind dealing with controversy. It is incredible that if the Jews and the early church were in such a serious error in their interpretation of the Old Testament and in their expectation of a righteous kingdom on earth following the second advent, that there should be no corrective, and that all the evidence should confirm rather than deny such an interpretation. The general context of the New Testament is entirely in favor of the premillennial viewpoint. The amillennial interpretation has not one verse of positive testimony in the New Testament and can be sustained only by spiritualizing the prophecies of the Old Testament as well as the teaching of the New.

IV. EXTRA-BIBLICAL PREMILLENNIALISM IN THE FIRST CENTURY

The available evidence in regard to the premillennialism of the first century is not extensive by most standards, but such evidence as has been uncovered points in one direction—the premillennial concept. Peters in his classic work, *The Theocratic Kingdom,* cites no less than fifteen advocates of premillennialism in the first century.[7] While his classification in some cases is debatable, in others it is undisputed. The notable testimony of Papias, who was associated with the Apostle John, is of special weight. Papias who lived in the first century and the beginning of the second lists as adherents of premillennialism Aristio, John the Presbyter and the Apostles Andrew, Peter, Philip, Thomas, James, John, and Matthew. He certainly was in a position to know their views, and his testimony is an important link in sustaining the fact that the disciples continued in the Jewish expectation of a kingdom on earth. Peters also lists as premillenarians Clement of Rome, Barnabas, Hermas, Ignatius, and Polycarp. In previous discussion of amillennialism, it was shown that the prevailing opinion of both amillenarians and premillenarians that Barnabas is premillennial in his views is fully justified. Hermas also is conceded by practically all parties as premillennial. In other words, there are clear and unmistakable evidences of premillennialism in the first century. Further, this viewpoint is linked extra-biblically with the apostles themselves. In contrast to these clear evidences, not one adherent, not one line of evidence is produced sustaining

---

[7]G. N. H. Peters, *The Theocratic Kingdom,* I., 494-95.

the idea that any first-century Christians held Augustinian amillennialism—that the interadvent period was the millennium. Further, there is no evidence whatever that premillennialism was even disputed. It was the overwhelming-majority view of the early church.

V. PREMILLENNIALISM IN THE SECOND CENTURY

The second century like the first bears a sustained testimony to the premillennial character of the early church. Even the amillenarians claim no adherents whatever by name to their position in the second century except in the allegorizing school of interpretation which arose at the very close of the second century. Premillennialism was undisputed for the first ninety years of the second century. Among those who can be cited in this century as holding premillennialism Peters names Pothinus, Justin Martyr, Melito, Hegesippus, Tatian, Irenaeus, Tertullian, Hippolytus, and Apollinaris.[8] Of these Justin Martyr (100-168) is quite outspoken. He wrote: "But I and whatsoever Christians are orthodox in all things do know that there will be a resurrection of the flesh, and a thousand years in the city of Jerusalem, built adorned, and enlarged, according as Ezekiel, Isaiah, and other prophets have promised. For Isaiah saith of this thousand years (ch. 65:17), 'Behold, I create new heavens and a new earth: and the former shall not be remembered, nor come into mind; but be ye glad and rejoice in those which I create: for, behold, I create Jerusalem to triumph, and my people to rejoice,' etc. Moreover, a certain man among us, whose name is John, being one of the twelve apostles of Christ, in that revelation which was shown to him prophesied, that those who believe in our Christ shall fulfill a thousand years at Jerusalem; and after that the general, and in a word, the everlasting resurrection, and last judgment of all together. Whereof also our Lord spake when He said, that therein they shall neither marry, nor be given in marriage, but shall be

---

Ibid., I, 495-96.

equal with the angels, being made the sons of the resurrection of God."[9]

While even modern premillenarians might not accept the details of Justin's interpretation, the notable fact is that he clearly states the essentials of premillennialism—the second advent, followed by a thousand-year reign and the separating of the resurrections before and after the millennium. Further, Justin declares that this view which he advocates is generally accepted as the orthodox view of the church. Peters accordingly cites the conclusion of Semisch in Herzog's Cyclopaedia, "Chiliasm constituted in the sec. century so decidedly an article of faith that Justin held it up as a criterion of perfect orthodoxy."[10]

The testimony of Justin is by no means unsustained by others, as Peters shows. Pothinus taught his churches at Lyons and Vienne premillennial doctrine which was continued by Irenaeus his successor. Melito, the bishop of Sardis, is declared a premillenarian by Shimeall in his *Reply*, based on Jerome and Genadius. Tertullian is generally regarded as a premillenarian. Others are less certain but the evidence, such as it is, seems to point to their holding similar positions.

In general, the second century, then, has a similar testimony to the first. All characters who have anything to say on the subject are premillennial and this is set forth as the orthodox opinion of the church. Those who may have denied it were classified as heretics, not simply for being opposed to premillennialism but for other reasons. The first opposition to premillennialism did not become vocal until the opening of the third century. Amillenarians and postmillenarians have not only no positive evidence in favor of their position but no evidence that there was even a reasonable minority in the church contending against premillennialism. Apparently none of the orthodox fathers thought of challenging this important doctrine in the first two centuries.

---

[9]*Ibid.*, I, 480.
[10]*Loc. cit.*

VI. Premillennialism in the Third Century

In the third century premillennialism began its historic decline, and it is admitted by all that opposition arose to premillennial ideas. Opponents of premillennialism are found in Gaius, Clement, Origen, Dionysius, and others. The form in which the attack came consisted in the adoption of the allegorizing method of interpreting Scripture in a manner which is no credit to amillennialism. Rutgers, though a determined foe of premillennialism, as previously noted in tracing the rise of amillennialism in the third century minces no words in denouncing Clement as one who is entirely erroneous in his use of the allegorical method and as one who is dominated by Greek philosophy. Though he as an amillenarian does not defend the literalism of the premillennial view, at the same time he recognizes that Clement was a heretic whom no intelligent scholar today would follow.[11]

It is not surprising that opposition to premillennialism should arise. All forms of true doctrine have opposition and even the majority view in the history of doctrine is not necessarily the right one. The point of great significance is the form in which the opposition arose. It was not the product of orthodox studies in the Scripture, nor of the application of tried and true hermeneutics. It was rather the subversion of the plain meaning of Scripture not only as applied to the millennial question but all other areas of doctrine. The church today with one voice condemns all of the early opponents of premillennialism as heretics. Opposition to premillennialism had its rise in the attackers of true Scriptural doctrine, and it was not until the time of Augustine (354-430) that a reputable adherent of amillennialism can be cited. The opposition to premillennialism in the third century is no asset to amillennialism. While amillenarians may hail the conclusions of the enemies of premillennialism, they accept neither the general method nor the theology of those who participated in the attack.

---

[11]Cf. W. H. Rutgers, *Premillennialism in America*, p. 64.

Usually, like Allis, amillenarians abandon the early centuries as a lost cause and begin with Augustine.

The third century had its own continued witness to premillennialism, however. Among those who can be cited are Cyprian (200-258), Commodian (200-270), Nepos (230-280), Coracion (230-280), Victorinus (240-303), Methodius (250-311), and Lactantius (240-330). Some of these like Commodian and Nepos are undisputed premillenarians. Nepos early recognized the heretical tendencies of the Alexandrian school of theology, which was the first effective opponent of premillennialism, and he attacked them with vigor. Methodius is conceded as premillenarian by Whitby himself. It is clear, however, that a rising tide of opposition was beginning to manifest itself against premillennialism and, while the church managed to extricate itself from much of the other bad doctrine of the Alexandrian school, premillennialism became in time one of the fatalities.

VII. Premillennialism from the Third Century
to Modern Times

All admit that premillennialism after the third century waned and lost its hold on the majority of the church. It was the time of the rising strength of the Roman Church. Both the theological and political atmosphere was against it. While there was a continued minority who held premillennialism both within and without the Roman Church, they were not very vocal and were quite ineffectual in continuing a strong testimony. The Reformers, while returning to true doctrine in many areas, accepted Augustine as the starting point for their theology, and for the most part accepted without much consideration his opposition to premillennialism. The fact that premillennialism was held by some fanatical sects did not give it much standing. It remained for the renewal of Scriptural studies some time after the Reformation to turn the attention of a large portion of the church again to the premillennial question. The last hundred years have brought premillennialism out of its partial eclipse, and among those who accept the inspiration of Scripture it continues to be an area of lively discussion.

VIII. MODERN PREMILLENNIALISM

The general features of modern premillennialism are highly significant and need to be outlined before assuming the larger task of the analysis and defense of premillennial doctrine. Even a casual observer of the premillennial movement in the twentieth century can see certain important tendencies.

Infallibility of Scripture. Premillennialism is based on the thesis of the infallibility of Scripture. It stands or falls not only on the method of interpretation of Scripture, but also on the question of the infallibility of the Holy Scripture. For this reason, premillennialism is entirely confined to those who are conservative in their general theological position. Premillennialism has always been the foe of liberal theology and of unbelief in the Scripture. It has often been attacked for this very reason. Much of the modern zeal of its opponents has not arisen in love for doctrinal purity, but in hatred of conservative Biblical theology. To be a premillenarian exposes one at once to all who have departed from conservative theology. Premillennialism remains a bulwark against the inroads of modern theology.

Literal interpretation. Modern premillennialism is dependent upon the principle of literal interpretation. Premillennialism is a result of the application of this method to Scriptural interpretation. It is accordingly the foe of modern liberal spiritualization of all areas of theology as well as the more confined spiritualization of conservative amillenarians. The literal method of interpretation is also vitally related to Biblical dispensationalism. The recognition of Biblical dispensations and the proper statement of dispensational distinctions is not in itself a method of interpretation but rather a result of a method—the application of the literal method. In this connection it should also be noted that extremes in dispensational distinctions do not have their rise in a more rigid literal method, but rather in the area of general interpretation. Extreme dispensationalism which divides the interadvent period into Jewish and Gentile churches, and makes much of the New Testament nonapplicable to modern churches, is not more or less literal than ordinary dispensationalism. It is misapplication of the literal method rather than its proper use.

Evangelicalism. Premillennialism has been definitely an evangelical movement. While often charged with pessimism regarding this world and with "other-worldliness," premillennialism has been a large factor in modern effective gospel preaching. A premillenarian is usually a believer in the orthodox gospel and an adherent of Biblical theology in all major areas. Premillennialism among other things has opposed legalism or the Galatian error as it exists today and has upheld the doctrine of grace both as the ground of salvation and as a rule of life for the believer.

Opposition to ecclesiasticism. Premillennialism has tended to be more independent of human and ecclesiastical opinions and more inclined to exalt the Scriptures and the guidance of the Holy Spirit as a basis for conduct. The modern tendency to exalt church programs often pursued in the energy of the flesh rather than in the power of the Spirit, and the trend to exalt submission to church authority rather than to the Holy Spirit have had no encouragement from premillennialism. Premillennialism has supported exegetical preaching, informal church services, the guidance of the Holy Spirit, and extemporaneous prayers in contrast to the ritualism, formalism, and mechanical tendency of modern Christianity.

Emphasis on prophetic studies. It is transparent that premillennialism has also exalted the study of prophetic truth. In contrast to the common neglect of even the essential doctrines of the second advent, heaven, hell, and final judgment, usually omitted from liberal theological preaching, premillennialism has focused the white light of careful investigation on Scriptural teachings concerning future things. Prophetic Bible conferences are inevitably premillennial in their doctrine. Neither amillennialism nor postmillennialism ever aroused much interest in prophecy.

Such is the historical context of modern premillennialism. Rooted in the Old and New Testaments, a product of literal interpretation, nurtured by the apostles and the early church, eclipsed for centuries by the dark shadows of pagan philosophies and allegorizing methods of interpretation, emerging once more as a dominant strain in Biblical theology in these eschatological times, premillennialism is more than a theory, more than a doctrine. It is a system of Biblical interpretation which alone honors the Word of God as infallibly inspired, literally interpreted, and sure of literal fulfillment. It has stirred the coals of evangelicalism, created interest in Biblical study, and constituted a preparation of God's people for the coming of the Lord for His saints. Premillennial truth has been an inestimable blessing to those who have received it. To them the Bible has become a living book to be interpreted in its ordinary sense. It is significant that the Bible study movements have usually been premillennial, and institutions which emphasize the study of the text of Scripture, as illustrated in the Bible institute movement, have often been an integral part of the premillennial movement.

Chapter XI

THE THEOLOGICAL CONTEXT OF PREMILLENNIALISM

I. Premillennialism a System of Theology

The oft-repeated charge that premillennialism is only a dispute over the interpretation of Revelation 20 is both understatement and a serious misrepresentation of the facts. Opponents of premillennialism delight to point out that the reference to the thousand years is found only in Revelation 20. Warfield observes in a footnote, " 'Once, and only once,' says the 'Ency. Bibl.,' 3095, 'in the New Testament we hear of a millennium.' "[1] The issues of premillennialism are neither trivial nor simple. Premillennialism is rather a system of theology based on many Scriptures and with a distinctive theological context. The reckless charge of Landis that European premillennialism is based only on Ezekiel 40-48 and the American premillennialism is based only on Revelation 20:1-7 is as unfair as his more serious charge that "actually their bases are both contra-Biblical," and that premillennialism "is a fungus growth of first-century Pharisaic rabbinism."[2] Most opponents of premillennialism have enough perspective to see that premillennialism has its own Biblical and theological context and that its origin in the early church as well as its restoration in modern times is based on Biblical and theological studies. It is the purpose of this phase of the study of premillennialism to examine the general features of premillennial theology in contrast to opposing views. Premillennialism involves a distinctive principle of interpretation of Scripture, a different concept of the present age, a dis-

[1] B. B. Warfield, *Biblical Doctrines*, p. 643.
[2] Ira D. Landis, *The Faith of Our Fathers on Eschatology*, p. 31.

tinct doctrine of Israel, and its own teaching concerning the
second advent and millennial kingdom.

II. Principles of Premillennial Interpretation

*The literal, grammatical-historical method applied to escha-
tology.* The debate between premillenarians and amillenarians
hangs to a large extent upon the principles of interpretation of
Scripture which each group employs. This is commonly recognized by all parties. The amillenarian Albertus Pieters states,
"The question whether the Old Testament prophecies concerning the people of God must be interpreted in their ordinary
sense, as other Scriptures are interpreted, or can properly be
applied to the Christian Church, is called the question of spiritualization of prophecy. This is one of the major problems in
biblical interpretation, and confronts everyone who makes a
serious study of the Word of God. It is one of the chief keys
to the difference of opinion between Premillenarians and the
mass of Christian scholars. The former reject such spiritualization, the latter employ it; and as long as there is no agreement
on this point the debate is interminable and fruitless."[3] In
principles of interpretation the crux of the controversy is revealed.

The premillennial position is that the Bible should be interpreted in its ordinary grammatical and historical meaning
in all areas of theology unless contextual or theological reasons
make it clear that this was not intended by the writer. Amillenarians use the literal method in theology as a whole but
spiritualize Scripture whenever its literal meaning would lead
to the premillennial viewpoint. This is obviously a rather subjective principle and open to manipulation by the interpreter
to sustain almost any system of theology. The conservative amillenarian claims to confine spiritualization to the field of prophecy and interpret other Scriptural revelation literally. Thus
a conservative amillenarian would interpret literally passages
teaching the deity of Christ, the substitutionary atonement, the

---

[3]Albertus Pieters, "The Leader," September 5, 1931, as cited by Gerrit
H. Hospers, *The Principle of Spiritualization in Hermeneutics*, p. 5.

resurrection of Christ, and similar doctrines. They would denounce as heretics anyone who would tamper with these fundamental doctrines—as Origen, the father of amillenarianism, most certainly did. Conservative amillenarians would, however, feel perfectly justified in proceeding to spiritualize passages speaking of a future righteous government on earth, of Israel's restoration as a national and political entity, of Israel's regathering to Palestine, and of Christ reigning literally upon the earth for a thousand years. Their justification is that these doctrines are absurd and impossible and that therefore they must be spiritualized. The wish is father of the interpretation, therefore, and amillennial interpretation of Scripture abundantly illustrates this.

While professing to confine spiritualization to prophecy, actually they invade other fields. For instance, they tend to spiritualize Israel to mean the church and make David's throne to be the throne of God in heaven. They hold up to ridicule as extremists those who want to interpret references to Israel literally. As Allis writes with considerable inaccuracy, as previously noted, "Carrying to an almost unprecedented extreme that literalism which is characteristic of Millenarianism, they [the Brethren Movement] insisted that Israel must mean Israel, and that the kingdom promises in the Old Testament concern Israel and are to be fulfilled to Israel literally."[4] In his zeal to load premillenarians with an extreme position, Allis finds it convenient to forget that the postmillennial Charles Hodge and the amillennial William Hendriksen both interpret reference to Israel in Scripture as belonging to God's ancient people, Israel, not to a Gentile church.

Premillenarians, on the other hand, insist that one general rule of interpretation should be applied to all areas of theology and that prophecy does not require spiritualization any more than other aspects of truth. They hold that this rule is the literal, grammatical-historical method. By this it is meant that a passage should be taken in its literal sense, in keeping with the grammatical meaning of the words and forms. History is

[4]Oswald T. Allis, *Prophecy and the Church*, p. 218.

history, not allegory. Facts are facts. Prophesied future events are just what they are prophesied. Israel means Israel, earth means earth, heaven means heaven.

Problems of the literal method. Attacks on premillennialism which recognize the central importance of the literal method of interpretation delight to show that premillenarians do not always interpret Scripture literally either. Landis asks, "How literal are the literalists?"[5] Allis confuses typical with spiritual interpretation and charges that premillennial use of typology destroys the literal principle. He writes, "While Dispensationalists are extreme literalists, they are very inconsistent ones. They are literalists in interpreting prophecy. But in the interpreting of history, they carry the principle of typical interpretation to an extreme which has rarely been exceeded by the most ardent allegorizers."[6] True typical interpretation, of course, always involves literal interpretation first. In drawing typical truth from the Old Testament sacrifices, for instance, the interpreter takes for granted the historical existence of the sacrifice. If Joseph is taken as a type of Christ, his historical life is assumed. It is surprising that a scholar of Allis' proportions should be confused on such a simple hermeneutical distinction. The dispute highlights, however, some of the problems of the use of the literal method.

Premillenarians recognize that all Scripture cannot be interpreted literally. All areas of theology are sometimes revealed in Scripture under symbolic terms. Such passages, however, are usually clearly identified. For instance, the "rod out of the stem of Jesse" and the "Branch" is the one who "shall smite the earth with the rod of his mouth, and with the breath of his lips shall he slay the wicked." It is clear from that context that a literal prophecy of judgment on the wicked in the earth at the second advent is intended even though some of the expressions are figurative. While the expression "rod of his mouth" is clearly figurative, such simple expressions as "earth" in the context of this passage in Isaiah 11 cannot be spiritualized on

---

[5] Landis, *op. cit.,* p. 45.
[6] Allis, *op. cit.,* p. 21.

the same grounds. We are not free to make "earth" arbitrarily an equivalent for heaven as amillenarians do, nor can we speak of the regathering of Israel "from the four corners of the earth" (Isa. 11:12) as the conversion of Gentiles and the progress of the church. While the expression "four corners" is figurative, the word "earth" is not. In other words, figures of speech which are clearly identified as such give no warrant whatever to spiritualize words and expressions which can be taken in their ordinary meaning.

The literal method sustained by literal fulfillment. The literal method of interpreting prophecy has been fully justified by the history of fulfillment. The most unlikely prophecies surrounding the birth of Christ, His person, His life and ministry, His death and resurrection have all been literally fulfilled. The prophetic vision of Daniel, however couched in symbols and dreams, has had the most concrete fulfillment down to the present hour in the history of Gentile nations. Hundreds if not thousands of prophecies have had literal fulfillment. A method that has worked with such success in the past is certainly worthy of projection into the future.

The interpreter of prophecy has, therefore, no more warrant to spiritualize prophecy than any other area of theology. If the details of the virgin birth, the character of the miracles of Christ, His very words on the cross, His form of execution, the circumstances of His burial, and His resurrection from the dead could be explicitly prophesied in the Old Testament, certainly there is no *a priori* reason for rejecting the literal interpretation of prophecy concerning His future righteous government on earth. The literal method is the method recognized in the fulfillment of prophecy and is the mainspring of the premillennial interpretation of the Scriptures.

The question of relative difficulty of interpreting prophecy. It may be admitted that there are problems in the interpretation of prophecy which are peculiar to this field. While the problems differ in character from the interpretation of history or theological revelation, they do not consist in the choice of spiritual or literal interpretation. It is not so much a question of whether the prophecy will be fulfilled, but rather concerning the unrevealed details of time and circumstance. While premillenarians have sometimes been guilty of making prophetic interpretation appear as too simple a process, amillenarians have erred in the other direction. After all, interpreting Scripture on such subjects as predestination, the decree of God, the doctrine of the Trinity, the person of the incarnate Christ, the sufferings of Christ on the cross, and similar doctrines is certainly difficult even though in the realm of specific revelation and historic fulfillment. The theologian should no more turn to spiritualization of Scripture to solve the doctrinal difficulties in these areas than he should spiritualize prophecy to fit a denial of a millennial kingdom on earth. Difficulty or even seeming contradiction is not sufficient justification for spiritualization. If the incongruous elements of the human and the divine in Christ can be accepted literally in spite of their seeming contradiction, the elements of prophecy which may seem confusing should not be sacrificed on the altar of spiritualization to remove the problem that arises from literal interpretation.

A general principle guiding the interpretation of prophecy is quite clear in the Scripture. This principle is that the whole doctrine of prophecy should be allowed to be the guide for the interpretation of details. The main elements of prophecy are far more clear than some of the details. Difficult passages are often solved by a study of related Scriptures. The book of Revelation, while admittedly difficult to interpret, has its symbols drawn from other portions of Scripture, and many questions of interpretation can be answered with the larger context of the entire Bible.

The problem of the time element in prophecy. One of the problems of interpretation of prophecy is that it involves time relationships. Events widely separated in fulfillment are often brought together in prophetic vision. Thus the first coming and the second coming of Christ are pictured in the same Scriptural context. Isaiah 61:1-2 as quoted in part by Christ in Luke 4:16-19 is an illustration of this. In the quotation in Luke, Christ quoted only the first part of the Isaiah passage, stopping just before the elements that dealt with the second coming. We can therefore expect in Old Testament prophecy the complete spanning of the present age with no inkling of the millenniums that separate the first and second advent. On the other hand, when time elements are included, they are intended to be taken literally. Hence, Daniel's "seventy weeks" are subject to literal interpretation even though the interval between the sixty-ninth and the seventieth week is only hinted at by Daniel himself. The rule does not justify spiritualization of that which is specifically revealed.

The problem of partial fulfillment. This, in a word, is the partial fulfillment of a prophecy first, followed by the complete fulfillment later. In Luke 1:31-33, for instance, there was fulfillment of the first part of the prophecy in the incarnation, but the prediction that Christ would rule over Israel on the throne of David forever has had no fulfillment. Amillenarians have succumbed to the temptation to spiritualize the throne of David. Such an interpretation violates the very integrity of Scripture. Mary certainly believed the prediction to refer to the literal kingdom on earth prophesied in the Old Testament. A spiritual throne in heaven, God's own throne, in no wise fulfills the prediction.

Premillennial principles of literal interpretation justified. The general features of premillennial interpretation are therefore evident. Its method is literal interpretation except for figures plainly intended to be symbols. Prophecies are therefore to be taken literally, the exact interpretation following the pattern of the law of fulfillment established by prophecies already fulfilled and in keeping with the entire doctrine. Time relationships in prophecy are seen to include the literal interpretation of time elements when given and at the same time the prophetic vision is seen to present events widely separated in time in the same revelation. Prophecies fulfilled in part are found to sustain the principle of literal fulfillment, with a partial fulfillment first and complete literal fulfillment to follow. Prophecy in general must follow the same hermeneutical principles of interpretation which govern other areas of theology.

III. The Premillennial Concept of the Present Age

The immediate and practical importance of premillennial interpretation can be seen at once in the comparison of concepts of the present age advanced by the various millennial views. Postmillennialism usually interprets the prophecies of the coming kingdom of righteousness on earth as being subject to a somewhat literal fulfillment in the period just preceding the second advent, a period still future from the contemporary viewpoint. This interpretation has almost vanished among contemporary conservative theologians, being continued mainly in the evolutionary principle of continued world-improvement to which some still resolutely cling in spite of trends to the contrary. Amillenarians, on the other hand, regard the kingdom prophecies as being fulfilled now, in the present age, either on earth or in heaven, or both. The premillennial interpretation denies both the postmillennial and amillennial views, affirming that the kingdom on earth will follow, not precede the second advent of Christ.

The premillennial concept of the present age makes the inter-advent period unique and unpredicted in the Old Testament. The present age is one in which the gospel is preached to all the world. Relatively few are saved. The world becomes, in fact, increasingly wicked as the age progresses. The premillennial view holds no prospects of a golden age before the second advent, and presents no commands to improve society as a whole. The apostles are notably silent on any program of political, social, moral, or physical improvement of the unsaved world. Paul made no effort to correct social abuses or to influence the political government for good. The program of the early church was one of evangelism and Bible teaching. It was a matter of saving souls out of the world rather than saving the world. It was neither possible nor in the program of God for the present age to become the kingdom of God on earth.

Central in the purpose of the present age in the premillennial view is the formation of the church, the body of Christ, out of believers in the gospel. This body of believers is quite distinct from Israel in the Old Testament and is not simply a revamped Judaism. The truth regarding the church as the body of Christ is declared to be a mystery, that is, a truth not revealed in the Old Testament. Composed of Jew and Gentile on an equal basis, and resting on New Testament promises of grace and salvation in Christ, the new entity is a new creation of God, formed by the baptism of the Holy Spirit, indwelt by the Spirit of God, united to Christ as the human body is united to its head. The main body of premillenarians regard the church as being at Pentecost, having its program and formation in the present age, and a prophetic future all its own, not to be confused with Israel or Old Testament saints.

IV. THE PREMILLENNIAL CONCEPT OF ISRAEL

There have been, in the main, three interpretations of the theological concept of Israel in Protestant theology. One of these, which can be identified with John Calvin, is the idea that the church is the true Israel and therefore inherits Israel's promises. This is the viewpoint advocated by amillenarians. Allis considers it the only possible amillenarian position. It considers Israel nationally and individually set aside forever and his promises of blessings transferred to the church. Under this concept there is no future hope for Israel whatever.

Some amillenarians such as William Hendriksen and some conservative postmillenarians such as Charles Hodge hold that Israel's promises of blessings will be fulfilled to those of Israel in the flesh who come to Christ and become part of the Christian church. The promises are to be fulfilled, then, to Israel, but to Israel in the church. Hodge takes this as a final triumph of the gospel and even envisions some regathering of Israel for this purpose. Under both of these forms of interpretation, no post-advent kingdom is required to fulfill Israel's promises. All will be fulfilled in the present age.

It is clear, however, even to opponents of premillennialism that many of the promises cannot be literally applied to present earth conditions. Two expedients are followed by the amillenarian and postmillenarian interpretation. Some promises are cancelled as having been conditional in the first place. Others are spiritualized to fit the pattern of the present age or of heaven. This interpretation is based upon a somewhat contradictory set of principles. One view is that the promises to Israel were never intended to be taken literally and hence are rightly spiritualized to fit the church. The other is that they were literal enough, but cancelled because of Israel's sin: The concept of Israel prevailing among amillenarians and postmillenarians is therefore confused and inherently contradictory. There does not seem to be any norm or central consistency except in their denial of a political and national future for Israel after the second advent. What unity exists in their system rests upon this denial.

The premillennial view concerning Israel is quite clear and simple it its important particulars. The prophecies given to Israel are viewed as literal and unconditional. God has promised Israel a glorious future and this will be fulfilled after the second advent. Israel will be a glorious nation, protected from her enemies, exalted above the Gentiles, the central vehicle of the manifestation of God's grace in the millennial kingdom. In the present age, Israel has been set aside, her promises held in abeyance, with no progress in the fulfillment of her program. This postponement is considered no more difficult than the delay of forty years in entering the promised land. Promises may be delayed in fulfillment but not cancelled. All concede that a literal interpretation of Israel's promises in the Old Testament present just such a picture. Again it resolves into a problem of literal interpretation and the defense of this interpretation as reasonable and consistent. The preservation of Israel as a racial entity and the resurrection of Israel as a political entity are twin miracles of the twentieth century which are in perfect accord with the premillennial interpretation. The doctrine of Israel remains one of the central features of premillennialism.

V. THE PREMILLENNIAL CONCEPT OF THE SECOND ADVENT

The general facts concerning the premillennial viewpoint of the second advent are well known. Premillenarians hold to a literal, bodily, visible, and glorious return of Christ to the earth, fulfilling the many Scriptural prophecies of this event. They hold that this event is the occasion for the deliverance and judgment of Israel, the downfall and judgment of the Gentiles, the inauguration of the kingdom of righteousness on earth. In contrast to both amillennialism and postmillennialism, they hold that the coming of Christ is before the millennium. Satan is bound at this time. The curse of sin is lifted from the material world. Righteousness, peace, and prosperity become the rule. Jerusalem becomes the capital for the whole world. The kingdom continues for one thousand years and then is merged into eternity attended by catastrophic events—the destruction of the present earth and heavens, the judgment of the wicked dead who are then raised, the establishment of the saints of all ages in the new earth and new heaven. All of these events are interpreted literally by the premillenarian and constitute the blueprint of things to come.

Premillenarians often distinguish between the second advent and the rapture of the church. Usually Scripture is interpreted to sustain the teaching that the rapture comes before the tribulation time, separated from the second advent by a period of about seven years. Some few hold that the rapture comes in the middle of the tribulation, the midtribulation theory. Others hold to the posttribulation view which identifies the rapture with the second advent proper.

VI. CONCLUSION

It should be clear from this survey of the field that premillennialism is a distinct system of theology. Opponents of premillennialism are right in part when they charge that premillennialism is essentially different from other forms of theology. The chief differences arise in ecclesiology, eschatology, and hermeneutics. Opponents of premillennialism are wrong when they claim that premillennialism is new, modern, or heretical. Even partisans in the millennial argument usually agree that premillenarians are evangelical, true to Biblical doctrine, and opposed to modern defections from the faith of our fathers.

The task that remains is the large undertaking of presenting the Scriptural evidence for premillennialism in a constructive way, showing that it is consistent with itself and its hermeneutical principles, and that it is the best system of interpretation of the entire Scriptures. The approach will be through the Biblical covenants, beginning with God's covenant with Abraham, which has become increasingly the crux of the millennial issue. The literal method of interpretation will be tested by its practical use in seeking solution of the millennial problem.

CHAPTER XII

INTERPRETATION OF THE ABRAHAMIC COVENANT

I. IMPORTANCE OF THE COVENANT

It is recognized by all serious students of the Bible that the covenant of God with Abraham is one of the important and determinative revelations of Scripture. It furnishes the key to the entire Old Testament and reaches for its fulfillment into the New. In the controversy between premillenarians and amillenarians, the interpretation of this covenant more or less settles the entire argument. The analysis of its provisions and the character of their fulfillment set the mold for the entire body of Scriptural truth.

Most of the discussions on the issue are distinguished for their disregard of the specific provisions of the covenant. Albertus Pieters in his closely reasoned book on this subject[1] is no exception. Like Louis Berkhof,[2] Oswald Allis,[3] Rutgers,[4] and other amillenarians, he finds it convenient and suited to his purpose to overlook the details of the promise and seize upon its general promises of blessings. This is of course necessary for the amillennial interpretation which does not provide any fulfillment of the details ignored. The premillennial interpretation on the other hand is able to account for the entire prophecy and its ultimate complete fulfillment.

The issue, in a word, is the question of whether Israel as a nation and as a race has a prophesied future. A literal interpretation of the Abrahamic covenant involves the permanent existence of Israel as a nation and the fulfillment of the promise

[1]Albertus Pieters, *The Seed of Abraham.*
[2]Louis Berkhof, *Systematic Theology,* p. 277.
[3]Oswald T. Allis, *Prophecy and the Church,* pp. 32 ff.
[4]W. H. Rutgers, *Premillennialism in America.*

that the land should be their everlasting possession. Amillenarians generally deny this. Premillenarians affirm it. What, then,
are the provisions of the covenant with Abraham and do they
promise what premillenarians affirm?

II. THE PROVISIONS OF THE COVENANT

The language of the Abrahamic covenant is plain and to
the point. The original covenant is given in Genesis 12:1-3, and
there are three principal confirmations and amplifications as
recorded in Genesis 13:14-17; 15:1-7; and 17:1-18. Some of the
promises are given to Abraham personally, some to Abraham's
seed, and some to Gentiles, or "all families of the earth" (Gen.
12:3).

The promise to Abraham. Abraham himself is promised that
he would be the father of a great nation (Gen. 12:2), compared
to the dust of the earth and the stars of the heaven in number
(Gen. 13:16; 15:5), and including kings and nations other than
the "seed" itself (Gen. 17:6). God promises His personal blessing on Abraham. His name shall be great and he himself shall
be a blessing. All of this has had already the most literal fulfillment and continues to be fulfilled.

The promise to Abraham's seed. In addition to the promises
to Abraham, the covenant includes blessings for Abraham's seed.
The nation itself shall be great (Gen. 12:2) and innumerable
(Gen 13:16; 15:5). The nation is promised possession of the
land. Its extensive boundaries are given in detail (Gen. 15:18-
21). In connection with the promise of the land, the Abrahamic
covenant itself is expressly called "everlasting" (Gen. 17:7) and
the possession of the land is defined as "an everlasting possession" (Gen. 17:8). It should be immediately clear that this
promise guarantees both the everlasting continuance of the seed
as a nation and its everlasting possession of the land.

Miscellaneous promises are included in the covenant. God
is to be the God of Abraham's seed. It is prophesied that they
would be afflicted, as fulfilled in the years in Egypt, and that
afterwards they would "come out with great substance" (Gen.

15:14). In the promise to Abraham, "In thee shall all families of the earth be blessed," it is anticipated that the seed should be a channel of this blessing. In particular this is fulfilled in and through the Lord Jesus Christ.

All the promises to the "seed" in Genesis are references to the physical seed of Abraham. General promises of blessing to Abraham's seed seem to include all his physical lineage, but it is clear that the term is used in a narrower sense in some instances. Eliezer of Damascus, while according to the customs of the day regarded as a child of Abraham because born in his house, is nevertheless disqualified because he is not the physical seed of Abraham (Gen. 15:2). Further, not all the physical descendants of Abraham qualify for the promises to the seed. Ishmael is put aside. When Abraham pleads with God, "Oh that Ishmael might live before thee!' God replies, "Sarah thy wife shall bear thee a son; and thou shalt call his name Isaac: and I will establish my covenant with him for an everlasting covenant for his seed after him" (Gen. 17:18-19). The line of the seed and its promises is narrowed to the one son of Abraham. Later when Jacob and Esau are born, God in sovereign choice chooses the younger as the father of the twelve patriarchs and confirms the covenant to Jacob. The particular Abrahamic promises and blessings are thereafter channelled through the twelve tribes.

While the promises to the "seed" must be limited to their application according to the context, it is clear that much of the general blessing attending the Abrahamic covenant such as the general blessing of God upon men is larger in its application. Thus the sign of circumcision (Gen. 17:10-14, 23-27) is administered not only to Isaac later, but also to Ishmael and the men in Abraham's house either born in the house or bought with money. Circumcision is wider in its application than the term *seed,* as far as the use in Genesis is concerned.

The promise to Gentiles. As a part of the Abrahamic covenant, "all the families of the earth" are promised blessing (Gen. 12:3). It is not specified what this blessing shall be. As a general promise it is probably intended to have a general fulfillment,

Abraham himself has certainly been a blessing to all nations and has the distinction of being honored alike by Jew, Mohammedan, and Christian. The seed of Abraham or the nation of Israel itself has been a great blessing as the channel of divine revelation and the historic illustration of God's dealings with men. The seed of Abraham, the Lord Jesus Christ Himself, has also been a blessing to all nations. The blessing bestowed includes not only the salvation of many but the revelation of God, the revelation of moral law, and the many by-products of Biblical Judaism and Christianity. This part of the promise has already been abundantly fulfilled.

A solemn part of the covenant as it deals with the Gentiles is the provision, "I will bless them that bless thee, and him that curseth thee will I curse" (Gen. 12:3). This of course would be true even of an Israelite, but the primary application is to Gentiles. Long sections of the Old Testament pronouncing judgment upon the Gentiles for their ill-treatment of Israel enlarge on this provision. History has recorded graphic fulfillment in the wrecks of Nineveh, Babylon, and Rome, to say nothing of smaller groups and peoples. Down to modern times, the nation that has persecuted the Jew has paid dearly for it.

Further distinctions. The promises to Abraham, to Abraham's seed, and to "all the families of the earth" are to be distinguished clearly. It breeds utter confusion to ignore these Scriptural divisions and to muddle the whole by reducing it to a general promise. Not only should these distinctions be observed, but it should be carefully noted what is left out of the covenant. While Abraham is personally justified by faith because of his trust in God's promise concerning his seed, it is obvious that the Abrahamic covenant itself is not the gospel of salvation even though the promised blessing anticipated the gospel (cf. Gal. 3:8). Those in the covenant are promised that God will be their God in the general and providential sense. It is true that Christ is the fulfillment of the promise of blessing to all nations. But the covenant does not contain the covenant of redemption, a revelation of the sacrifice of Christ, a promise of forgiveness of sin, a promise of eternal life, or any of the elements of salvation. The promise to Adam and Eve in Genesis 3:15 is, by way of example, a far clearer picture of the promise of redemption than any of the long passages dealing with the Abrahamic covenant. While the Abrahamic covenant is essentially gracious and promises blessings, it deals for the most part with physical blessing and with a physical seed. To make the covenant a phase or a statement of the covenant of redemption is hardly justified by the study of its precise provisions.

III. LITERAL VERSUS SPIRITUAL INTERPRETATION

While the premillennial interpretation of the Abrahamic covenant distinguishes the promises to Abraham, to Abraham's seed, and to "all the families of the earth," the amillennial view largely blurs this distinction. In order to understand the amillennial view, it will be necessary to summarize its main arguments.

The amillennial position. Albertus Pieters in his work, *The Seed of Abraham,* has summarized the amillennial position as follows: "The expression 'Seed of Abraham,' in biblical usage, denotes that visible community, the members of which stand in relation to God through the Abrahamic Covenant, and thus are heirs to the Abrahamic promise."[5] In other words, all who are heirs of the covenant in any sense are the seed of Abraham. In discussing the circumcision of Abraham's entire house including the servants, Pieters concludes, "Yet they were all accounted, for covenant purposes, to be 'The Seed of Abraham.' "[6] He states further in regard to the question of whether promises were made to Abraham's physical seed, "Whenever we meet with the argument that God made certain promises to the Jewish race, the above facts are pertinent. God never made any promises to any race at all, as a race. All his promises were to the continuing covenanted community, without regard to

---

[5]Albertus Pieters, *op. cit.,* p. 20.
[6]*Ibid.,* p. 17.

its racial constituents or to the personal ancestry of the individuals in it."[7]

The expression *seed of Abraham* under this interpretation loses its literal meaning and is considered the seed of Abraham only in a spiritual sense. Coupled with this spiritualizing of the term is the general assumption that the covenant as a whole is entirely conditioned upon the faith of the individual. Hence the promise of everlasting possession of the land by the seed of Abraham is thrown out as having been forfeited by Israel's failures in the Old and New Testament. To all practical purposes the Abrahamic covenant has its fulfillment in the church according to the amillennial viewpoint.

The premillennial view of the covenant. As distinguished from the amillennial position, the premillennial interpretation of the Abrahamic covenant takes its provisions literally. In other words, the promises given to Abraham will be fulfilled by Abraham; the promises to Abraham's seed, will be fulfilled by his physical seed; the promises to "all the families of the earth," will be fulfilled by Gentiles, or those not the physical seed. While possession of the land forever is the promise to the physical seed, the promise of blessing is to "all the families of the earth." Both are to be fulfilled exactly as promised.

While the premillennial position insists upon fulfillment of promises to Israel as the physical seed, and thereby its national preservation and future hope of possession of the land, the premillenarian recognizes that there is a spiritual as well as a natural seed of Abraham. The New Testament in numerous passages refers to the spiritual seed of Abraham. Abraham is called "the father of all them that believe" (Rom. 4:11). In Galatians 3:7, it is noted, "Know therefore that they that are of faith, the same are sons of Abraham." Again in Galatians 3:29 it is revealed, "And if ye are Christ's, then are ye Abraham's seed, heirs according to promise." These passages teach beyond doubt that there is a spiritual seed of Abraham, those

[7]*Ibid.*, pp. 19-20.

who like Abraham of old believe in God, and are children of faith.

Premillenarians also recognize the distinction between the natural and the spiritual seed within Israel itself. In Romans 9:6, this is stated in a few words, "For they are not all Israel, that are of Israel." This is defined later, "That is, it is not the children of the flesh that are children of God; but the children of the promise are reckoned for a seed" (Rom. 9:8). Within Israel, then, there is a believing remnant who are both natural and spiritual children of Abraham. These inherit the promises.

Threefold reference to the seed of Abraham. There are, then, three different senses in which one can be a child of Abraham. First, there is the natural lineage, or natural seed. This is limited largely to the descendants of Jacob in the twelve tribes. To them God promises to be their God. To them was given the law. To them was given the land of Israel in the Old Testament. With them God dealt in a special way. Second, there is the spiritual lineage within the natural. These are the Israelites who believed in God, who kept the law, and who met the conditions for present enjoyment of the blessings of the covenant. Those who ultimately possess the land in the future millennium will also be of spiritual Israel. Third, there is the spiritual seed of Abraham who are not natural Israelites. Here is where the promise to "all the families of the earth" comes in. This is the express application of this phrase in Galatians 3:6-9, "Even as Abraham believed God, and it was reckoned unto him for righteousness. Know therefore that they that are of faith, the same are sons of Abraham. And the scripture, foreseeing that God would justify the Gentiles by faith, preached the gospel beforehand unto Abraham, saying, In thee shall all the nations be blessed. So then they that are of faith are blessed with the faithful Abraham." In other words, the children of Abraham (spiritually) who come from the "heathen" or the Gentiles fulfill that aspect of the Abrahamic covenant which dealt with Gentiles in the first place, not the promises pertaining to Israel. The only sense in which Gentiles can be Abraham's seed in the Galatians context is to be "in Christ Jesus" (Gal. 3:28). It follows: "And if ye are Christ's, then are ye Abraham's seed, heirs according to promise" (Gal. 3:29). They are Abraham's seed in the spiritual sense only and heirs of the promise given "to all the families of the earth."

While premillenarians can agree with amillenarians concerning the fact of a spiritual seed for Abraham which includes Gentiles, they deny that this fulfills the promises given to the natural seed or that the promises to the "seed of Abraham" are fulfilled by Gentile believers. To make the blessings promised all the nations the same as the blessings promised the seed of Abraham is an unwarranted conclusion.

Weakness of amillennial exegesis of covenant passages. The weakness of the amillennial position is shown by examination of their exegesis of such passages as Genesis 15:18-21, where the exact boundaries of the promised land are given, and the kindred passage in Genesis 17:7-8 where the covenant is called everlasting and the land is promised as an everlasting possession. Albertus Pieters, in his discussion of "The Seed of Abraham in the Patriarchal Period,"[8] finds it convenient to pass over these passages entirely. His argument is that modern Jews have lost their lineage and therefore nobody today is qualified to claim the promises given to the Jew anyway—a radical and questionable line of argument to say the least. Most amillenarians as well as premillenarians recognize the modern Jew as having some racial continuity with ancient Israel, however polluted by intermarriage with Gentiles.

Oswald Allis,[9] on the other hand, while an ardent amillenarian, faces these promises on an entirely different basis. His argument is that the promises have either been fulfilled literally for Israel or that they were conditional promises and Israel failed to meet the conditions. The contrast between the approach of Allis and that of Pieters illustrates that amillenarians are quite at odds among themselves not only on details but on the main principles of their interpretation.

[8]*Ibid.*, pp. 11-23.
[9]Oswald T. Allis, *op. cit.*, pp. 31-36.

IV. Partial Fulfillment as a Proof of Future Fulfillment

One of the important guides in the interpretation of prophecy is the law of fulfillment. If prophecy is fulfilled literally, it is evidence that it was intended to be interpreted literally. In the study of the Abrahamic covenant, it is of great significance that those portions of the covenant which have been fulfilled in history have followed the literal pattern. Abraham had been promised that his seed would become a great nation. This was not simply fulfilled spiritually—i.e., the many believers who followed Abraham's example of faith—but it was fulfilled literally. Israel became a great nation in a physical and literal sense. It was also promised Abraham that other nations would come from him (Gen. 17:6, 20). This too had a most literal fulfillment in the descendants of Ishmael, Esau, and the children of Keturah, Abraham's second wife. Abraham was promised personal blessings (Gen. 12:2), which again have had the most literal fulfillment. Kings have descended from him in literal fulfillment of the promise (Gen. 17:6). Abraham to this day is remembered as a great man. Gentiles were promised blessing through Abraham's seed (Gen. 12:3). While the blessings were spiritual in character, at the same time it very literally fulfilled the prophecy which offered no physical promises to the Gentiles. There is no necessity to explain away the ordinary and plain meaning of the text to find the most accurate and complete fulfillment. The nations who blessed Israel have been blessed; the nations who cursed Israel have been cursed (Gen. 12:3). Babylon, Assyria, and Egypt are clear Biblical examples, and in profane history it has been fulfilled ever since. The nations which have been notably friendly to Israel have been blessed, and the nations notably persecuting Israel have paid for it, witnessed in modern Russia, Germany, and Spain. As each detail of the provisions of the covenant is noted, fulfillment has followed the literal pattern.

The issue which divides premillenarians and amillenarians in the interpretation of the Abrahamic covenant is the familiar question of literal versus spiritualized interpretation. If taken in its ordinary literal sense, the sense which Abraham no doubt understood it, the covenant promised the land of Abraham's seed as a lasting possession and along with this the promise of being in a special way the object of God's care, protection, and blessing. The Scriptures give adequate indication that the Abrahamic covenant was intended to be interpreted literally as indicated in its partial fulfillment and the frequent prophetic revelation of Israel's glorious future and repossession of the land. Before considering this evidence, it is necessary first to examine the amillennial claim that the Abrahamic covenant does not require literal fulfillment because it was intended to be fulfilled only if conditions were met. In other words, Israel's failure being what it was, amillenarians feel that there is no need for the promises to be fulfilled. Only spiritual blessings are left and these are for those who are Abraham's spiritual children.

Chapter XIII

IS THE ABRAHAMIC COVENANT
UNCONDITIONAL?

I. The Issue Stated

Amillenarians believe that the Abrahamic covenant is based on certain conditions, and its fulfillment hinges on these conditions being met. Premillenarians hold that the Abrahamic covenant is a declaration of God's intention which is not conditional upon the obedience of individuals or nations for its fulfillment—an unconditional plan of God.

As given in the Scriptures, the Abrahamic covenant is hinged upon only one condition. This is given in Genesis 12:1, "Now Jehovah said unto Abram, Get thee out of thy country, and from thy kindred, and from thy father's house, unto the land that I will show thee." The original covenant was based upon Abraham's obedience in leaving his homeland and going to the land of promise. No further revelation is given him until he was obedient to this command after the death of his father. Upon entering Canaan, the Lord immediately gave Abraham the promise of ultimate possession of the land (Gen. 12:7), and subsequently enlarged and reiterated the original promises.

The one condition having been met, no further conditions are laid upon Abraham; the covenant having been solemnly established is now dependent upon divine veracity for its fulfillment. A parallel can be found in the doctrine of eternal security for the believer in the present dispensation. Having once accepted Jesus Christ as Savior, the believer is assured a complete salvation and eternal bliss in heaven on a gracious principle quite independent of attaining a degree of faithfulness or obedience during this life. The original condition having been met, the promise continues without further conditions.

II. EVIDENCE THAT THE COVENANT IS UNCONDITIONAL

The Scriptures afford a most complete line of evidence in support of the unconditional character of the covenant. This evidence is commonly ignored by amillenarians who usually do not even bother to refute it. For those willing to examine all the evidence, it constitutes proof of the premillennial position.

All Israel's covenants unconditional except the Mosaic. The Abrahamic covenant is expressly declared to be eternal and therefore unconditional in numerous passages (Gen. 17:7, 13, 19; 1 Chron. 16:17; Ps. 105:10). The Palestinian covenant is likewise declared to be everlasting (Ezek. 16:60). The Davidic covenant is described in the same terms (2 Sam. 7:13, 16, 19; 1 Chron. 17:12; 22:10; Isa. 55:3; Ezek. 37:25). The new covenant with Israel is also eternal (Isa. 61:8; Jer. 32:40; 50:5; Heb. 13:20).

No conditions stated. Except for the original condition of leaving his homeland and going to the promised land, the covenant is made with no conditions whatever. It is rather a prophetic declaration of God of what will certainly come to pass, and is no more conditional than any other announced plan of God which depends upon God's sovereignty for its fulfillment.

Confirmation not conditional. The Abrahamic covenant is confirmed repeatedly by reiteration and enlargement. In none of these instances are any of the added promises conditioned upon the faithfulness of Abraham's seed or of Abraham himself. While God promises in some instances the larger aspects of the covenant in recognition of Abraham's faithfulness, nothing is said about it being conditioned upon the future faithfulness of either Abraham or his seed.

Confirmed by unqualified oath of God. The Abrahamic covenant was solemnized by a divinely ordered ritual symbolizing the shedding of blood and passing between the parts of the sacrifice (Gen. 15:7-21; Jer. 34:18). This ceremony was given to Abraham as an assurance that his seed would inherit the land in the exact boundaries given to him in Genesis 15:18-21.

No conditions whatever are attached to this promise in this context.

Circumcision not a condition. To distinguish those who would inherit the promises as individuals from those who were only physical seed of Abraham, the visible sign of circumcision was given (Gen. 17:9-14). One not circumcised was considered outside the promised blessing. The ultimate fulfillment of the Abrahamic covenant and possession of the land by the seed is not hinged, however, upon faithfulness in the matter of circumcision. In fact the promises of the land were given before the rite was introduced.

No conditions required of Isaac and Jacob. The Abrahamic covenant was confirmed by the birth of Isaac and Jacob to both of whom the promises are repeated in their original form (Gen. 17:19; 28:12-13). To them again no conditions were delineated for the fulfillment of the covenant. The added revelation is that the promised seed would be channeled through them.

Confirmation in spite of disobedience. Notable is the fact that the reiterations of the covenant and the partial early fulfillments of the covenant are in spite of acts of disobedience. It is clear that on several instances Abraham strayed from the will of God, as for instance in his departure out of the land and sojourn in Egypt. Jacob has the promise given him in spite of his disobedience, deceit, and unbelief. In the very act of fleeing the land the promises are repeated to him.

Even apostasy does not destroy the covenant. The latter confirmations of the covenant are given in the midst of apostasy. Important is the promise given through Jeremiah that Israel as a nation will continue forever (Jer. 31:36). The place of the new covenant given through Jeremiah in its relation to the Abrahamic covenant and the extensive and numerous predictions in the Minor Prophets concerning Israel's gathering and restoration to fulfill the Abrahamic covenant will be considered in later discussion. The very existence of this large body of Scripture is an important link in the proof of the unconditional character of the Abrahamic covenant.

The covenant declared immutable. The New Testament declares the Abrahamic covenant immutable (Heb. 6:13-18; cf. Gen. 15:8-21). It was not only promised but solemnly confirmed by the oath of God.

Israel's revealed program confirms it. The entire Scriptural revelation concerning Israel and its future as contained in both the Old and New Testament, if interpreted literally, confirms and sustains the unconditional character of the promises given to Abraham.

Additional arguments. There are then many and weighty reasons for considering the Abrahamic covenant unconditional. The latter discussion of the Davidic covenant and the New covenant constitutes a further indication of the unconditional character of God's promises to Abraham's seed. The fulfillment of the Abrahamic covenant in history down to the present day adds its weight to all the other arguments. In spite of these important considerations, the amillenarian insists that the covenant must be interpreted spiritually and that it will never be completely fulfilled because of the failure to meet the supposed conditions.

III. The Amillennial Argument for a Conditional Covenant

Obedience assumed as a condition. The amillennial point of view almost takes for granted that the Abrahamic covenant is subject to conditions. In fact the statement is frequently made that obedience is always the prerequisite for blessing. In the words of Oswald Allis: "It is true that, in the express terms of the covenant with Abraham, obedience is not stated as a condition. But that obedience was presupposed is clearly indicated by two facts. The one is that obedience is the precondition of blessing under all circumstances. . . . The second fact is that in the case of Abraham the duty of obedience is particularly stressed."[1]

Fallacy of amillennial position. Allis is guilty here of begging the question with a very hasty dogmatism. It is not true

---

[1]Oswald T, Allis. *Prophecy and the Church,* p. 33.

that obedience is always the condition of blessing. The seed of Abraham have been disobedient in every moral category. Yet in spite of that disobedience they have fulfilled many of the promises of the covenant. The very principle of grace is that God blesses the unworthy. The individual is not saved on the ground of moral obedience or of attaining moral perfection. The security of the believer, a doctrine which Allis certainly believes, is quite independent of human worth or faithfulness. Allis is saying in effect that God can make no certain promises where human agency is concerned. As a Calvinist, where is Allis' doctrine of unconditional election? Is it not better to avoid such a sweeping universal and to recognize that, while covenants may be conditional as for instance the Mosaic covenant was, covenants can also be unconditional? The Abrahamic covenant is a declaration of God's purpose and, while human agency is involved, the main point of the covenant is that God will fulfill it in spite of human failure.

Amillennial misconception of the place of obedience. Amillenarians while admitting that obedience is never made the condition of the covenant—which ought to be decisive in itself —point out that obedience is stressed. An examination of various references to human obedience reveals that Abraham had promises reiterated and further revelation given concerning them because of his obedience. It is never stated or implied, however, that the covenant was in abeyance until Abraham was obedient.

Obedience related to personal blessing. The role of obedience was important for individual blessing under the covenant. An individual could deprive himself of the immediate blessings of the covenant through gross disobedience. The point is that in spite of such individual actions the covenant would have its complete fulfillment. It is anticipated that there would be a godly remnant, as there was, in whom the covenant would have its complete fulfillment (cf. Gen. 18:18-19); but in the renewal of the covenant to Isaac, certainty of it is not built upon the future obedience of the seed of Abraham, but upon the past obedience of Abraham (Gen. 26:3-5). In recognizing the obedience of Abraham in offering Isaac, God repeated the same promises given before (Gen. 22:16-18). Obviously if these promises were conditioned on the worthiness of Abraham's seed, the large probability of human failure would have robbed the promises of any real hope of fulfillment.

Obedience related to foreordination. It is of course anticipated in the sovereignty and foreknowledge of God that, to the extent that obedience entered into the fulfillment of the covenant, such obedience was predestined and determined. The agency and circumstances of the fulfillment of the covenant are not the important point. God was promising that the covenant would be fulfilled, and the premillenarian believes that it would be fulfilled exactly as promised.

Amillennial arguments in detail. Most of the other amillennial objections to considering the covenant unconditional stem from their main premise that all covenants are conditional. In support of this idea, numerous smaller claims are made. Attention is directed to Jonah's command to preach judgment on Nineveh, "Yet forty days, and Nineveh shall be overthrown" (Jonah 3:4), a promise cancelled when Nineveh repented. The answer, of course, is that this is not a covenant but a warning. The very fact that Nineveh was brought to repentance shows that they understood it in this light. This at best is argument by analogy, and the circumstances show it is not a parallel case.

The judgment on Eli's house for its sin is cited by Allis[2] to prove that an unstated condition is implied in every covenant (1 Sam. 2:30 with Ex. 29:9. Cf. Jer. 18:1-10; Ezek. 3:18-19; Ex. 32:13 ff.). In this case, premillenarians will agree with the illustration, disagree with the principle which it is supposed to illustrate. The covenant with Eli's house was a part of the Mosaic covenant, which all agree is a conditional covenant which was not intended to be eternal. This has no bearing whatever upon the Abrahamic covenant. In God's dealings with nations other than Israel He is free to pluck up and cast down. In Israel's case, He has pledged His word, and Moses is

---

[2]*Ibid.*, p. 32.

quick to remind God of His unalterable covenant in the face of Israel's sin (Ex. 32:13-14).

The rite of circumcision is cited as proving the covenant is conditional. All agree that the individual enjoyment of blessing under the covenant is to a large degree dependent upon the individual's faith and obedience. That is quite different than stating that the fulfillment of the covenant as a whole is conditioned upon obedience of the nation as a whole. This also explains what seems to Allis to be a contradiction, that C. I. Scofield taught that Israel must be in the land of promise to be fully blessed.[3] The issue here again is individual blessing or blessing on any one generation of Israel. The question of ultimate fulfillment is not in view.

Esau is also cited by amillenarians as proof that the covenant is conditional. Allis says, "That Dispensationalists do not regard the Abrahamic covenant as wholly unconditional is indicated also by the fact that we never hear them speak of the restoration of Esau to the land of Canaan and to full blessing under the Abrahamic covenant. . . . But if the Abrahamic covenant was unconditional why is Esau excluded from the blessings of the covenant?"[4] The answer is quite simple, of course, and Allis anticipates it somewhat in his discussion. The promises to Abraham are not fulfilled by *all* the natural seed of Abraham, but by *some* of them. Those who will fulfill the covenant descend from Jacob, and Esau is excluded. Allis should be reminded that Esau is excluded by solemn choice of God before obedience became an issue, a fact clearly brought out in Romans 9:11-13.

Allis in his argument changes pace quite rapidly in his next objection to the premillennial view. He states: "The certainty of the fulfillment of the covenant and the security of the believer under it, ultimately depend wholly on the obedience of Christ."[5] This is, of course, absolutely true, but it has no bearing on the argument here and is actually against the amil-

---

[3]*Ibid.*, p. 34.
[4]*Ibid.*, pp. 35-36.
[5]*Ibid.* p. 36.

lennial position. If it all hinged upon the obedience of Christ, and that obedience was absolutely certain, it would follow that the fulfillment of the Abrahamic Covenant was also absolutely certain, which is exactly what premillenarians are trying to uphold and mean by its being unconditional. The main issue is whether the complete fulfillment of the covenant is certain in spite of human failure.

Allis employs a premillennial form of argument on another point. He holds in effect that the covenant has already been fulfilled and that the promise of the multiplied seed was already realized by Solomon's day (cf. Gen. 13:16; 15:5; 22:17; 1 Kings 4:20; 1 Chron. 27:23; 2 Chron. 1:9; Heb. 11:12). This, of course, all concede. It is in fact a stock premillennial argument that partial fulfillment of the covenant in a literal way demands literal fulfillment of the rest of it.

Allis goes right on to state, however, "As to the *land,* the dominion of David and of Solomon extended from the Euphrates to the River of Egypt (1 Kgs. iv. 21), which also reflects the terms of the covenant. Israel did come into possession of the land promised to the patriarchs. She possessed it, but not 'for ever.' Her possession of the land was forfeited by disobedience, both before and after the days of David and Solomon."[6] Allis admits, however, that the possession of the land did not really fulfill the covenant.

According to the Abrahamic covenant, the land would be *completely* possessed, and would be permanently possessed as "an everlasting possession" (Gen. 17:8). The fulfillment under Solomon breaks down under every requirement. As Allis very well knows, neither David nor Solomon "possessed" all the land for which the boundaries are given with precision in Genesis 15:18-21. At best much of this land was put under tribute, but was never possessed. Further as Allis admits, it was soon lost again, which in no wise fulfilled the promise of permanent or everlasting possession (Gen. 17:8). Besides, Allis is quite oblivious to a fact that nullifies his entire argument here. The prophets who lived after Solomon were still anticipating the

---

[6]*Ibid.,* p. 58.

future fulfillment of the promises of the everlasting possession of the land (cf. Amos 9:13-15) and reiterate in practically all
the Minor Prophets the theme song that Israel is to be restored
to the land, to be regathered there, and to continue under the
blessing of God. While the promises relative to a large progeny
may have been fulfilled in Solomon's day, the promises relative to the land were not.

Summary of amillennial argument. The amillennial argument, then, is based on the principle that the Abrahamic
covenant is a conditional covenant, that its promises are therefore uncertain as depending upon obedience of men for fulfillment. On this basis they are sure that no literal fulfillment
of the covenant is necessary, and in fact hold that the only possible fulfillment in our day is a spiritual one of inheriting
spiritual blessings. By contrast, the premillennial view holds
that the covenant will be fulfilled literally, that the covenant
itself does not contain any conditions for its ultimate fulfillment, but is the unalterable purpose of God revealed to Abraham. The constant reference to the Abrahamic covenant in
the Old Testament, the common understanding of this covenant down to the lifetime of Christ, and the explicit teachings
of the New Testament all confirm a future for Israel and sustain the principle of a future fulfillment of the Abrahamic
covenant.

All agree that certain provisions of the covenant are unfulfilled. The unfulfilled portions coincide with the future
program for the world and for Israel as set forth by premillenarians. The promise of complete and everlasting possession
of the land is to be fulfilled in the future millennial kingdom
and will issue in possessions in the eternal new earth. Israel
will continue as a nation and will be dealt with as a nation by
God. Israel's distinct place and promises are apparently eternal.
The day of full blessing, Israel's regathering, her exaltation
over the Gentiles, and her bliss under the righteous reign of
the Son of David will provide the ultimate fulfillment which
will complete the story of God's faithfulness to His covenant.
Because of the decisive importance of the issue of Israel's future

fulfillment of the Abrahamic covenant, this will be considered next. Her continuance as a nation, her possession of the land, and her restoration are important themes of Scripture which fully confirm the premillennial concept of the Abrahamic covenant.

CHAPTER XIV

WILL ISRAEL CONTINUE AS A NATION?

I. THE POINT AT ISSUE

In previous discussion of the Abrahamic covenant, it was shown that the term *seed of Abraham* had three distinct meanings as used in Scripture. It is used (1) of the natural seed of Abraham, limited in some contexts to the seed of Jacob or Israel; (2) it is used of the spiritual seed of Abraham within the natural seed—spiritual Israel; (3) it is used of those who are spiritual seed of Abraham but not natural descendants, i.e., Gentile believers. Premillenarians concede to amillenarians the existence of a spiritual seed of Abraham. The point at issue is that amillenarians insist that the Abrahamic covenant is fulfilled *only* through the spiritual seed of Abraham and that therefore Israel racially and nationally has no covenant promises.

II. THE MEANING OF THE TERM "SEED OF ABRAHAM"

Amillennial definition. The usual amillennial position is stated by Albertus Pieters in these words, as quoted in part previously: "Whenever we meet with the argument that God made certain promises to the Jewish race, the above facts are pertinent. God never made any promise to any race at all, as a race. All His promises were to the continuing covenanted community, without regard to its racial constituents or to the personal ancestry of the individuals in it. Hence no proof that those whom the world now calls 'the Jews' are descended from Abraham if it could be supplied (which it can not), would be of any avail to prove that they are entitled to the fulfillment of any divine promise whatsoever. Those promises were made to the covenanted group called 'The Seed of Abraham,' and to that community they must be fulfilled. What is needed is that one shall bring forward proof of his membership in that group."[1]

The amillennial viewpoint as represented by Pieters holds, then, to the following position: (1) God never made any promises to the physical seed of Abraham as a race; (2) the Abrahamic promises are given only to the spiritual seed of Abraham or the "continuing covenanted community"; (3) Jews today have no claim on the promise to Abraham because (a) they are not the spiritual seed; (b) they could not prove that they are the physical seed anyway.

To say the least, these are sweeping statements for which the most complete proof should be available. An examination of Pieters' arguments fails to produce any conclusive proof. What is his proof for the statement that God made no promises to the physical seed of Abraham as a race? A search of his book produces no proof whatever. Pieters shows what premillenarians concede: that there is a spiritual seed of Abraham who are blessed with Abraham and for the same reason, that they believe in God. He shows that the blessings of the covenant go beyond the physical seed of Abraham, which also everyone concedes. What he fails to show, and this is the point of the whole issue, is that no promises are given to the physical seed.

Are promises given to the physical seed of Abraham? An examination of the whole context of the Abrahamic covenant shows that first of all it was vitally connected with Abraham's physical seed, Isaac. God said of Isaac before he was born, "I will establish my covenant with him for an everlasting covenant for his seed after him" (Gen. 17:19). How did Abraham understand the term *seed* here? Obviously, it had reference to the physical seed, Isaac, and his physical descendants. God did not say that no spiritual blessing would come to those outside the physical seed, but the physical line of Isaac would inherit the promises given to the "seed of Abraham."

Later God made the same promise to Jacob (Gen. 28:13-14) reiterating the particular promises peculiar to the physical seed

---

[1]Albertus, Pieters. *The Seed of Abraham*, pp. 19-20.

of Abraham: possession of the land; a great posterity as to number, and that "in thee and in thy seed shall all the families of the earth be blessed." Nothing should be plainer than that Abraham, Isaac, and Jacob understood the term *seed* as referring to their physical lineage. While blessing is promised those outside the seed of Abraham if they believe as godly Abraham believed, the particular promises of a great posterity, of possession of the land, and being the channel of blessing to Gentiles is never given to any except the physical seed. Again it should be made clear that God is not undertaking to fulfill the promise to *all* the physical seed of Abraham, but through *some* of them, chosen as the line of the seed. While the line of the seed culminates in Christ, who fulfills much of the promise of blessing to the Gentiles, it is clear that all the twelve tribes, not only Judah, were considered the seed of Abraham and in particular the seed of Israel.

While Pieters' presentation of the amillenarian position accomplishes about all that could be asked for that viewpoint, it must be rejected as lacking any positive proof. The arguments, however cogently presented, do not prove the point at issue. The Scriptural use of the term *seed of Abraham* while it justifies the concept of a spiritual seed does not exclude the promises to the physical seed. The amillenarian arguments beg the question by assuming what they are trying to prove. The fact is that Pieters and most amillenarians seem to avoid the real issues and in their discussion of the Abrahamic covenant do not deal with that aspect that concerns the physical seed.

Does Abraham have a physical seed today? The concluding point of Pieters, that the Jews have no racial continuity, is an illustration of the extremes to which amillenarians are forced to go to sustain their position. Certainly the world today is bearing witness to the continuing physical strain of Jewish blood, however contaminated by marriage with Gentiles. The Jews themselves acknowledge this physical lineage. Most Biblical scholars who are conservative acknowledge it whether premillennial, postmillennial, or amillennial. Certainly the

Scriptures continue the recognition of this people even after centuries of intermarriage with Gentiles. The book of Revelation in its prophetic account of things future speaks of the twelve tribes being again identified by God. In modern history we have witnessed the creation of the political state of Israel in Palestine, the persecution of Jews as such in Europe, the continued teachings of orthodox Judaism as well as its reformed counterparts. Anyone in the face of such overwhelming evidence for recognition of the physical seed of Abraham in the world today who in effect denies them right and title to the name *Israel* is shutting his eyes to some very plain facts. One of the greatest of modern miracles has been the preservation of the identity of Israel as a race and nation, a fact which has been the stumbling stone for the amillennial denial of Israel's future. To deny that Israel has a bona fide existence today is to ignore that which is plain to everyone else.

III. The Term "Israel"

Meaning of the term. The millennial controversy over the meaning of the term *seed of Abraham* carries over into the term *Israel*. As a title given to Jacob, meaning *prince of God,* it has commonly been used to designate the physical descendants of Jacob. While amillenarians tend to deny that the seed of Abraham has any physical reference, as we have seen, they concede that the term *Israel* has some physical reference. The question at issue does not concern the Old Testament use of the term so much as it concerns the New Testament meaning of Israel.

Amillennial view. Amillenarians characteristically do not agree among themselves on even the essentials of their theology, and their concept of Israel is a good illustration. The older and more familiar type of amillenarians, of which Calvin may be taken as a representative, holds that when Israel rejected Christ they lost their promises and that the New Testament church has become the inheritor of Israel's covenants. The church of the New Testament, they hold, is Israel. Oswald Allis, for instance, is a staunch defender of Calvin's viewpoint and goes so far as to label literal interpretation of the term *Israel* as "an almost unprecedented extreme."[2] As pointed out previously, the idea that Israel means Israel is not unprecedented, nor is it confined to the Brethren movement. It is held in its essentials by postmillenarians[3] and avowed amillenarians.[4] Allis seems unaware that he himself is the one out of step. The whole tendency of modern theology both conservative and liberal is toward the position of distinguishing rather than merging Biblical Judaism and Christianity.

The newer amillennial approach to the meaning of the term *Israel* is to regard it as always being basically a reference to those physically Israel. They may regard them like Hendriksen as spiritual Israel or elect Israel down through the ages, or like the postmillenarian Charles Hodge as Israelites who become Christians—certainly one of the Biblical usages, but there is no longer much zeal to make the church the inheritor of all Israel's promises.

There are a number of good reasons for this trend away from Calvin and his modern disciple Allis. Obviously the church does not fulfill in any literal way the great bulk of Israel's promises which had to do with repossession of the land, Israel's regathering, and a glorious kingdom on earth. It is much easier and more logical to seal off these promises as conditional and therefore no longer subject to fulfillment. This permits a more logical exposition of the passages without embarrassment by comparison with the history of the church. Further, Israel is promised curses as well as blessings under her covenants. To qualify for the blessings puts the church in a compromising position of being involved in Israel's curses also. Modern amillennialism prefers to stand on New Testament rather than Old Testament promises.

Within the ranks of amillennialism there is, then a decisive and basic difference of opinion on the meaning of the term *Israel*.

---

[2]Oswald T. Allis, *Prophecy and the Church*, p. 218.
[3]Charles Hodge, *Commentary on Romans*, p. 589.
[4]William Hendriksen, *And So All Israel Shall Be Saved*, p. 33.

The older opinion is that the church today inherits Israel's promises; the more modern amillennial position is that Israel means Israel even in the New Testament.

Premillennial view. The premillennial position on the term *Israel* is that it *always* has reference to those who are physical descendants of Jacob. Within this larger definition, however, there are distinctions. There is a godly or spiritual Israel in the Old Testament who are true believers in God, and there is a godly Israel in the church consisting of Israelites who are believers in Jesus Christ. The premillennial position is demonstrated by a careful study of all the New Testament references to Israel and by the contrast between Israel and other terms.

IV. ISRAEL AND GENTILES CONTRASTED

Distinctions continue after Pentecost. It should be obvious to anyone making even a casual study of the subject that the terms *Israel* and *Gentiles* continue to be used after the institution of the church at Pentecost and that the terms are mutually exclusive. Both Gentiles and Israelites continued to exist after the church began, and while some of each came into the church, the Gentiles and Israelites continued as such. Israel as a nation is addressed again and again *after* the institution of the church (Acts 3:12; 4:8, 10; 5:21, 31, 35; 21:28, etc.). A notable instance is Paul's prayer for Israel that they might be saved (Rom. 10:1) —obviously a reference to Israel outside the church.

The term *Jew* also continues in the New Testament after the beginning of the church. In 1 Corinthians 10:32 it is specifically mentioned: "Give no occasion of stumbling, either to Jews, or to Greeks, or to the church of God." Here is a clear threefold division of humanity into (1) Jews, (2) Gentiles, (3) church of God.

Israel's continued privileges. The Apostle Paul calls attention to Israel's unique place and privilege constantly in his epistles. He declares that their peculiar promises include the adoption, the glory, the covenants, the giving of the law, the service of God, the promises, the fathers, and the privilege of being the people of whom Christ should come (Rom. 9:4-5).

Now, it is obvious that Paul is referring to Israel *in unbelief* when he refers to those who have these privileges, for he declares: "For I could wish that I myself were anathema from Christ for my brethren's sake, my kinsmen according to the flesh: who are Israelites. . . ." (Rom. 9:3-4). He declares that they even in unbelief "are Israelites," and relates to them all the peculiar privileges of Israel. It is evident that the institution of the church did not rob Israel in the flesh of its peculiar place of privilege before God.

Gentiles continue to be excluded from Israel's privileges. The declaration of Romans 9:3-4 is given added weight by the fact that in Ephesians 2:12 Gentiles are expressly declared to have been excluded from the promises given to Israel: "That ye [Gentiles] were at that time separate from Christ, alienated from the commonwealth of Israel, and strangers from the covenants of the promise, having no hope, and without God in the world." The passage goes on to state their privilege as Christians in the church. It is noteworthy that Paul does *not* say that the Gentiles came into these same Israelitish promises when they were converted; rather he pictures a work of God bringing Jew and Gentile into a new order entirely—"one new man" (Eph. 2:15). It may be concluded without further argument that the distinction between natural Israel and Gentiles is continued after the institution of the church—Israel is still a genuine Israel, and the Gentiles continue to fulfill their part. While this fact of the Scripture is more or less admitted even by the amillennialist, the significance is not adequately realized. The continuance of Israel and Gentiles as such is a strong argument against either one being dispossessed of their own place. Israel is not reduced to the bankruptcy of the Gentiles—to become "strangers from the covenants of promises" (Eph. 2:12), and the distinction between the two groups is maintained on the same sharp lines as before the church was instituted.

V. NATURAL ISRAEL AND THE CHURCH CONTRASTED

Amillennial position untenable. Not only is natural Israel contrasted to Gentiles, but it is also contrasted to the church as such. The amillennial position fully agrees to this contrast, but in doing so its supporters do not realize that the basis of their own argument is jeopardized. If natural Israel continues as an entity apart from the church with its own program and destiny, it becomes at once an interesting and vital argument against the transfer of Israel's promises to the church or their loss by any other means. Amillenarians are forced to a position which by its nature is untenable. They must admit the existence of natural Israel apart from the church because it is too evident that this is a fact of Scripture and history.[5] They cannot admit any program for them or any possibility of a national future for them.

New Testament testimony to future for Israel. The Scriptures, however, speak of a future for Israel, and that in the New Testament. The testimony of Scripture is confirmed by the obvious fact that Israel in the flesh has continued to exist as a distinct people even in centuries of dispersion. The Scriptures reveal that God has placed Israel in the present age in a peculiar relation to Himself and that He contemplates a renewal of His mercies to them at a future period.

The classic passage found in Romans eleven deals specifically with the problem before us. Has God no program for Israel as such? Paul raises the question himself: "I say then, Did God cast off his people?" (Rom. 11:1). He goes on to answer in the negative, indicating that at the time of the writing of Romans there was a remnant out of Israel saved by grace who had their part in the church. Unbelieving Israel is declared to have been blinded: "What then? That which Israel seeketh for, that he obtained not; but the election obtained it, and the rest were hardened" (Rom. 11:7). He speaks of this hardening or spiritual blinding as their "fall," which, because of the present privilege of Gentiles to receive the gospel and salvation on the same terms as Israel, becomes "the riches of the Gentiles" (Rom. 11:12). He then goes on to compare their fall with their full-

---

[5]Pieters' denial of a natural Israel is an exception to the rule. Cf. *loc. cit.*

ness: "Now if their fall is the riches of the world, and their loss the riches of the Gentiles; how much more their fulness?" (Rom. 11:12). In other words, if the blindness which has fallen upon Israel nationally during this present age was the occasion for great blessing for the Gentiles, the "fulness" of Israel will bring a richness of blessing which will be "much more." Now, obviously, there can be no fullness of Israel if they have no future. Their fullness will come when the present condition of blindness is lifted.

Israel's future program to follow present Gentile blessing. He takes occasion to warn the Gentiles of their present privileges on the basis of this argument. In Romans 11:15 he refers again to the future blessing of Israel: "For if the casting away of them is the reconciling of the world, what shall the receiving of them be, but life from the dead?" It is true that he speaks of Israel being broken off that the Gentiles might be grafted in (Rom. 11:17-24), but he also speaks of the *future* ingrafting of Israel back into "their own olive tree" (Rom. 11:24). This is contingent upon the "blindness" being lifted, and it is declared that the blindness will continue "until the fulness of the Gentiles be come in" (Rom. 11:25). The use of the word *until* signifies not only that the period of Gentile blessing will end, but it also indicates that a future period of Israel's ingrafting will follow. Samuel H. Wilkinson has brought this out: "If and when an 'until' sets a time-limit to any group of conditions, it makes the said group of conditions to be *temporary* not *everlasting*, to be *preliminary*, not *final*. And the change, whatever it be, which is to occur when the time-limit is reached and passed, must surely refer to the same object as that which was submitted to the temporary conditions. With these two reasonable considerations in view, it will be found that all the time-limits described in the New Testament leave room for the full scope of Old Testament prophecy to become in due time realized."[6]

The distinction between Israel outside of the church and

---

[6]*The Israel Promises and Their Fulfillment* (London: John Bale, Sons & Danielsson, Ltd., 1936), p. 78.

the church itself, then, is a highly significant fact of Scripture
The Scriptures clearly state that Israel in unbelief is blinded,
that this blinded condition is temporary not final, that the
blindness will be lifted when the present period of Gentile
blessing is concluded. The fulfillment of the covenants with
Israel will follow, as Romans 11:26-32 indicates. Not only the
fact of Israel's continuance is revealed, but Israel's present program and future blessings are specifically outlined in Romans
eleven and other portions of Scripture which need not be discussed at this time.

VI. SPIRITUAL ISRAEL AND GENTILE CHRISTIANS CONTRASTED

Are Gentile Christians designated Israelites? While the contrasts between Israel, Gentiles, and the church are severally
important, the crux of the argument is the contrast between
spiritual Israel, that is, those who have become Christians, and
Gentile Christians is obvious to all. In the attempt to disfran-
chise Israel of her promises, however, some amillenarians claim
that the church, composed of both Gentiles and Jews, takes
Israel's place of blessing completely. It is pointed out that there
has always been an inner circle of Israelites who were the "true
Israel" and that these were the genuine inheritors of the promises, not the nation as a whole. It is' the purpose of this discussion to inquire into only one phase of the problem—Is the
church ever identified with true or spiritual Israel, that is, are
Gentile Christians ever included in the designation *Israel?* The
problem of whether the church actually inherits Israel's promises and realizes them is reserved for later treatment.

Romans 9-11. Two principal passages are the foundation for
the discussion. In Romans 9-11 the problem comes up repeatedly.
In Romans 9:6 it is revealed: "For they are not all Israel, that are
of Israel." Those who have opposed a future for Israel find in
this passage a proof-text for their theory that only a portion of
Israel, that is, those who are "spiritual," inherit the promises,
and the rest are excluded from the promises. An examination of
this passage, however, will reveal that the real contrast is not

between those who inherit Abraham's promises and those who do not. It is rather that the promises to Abraham are classified as belonging either to Israel according to the flesh or Israel which enters into the spiritual promises by faith—which are given also to Gentile believers (Gal. 3:6-9, 14). It is not, therefore, a contrast between those who are excluded and those who are included, but rather a contrast between those who inherit only the national promises and those who inherit the spiritual promises also. The line of national promises is narrowed to Isaac and his seed (Rom. 9:7), and the line of spiritual promises is narrowed to those who believe. In the present age, Israel as a nation is blinded, which blindness will be lifted. As individuals, Israelites who believe belong to the election of grace (Rom. 11:5-10). Both Israelites in the flesh (unbelievers) and Israelites who believe are genuine Israelites. They are sharply distinguished as to present blessings. Unbelieving Israelites are lost and blinded, while believing Israelites come into all the present blessings of the church. The distinction is always on the ground of whether or not they believe in Christ, not on whether they are true Israelites.

Galatians 6:15-16. The second principal passage is found in Galatians 6:15-16, "For neither is circumcision anything, nor uncircumcision, but a new creature. And as many as shall walk by this rule, peace be upon them, and mercy, and upon the Israel of God." It has been alleged on the basis of this passage that the church as such is specifically called the "Israel of God." To this is opposed the fact that everywhere else in the Scriptures the term Israel is applied only to those who are the natural seed of Abraham and Isaac, never to Gentiles. If it can be sustained that in this passage the church is called *Israel,* it would, of course, be an argument for the identification of the church with Israel in the present age—though by no means conclusive, in the face of constant use of the term *Israel* in the Scriptures in reference to unbelieving Jews. An examination of Galatians 6:15-16, however, instead of proving any such identification is rather a specific instance where Jewish believers are distinguished from Gentile believers, and this by the very term *Israel of God.*

In Galatians 6:15 the contrast is brought out between "circumcision" and "uncircumcision," i.e., between Jew and Gentile. This contrast is declared to avail not in Christ Jesus, but that rather the issue is a new creation when either Jew or Gentile becomes a believer. God's blessing is declared on those who walk according to this rule (among the Galatians who were Gentiles), and also "upon the Israel of God." The use of *and* (Greek *kai*) is difficult to explain apart from the intention of the writer to set off the "Israel of God" from those considered in the first half of the verse. It is rather another indication that Gentile and Jewish believers are on the same level, as *and* is used principally to link co-ordinate parts of a sentence.

In any case, the argument of those who would destroy Israel's national hope based upon this verse is not founded on sound exegesis. The passage does not state explicitly, even if strained to accommodate their view, that the "Israel of God" and the "new creation" are identical. It is safe to say that if these key passages which are claimed as special proof of the identification of Israel and the church do not teach this doctrine then there is no passage in the New Testament in which the term *Israel* is used as synonymous with the church. In every case the term is used either of the nation Israel as such, still in unbelief, or of that believing remnant which is incorporated into the church without destroying the national promises to Israel in the least.

VII. Is the Nation Israel Disinherited?

The point at issue. One of the assertions which is made confidently by those opposed to a future for Israel is that Israel through their rejection of Christ has been rejected by God as a nation. Now it is clear from both Scripture and history that Israel as a race is scattered throughout the world up to this hour, preserved in their identity but until recently without a national home. The question is whether they will ever be restored as a chosen nation and whether the promises given to them as a nation will be fulfilled. Amillenarians assert, however, that Israel's promises are transferred to the church and that no spiritual Israel will ever exist apart from the present order found in the church. It is claimed that Israel is expressly disinherited.

In refutation of this theory, a host of Scriptures can be found having more or less bearing on the problem. It has already been demonstrated, at least in part, that there is a New Testament basis for believing Israel has a future and, if so, then Israel is not disinherited. Two principal passages will suffice to deal with the crux of the problem.

Matthew 21:43. Christ said, after the parable of the householder, "Therefore say I unto you, The kingdom of God shall be taken away from you, and shall be given to a nation bringing forth the fruits thereof." This seems, at first glance, to be a categorical disinheriting of Israel. A further examination of the passage will bring up several important questions, however. What did Christ refer to by "you," the nation (present and future) of Israel or the immediate generation and individuals to whom He was speaking? What "nation" is going to receive the "kingdom of God"? What does He mean by the "kingdom of God" anyway?

These questions are not easily answered in a few words. It will be noted, first, that there is used in this passage the expression "kingdom of God" in contrast to the usual expression for Matthew, "kingdom of heaven." The "kingdom of God" is apparently the sphere of genuine faith in God and the sphere of genuine rule. It is never used in the Scriptures to include unbelievers whether in Matthew or other New Testament books. On the other hand, the "kingdom of heaven" seems to be concerned with the outward display of God's government and *appearance* rather than reality. The wheat and the tares of Matthew thirteen are both in the kingdom of heaven—the wheat representing genuine believers, the tares representing those who are merely professing believers. The taking of the kingdom of God from the Jew was, then, a declaration that they, that is, the scribes and Pharisees represented in the parable as the wicked husbandmen, would never enter the kingdom of God, i.e., would never be saved. It is obvious that this was true *ipso facto,* but on the other hand it is also clear that *some* Jews did enter the kingdom of God, and that the *nation* of Israel as such never did enter the kingdom of God even in the Old Testament. It had always been limited to those who were genuine believers in the true God. Further, the "kingdom of God" is not to be identified with the millennial kingdom prophesied for Israel and the Gentile nations, though the millennial kingdom is an important manifestation and phase of the kingdom of God.

The declaration of Christ in this passage resolves itself into an affirmation that the unbelieving scribes and Pharisees would never be saved because of their rejection of the "son" of the "householder," and that others would take their place. Gaebelein suggests that the "nation" which will take their place will be other Israelites: "The nation to whom the Lord promises the Kingdom is not the Church. The Church is called the Body of Christ, the Bride of Christ, the Habitation of God by the Spirit, the Lamb's Wife, but never a nation. The nation is Israel still, but that believing remnant of the nation, living when the Lord comes."[7] Whether or not Gaebelein is correct, it is certain that Gentiles as a whole do not inherit the kingdom of God.

Romans 11:1-32. This chapter deals with the question whether God has cast off Israel. To this leading question Paul replies in positive terms, "God forbid." His argument may be summarized as a denial of this question. God has not cast away His people. There has always been a remnant in every age true to God. The unbelief of the nation Israel has never caused God to cast off His people as a whole (Rom. 11:3-4). There has always been a continuing program for Israel as witnessed in the present election of grace. Some Jews are being saved. While unbelieving Jews are blinded now, their present

---

[7]A. C. Gaebelein, *The Gospel of Matthew* (New York: Our Hope, 1910), II. 138.

blindness will be lifted and replaced by sight and faith. When this glad day comes "all Israel shall be saved" (Rom. 11:26), meaning a group or national deliverance in contrast to the individual salvation offered now. At that time God's covenants with Israel will be fulfilled, for the gifts and calling of God are without repentance, sure and irrevocable. The whole tenor of the chapter is against either the idea that Israel has lost all future hope of fulfillment of their promises through cancellation or that the church has received these promises and Israel is disinherited.

VIII. Conclusion

On the basis of this brief study of terminology, the evidence has been examined and found to produce nothing indicating that the term *Israel* is ever used of Gentiles. Rather it is used of the godly remnant in all ages, Christian Jews, and the future national entity anticipated through the Scriptures. None of these usages support the amillennial contention that Israel has no national future. With this as a foundation, Israel's precise promises relative to the land, her regathering and repossession of it, may be considered.

Chapter XV

WILL ISRAEL POSSESS THE PROMISED LAND?

I. THE PROMISE TO ABRAHAM

One of the important provisions of the Abrahamic covenant is the promise of possession of the land. From Abraham's point of view, this was undoubtedly one of its main features. In the original promise he was told, "Get thee out. . . unto the land that I will show thee" (Gen. 12:1). This anticipation of possessing the land is given more content in Genesis 13:15, where Abraham is promised, "For all the land which thou seest, to thee will I give it, and to thy seed for ever." This promise of the land is subsequently enlarged and given specific boundaries (Gen. 15:18-21), and the land is promised as an everlasting possession (Gen. 17:7-8).

All interpreters of the Abrahamic Covenant are faced with the question of the interpretation and fullfillment of these promises. In general, amillenarians tend either to make these promises conditional, and therefore not requiring fulfillment, or to spiritualize them and point to past possessions of the land as fulfilling the promise. Premillenarians consider the promises as given unconditionally as far as ultimate fulfillment is concerned and therefore hold that Israel has a bona fide ground for future possession of the land, particularly in the millennial kingdom period. For practical purposes the problem resolves into the question of whether Israel will ever possess all the promised land.

It has been previously shown that the Abrahamic covenant is basically unconditional, though the present enjoyment of it by an individual or a nation may have certain conditions. It has also been shown that Israel shall continue as a nation forever. If these two conclusions be sustained, it follows that

Israel as such will possess the land. It also is true that all the evidence pointing to ultimate possession of the land confirms and supports the idea that the covenant is unconditional and that Israel will continue as a nation forever.

II. The Character of the Promise of the Land

The promise of possession of the land by the seed of Abraham is a prominent feature of the covenant, and the way the promise is given enhances its significance. The promise as given emphasizes that (1) it is gracious in its principle; (2) the land is an inheritance of the seed; (3) its title is given forever; (4) the land is to be possessed forever; (5) the land promised includes specific territory defined by boundaries. It is difficult to imagine how God could have made it clearer that the covenant was sure of its literal fulfillment.

The promise is gracious in its principle. Unlike the Mosaic covenant, which conditions the promises of blessings upon obedience, the Abrahamic covenant simply pronounces God's intention to give the land to Abraham and his seed forever. Its character as an inheritance of the seed is repeated in the subsequent enlargement of the promise and is linked to the physical lineage. The emphasis upon its unending application as seen in the words "for ever" (Gen. 13:15), "everlasting covenant" (Gen. 17:7), and "everlasting possession" (Gen. 17:8) carries with it the necessity of complete and unconditional fulfillment. The extent of the possession of the land as defined in Genesis 15:18-21, including the great area from the river of Egypt to the river Euphrates, can hardly be spiritualized without abandoning any pretense of sensible exegesis. If this covenant means what it appears to mean, the only proper interpretation is that given by the premillenarians.

III. The Dispersions of Israel

Like the Abrahamic covenant as a whole, the promise of the land is never conditioned upon human obedience. As has been shown, the pronouncements are unequivocal in character.

God is revealing what He will fulfill. All agree, however, that prior to the ultimate fulfillment of the promise, possession and enjoyment of the land by any generation of Israelites *is* conditioned upon certain requirements. These are set forth in both the Mosaic covenant and the Palestinian covenant (cf. Deut. 28:1—30:10). Israel is promised rich blessings in the land for obedience, but is promised curses for disobedience. Among the curses are plagues and disasters if they are in the land, and dispersion to various places out of the land. As early as Genesis 15:13, the dispersions of Israel are anticipated.

In general, three dispersions of Israel are prophesied in the Scripture. The first of these was the sojourn in Egypt when Jacob and his family followed Joseph in leaving the land of promise. This is foretold in Genesis 15:13, and it is promised that they would return to the land with great substance (Gen. 15:14-16). The second dispersion was that of the captivities of Assyria and Babylon, when first the ten tribes and then the remaining tribes were in large measure removed from the promised land because of sin. This dispersion is a large theme of both the major and minor prophets and was prophesied by Moses (Deut. 28:62-65; 30:1-3; Jer. 25:11). There are frequent promises of restoration from this dispersion (Jer. 29:10-14; Dan. 9:2).

Historically Israel returned to the land under Zerubbabel and Ezra. The final dispersion took place in A.D. 70 at the destruction of Jerusalem, and Israel only in recent years has taken any important steps to return to the land.

IV. THE FINAL REGATHERING

One of the phenomena of the modern world is the creation of the state of Israel and the large movement of Jews from all over the world back to their ancient land. As the three dispersions are history along with the two historic returns, the theological question hangs on the issue of whether Israel is to be regathered for the third time and brought back to possess the land of promise. History has shown that the previous returns of Israel, while involving human contingencies, nevertheless were carried out on schedule according to the prophetic Word. The return from Egypt, while not without chronological difficulties, can be reconciled to the prophetic pattern laid out in Genesis. The return of Israel from the second dispersion is clearly linked with the chronology of the seventy years of the captivity, and difficulties are merely with the details and questions of actual dates. The third dispersion is nowhere dated in the Word of God but like the previous returns is certain as to its ultimate fulfillment.

V. Unconditional Promise Includes Contingencies

From the study of the dispersions of Israel and the two regatherings which have already been fulfilled it can be seen that as a general principle divine certainty is given both the dispersions and the regatherings. Premillenarians do not deny that there are human contingencies involved. Obviously the dispersions themselves depended upon Israel's disobedience and the dispersions were a form of judgment from God.

In this sense they were conditional though nevertheless certain. The regatherings are also hinged upon Israel turning back to God in a measure. It is inherent in the pronouncements of Moses that the return to the land would follow a return to God (cf. Deut. 30:1-5). The point is that not only the dispersions were predicted definitely before human failure appeared, but the regatherings of Israel were clearly predicted before Israel returned to God spiritually. In other words, the human contingencies are fully recognized, but the certainty of the prophetic plan is nevertheless affirmed. It is in this sense that the promise of ultimate fulfillment is unconditional. The doctrine of the third regathering of Israel and their possession of the land depends, then, on the question whether the promises of regathering and possession of the land are already fulfilled by Israel's history or whether the Scriptures require a future fulfillment—a third regathering followed by possession of the land.

VI. HAVE HISTORIC POSSESSIONS OF THE LAND FULFILLED THE SCRIPTURES?

The amillenarian position on Israel's possession of the land is that the promise has already been fulfilled. George L. Murray[1] cites 1 Kings 4:21, 24 as evidence that the promise was fulfilled in Solomon's day, "And Solomon ruled over all kingdoms from the River unto the land of the Philistines, and unto the border of Egypt: they brought tribute, and served Solomon all the days of his life. . . . For he had dominion over all the region on this side of the River . . . and he had peace on all sides round about him."

Murray[2] further cites Joshua 21:43, 45 to the same point, and concludes with a reference to Nehemiah 9:7-8 which to him is conclusive. He states, "Whatever political movements we may witness now or in the future by way of a restoration of Hebrew economy in the land of Palestine, these will not come by way of fulfillment of God's promises to Abraham of possession of the land, for we have conclusive evidence that these promises have been fulfilled."[3] Oswald Allis takes essentially the same position quoting only the Solomon reference.[4]

The amillenarian position is often distinguished for its blindness to facts which would upset its own argument. The present instance is a good illustration. If its promises regarding the land were fulfilled in Joshua's time or in Solomon's, why do the Scriptures which were written later still appeal to the hope of future possession of the land? Practically every one of the Major and Minor Prophets mention in some form the hope of future possession of the land. All of them were written after Solomon's day. This is an obvious rebuttal to the amillennial position and points to the amillennial failure to face the real issues of the millennial debate with a view to all the evidence.

The case of Nehemiah is an illustration of faulty logic. In

---

[1]George L. Murray, *Millennial Studies*, p. 27.
[2]*Ibid.*, p. 28.
[3]*Ibid.*, pp. 29-30.
[4]Oswald T. Allis, *Prophecy and the Church*, p. 58.

the confession of the priests, tribute is given to God as one who had been faithful in giving Israel the land of the Cannaanites, Hittites, Amorites, Perizzites, Jebusites, and the Girgashites. On the basis of the statement, "and hast performed thy words; for thou art righteous" (Neh. 9:8), Murray contends that the Abrahamic promise has been completely fulfilled.

A careful reading of all these related passages of Scripture will show that they do not prove what is claimed of them. The original promises of the land involved (1) possession of the land, (2) permanent possession, (3) and occupying the land. Even in Solomon's day at the height of his kingdom the land was not all possessed. At best it was placed under tribute as the very passage cited by the amillennarians indicates (1 Kings 4:21). Certainly all must agree that possession was not permanent. Further at no time was all the land actually occupied by Israel.

The priests in the Nehemiah reference do not claim complete fulfillment. They merely state that God had given the land to them—i.e., had done His part. The past occupancy of the land was a partial fulfillment but not a complete fulfillment of the promise. Certainly, in the light of the Nehemiah context, it is reaching an unwarranted conclusion to press the words of Nehemiah, "and hast performed thy words; for thou art righteous," to mean that all the promises had already been fulfilled relating to the land of Palestine. It refers rather to the general faithfulness of God revealed in the following context (Neh. 9:9-38) to include not only acts of mercy but all righteous judgments of God for the sins of Israel. To follow Murray in his interpretation of Nehemiah would involve the spiritualization of all the prophecies about the land subsequent to Solomon as well as those before Solomon. The real issue remains whether the Scriptures after Solomon continue to anticipate a future and glorious regathering of Israel and occupancy of the promised land.

VII. The Scriptural Testimony Concerning Israel's
Final Regathering

The abundant testimony of Scripture on the subject of
Israel's regathering provides material for a book on this subject alone. It is the dominant strain of both the Major and
Minor Prophets. Isaiah after dealing with the character of the
kingdom reign of Christ on earth (Isa. 11:1-11), goes on, "And
it shall come to pass in that day, that the Lord will set his hand
again the second time to recover the remnant of his people,
that shall remain, from Assyria, and from Egypt, and from
Pathros, and from Cush, and from Elam, and from Shinar,
and from Hamath, and from the islands of the sea" (Isa. 11:11-
12). The same theme is repeated in other words in many other
passages in Isaiah (12:1-3; 27:12-13; 43:1-8; 49:8-16; 66:20-22).
The promise of regathering is not only reiterated again and again
but it is linked to the continuance of Israel as a nation forever:
"For as the new heavens and the new earth, which I will make,
shall remain before me, saith Jehovah, so shall your seed and
your name remain" (Isa. 66:22).

The Prophet Jeremiah, living in the days of Israel's apostasy, writes graphically, "Therefore, behold, the days come, saith
Jehovah, that it shall no more be said, As Jehovah liveth, that
brought up the children of Israel out of the land of Egypt; but,
As Jehovah liveth, that brought up the children of Israel from
the land of the north, and from all the countries whither he
had driven them. And I will bring them again into their land
that I give unto their fathers. Behold, I will send for many
fishers, saith Jehovah, and they shall fish them up; and afterward I will send for many hunters, and they shall hunt them
from every mountain, and from every hill and out of the clefts
of the rocks" (Jer. 16:14-16). This certainly has had no fulfillment to the present hour, but it foreshadows the complete
regathering in connection with the millennial kingdom. The
theme of regathering is reiterated in connection with the coming of the righteous branch of David to reign over the earth
(Jer. 23:3-8).

Again in Jeremiah 30:10-11, the prophet speaks: "Therefore fear thou not, O Jacob my servant, saith Jehovah; neither be dismayed, O Israel: for, lo, I will save thee from afar, and thy seed from the land of their captivity; and Jacob shall return, and shall be quiet and at ease, and none shall make him afraid. For I am with thee, saith Jehovah, to save thee. . . ." Most of the thirty-first chapter of Jeremiah is devoted to this theme. Jehovah declares, "Behold, I will bring them from the north country, and gather them from the uttermost parts of the earth" (Jer. 31:8). The theme of regathering is linked in this chapter with the new covenant with the house of Israel (Jer. 31:31-34) and the solemn pledge that Israel shall continue as a nation as long as the sun, moon, and stars continue (Jer. 31:35-37).

The prophet Ezekiel adds his testimony (11:17-21; 20:33-38; 34:11-16; 39:25-29). Included in his testimony is the purging judgment of Israel which follows their regathering (20:33-38) and the pledge that God will leave not a single Israelite in the lands of the Gentiles after the regathering (Ezek. 39:28). There has never been any fulfillment of these prophecies in the regatherings after the captivities when most of the Israelites were left behind. If these Scriptures are to have any reasonable fulfillment it demands a future regathering of Israel and the fulfillment of all the related promises.

The testimony of the Minor Prophets to the regathering of Israel is often repeated. It is sustained by many references which imply the regathering, such as the pictures of Israel in the land, or sometimes general promises of restoration. A study of these passages will fully sustain the doctrine of Israel's regathering (Hos. 1:10-11; Joel 3:17-21; Amos 9:11-15; Micah 4:4-7; Zeph. 3:14-20; Zech. 8:4-8). Of note is the promise of Amos, "And I will plant them upon their land, and they shall no more be plucked up out of their land which I have given them, saith Jehovah thy God" (Amos 9:15). The regathering and possession of the land here prophesied is the final regathering attended by the promise that Israel will no more be dispersed.

This could apply only to a future regathering as the past regatherings all ended in further dispersion.

The united testimony of the prophets is all to the same point, that Israel will yet be regathered from the nations of the world and reassembled in their ancient land. The beginnings of this final regathering are already apparent in contemporary history with almost two million Jews, or approximately one in six of all the Jewish population of the world, now living in Palestine. Scriptures make clear that the regathering will continue until consummated after the second advent of Christ. The promises of regathering linked as they are in Scripture to the original promise of the land as an everlasting possession of Israel, coupled with the fact that no possession of the land in history has approached a complete fulfillment of these Scriptural promises, make it clear that Israel has a future, and in that future will actually possess all the land promised Abraham's seed as long as this present earth continues.

Chapter XVI

WILL ISRAEL BE RESTORED AS A NATION?

I. Testimony of the Old Testament Prophets

Most of the prophets of the Old Testament with enraptured gaze contemplated the glory of a millennial kingdom in which Israel would be restored and be head of all nations. In the darkest hours of Israel's apostasy and sin, in the very hour of her captivity and disgrace, the prophets uttered their message of hope. Jeremiah's word may be taken as typical: "Yea, I have loved thee with an everlasting love: therefore with lovingkindness have I drawn thee. Again I will build thee, and thou shalt be built, O Virgin of Israel: thou shalt again be adorned with tabrets, and shalt go forth in the dances of them that make merry. Again thou shalt plant vineyards upon the mountains of Samaria; the planters shall plant, and shall enjoy the fruit thereof. . . . Behold, I will bring them from the north country, and gather them from the uttermost parts of the earth, and with them the blind and the lame, the woman with child and her that travaileth with child together: a great company shall return thither. They shall come with weeping, and with supplications will I lead them: I will cause them to walk by rivers of waters, in a straight way wherein they shall not stumble: for I am a father to Israel, and Ephraim is my firstborn. . . . And it shall come to pass that, like as I have watched over them to pluck up and to break down, and to throw down and to destroy and to afflict, so will I watch over them to build and to plant, saith the Lord. . . . Behold, the days come, saith Jehovah, that I will make a new covenant with the house of Israel, and with the house of Judah. . . . But this is the covenant that I will make with the house of Israel after those days, saith Jehovah: I will put my law in their in-

ward parts, and in their heart will I write it; and I will be
their God, and they shall be my people. And they shall teach
no more every man his neighbor, and every man his brother,
saying, Know Jehovah; for they shall all know me, from the
least of them unto the greatest of them, saith Jehovah: for I
will forgive their iniquity, and I will remember their sin no
more" (Jer. 31:3-5, 8-9, 28, 31, 33-34).

The Abrahamic covenant required that Israel continue as
a nation forever in order to fulfill the "everlasting covenant"
(Gen. 17:7) and in order to have the land as "an everlasting
possession" (Gen. 17:8). All the facts discussed previously, to
the point that Israel continues as a nation forever, possesses
the land forever, is not disinherited, is not supplanted by the
church, and that Israel's basic covenants are dependent upon
God's faithfulness alone for fulfillment, combine to require
Israel's restoration after these centuries of dispersion and chas-
tening. The conclusion that Israel has a future restoration is
based upon these facts along with the voluminous testimony
of the prophets concerning Israel's coming golden age.

II. THE DENIAL OF THIS TESTIMONY

The present discussion must confine itself to the simple
question of the fact of Israel's restoration. This fact has been
doubted in proportion as expositors have questioned the Scriptures upon which Israel's restoration is based. The opposition
has come from two principal sources: those who deny the prophetic portions of the Word of God on the basis of rejection of
their inspiration and authority, and those who deny the literal
interpretation of these prophecies while accepting their authority and inspiration.

Within the ranks of those who accept inspiration the restoration of Israel is recognized in exact proportion to the degree of literal interpretation allowed. Amillenarians who follow
Augustine usually spiritualize the restoration of Israel as
meaning merely the growth and progress of the church. Into
this pattern fall Oswald Allis, B. B. Warfield, and Louis Berk-

hof. Some contemporary amillenarians such as William Hendriksen and some postmillenarians such as Charles Hodge interpret the promises of Israel's restoration as a picture of the revival of Israel within the church, i.e., the conversion of the Jews to Christianity in large numbers. This tends toward a more literal interpretation as it refers the promises to Israel rather than the church as a whole. Any attempt to interpret the promises given to Israel literally, however, points to a future restoration coincident to the establishment of the millennial kingdom upon the earth at the second advent of Jesus Christ. This future restoration of Israel is in harmony with and supported by the great body of revelation concerning Israel much of which has already been discussed. By way of summary certain leading facts may be mentioned.

III. Israel's Continuance as a Nation

The provision of the Abrahamic covenant for an everlasting covenant relation and the promises of God for Israel's continuance as a nation to inherit these covenant promises combine to assure Israel's continuance as a nation. The thought of Israel ceasing "from being a nation" is as unthinkable to the Prophet Jeremiah as the revocation of ordinances of the sun, moon, and stars and as impossible as it is to measure the heavens or search out the foundations of the earth (cf. Jer. 31:35-37). The historic fact is that Israel has continued as a recognizable entity in the world in spite of centuries of dispersion and corruption of the physical seed. The twentieth century has witnessed the miracle of this ancient people establishing after the lapse of nineteen hundred years a political state bearing its name and embodying at least a portion of their ancient geographical possessions. This is all the more remarkable because those who are accomplishing this phenomenon are not for the most part believers in the Scriptures and do not recognize the prophetic significance of what they are doing.

IV. Israel's Regathering After Dispersion

The foundation of the state of Israel in recent years has

been a part of the predicted regathering of scattered Israel back
to their ancient land. Previous discussion has pointed out the
three predicted dispersions of Israel as already having been fulfilled along with two predicted regatherings. The present movement of Jews back to Palestine in a movement that parallels in
many ways the Exodus from Egypt is tangible evidence which
cannot be ignored reasonably. The significance of the regathering is that it justifies the literal interpretation of prophecy which
anticipated just such a movement. If the regathering is to be
taken literally, as present history would indicate, it would naturally follow that the predicted golden age is ahead following
the second advent of Christ. Just as the second gathering was
the prelude for the first advent of Christ, so the third regathering is the prelude for the second advent.

V. Israel's Possession of the Promised Land

An integral part of the original Abrahamic covenant was
the promise of everlasting possession of the land. Specific boundaries given to Abraham (Gen. 15:18-21) indicate the extent
of the promise. Previous discussion of this has shown that these
promises have never been fulfilled, that they are unconditionally promised to Israel, that delays, dispersions, and Israel's failures do not abrogate the promises. The present partial possession of the land is a token. The complete possession awaits
the coming of Israel's Redeemer. The possession of the land
anticipates also Israel's restoration. One is antecedent to the other.
The cumulative force of all the Abrahamic promises strengthened and enlarged by extensive prophetic portions of Scripture
focuses upon the conclusion that Israel is to be restored as a
nation.

VI. The Restoration of Israel in the New Testament

The teaching of Christ. The teaching of Christ and the expectation of the apostles anticipated the fulfillment of the prophecies relative to Israel's kingdom. The bulk and content of
the coming kingdom is given so largely in the Old Testament

that the New Testament confines itself for the most part to confirmation. As shown in previous discussion, Christ when questioned about the coming kingdom never denied and rather confirmed that it remained the sure expectation of the people of Israel. Mary the mother of our Lord was assured that her son would sit upon the throne of David and reign over the house of Jacob forever (Luke 1:32-33). The ambitious mother of James and John was denied her petition that her sons sit on either side of Christ in the kingdom, not because her hope of the earthly kingdom was an error, but on the ground that this honor was only for those whom the Father chose (Matt. 20:19-23). The apostles had been previously assured that they would sit on thrones judging the twelve tribes in the day of restoration (Matt. 19:28), and would eat at His table (Luke 22:30). When on the day of ascension they asked the Christ, "Lord, wilt thou at this time restore again the kingdom to Israel?" (Acts 1:6), they were not rebuked for doctrinal error but informed merely that the "times or seasons" were in the hands of the Father. In other words, the teaching of Christ never refutes the common expectation of the Jews and the apostles for literal fulfillment of the promises of an earthly kingdom for Israel, but rather confirms it.

The general teaching of Romans 11. The classic passage in the New Testament on the issue of Israel's restoration is Romans 11, which has already been referred to repeatedly. The general teaching of Romans 11 is that Israel is to be restored. Paul asks the question, "Hath God cast away his people?" In answer to that question, Paul states categorically, "No"—"God forbid." The arguments are then piled up in confirmation of this answer. God has never cast away His people. In the time of apostasy prior to the captivities, Elijah is assured that there was a godly remnant of 7,000 who had not bowed the knee to Baal (Rom. 11:2-4). During the lifetime of Paul himself there was "a remnant according to the election of grace" (Rom. 11:5), i.e., Jewish Christian believers. The fact that the nation Israel as a whole is unconverted and blinded is plainly faced (Rom. 11:6-10). The purpose of allowing Israel's failure is revealed as an act of mercy to the Gentiles: "I say then, did they stumble that they might fall? God forbid: but by their fall salvation is come unto the Gentiles, to provoke them to jealousy" (Rom. 11:11).

From the very fact of the fall of Israel resulting in great Gentile blessing, the argument continues that Israel is destined for a glorious future: "Now if their fall is the riches of the world, and their loss the riches of the Gentiles; how much more their fulness?" (Rom. 11:12). Israel's time of fullness is still ahead. Using the figure of an olive tree as the fountain of blessing, Israel is pictured as being cut off the olive tree and the Gentiles are grafted in. But, Paul argues, if Gentiles who are like branches from a wild olive tree can be grafted into a good tree, how much more can Israel who is of the good tree naturally be grafted back in? Gentiles are warned that if they continue not in faith they too shall be cut off. It is clear that he is not talking about individual Gentiles or individual Israelites, but rather to each entity as a group. Today is the time of Gentile opportunity while the Israel promises are suspended. The day is coming when the present time of Gentile blessing or fullness will come in and then Israel's hour of blessing will follow.

Israel promised deliverance from blindness. The subject of Israel's blindness as now imposed and as scheduled for removal is to a large extent the key to the passage. It is not strange that a number of interpretations should be given to Romans 11:25, "For I would not, brethren, have you ignorant of this mystery, lest ye be wise in your own conceits, that a hardening in part hath befallen Israel, until the fulness of the Gentiles be come in." According to Origen, the father of allegorical interpretation, "all Israel" means simply "all believers." The Reformers like Origen attempted to eliminate Israel from the passage entirely. Calvin changed the "until" to "that"—a deliberate interpretation rather than a translation—so that the passage read, "a hardening in part is happened to Israel *that* the fulness of the Gentiles be come in."[1] Luther labeled the Jews as the devil's

---

[1] John Calvin, *Commentary on Romans, in loc.*

children impossible to convert.[2] Origen, Calvin, and Luther unite in opposition to considering Israel as meaning Israel. On the other hand, Charles Hodge interpreted Romans 11:25 as predicting "a great and general conversion of the Jewish people, which should take place when the fulness of the Gentiles had been brought in, and then and not till then, those prophecies should be fully accomplished which speak of the salvation of Israel."[3] Charles Hodge goes on to prove by eight formal arguments that his position is that of the historic church and that the Reformers are the exception rather than the rule in their interpretation.

Premillenialism holds that Israel as used in this passage refers to the nation Israel and that what is predicted here is their release from the blindness or obtuseness of spiritual discernment which fell on them as a judgment of unbelief. Robertson cites Hippocrates as using the term in a medical sense and concludes that it means "obtuseness of intellectual discernment, mental dullness."[4] This judgment had fallen upon Israel. While Israel in the Old Testament had been guilty of unbelief in the prophetic Word, in the New Testament they had been guilty of unbelief in the fulfillment in Christ. For this reason it is designated a "mystery"—a doctrine not revealed prior to the New Testament but now revealed. Robertson defines *mystery*, "the revealed will of God now made known to all."[5] The mystery consisted in the special judicial blindness or hardening which had befallen Israel over and above any natural blindness common to Israel or Gentiles in the past.

The blindness which befell Israel is scheduled for removal when "the fulness of the Gentiles be come in." This expression has been variously defined by commentators. According to the context the fall of Israel is a parallel to the fullness of the Gentiles, and the end of the fullness of the Gentiles would parallel the restoration of Israel. The "until" marks, then, the terminus of Gentile blessing, and the beginning of Israel's restoration.

---

[2] Cf. Charles Hodge, *Epistle to the Romans*, pp. 584-85.
[3] *Ibid.*, p. 584.
[4] A. T. Robertson, *Word Pictures in the New Testament*, IV, 398.
[5] *Ibid.*, IV, 397.

This in turn can be identified as the time of the Lord's coming for the church and the end of the age of grace.

Israel's national salvation. Subsequent to the lifting of Israel's blindness, it is predicted, "And so Israel shall be saved: even as it is written, There shall come out of Zion the Deliverer; he shall turn away ungodliness from Jacob" (Rom. 11:26). Here is a specific declaration that Israel will be restored. This interpretation hangs upon the interpretation of the term "all Israel," upon the character of the salvation or deliverence of Israel, and upon the question of the time of the deliverance.

The term *Israel* as it is used here is defined by the context as a genuine reference to the Jewish people. It is used in contrast to Gentiles throughout the preceding context. Except for Origen and Calvin and those who completely spiritualize the term, this is generally accepted. Previous discussion has shown that the word *Israel* means the Jewish people, not the church as such.[6] Charles Hodge states plainly, "Israel, here, from the context, must mean the Jewish people, and *all Israel,* the whole nation. The Jews, as a people, are now rejected; as a people, they are to be restored. As their rejection, although national, did not include the rejection of every individual; so their restoration, although in like manner national, need not be assumed to include the salvation of every individual Jew. Israel is not therefore to be here understood to mean, all the true people of God, as Augustine, Calvin, and many others explain it; nor all the elect Jews, i.e., all that part of the nation which constitute 'the remnant according to the election of grace'; but the whole nation, as a nation."[7] The term "all Israel" may be taken, then, as a reference to the people as a whole.

The nature of the salvation of Israel indicated here is described by a citation of Old Testament prophecy, "There shall come out of Zion the Deliverer, he shall turn away ungodliness from Jacob: and this is my covenant unto them, when I shall take away their sins" (Rom. 11:26-27). The quotation is from

---

[6]Cf. A. T. Robertson, *op cit.,* IV, 398; Charles Hodge, *op. cit.,* p 589; William Hendriksen, *And So All Israel Shall Be Saved,* p. 33.
[7]Charles Hodge, *op. cit.,* p. 589.

Isaiah 59:20-21 and a comparison will show at once the identity of the two passages and at the same time show the quotation is only in part and with variations.

Three things are singled out in the Romans quotation: (1) the Redeemer shall come *out of* Zion. The LXX has it "for Zion." (2) He shall turn away ungodliness from Jacob. (3) The deliverance shall be a fulfillment of the covenant with Israel including taking away their sins. The phrase "out of Zion" in Romans 11:26 has been seized upon because the Isaiah passage reads, "to Zion." The LXX has it "for Zion." Paul uses neither the Hebrew nor the LXX. Where did Paul get this phrase? The answer is that Paul is not attempting direct quotation. The reference to turning away ungodliness is not in the Isaiah passage either. Paul is appealing rather to the general doctrine. The Scriptures speak of Christ as both coming *to Zion* and coming *from Zion* (cf. Ps. 14:7; 20:2; 53:6; 110:2; 128:5; 134:3; 135:21; Isa. 2:3; Joel 3:16; Amos 1:2). Certainly Paul is justified in his declaration that what he quoted "was written." Further, the change in wording gives no comfort to the amillenarian though Allis tries to make it imply that only a heavenly Zion is in view.[8]

Even if Allis were right, the action is subsequent to the second advent and deals with Israel on earth, not in heaven. It should be obvious, however, that Christ in His second advent comes both to Zion and from Zion. He comes to Zion in His second advent, and goes forth from Zion to bring deliverance to Israel.

Zion, as it is used in the Scripture, has reference to Jerusalem and is often used in this sense as synonymous. Its use in the Old Testament as in the New is literal in every instance. Amillenarians find it necessary to spiritualize the term in Hebrews 12:22 and Revelation 14:1 in order to avoid premillennial ideas, but if the doctrine of premillennialism be established on other grounds, these passages like all others yield to an ordinary literal usage.

The Deliverer "shall turn away ungodliness from Jacob" and "take away their sins." Here again is an event, not a process, spe-

---

[8]Oswald T. Allis, *Prophecy and the Church*, p. 505.

cified as subsequent to the second advent. According to the Scripture, Israel will also be delivered in that day from her persecutors, regathered from all over the earth and brought back to her ancient land, and there blessed spiritually and materially. All these events are not mentioned here. To conclude as Allis does that items not mentioned are therefore not included is a precarious argument from silence.[9] The purpose of Romans 11 is not to summarize all the future of Israel but to speak to the point of whether Israel is "cast away." The evidence is complete and decisive: Israel has a future a glorious one, which will be fulfilled subsequent to the return of her Deliverer.

Israel's restoration fulfills Abrahamic covenant. The restoration of Israel is the capstone of the grand structure of doctrine relating to the Abrahamic covenant. In bringing to a close the consideration of this covenant as it pertains to premillennialism, attention should be directed again to the strategic importance of this revelation to Scriptural truth. It has been seen that the covenant included provisions not only to Abraham but to Abraham's spiritual seed, i.e., all who follow the faith of Abraham whether Jew or Gentile in this age. It has been shown that Abraham interpreted the covenant literally as pertaining primarily to his physical seed. The unconditional character of the covenant has been demonstrated—a covenant resting upon God's promise and faithfulness alone. The partial fulfillment recorded to the present has confirmed the intent of God to give literal fulfillment to the promises. It has been shown that Israel's promise of perpetual possession of the land is an inevitable part and conclusion of the general promises given Abraham and confirmed to his seed. Israel's continuance as a nation, implied in these promises, has been sustained by the continued confirmation of both Testaments. It was shown that the New Testament church in no wise fulfills these promises given to Israel. Finally, Israel's restoration as the natural outcome of these promises has been presented as the express teaching of the entire Bible. If these conclusions reached after care-

---

[9]*Loc. cit.*

ful examination of the Scriptural revelation are sound and reasonable, it follows that premillennialism is the only satisfactory system of doctrine that harmonizes with the Abrahamic covenant.

These conclusions are further strengthened and supported by the other Biblical covenants given to David and the new covenant given to Israel. Next in order of consideration will be the promises given to David concerning his seed, throne, and kingdom.

CHAPTER XVII

THE KINGDOM PROMISES TO DAVID

I. Importance of Davidic Covenant

Next in importance to the Abrahamic covenant in the Old Testament doctrine of premillennialism stands the Davidic covenant—the promises of God to David that his seed, throne, and kingdom would endure forever. This covenant has been obscured and ignored by most amillenarians and again and again statements are made that premillennialism rests solely upon the interpretation of Revelation 20. Louis Berkhof in his discussion of "the premillennial theory" states, "The only Scriptural basis for this theory is Rev. 20:1-6, after an Old Testament content has been poured into it."[1] In other words it is expressly denied that the Old Testament or the New provides any teaching at all on an earthly millennial kingdom.

One of the reasons for such an unwarranted conclusion is the neglect of the Biblical covenants of the Old Testament of which the Davidic is prominent. The principle of spiritualization of all prophecies which teach premillennialism is carried through with precision by the amillenarians with the result that by a process of changing the meaning of the promises they are robbed of their content. A study of amillenarian interpretation of the Davidic covenant well illustrates this method. Accepting as literal those prophecies which do not affect the premillennial argument and spiritualizing all others, they are able with straight face to declare that the Old Testament does not teach a millennial kingdom on earth. On the contrary, premillenarians believe these promises were intended to be interpreted literally as most certainly David understood them and as the Jews living in the time of Christ anticipated. A study of this

---

[1]Louis Berkhof, *Systematic Theology*, p. 715.

194

covenant will afford another strong confirmation of premillennial doctrine.[2]

II. ANALYSIS OF THE PROMISE TO DAVID

David had the godly ambition to build a temple to Jehovah. The incongruity of allowing the ark of God to remain in a temporary tentlike tabernacle while he himself lived in the luxury of a house of cedar seemed to call for the erection of a suitable permanent building to be the center of worship. To Nathan, the prophet, was revealed that God intended David to build something more enduring than any material edifice. David's "house" was to be his posterity and through them his throne and his kingdom were to continue forever. The main features of the covenant are included in the following passage: "When thy days are fulfilled, and thou shalt sleep with thy fathers, I will set up thy seed after thee, that shall proceed out of thy bowels, and I will establish his kingdom. He shall build a house for my name, and I will establish the throne of his kingdom for ever. I will be his father, and he shall be my son: if he commit iniquity, I will chasten him with the rod of men, and with the stripes of the children of men; but my loving-kindness shall not depart from him, as I took it from Saul, whom I put away before thee. And thy house and thy kingdom shall be made sure for ever before thee: thy throne shall be established for ever" (2 Sam. 7:12-16).

The provisions of the Davidic covenant include, then, the following items: (1) David is to have a child, yet to be born, who shall succeed him and establish his kingdom. (2) This son (Solomon) shall build the temple instead of David. (3) The throne of his kingdom shall be established forever. (4) The throne will not be taken away from him (Solomon) even though his sins justify chastisement. (5) David's house, throne, and kingdom shall be established forever.

---

[2]The classic work on this theme is George N. H. Peters' *The Theocratic Kingdom*, published by Kregel Publications in three volumes of over 2,000 pages.

To Solomon, then, was promised a throne which would be established forever. To David was promised a posterity, a throne, and a kingdom to be established forever. The promise is clear that the throne passed on through Solomon to David's posterity was never to be abolished. It is not clear whether the posterity of David should be through the line of Solomon. It will be shown that this fine point in the prophecy was occasioned by the cutting off of the posterity of Solomon as far as the throne is concerned.

What do the major terms of the covenant mean? By David's "house" it can hardly be doubted that reference is made to David's posterity, his physical descendants. It is assured that they will never be slain *in toto*, nor displaced by another family entirely. The line of David will always be the royal line. By the term "throne" it is clear that no reference is made to a material throne, but rather to the dignity and power which was sovereign and supreme in David as king. The right to rule always belonged to David's seed. By the term "kingdom" there is reference to David's political kingdom over Israel. By the expression "for ever" it is signified that the Davidic authority and Davidic kingdom or rule over Israel shall never be taken from David's posterity. The right to rule will never be transferred to another family, and its arrangement is designed for eternal perpetuity. Whatever its changing form, temporary interruptions, or chastisements, the line of David will always have the right to rule over Israel and will, in fact, exercise this privilege. This then, in brief, is the covenant of God with David.

III. OLD TESTAMENT CONFIRMATION

It should be clear to anyone who interprets the Old Testament prophecies literally that the entire theme of Messianic prophecy confirms the Davidic promises. The great kingdom promises of Isaiah, Jeremiah, Ezekiel, and Daniel combine with the Minor Prophets in reiterating the theme of the coming Immanuel and His kingdom upon the earth. Isaiah wrote of this, "Of the increase of his government and peace there shall be no end, upon the throne of David and upon his kingdom, to establish it, and to uphold it with justice and with righteousness from henceforth even for ever" (Isa. 9:7). Again Isaiah writes "With righteousness shall he judge the poor, and decide with equity for the meek of the earth; and he shall smite the earth with the rod of his mouth: and with the breath of his lips shall he slay the wicked" (Isa. 11:4). Such passages can be multiplied.

Not only are there many general kingdom promises but there is also specific confirmation of the Davidic covenant. Psalm 89 reiterates the content and makes the covenant immutable and sure even though Israel sins: "I have made a covenant with my chosen. I have sworn unto David my servant. Thy seed will I establish for ever, and build up thy throne to all generations. Selah. . . . My lovingkindness will I keep for him for evermore; and my covenant shall stand fast with him. His seed also will I make to endure for ever. And his throne as the days of heaven. If his children forsake my law, and walk not in my judgments; if they break my statutes, and keep not my ordinances . . . then will I visit their transgression with the rod, and their iniquity with stripes. But my lovingkindness will I not utterly take from him, nor suffer my faithfulness to fail. My covenant will I not break, nor alter the thing that is gone out of my lips. Once have I sworn by my holiness: I will not lie unto David. His seed shall endure for ever, and his throne as the sun before me. It shall be established for ever as the moon, and as the faithful witness in the sky" (Ps. 89:3-4, 28-30, 32-37).

IV. FULFILLMENT AT THE FIRST ADVENT OF CHRIST

While modern liberalism does not concern itself with the fulfillment of the promises to David, conservative scholars whether amillennial or premillennial are agreed that Jesus Christ is the one who fulfills the Davidic covenant. This is the import of the testimony of the angel to Mary: "And behold, thou shalt conceive in thy womb, and bring forth a son, and shalt call his name JESUS. He shall be great, and shall be called the Son of the Most High: and the Lord God shall give unto him the throne of his father David: and he shall reign over the house of Jacob for ever; and of his kingdom there shall be no end" (Luke 1:31-33). The promises to David are therefore transferred to Jesus Christ and we do not need to look for another.

The problem of fulfillment does not consist in the question of whether Christ is the one who fulfills the promises, but rather on the issue of *how* Christ fulfills the covenant and *when* He fulfills it. Concerning this question, there have been two principal answers: (1) Christ fulfills the promise by His present session at the right hand of the Father in heaven; (2) Christ fulfills the promise of His return and righteous reign on earth during the millennium. Interpreters of Scripture have usually adopted an answer to the problem which fits their larger system of doctrine. Those who deny a millennium or who identify Israel and the church are apt to insist that Christ is fulfilling the covenant by His present session.[3] Those who believe in a literal millennium and a reign of Christ on earth affirm the second answer. In this obvious contradiction between two systems of interpretation, there are certain issues which determine the outcome. These issues may be reduced for our purpose to the following: (1) Does the Davidic covenant require *literal* fulfillment? (2) Does the partial fulfillment, already a matter of history, permit a literal fulfillment? (3) Is the interpretation of this covenant in harmony with other covenant purposes of God? (4) What does the New Testament teach regarding the present reign of Christ?

V. DOES THE DAVIDIC COVENANT REQUIRE LITERAL FULFILLMENT?

If it were not for the difficulty of contradicting certain systems of interpretation of Scripture, it is doubtful whether anyone would have thought of interpreting the Davidic covenant otherwise than as requiring a literal fulfillment. The arguments in favor of literal interpretation are so massive in their construction and so difficult to waive that they are more commonly ignored by those who do not want to believe in literal fulfillment than answered by argument.

---

[3] Cf. Louis Berkhof, *The Kingdom of God,* and Geerhardus Vos, *The Kingdom and the Church.*

Peters in *The Theocratic Kingdom,* Proposition 52, has listed no less than twenty-one arguments in favor of literal interpretation, not to include collateral material. His important arguments for literal interpretation may be summarized as follows: (1) The solemn character of the covenant which was confirmed by an oath. (2) A spiritual fulfillment would not be becoming to a solemn covenant. (3) Both David and Solomon apparently understood it to be literal (2 Sam. 7:18-29; 2 Chron. 6:14-16). (4) The language used, which is also used by the prophets, denotes a literal throne and kingdom. (5) The Jews plainly expected a literal fulfillment. (6) The throne and kingdom as a promise and inheritance belong to the humanity of Christ as the seed of David rather than belong to His deity. (7) There is no ground for identifying David's throne and the Father's throne. (8) A symbolical interpretation of the covenant leaves its interpretation to man. (9) The literal fulfillment is requisite to the display of God's government in the earth, necessary to the restoration and exaltation of the Jewish nation and deliverance of the earth from the curse. (10) Literal fulfillment is necessary to preserve the Divine unity of purpose.

Unless all of these weighty arguments be dismissed as utterly without foundation, it must be clear that there are good and important reasons for adopting a literal interpretation of the covenant promises. If a literal interpretation be adopted, the present session of Christ is *not* a fulfillment of the covenant, and it must be referred to the future. It is clear that at the present time Christ is not in any literal sense reigning over the kingdom of David. From the content and circumstances surrounding the Davidic covenant, it is evident that a literal fulfillment is anticipated.

VI. Does the Historical Partial Fulfillment Permit

a Literal Interpretation?

There are, however, obvious difficulties in interpreting the Davidic covenant in a literal way and expecting a literal fulfillment. The covenant was given almost three thousand years ago, and history has not contained any continuous development or continuous authority of the political kingdom of David. A question may be raised whether history permits a literal fulfillment of the covenant. Does not the fact, viz., of Israel's captivity, with the downfall of the kingdom of Israel, argue against a literal fulfillment? Do not the centuries which have elapsed since the coming of Christ prove that no literal fulfillment is intended? If we believe that no word of God is broken, it is obvious that an interpretation which is not sustained by historic fulfillment is a wrong interpretation. The amillennial solution to this problem is that there is both a historical and a spiritual fulfillment. It is historical in that a literal descendant of David was born—Christ; it is spiritual in that the kingdom perpetuated and the throne are not literally David's but God's.[4]

The difficulty with the interpretation of the Davidic covenant as fulfilled partly by temporal events and partly by a spiritualized interpretation is that it does not actually fulfill the covenant. *A literal promise spiritualized is exegetical fraud.* The point of the Davidic covenant is that the Son of David will possess the throne of His father David. To make His person literal but His throne a spiritualized concept is to nullify the promise.

This point is crystallized in the pronouncement of the angel Mary quoted above (Luke 1:32-33). It should be perfectly obvious to any Bible student that Mary would understand the promise literally. She actually expected her prophesied Son to reign on an earthly Davidic throne. This expectation seems to have been shared by many others in the first century. How can anyone formulate a theodicy for the obvious deception that was perpetrated if Mary's idea was utterly wrong and it was never intended to perpetuate the earthly throne of David? The force of the prophecy to Mary is a precise and dramatic

---

[4]Cf. Jamieson, Fausset, and Brown, *A Commentary, Critical, Experimental, and Practical on the Old and New Testaments*, unabridged edition (Glasgow: William Collins, Sons, & Company, 1868), II, 235.

confirmation of the promise to David in spite of Israel's centuries of wandering, captivities, and sin.

In the mind of God it is evident that there is no contradiction in the literal interpretation of the covenant and the temporary enslavement of the Jewish nation in the captivity and under the dominion of Rome. In what sense, then, can we expect a literal fulfillment?

A clue can be taken in a significant accuracy in the covenant and its subsequent fulfillment. In proclaiming the covenant, the language of the prophet carefully distinguishes between the seed of David, Solomon, and the throne. David is assured that his seed will reign forever. Solomon is assured only that his throne will continue forever. In this fine point is an illustration of God' intention. In subsequent history of Israel, Solomon's line is specifically cut off from the throne at the time of the captivity of Judah (Jer. 22:30; 36:30). In the lineage of Christ found in Matthew and Luke, it is clear that Joseph descended from Solomon and the line which is cut off, while Mary descended from another son of David entirely, Nathan—by curious coincidence the same name as the prophet's who gave the Davidic covenant, though undoubtedly two different individuals. Accordingly, while the legal lineage came to Christ through Joseph, his *legal* father and a descendant of Solomon and his heirs, the actual seed of David was transmitted through Nathan and Mary.

This leads us to an important conclusion: the line which was to fulfill the promise of the eternal throne and eternal kingdom over Israel was preserved by God through the lineage which in fact did not sit on the throne at all, from Nathan down to Christ. It is, then, not necessary for the line to be unbroken as to actual conduct of the kingdom, but it is rather that the lineage, royal prerogative, and right to the throne be preserved and *never lost,* even in sin, captivity, and dispersion. It is not necessary, then, for continuous political government to be in effect, but *it is necessary that the line be not lost.*

All conservatives agree that the line is not lost. It came to its fulfillment in Christ. In the destruction of Jerusalem, the genealogies were destroyed and it would be impossible for Jews of today to trace their lineage back to the line of David. Accordingly, in the wisdom of God, the proof that Christ was of the line of David has been preserved, but at the same time the evidence has been destroyed for any future contenders for the honor. The Jews of today must admit that they could not positively identify the lineage of a Messiah if he did appear now. Only Christ has the evidence necessary, and the line is preserved with Him.

The partial fulfillment of the covenant, in that Christ is identified as the one through whom it will be fulfilled, instead of indicating a spiritual fulfillment rather lays the foundation for a literal fulfillment. The purpose of God is seen to be preserved in maintaining the line of David which has the right to rule. The postponement or delay in assuming political power in no wise invalidates the promise. The partial fulfillment does not hinder the literal fulfillment of all the covenant.

VII. Is Literal Fulfillment in Harmony with Other Covenants?

The interpretation of the Davidic covenant inevitably is colored by the construction placed on other covenants of Scripture. If the premillennial viewpoint of Scripture be sustained, it is clear that the Davidic covenant fits perfectly into the picture. It is the covenant ground for the earthly rule of Christ. All the promises regarding the nation Israel, the possession of the land, the millennial blessings in general, and the return of Christ to reign are in perfect harmony with a literal fulfillment of the covenant. The purpose of God in David is fulfilled in the reign of Christ. This has two aspects: His millennial reign and the continued rule of God in the new earth for eternity. The premillennial viewpoint provides a fully adequate literal fulfillment of the covenant.

Wilkinson has written a forceful summary of this point: "Nevertheless, facts are stubborn things. It is a fact that God has declared that Israel is not to cease from being a nation before Him for ever. It is a fact that the Jewish nation, still in unbelief, survivor of all others, alone retains its national identity.

. . . It is a fact that the promise of a land (the territorial limits of which were defined) to the posterity of Abraham, as also the promise of a son of David's own line to occupy David's throne for ever, were *unconditional* promises, ratified by covenant and oath. It is a fact that the posterity of Abraham has never yet fully possessed and enjoyed the whole of the land so granted and that no son of David occupies David's throne. . . . The O. T. promises are all as certain of fulfilment in their O. T. sense and meaning and purpose to Israel, as are the N. T. promises certain of fulfilment to the Church."[5]

The literal fulfillment of the Davidic covenant is in harmony with the larger covenant purpose of God. In fact, its plain intent and the nature of the promises are another confirmation of the premillennial interpretation of Scripture. It provides an interpretation fully honoring to God and His Word.

VIII. THE NEW TESTAMENT TEACHING ON THE REIGN OF CHRIST

Attention has already been called to the New Testament confirmation of the purpose of God to fulfill the Davidic covenant literally (Luke 1:32-33). The New Testament has fifty-nine references to David. It also has many references to the present session of Christ. A search of the New Testament reveals that *there is not one reference connecting the present session of Christ with the Davidic throne.* While this argument is, of course, not conclusive, it is almost incredible that in so many references to David and in so frequent reference to the present session of Christ on the Father's throne there should be not one reference connecting the two in any authoritive way. The New Testament is totally lacking in positive teaching that the throne of the Father in heaven is to be identified with the Davidic throne. The inference is plain that Christ is seated on the Father's throne, but that this is not at all the same as being seated on the throne of David.

About the only reference which can be construed as having any connection with the identification of David's kingdom reign

---

[5]Samuel Hinds Wilkinson, *The Israel Promises and Their Fulfillment* (London: John Bale, Sons and Danielsson, Ltd., 1936), pp. 56-57.

and the present session of Christ is that found in Acts 15:14-17. After Paul's testimony of wonders wrought among the Gentiles, James addressed the council in these words: "Simeon hath rehearsed how first God visited the Gentiles, to take out of them a people for his name. And to this agree the words of the prophets; as it is written, After these things I will return, and I will build again the tabernacle of David, which is fallen; and I will build again the ruins thereof, and I will set it up: that the residue of men may seek after the Lord, and all the Gentiles, upon whom my name is called" (Acts 15:14-17).

The problem of this passage resolves into these questions: (1) What is meant by the "tabernacle of David"? (2) When is the "tabernacle of David" to be rebuilt? The first question is settled by an examination of its source, Amos 9:11, and its context. The preceding chapters and the first part of chapter nine deal with God's judgment upon Israel. It is summed up in the two verses which immediately precede the quotation: "For, lo, I will command, and I will sift the house of Israel among all the nations, like as grain is sifted in a sieve, yet shall not the least kernel fall upon the earth. All the sinners of my people shall die by the sword, who say, The evil shall not overtake nor meet us" (Amos 9:9-10).

Immediately following this passage of judgment is the promise of blessing *after* the judgment, of which the verse quoted in Acts fifteen is the first: "In that day will I raise up the tabernacle of David that is fallen, and close up the breaches thereof; and I will raise up its ruins, and I will build it as in the days of old; that they may possess the remnant of Edom, and all the nations that are called by my name, saith Jehovah that doeth this. Behold, the days come, saith Jehovah, that the plowman shall overtake the reaper, and the treader of grapes him that soweth seed; and the mountains shall drop sweet wine, and all the hills shall melt. And I will bring back the captivity of my people Israel, and they shall build the waste cities, and inhabit them; and they shall plant vineyards, and drink the wine thereof; they shall also make gardens, and eat the fruit of them. And I will plant them upon their own land, and they shall no more be plucked up out of their land which I have given them, saith Jehovah thy God" (Amos 9:11-15).

The context of the passage deals, then, with Israel's judgment. After this period, which is the period of Gentile opportunity, God will raise up the tabernacle of David, give Israel supremacy over Edom and the nations, bless their crops, regather Israel, restore their cities, and assure them that they will never again be dispersed. The entire passage confirms that the "tabernacle of David" is an expression referring to the whole nation of Israel and that in contrast to the Gentile nations. By no possible stretch of the plain meaning of this passage can the "tabernacle of David" be made to be an equivalent of the New Testament church. The prophecy concerns the *rebuilding* of that which was fallen down. The "ruins" are to be rebuilt "as in the days of old." The nature of the blessings are *earthly, territorial,* and *national,* and have nothing to do with a spiritual church to which none of these blessings has been promised.

What then is the meaning of the quotation of James? What relation does it have to the problem faced by the council at Jerusalem? The question considered by the council was one of Gentile participation in the church. It apparently was difficult for the apostles to adjust themselves to equality with Gentiles in the gospel. The evident blessing of God upon the Gentiles, their salvation, and spiritual gifts were indisputable evidence that a change in approach to the Gentiles was necessary. They must face the fact that both Jew and Gentile were saved by grace in exactly the same manner. How was this to be reconciled with the promises of God to Israel? It is this which James answers.

He states, in effect, that it was God's purpose to bless the Gentiles as well as Israel, but in their order. God was to visit the Gentiles *first,* "to take out of them a people for his name." James goes on to say that this is entirely in keeping with the prophets, for they had stated that the period of Jewish blessing and triumph should be *after* the Gentile period: "After these things I will return, and I will build again the tabernacle of David, which is fallen." Instead of identifying the period of

Gentile conversion with the rebuilding of the tabernacle of David, it is carefully distinguished by the *first* (referring to Gentile blessing), and *after* this (referring to Israel's coming glory). The passage, instead of identifying God's purpose for the church and for the nation Israel, established a specific time order. Israel's blessing will not come until "I return," apparently reference to the second coming of Christ. That it could not refer either to the incarnation or to the coming of the Spirit at Pentecost is evident in that neither is a "return." The passage under consideration constitutes, then, an important guide in determining the purpose of God. God will first conclude His work for the Gentiles in the period of Israel's dispersion; then He will return to bring in the promised blessings for Israel. It is needless to say that this confirms the interpretation that Christ is not now on the throne of David bringing blessing to Israel as the prophets predicted, but He is rather on His Father's throne waiting for the coming earthly kingdom and interceding for His own who form the church.

It is highly significant that as late as Acts 15 the disciples still needed instruction on the distinctions between the kingdom promises and the church. They had been encouraged throughout the earthly ministry of Christ to expect a literal fulfillment of the kingdom promises. As discussed in the previous treatment of the restoration of Israel, the promise given to Mary and Luke was embraced by the disciples as well. They expected the promise of the Davidic kingdom to be fulfilled immediately. They had been promised thrones from which they would judge the twelve tribes of Israel (Matt. 19:28). The aspiring mother of James and John while rebuked in her hope that her sons would sit on either side of Christ in His kingdom was told that the place was for others—a confirmation of the fundamental kingdom hope. The disciples were promised a place at the King's table in the kingdom as a reward for their sufferings in this life (Luke 22:30). As late as Acts 1:6, the disciples were still looking for a literal kingdom. While refused revelation concerning the "time" of the kingdom, their hope is not denied, spiritualized, or transferred to the church. The kingdom hope is postponed and the new age of which they never dreamed was interposed, but the promises continued undimmed. Israel's day of glory is yet to come and the Christ will reign on earth.

Chapter XVIII

THE NEW COVENANT WITH ISRAEL

Among the Biblical covenants of the Old Testament, the new covenant with Israel takes its place in importance with the Abrahamic and the Davidic covenants as determining the course and destiny of the nation Israel. In the study of premillennialism it is another important evidence for a future millennial kingdom in which its promises can find literal fulfillment.

I. The Promises of the New Covenant with Israel

The promises of the new covenant with Israel are among the most specific of the Scriptures. The major passage is found in Jeremiah 31:31-34: "Behold, the days come, saith Jehovah, that I will make a new covenant with the house of Israel, and with the house of Judah: not according to the covenant that I made with their fathers in the day that I took them by the hand to bring them out of the land of Egypt; which my covenant they brake, although I was a husband unto them, saith Jehovah. But this is the covenant that I will make with the house of Israel after those days, saith Jehovah: I will put my law in their inward parts, and in their heart will I write it; and I will be their God, and they shall be my people. And they shall teach no more every man his neighbor, and every man his brother, saying, Know Jehovah; for they shall all know me, from the least of them unto the greatest of them, saith Jehovah: for I will forgive their iniquity, and their sin will I remember no more."

II. The Problems of Interpretation

Postmillennial interpretation. Three principal interpretations are found of this strategic Scripture corresponding to the postmillennial, amillennial, and premillennial interpretations. The view of Charles Hodge may be taken as representative of the postmillennial view, which is now discarded almost completely, though its optimism is preserved somewhat in modern liberalism. While abiding with the literal concept of the word *Israel*, Hodge finds the fulfillment of the promise in the latter part of the interadvent age in blessing on Jews who believe in Christ. To put it in different words, he believed the new covenant would be fulfilled to Israel in the millennium or golden age just preceding the second advent.[1]

Amillennial interpretation. A second interpretation characterizes the amillennial view as illustrated in the writings of Oswald T. Allis which expresses the sentiment of a considerable element of Reformed theology since Calvin. He identifies Israel with the church and transfers the promises of the new covenant to believers in Christ in this dispensation, both Jews and Gentiles. Allis states, "For the gospel age in which we are living is that day foretold by the prophets when the law of God shall be written in the hearts of men (Jer. xxxi.33) and when the Spirit of God abiding in their hearts will enable them to keep it (Ezek. xi.19, xxxvi 26f.)."[2] This view differs from the position of Hodge in that it is a denial that the promises refer to Israel nationally and transfers them entirely to believers of this age.

Premillennial interpretation. In contrast to the postmillennial and amillennial views, the premillennial position is that the new covenant is with Israel and the fulfillment in the millennial kingdom after the second coming of Christ. Minor variations are found in the premillennial view of the new covenant based largely on the further light given in the New Testament. The premillennial view popularized by the *Scofield Reference Bible*[3] regards the new covenant as having a twofold applica-

---

[1]Charles Hodge, *Commentary on the Epistle to the Romans* (New York: A. C. Armstrong and Son, 1909), p. 589.
[2]Oswald T. Allis, *Prophecy and the Church* (Philadelphia: The Presbyterian and Reformed Publishing Company, 1945), p. 42.
[3]*Scofield Reference Bible*, pp. 1297-98, note.

tion, first to Israel fulfilled in the millennium, and, second, to the church in the present age.

Another point of view is taken by Lewis Sperry Chafer who believes the new covenant in the Old Testament will be fulfilled only in the millennium, but finds also another new covenant revealed in the New Testament which has reference to the church in the present age. This conceives the sacrifice of Christ as making possible two covenants, a new covenant for Israel as well as a new covenant for the church.[4] This view has the advantage of not complicating the promises given expressly to Israel with promises given to the church.

A third position, also premillennial, was advocated by J. N. Darby who held that the new covenant belonged to Israel alone in both Old and New Testaments though the church participates in the benefits of the sacrifice of Christ.[5] Darby holds that "the gospel is not a covenant, but the revelation of the salvation of God."[6]

The premillennial view, though varying in details in the interpretation of the new covenant, insists that the new covenant as revealed in the Old Testament concerns Israel and requires fulfillment in the millennial kingdom. This is substantiated by a study of the contents of the covenant.

III. THE PROVISIONS OF THE NEW COVENANT

According to Jeremiah 31:31-34 previously quoted, at least seven aspects are found contained in the new covenant with Israel.

(1) It is specifically a covenant with "the house of Israel, and with the house of Judah." This was certainly understood by the Jews living in the Old Testament period as referring to Israel.

(2) The new covenant is contrasted to the Mosaic covenant, which was made with Israel only.

[4]Lewis Sperry Chafer, *Systematic Theology* IV, 325. Cf. Charles C. Ryrie, *The Basis of the Premillennial Faith*, pp. 105 ff.
[5]J. N. Darby, *Synopsis of the Books of the Bible*, New Edition—revised, V, 286.
[6]*Loc. cit.*

(3) The covenant promised fulfillment after the days of Israel's trouble (Jer. 30:7) or the great tribulation which Christ predicted (Matt. 24:21). It is further synchronized with the time of Israel's regathering which is regarded as a preparation for fulfillment of the covenant (cf. Jer. 31:1-30) and constitutes the immediate context of the revelation of the new covenant.

(4) The new covenant is designed to supplant and be superior to the Mosaic covenant in that it will be written "in their heart" instead of tables of stone.

(5) The new covenant will bring in great spiritual blessing in that God and Israel will be publicly identified and Israel will be God's people.

(6) The new covenant will be fulfilled in a period of universal knowledge of the Lord in that it will not be necessary to instruct one's neighbor concerning the Lord for "they shall all know me, from the least of them unto the greatest of them." It is obviously the same time referred to by Isaiah when "the earth shall be full of the knowledge of Jehovah, as the waters cover the sea" (Isa. 11:9). This is a strong contrast to the prevailing ignorance of the Lord in the present age and the contemporary failure of missionary effort to reach everyone even in Christian countries. Only a millennial kingdom in which Christ is visibly and gloriously present could provide such a context for the fulfillment of this covenant.

(7) The new covenant involves forgiveness of sins, specifically the sins mentioned in the preceding context as having merited God's judgment upon Israel. It is therefore a gracious covenant.

It should be obvious to every candid expositor of this passage that only the premillennial interpretation provides possibility of a literal fulfillment of all these provisions. To spiritualize the passage to the extent of making Israel mean the church and to restrict the passage to a spiritualized fulfillment of the details of the covenant robs the covenant of its essential features. The facts are not only stated closely in Jeremiah 31

and intended to be taken literally, but similar passages elsewhere have the same features.

Isaiah 61:8-9 declares that the covenant is everlasting and
especially designed to reveal to all observers that God has
blessed the seed of Israel. The context is the same as in Jeremiah
—the covenant will be fulfilled following a period of trial and
judgment and preceded by the regathering of Israel. Jeremiah
repeats the same promises in Jeremiah 32:37-40 where again the
everlasting character of the covenant and its relation to Israel's
regathering are reiterated.

Ezekiel 37:21-28 adds further confirmation: (1) Israel to
be regathered; (2) Israel to be one nation, ruled by one king;
(3) Israel no longer to be idolatrous, to be cleansed, forgiven;
(4) Israel to dwell "forever" in the land after regathering;
(5) the covenant of peace with them to be everlasting; (6)
God's tabernacle to be with them, i.e., He will be present with
them in a visible way; (7) Israel to be known among Gentiles as
a nation blessed of God. All of these promises are implicit in
the basic passage of Jeremiah, but they confirm, enrich, and
enlarge the covenant.

The present age of grace does not fulfill these provisions in
many particulars. The events preceding the fulfillment have not
taken place. Israel as a nation is not regathered, though many
have returned to Palestine in our day. The great tribulation
or the time of Jacob's trouble is yet future. It is therefore impossible for the new covenant with Israel to be realized now.
Israel today is not publicly recognized as God's people, indeed,
they do not claim any special privilege themselves. Certainly
Israel as a nation is not being blessed of God in spiritual ways.
Most obvious too is the fact that all do not know the Lord
which would make missionary effort or witness unnecessary. All
do not know the Lord, and our neighbors still need to know
Him. This is an age of missionary effort in contrast to the
prophesied situation under which the new covenant will operate.
Israel today is not being ruled by one king. God is not taber-
nacling with Israel now. All of these plain statements have to

be ignored or spiritualized to avoid the premillennial teaching that the new covenant is designed for millennial conditions.

If taken in their ordinary literal sense, the promises of the new covenant as contained in Old Testament prophecy correspond precisely to the premillennial interpretation. Amillenarians have indirectly admitted this, first, by acknowledging that "Jewish" interpretation anticipated an earthly, literal reign of the Messiah in which the covenant would be fulfilled. It is their contention that the Jewish expectation was an error. Second, amillenarians indirectly admit the force of the premillennial argument by consistently avoiding exegesis of the precise promises given. The promises are usually grouped in a broad generality of promised spiritual blessing and appropriated by the device of making Israel mean the church or body of believers. Third, amillenarians have turned for the most part from exegesis of the new covenant in the Old Testament to supposed confirmation of their view in the New Testament. An illustration of this is the work of Allis.[7] While he refers to it and identifies it with the grace extended to the church in the present age, he nowhere in his extensive treatment of premillennialism attempts to give a reasonable exegesis of the passage and explain the particulars of the covenant. It is safe to say that this is an impossibility without spiritualization of its provisions. The Old Testament taken alone would never have suggested the spiritualized interpretation adopted by the amillenarians. The question remains. What does the New Testament teach?

IV. GENERAL TEACHING OF THE NEW TESTAMENT ON THE NEW COVENANT

The term *new covenant* (*kaine diatheke*) is used only five times in the best texts of the New Testament (Luke 22:20; 1 Cor. 11:25; 2 Cor. 3:6; Heb. 8:8; 9:15). Other references to the new covenant without the precise designation include at least seven more instances (Matt. 26:28; Mark 14:24; Rom. 11:27;

---

[7]Allis, *op. cit.*, p. 154.

Heb. 8:10; 8:13; 10:16; 12:24). The references in the Gospels obviously refer to the new covenant as stated in Luke and also in some texts of Matthew and Mark. The context makes the reference clear in the other instances. Of special interest is Hebrews 12:24 where the expression *diatheke nea* is used for the new covenant—new in the sense of recent, the only such instance in the New Testament.

Of the five direct references to a new covenant, only one (Heb. 8:8) is connected by the context directly with the new covenant of Jeremiah. While this does not solve the problem, as will be seen later, it certainly narrows the area of direct revelation. Of the auxiliary texts judged referring to the new covenant, Romans 11:27; Hebrews 8:10, 13, and 10:16 seem to have reference to the new covenant with Israel. The other references at least are not specific.

The general teaching of New Testament passages bearing upon the New Covenant is that the new covenant has been made possible by the sacrifice of Christ. Attention is drawn to this central aspect in passages dealing with the Lord's Supper (Matt. 26:28; Mark 14:24; Luke 22:20; 1 Cor. 11:25). Other passages enlarge on the grace of God and forgiveness of sins made possible by the death of Christ (Rom. 11:27; Heb. 8:8-13; 10:16-18). Christ is declared to be the Mediator of the new covenant (Heb. 12:24). Whether the church of the present age or Israel is in view, the new covenant provides a basis in grace for forgiveness and blessing secured by the blood of Jesus Christ. On this all conservative theologians agree whether premillennial, amillennial, or postmillennial. The difference in point of view is occasioned by the question of whether the new covenant promised Israel is being fulfilled now, in the present interadvent age, as the amillenarians contend, or whether Israel's new covenant will be fulfilled after the second coming of Christ in the millennial kingdom, as the premillenarians contend. Most premillenarians (Darby excepted) would agree that *a* new covenant has been provided for the church, but not *the* new covenant for Israel. The question resolves itself into one of exegesis of the principal passages.

V. THE NEW COVENANT FOR ISRAEL IN THE NEW TESTAMENT

Eliminating for the time being references to the new covenant in relation to the Lord's Supper, which are not determinative in the present argument, what do the other passages of the New Testament teach? Romans 11:27 refers to the covenant as taking away sin from Israel. The context is illuminating. The *time* for the fulfillment of this covenant is stated in the preceding verse as being when the Deliverer shall come out of Zion. This is clearly identified with the second coming of Christ, the time when "all Israel shall be saved" (Rom. 11:25). According to this passage the new covenant will have its fulfillment as a result of the second advent. This, of course, is precisely what the premillenarian believes and is absolutely contrary to the thought that the new covenant is in force for Israel now. The explicit teaching of this passage confirms the premillennial view.

Amillenarians find it convenient to ignore Romans 11:27. Wyngaarden, who has written extensively on the new covenant covering almost every Scripture reference, omits Romans 11:27 completely in his discussion in the *Calvin Forum* on "The New Covenant in Biblical Theology."[8] In his book, *The Future of the Kingdom in Prophecy and Fulfillment,* which on the whole is one of the best amillennial works on the subject, again there is no consideration whatever of the connection of the fulfillment of the new covenant with the second advent, and only one reference of any character at all to this verse.[9]

Oswald Allis, while discussing Romans 11:25-26, does not even mention Romans 11:27 in his entire work in defense of amillenarianism.[10] This illustrates a tendency in amillennial literature to avoid Scriptures which support the premillennial view.

Both Allis and Wyngaarden, however, devote considerable attention to the reference in Hebrews 8, and consider it an unanswerable argument in favor of their interpretation. It is, in fact, the only passage which provides any difficulty to the pre-

---

[8]Martin J. Wyngaarden "The New Covenant in Biblical Theology," *The Calvin Forum*, XI (May, 1946), 208-12.

[9]Martin J. Wyngaarden, *The Future of the Kingdom in Prophecy and Fulfillment* (Grand Rapids: Zondervan Publishing House, 1934), p. 188.

[10]Allis, *op. cit.*

millennial view, and this difficulty vanishes if the passage is carefully studied.

The argument of Hebrews 8 reveals the truth that the Christ is the Mediator of a better covenant than Moses, established upon better promises (Heb. 8:6). The argument hangs on the point that the Mosaic covenant was not faultless—was never intended to be an everlasting covenant (Heb. 8:7). In confirmation of this point, the new covenant of Jeremiah is cited at length, proving that the Old Testament itself anticipated the end of the Mosaic law in that a new covenant is predicted to supplant it. The writer of Hebrews singles out of the entire quotation the one word *new* and argues that this would automatically make the Mosaic covenant old (Heb. 8:13). A further statement is made that the old covenant is "becoming old" and "is nigh unto vanishing away." It should be noted that nowhere in this passage is the new covenant with Israel declared to be in force. The only argument is that which was always true— the prediction of a new covenant automatically declares the Mosaic covenant as a temporary, not an everlasting covenant.

Amillenarians, however, completely ignore the silence of the passage on the very point they are trying to prove. Allis writes enthusiastically: "The passage speaks of the new covenant. It declares that this new covenant has been already introduced and that by virtue of the fact that it is called 'new' it has made the one which it is replacing 'old,' and that the old is about to vanish away. It would be hard to find a clearer reference to the gospel age in the Old Testament than in these verses in Jeremiah."[11]

While Allis has done all he could to claim this passage in support of his amillennial position, he has also indicated the fallacy of the amillennial argument by flagrantly begging the question. He states that the passage "declares that this new covenant has been already introduced."[12] A careful reading of the passage will reveal it makes no such statement. It declares a "better covenant" than the Mosaic covenant has been made pos-

[11]Allis, *ibid.*, p. 154.
[12]*Loc. cit.*

sible (Heb. 8:6), but it does not state here or anywhere else that this better covenant is "the new covenant with the house of Israel," or that Israel's new covenant has been introduced. Allis not only reads in statements which are not to be found in this passage, but also ignores the argument of the writer of Hebrews. The argument does not depend upon the introduction of the new covenant for Israel, but only on the question of whether the Old Testament anticipates an end to the Mosaic covenant. The fact that the Old Testament predicts a new covenant for Israel establishes this point.

It should be further noted that if the writer had intended to argue that the provisions of the new covenant were already in force, he would certainly have used the various aspects of the new covenant as quoted. Instead, no use whatever is made of the details of the covenant except for the one word *new*. It would have been a crushing argument to contenders for the law of Moses if, in fact, the new covenant was already in force and its prophecy fulfilled. This would have ended the argument quickly. Instead, the writer contends merely for the superiority of the Christians order as superseding the Mosaic covenant. The new covenant in force in the present age is not claimed to fulfill the new covenant with Israel at all.

While amillenarians are usually content to argue from Hebrews 8, another passage of the same character is found in Hebrews 10:16-17 (which Allis does not mention). Here the argument hangs upon the essential grace character of the new covenant with Israel, which is again quoted in part. The point is made that the new covenant with Israel not only anticipated the abrogation of the law but also the end of Mosaic sacrifices as a basis for forgiveness. In that God promises to remember their sins no more, it requires a sacrifice for sin which does not need to be repeated. It is agreed that the death of Christ provides the gracious basis both for the new covenant with the church and the new covenant with Israel. The death of Christ has ushered in a day of grace enjoyed now by every believer, and to be enjoyed by the nation Israel in the millennial kingdom also.

Further light is cast on the problem in the unusual reference in Hebrews 12:24 where *new* is the translation of the *nea* meaning *recent*. Jesus is declared to be the Mediator of the new covenant in the sense of a *recent* covenant. The time element is in contrast to the old covenant, i.e., the Mosaic, which has been in force for many centuries. Reference is apparently to the covenant with the church and not to Israel's new covenant. Hebrews 9:15 likewise declares that Christ is the Mediator "of a new covenant," which is true, of course, both for a covenant with the church or a covenant with Israel.

VI. The New Covenant with Believers of This Age

Premillenarians are in agreement that the new covenant with Israel awaits its complete fulfillment in the millennial kingdom. However, there exists some difference of opinion how the new covenant relates to the present interadvent age. Particular attention is paid to Luke 22:20 and the parallel synoptic passages (Matt. 26:28; Mark 14:24) where the disciples are introduced to the Lord's Supper and informed that the cup represents the blood of the new covenant. Some premillenarians like Darby[13] believe the church is related only to the *blood* of the new covenant—the gracious ground of the new covenant, rather than the new covenant itself. It is true, of course, that the Old Testament covenants in general belonged to Israel, as brought out in Romans 9:4 (cf. Eph. 2:12); Scofield, however, regards the new covenant with Israel as having an oblique reference to the believers of this age, though concerned primarily with Israel.[14] Preference was stated earlier in this study for another view advanced by Lewis Sperry Chafer[15] advocating two new covenants, one for the nation Israel to be fulfilled in the millennium, the other for the church to be fulfilled in the present age.

The point of view that holds to two covenants in the present age has certain advantages. It provides a sensible reason for establishing the Lord's supper for believers in this age in commemoration of the blood of the new covenant. The language of

---

[13]Darby, *loc. cit.*
[14]*Scofield Reference Bible, loc. cit.*
[15]Chafer, *loc. cit.*

1 Corinthians 11:25 seems to require it: "This cup is the new covenant in my blood: this do, as often as ye drink it, in remembrance of me." It hardly seems reasonable to expect Christians to distinguish between the cup and the new covenant when these appear to be identified in this passage. In 2 Corinthians 3:6, Paul speaking of himself states: "Our sufficiency is of God: who also made us sufficient as ministers of a new covenant." It would be difficult to adjust the ministry of Paul as a minister of the new covenant if, in fact, there is no new covenant for the present age. Even Darby, who seems to have originated this idea, states, "We enjoy indeed all the essential privileges of the new covenant, its foundation being laid on God's part in the blood of Christ, but we do so in spirit, not according to the letter."[16] It can be seen that this is not far from Scofield's idea of a double application.

The issues of premillennialism have been focused with increasing sharpness in recent years until the line has been drawn between Israel's promises and those belonging to the church. The concept of two new covenants is a better analysis of the problem and more consistent with premillennialism as a whole. The amillennial argument breaks down, however, not on the basis of these finer distinctions but the obvious failure to find in the present age any literal fulfillment of the covenant with Israel. As in other particulars of prophecy concerning the millennium, a literal fulfillment demands a future millennial dispensation.

VII. CONCLUSION

The conclusions drawn from this study of the new covenant, while only a partial analysis of the covenant itself, point to future fulfillment of Jeremiah's covenant. The key texts such as Hebrews 8, upon which the amillennial theory bases most of its argument, upon analysis fail to provide any proof for its contentions. Further, such passages as Romans 11:27 in the New Testament predict fulfillment of the new covenant as an outgrowth of the second advent, not the first coming of Christ,

---

[16]Darby, *loc. cit.*

and therefore awaiting the return of Christ to establish His kingdom on earth. As in other areas of the millennial doctrine, the argument hangs upon the question of literal interpretation. Only by spiritualizing the promises and ignoring contradictory Scripture can the amillennial concept of the new covenant be sustained.

Chapter XIX

PREMILLENNIALISM AND THE CHURCH

I. Bearing of Ecclesiology on Premillennialism

The doctrine of the church has always rightly been considered an important part of theology. Embraced within its revelation are the principal items of the present divine program as well as the ultimate purpose of God. According to Lewis Sperry Chafer, the truth concerning the church is one of the two major Pauline revelations given in the New Testament, the other being the gospel of salvation by faith.[1]

It is strange that more attention has not been paid to the relation of ecclesiology to premillennialism. Various views on the millennium have their corresponding concepts of the church in the present age. Amillennialism identifies the present church age with the predicted millennial kingdom on earth. Premillennialism places the millennium after the second advent and therefore divorces it from the present church age. It is not too much to say that ecclesiology may be characterized as being either amillennial or premillennial.[2] Premillennialism has, then, an important bearing on the doctrine of the church, and vice versa. Many of the important aspects of premillennialism are determined in ecclesiology rather than in eschatology. The doctrine of the church must, therefore, be carefully examined before eschatology can be understood.

II. Major Types of Ecclesiology

Various points of view of the doctrine of the church are afforded respectively in the Roman, Greek, and Protestant churches. Again distinctions are raised in regard to the church as an

---

[1]Lewis Sperry Chafer, *Systematic Theology*, IV, 3-4.
[2]Cf. previous discussion of amillennial ecclesiology.

institution and as an organism, and the church as visible and invisible.[3] The church can also be considered in regard to its form of church government, officers, and sacraments. There are few doctrines which have as many facets as ecclesiology. As bearing on premillennialism, however, ecclesiology can be classified into three types: covenant theology, kingdom theology, and dispensational theology.

Covenant theology in relation to premillennialism. As indicated in earlier studies of the Biblical covenants, covenant theology characteristically belongs to amillennial and postmillennial theology, but there have always been adherents of covenant theology who could be classified as premillennial. Covenant theology, in a word, conceives the purpose of God as essentially soteriological, or concerned with the salvation of the elect. The unfolding of the successive ages of God's dealing with men is, then, the fulfillment of the divine purpose supposedly embraced in an eternal covenant within the Godhead. This normally issues in a merging of Israel and the church and the point of view which considers the Old Testament, the present age, and the future millennium essentially parts of one progressive purpose. The strongest proponents of covenant theology today are Reformed churches still adhering clearly to Calvin and conservative theology. These are usually amillennial rather than premillennial and are opposed to dispensational theology. Premillenarians who hold to covenant theology are often quite similar to amillenarians in their exegesis of passages relating to the present age, but as premillenarians they add a millennial age after the second advent on the basis of Revelation 20 and many other passages.

Kingdom theology. Another type of ecclesiology is afforded by those who emphasize kingdom ideology in the Scriptures. While this is often identical with covenant theology, it is not necessarily so. The kingdom of God is regarded as the embracive term including the church in the present age and the millennium in the future. Like covenant theology, however, it tends to identify the kingdom as soteriological rather than govern-

---

[3]Cf. Louis Berkhof, *Systematic Theology*, pp. 562-78.

mental and to all practical purposes it is covenant theology all over again but without the covenantal background specifically.[4] To some extent kingdom theology has been carried over into modern liberalism with its identification of the kingdom as the whole purpose of God in human history, often reducing it to a simple moral concept. Kingdom theology as a whole tends to minimize the distinctive character of the millennial kingdom and to make it an aspect of kingdom truth such as is found throughout human history. Like covenant theology it is more in harmony with amillennial theology than with premillennial, but it has nevertheless had its place within premillennialism.

Dispensational theology. While the dispensational idea is as old as theology itself, with elaborate dispensational systems being evolved even before Christ, in recent years the term has been applied to a specific point of view taught by modern dispensationalism. Dispensationalism in the past was not confined to premillennialism, and well-defined systems of dispensationalism are found in Augustine, an amillenarian, in Hodge, a postmillenarian, and in practically all Protestant systematic theologians. In the contemporary meaning of the term, however, dispensationalism is largely confined to premillennialism. While not denying an essential unity to divine dealings in human history, it distinguishes major stewardships or purposes of God, particularly as revealed in three important dispensations of law, grace, and kingdom. Saints of the present age are regarded as fulfilling the present purpose of God to call out a body of saints from Jew and Gentile alike. By contrast Old Testament saints are considered a separate people and in particular Israel is regarded as fulfilling a purpose of God peculiarly for them. The future millennium is considered a separate age, different from either the law or grace periods, and having a form of stewardship distinct from all previous dispensations.

The dispensations deal primarily with divine testing under a specific rule of life, but do not constitute separate ways of salvation as often misrepresented by opponents. Dispensational

---

[4]Cf. George E. Ladd, *Crucial Questions about the Kingdom of God*, pp. 80-85, 92-94.

ecclesiology is more consistent with premillennialism as it maintains sharply the distinctions between law and grace, between Israel and the church, between the earthly and the heavenly, and between prophecies being fulfilled and those which will be fulfilled in the millennium. Only dispensational ecclesiology has much to offer by way of support of premillennialism. While kingdom theology and covenant theology are easily harmonized with amillennialism, dispensationalism will not be, and the contrast between the present age and the future millennium is sharp and decisive.

III. The Church as a Distinct Body of Saints of This Age

Dispensational ecclesiology defines the church as a distinct body of saints in the present age, having its own divine purpose and destiny and differing from the saints of the past or future ages. This concept is based on a number of Scripture doctrines and the use of *ecclesia* itself.

Use of ecclesia. This word translated *church* or *assembly* is found in at least four important meanings in the New Testament. It is used (1) to mean an assembly of people. In this sense it has no special theological meaning. It can refer to Israel as a gathered people in the wilderness (Acts 7:38) or a regular assembly of citizens (Acts 19:39) or a group of people gathered for a religious worship (Heb. 2:12). (2) The same word is used for an assembly of Christians in a local church (Acts 8:1, 3; 11:22, 26) and in the plural for a group of such churches (1 Cor. 16:19; Gal. 1:2). Each assembly or church has a local gathering composed of professed Christians. That all in the assembly are not necessarily true believers is clear from the messages to the seven churches of Asia (Rev. 2—3).

(3) *Ecclesia* is also used of the total of professing Christians without reference to locality and is practically parallel in this sense to Christendom (Acts 12:1; Rom. 16:16; 1 Cor. 15:9; Gal. 1:13; Rev. 2:1—3:22; etc.).

The same word is used (4) of the body of Christ, composed of those baptized by the Holy Spirit into the church (1 Cor. 12:13). *Ecclesia* used in this connection becomes a technical word referring to the saints of this age.

All agree that *ecclesia* as in (1) above is used of Israel in the Old Testament. The issue is whether *ecclesia* is ever used of Israel in the sense of (2), (3), and (4). A study of every use of *ecclesia* in the New Testament shows that all references where *ecclesia* is used in the New Testament in reference to people in the Old Testament can be classified under (1). Of particular importance is the fact that *ecclesia* is never used of an assembly or body of *saints* except in reference to saints of the present age.

Use of ecclesia *in the Septuagint.* Three Hebrew words are used in the Old Testament for the concept of a congregation. Only one, the Hebrew word *kahal,* is translated *ecclesia* in the LXX. It is the broadest term for congregation in the Old Testament, and is translated by seven Greek words in the LXX. When translated *ecclesia,* as it is in most instances, it is invariably in connection with a physical assembly involving the physical presence of participants in one place. It is not specifically religious, and though used of Israel is also used of an assembly of evil doers (Ps. 26:5) and of an army (Ezek. 32:22-23). It is clearly not a technical word and must be interpreted by the context. It is never used in the sense of spiritual presence or relationship.

The church future in Matthew 16:18. The teaching that the body of Christ in the New Testament is a separate entity is supported by the predictive statement of Christ in Matthew 16:18, "Upon this rock I will build my church." The figure of speech rests upon a concept of a *future* undertaking. Christ did not say, "I am building," but "I will build." It is significant that this is the first reference to the church in the New Testament, and is here regarded as a future undertaking of Christ Himself.

The body of Christ formed at Pentecost. In Acts 1:5, Christ predicted, "John indeed baptized with water but ye shall be baptized in the Holy Spirit not many days hence." Ten days later was the Day of Pentecost. As far as the record of Acts 2 is concerned, nothing is said of the baptism of the Spirit. In Acts 11:15, however, in relating the story of the conversion of Cornelius Peter states, "And as I began to speak, the Holy Spirit fell on them, even as on us at the beginning." In the next verse he cites this as fulfilling the prophecy of Christ in Acts 1:5. The baptism of the Spirit which is the subject of predictive prophecy in the Gospels and in Acts 1 finds its first fulfillment in Acts 2.

The classic passage on the baptism of the Holy Spirit, 1 Corinthians 12:13, declares: "For in [by] one spirit were we all baptized into one body, whether Jews or Greeks, whether bond or free; and were all made to drink of one Spirit." The baptism of the Spirit is the act of God by which the individual believer of Christ is placed into the body of Christ. The Greek preposition *en,* translated "in" in the American Standard Version, is properly rendered "by" in both the Authorized and the Revised Standard Version in recognition of its instrumental use. The Spirit is the agent by whom the work of God is accomplished.

In virtue of these significant truths, it becomes apparent that a new thing has been formed—the body of Christ. It did not exist before Pentecost, as there was no work of the baptism of the Spirit to form it. The concept of the body is foreign to the Old Testament and to Israel's promises. Something new had begun. Peter declares that Pentecost was a new beginning (Acts 11:15). Saved Israelites under the old economy were placed into the body of Christ at Pentecost. (cf. Gal. 3:28; Eph. 2:14-15). Thereafter the church is distinguished from both Jew and Gentile (1 Cor. 10:32; Heb. 12:22-24). The church as the body of Christ is therefore a new entity, and the term *ecclesia* when used in this sense is used only of saints of the present dispensation.

IV. THE CHURCH AGE AS A PARENTHESIS

One of the important questions raised by the amillenarians is whether the present age is predicted in the Old Testament. This they confidently affirm and find the kingdom promises fulfilled in the present church age. Premillenarians have not always given a clear answer to the amillennial position. While dispensationalists have regarded the present age as a parenthesis unexpected and without specific prediction in the Old Testament, some premillenarians have tended to strike a compromise interpretation in which part of the Old Testament predictions are fulfilled now and part in the future. In some cases they have conceded so much to the amillenarians that for all practical purposes they have surrendered premillennialism as well. It is the purpose of the present investigation to show the reasonableness and Scriptural support of the parenthesis concept.

Daniel's seventieth week for Israel. One of the classic passages related to this problem is Daniel 9:27, defining the last of Daniel's weeks for the fulfillment of Israel's program. As generally interpreted the time unit in the "weeks" or "sevens" is taken to be a year. Conservative scholars usually trace the fulfillment of the first sixty-nine sevens of years as culminating in the crucifixion of Christ, predicted in the terms that "the anointed one be cut off and shall have nothing" (Dan. 9:26). While the most literal interpretation of the first sixty-nine sevens is thus afforded a literal fulfillment, nothing can be found in history that provides a literal fulfillment of the last seven or the seventieth week. It has been taken by many that this indicates a postponement of the fulfillment of the last seven years of the prophecy to the future preceding the second advent. If so, a parenthesis of time involving the whole present age is indicated.

This proposal has been rejected by the liberal, by the amillenarian, and by some premillenarians, particularly those who are not dispensationalists. Philip Mauro, an amillenarian, states flatly, "Never has a specified number of time-units making up a described stretch of time, been taken to mean anything but continuous or consecutive time units."[5]

It should be obvious to careful students of the Bible that Mauro is not only begging the question but is overlooking abundant evidence to the contrary. Nothing should be plainer to one reading the Old Testament than that the foreview therein provided did not predict a period of time between the two advents. This very fact confused even the prophets (cf. 1 Pet. 1:10-12). At best such a time interval was only implied. In the very passage involved, Daniel 9:24-27, it is indicated that there would be a time interval. The anointed one, or the Messiah, is cut off after the sixty-ninth week, but not in the seventieth. Such a circumstance could be true only if there were a time interval between these two periods.

Many illustrations of parentheses in the Old Testament. As H. A. Ironside has made clear in his thorough study of this problem,[6] there are more than a dozen instances of parenthetical periods in the divine program. In Luke 4:18-20, quoting Isaiah 61:2, obviously the present age now extending over 1900 years intervenes between the "acceptable year of the Lord" and the "day of vengeance of our God." There is no indication in the Isaiah passage of any interval at all, but Christ stopped abruptly in the middle of the sentence in His quotation in Luke thus indicating the division. A similar spanning of the entire church age is found in Hosea 3:4 as compared to 3:5 and Hosea 5:15 as compared with 6:1. Psalm 22 predicts the sufferings of Christ (Ps. 22:1-21), anticipates the resurrection of Christ (Ps. 22:22), and then in the remainder of the psalm deals with millennial conditions without a reference to the present age. This characteristic is found in much of Messianic prophecy in the Old Testament.

The prophetic foreview of Daniel 2 in Nebuchadnezzar's image and the fourth beast of Daniel 7:23-27 likewise ignores

---

[5]Philip Mauro, *The Seventy Weeks and the Great Tribulation*, p. 95.
[6]H. A. Ironside, *The Great Parenthesis*, 131 pp.

the present age. Daniel 8:24 seems to refer to Antiochus Epiphanes (B.C. 170), whereas Daniel 8:25 leaps the entire present age to discuss the future beast of Revelation 13:1-10, who will appear after the church age is concluded. A similar instance is found in Daniel 11:35 as compared with Daniel 11:36. Psalm 110:1 speaks of Christ in heaven and Psalm 110:2 refers to His ultimate triumph at His second advent.

Ironside suggests that Peter stops in the middle of his quotation of Psalm 34:12-16 in 1 Peter 3:10-12 because the last part of Psalm 34:16 seems to refer to future dealings of God with sin in contrast to present discipline.[7] The truth of a parenthesis is implied in Matthew 24 where the present age is described as preceding and intervening between the cross and the sign foretold by Daniel 9:27 (cf. Matt. 24:15). Acts 15:13-21, discussed in previous study of premillennialism, makes sense when it is understood that the present age intervenes between the cross and the future blessing of Israel in the millennium.

Even in types, the interval is anticipated. The yearly schedule of feasts for Israel separates widely those prefiguring the death and resurrection of Christ and those anticipating Israel's regathering and glory. In the New Testament, the use of the olive tree as a figure in Romans 11 involves the three stages: (1) Israel in the place of blessing; (2) Israel cut off and the Gentiles in the place of blessing; (3) the Gentiles cut off and Israel grafted in again. The present age and Israel's time of discipline and judgment coincide and constitute a parenthesis in the divine program for Israel.

Sir Robert Anderson in regard to 1 Kings 6:1 finds the discrepancy of 480 years as opposed to 573 years, which was the actual length of time for the period from the departure from Egypt to the building of the temple, is solved by subtracting 93 years during which Israel was cast off as a nation—five different periods of time (Judges 3:8, 14; 4:2-3; 6:1; 13:1). If Anderson's findings are accepted, it provides a clear illustration

[7]*Ibid.*, p. 44.

of time intervals embedded in a chronological program of the Old Testament.

The ultimate proof of the teaching that the present age is a parenthesis is in the positive revelation concerning the church as the body of Christ, the study of which will be undertaken next. The evidence for a parenthesis in the present age interrupting God's predicted program for Jew and Gentile as revealed in the Old Testament is extensive, however. The evidence if interpreted literally leads inevitably to the parenthesis doctrine. The kingdom predictions of the Old Testament do not conform to the pattern of this present age. Amillenarians from Augustine down to the present make no pretense of interpreting these prophecies in the same literal way as premillenarians. Those among the premillennial group who see clearly the issues involved would do well to divorce themselves from the amillennial method in dealing with the prophetic word, and interpret the prophecies of the Old Testament in relation to the millennium rather than the present age.

CHAPTER XX

PREMILLENNIALISM AND THE CHURCH
AS A MYSTERY

In the previous study of premillennialism and the church, it was brought out that the church is a body of believers in this age distinct in character from the Old Testament saints. Further, it was shown that the present age is a parenthesis or a time period not predicted by the Old Testament and therefore not fulfilling or advancing the program of events revealed in the Old Testament foreview. The present study occupies itself with the positive revelation in the New Testament of the church in its character as a mystery.

I. Is the Church a Separate Purpose?

The question is whether the main elements of the church in the present age which are revealed as mysteries support the conclusion that the church is a purpose of God separate from Israel. It should be obvious that this is vital to premillennialism. If the church fulfills the Old Testament promises to Israel of a righteous kingdom on earth, the amillenarians are right. If the church does not fulfill these predictions and in fact is the fulfillment of a purpose of God not revealed until the New Testament, then the premillenarians are right. A study of the mysteries related to the church which are revealed in the New Testament is an important contribution to the positive evidence in favor of premillenialism.

The church is never expressly called a mystery. The term *mystery* is used, however, of the distinctive elements of the truth concerning the church as the body of Christ. Contemporary with the apostolic age, various mystery cults held sway. They were so called because their rites of initiation were mysteries or secrets to those not in the cult. Initiation consisted of various rites in which the novitiate was introduced to these mysteries. The word came therefore to be used of significant facts once hidden but now revealed.

This idea is carried forward in the New Testament in passages where pivotal truths concerning the church as the body of Christ are described as mysteries. The truths thus revealed are not incomprehensible or obscure, as is sometimes meant by the modern use of the word *mystery*. It is rather that the truth relating to the church was once hidden, i.e., in the Old Testament, but is now revealed in the New Testament. Edwards correctly defines the word *mystery*, "a secret imparted only to the initiated, what is unknown until it is revealed, whether it be easy or hard to understand."[1]

II. THE MYSTERY OF THE ONE BODY

The New Testament revelation concerning the mystery of the one body is given in express terms in Ephesians 3:1-12. While the truth is an unfolding of the nature of the church in the present age and the relation of Gentiles to it, this passage has a vital bearing on the millennial issue. Allis devotes a whole chapter on "Paul's Doctrine of the Church" to the exegesis of this one passage in an effort to sustain his attack on the premillennial position.[2] It is lamentable, however, that he ignores so many other pertinent passages in the process.

Content of the mystery. In the Ephesian passage the content of the mystery is stated: ". . . by revelation was made known unto me the mystery, as I wrote before in few words, whereby, when ye read, ye can perceive my understanding in the mystery of Christ; which is other generations was not made known unto the sons of men, as it hath now been revealed unto his holy apostles and prophets in the Spirit; to wit, that the Gentiles are fellow-heirs, and fellow-members of the body, and fellow-partakers of the promise in Christ through the gospel" (Eph.

---

[1] D. Miall Edwards, "Mystery," *International Standard Bible Encyclopaedia*, III, 2104.
[2] Oswald T. Allis, *Prophecy and the Church*, pp. 90-110.

3:3-6). The purpose of the revelation is given in the words: "to make all men see what is the dispensation of the mystery which for ages hath been hid in God who created all things" (Eph. 3:9).

Even an ordinary reading of this passage will reveal the central feature of the mystery. It is that Gentiles should have an absolute equality with the Jews in the body of Christ: "fellow-heirs," "fellow-members," and "fellow-partakers of the promise in Christ through the gospel." This central fact is admitted by Allis in these words; "The mystery is, that the Gentiles are to enjoy, actually do enjoy, a status of *complete* equality with the Jews in the Christian Church. . . . They belong to the same body. . . . This important feature of the Christian Church was the mystery."[3]

Was the mystery partially revealed in the Old Testament? Having agreed with premillenarians on the central meaning of the passage, however, Allis takes back with his left hand what he has conceded with his right. His thought is that the mystery was not completely hidden, but only partially hidden: "It was a mystery in the sense that, like other teachings which are spoken of as such, it was not fully revealed in the Old Testament and was completely hidden from the carnally minded."[4] He believes that this point of view is sustained by two arguments: first, in the text itself by the qualifying "as" clause, and, second, by his argument that "Clearly the equality of Gentile with Jew was predicted in the Old Testament."[5]

According to Allis, there are three limitations on the thought that the mystery was a new truth: "This declaration taken by itself would seem to imply that it was absolutely new. So we must note that it is at once qualified by three supplementary and limiting statements: (1) 'as it hath now been revealed,' (2) 'unto his holy apostles and prophets in Spirit,' (3) 'that the Gentiles are fellow-heirs, and fellow-members of the body, and fellow-partakers of the promise in Christ Jesus through the gospel.'"[6] It should be clear to any impartial ob-

---

[3]*Ibid.*, p. 92.
[4]*Ibid.*
[5]*Ibid.*, p. 95.

server that Allis is straining to tone down and qualify the tremendous revelation given in this passage. The second and third points of his "supplementary and limiting statements" are nothing of the sort, but rather very important details of the mystery itself. Point two indicates the channel—New Testament apostles and prophets, and point three the content of the mystery itself. Referring to these points as limitations would be like considering the deity and humanity of Christ as "supplementary and limiting" attributes of the Second Person.

The first point of his series of three is the only point worthy of debate. Just what is the significance of the clause "as it hath now been revealed"? According to Allis, the meaning is that the mystery was not revealed in the Old Testament *as* it is now revealed—i.e., it was revealed but in lesser detail and was not comprehended then.

Any student of the New Testament Greek will find it rather amazing that a scholarly writer would in this way ignore the other possibilities in this grammatical construction. Allis is assuming that the only possible interpretation is a restrictive clause. The Greek word *hos,* here translated "as," is subject to many interpretations. It is used principally as a relative adverb of manner and as a conjunction in the New Testament. A. T. Robertson in one of many discussions of this word lists its various uses as "exclamatory," "declarative," "temporal," and used with superlatives, comparatives, and correlatives.[7] He notes further than basically most clauses of this kind are "adjectival."[8] While used in an adverbial clause in this passage, the force grammatically is relative.[9] Robertson says significantly in this connection, "The relative clause may indeed have the resultant effect of cause, condition, purpose or result, but in itself it expresses none of these things. It is like the participle in this respect. *One must not read into it more than is there"* (italics added).[10] This warning evidently has not been heeded by Allis in his discussion. He has assumed that a clause which is nor-

---

[7] A. T. Robertson, *A Grammer of the Greek New Testament*, pp. 967-69.
[8] *Ibid.*, pp. 953-54.
[9] *Ibid.*
[10] *Ibid.*, p. 956.

mally an adjectival idea, i.e., merely giving additional information, is a restrictive—qualifying absolutely the preceding statement. In support of his arbitrary classification of this clause, he supplies no grammatical argument whatever, and gives the impression that his interpretation is the only possible one.

Stifler in his discussion of the "as" clause refutes the position of Allis and cites Acts 2:15 and 20:24 as substantiating evidence: "the contrast here, as Colossians i. 26 shows, is between the other ages and 'now.' It may be further remarked on this Ephesian passage that the 'as' does not give a comparison between degrees of revelation in the former time and 'now.' It denies that there was any revelation at all of the mystery in that former time; just as if one should tell a man born blind that the sun does not shine in the night as it does in the daytime. It does not shine at all by night. Certainly there is no comparison by 'as' in Acts ii. 15; xx. 24. 'As' with a negative in the preceding clause has not received the attention which it deserves. It is sometimes almost equivalent to 'but' (1 Cor. vii. 31)."[11]

In other words, the "as" clause is purely descriptive and does not qualify the mystery as only partially hidden in the Old Testament. The evidence is definitely in favor of the interpretation which regards the mystery as completely hidden until revealed in the New Testament.

Allis states in the early part of his discussion that the word *mystery* occurs "29 times in the New Testament."[12] Of these many instances the passage in Ephesians is the *only* one with the "as" clause. The others make the most absolute statements about the mystery being hidden. Allis carefully avoids a passage like Colossians 1:26 where the mystery is stated in absolute terms as completely hidden: "even the mystery which hath been hid for ages and generations: but now hath it been manifested to his saints." If there is any question about the interpretation of this clause it should be settled by parallel passages which point

---

[11]James M. Stifler, *The Epistle tc the Romans, a Commentary Logical and Historical*, p. 273.
[12]Allis, *op. cit.*, p. 90.

clearly to the idea that the "as" clause is merely added information—descriptive or adjectival rather than restrictive.

Allis justifies his exegesis by claiming that the general equality of Gentile and Jew is predicted clearly in the Old Testament. In his own words he states, "Clearly, the equality of Gentile with Jew was predicted in the Old Testament."[13] A search of his argument for proof-texts on this point reveals none whatever. In other words, the two most important aspects of his argument are asserted but not proved.

The fact is that the thought of equality of Jew and Gentile is never mentioned in the great kingdom passages of the Old Testament. The Jews correctly interpreted such passages as Isaiah 61:5-6 as indicating their supremacy in the predicted kingdom age: "And strangers shall stand and feed your flocks, and foreigners shall be your plowmen and vinedressers. But ye shall be named priests of Jehovah; men shall call you the ministers of our God: ye shall eat the wealth of the nations, and in their glory shall ye boast yourselves." Isaiah 2:1-4 teaches the same truth of Israel's exaltation in the kingdom age. The seat of government shall be in Jerusalem and from Zion the law will go forth.

It is true, as Allis points out, that Gentiles are promised great blessing in the kingdom age. They are promised salvation, material blessing, peace, tranquillity, and a share in the glory of that era. None of these promised blessings are extended to Gentiles on the ground of equality, however, and this is the point of the mystery.

Does the Old Testament teach the doctrine of the one body? The crux of the issue is whether Jews and Gentiles are presented as the same body in the Old Testament. Any literal interpretation of the Old Testament will make plain that the purpose of God revealed for Israel in the millennial kingdom is quite different from the purpose of God in the present age in relation to the church as the body of Christ. Only by spiritualizing the Old Testament prophetic passages can the viewpoint of Allis be sustained. Allis himself admits this in the following state-

---

[13]*Ibid.*, p. 95.

ment: "This conception of the mystery is entirely due to the insistence of Dispensationalists that the kingdom promises to Israel must be literally fulfilled, and therefore that the complete equality of Jew with Gentile in the Church is utterly at variance with the Old Testament and necessitates the view that the church age is quite distinct from the kingdom age."[14] In other words, the only way he can sustain his contention that the mystery is not wholly new is by application of the spiritualizing principle of interpretation to the key passages of the Old Testament. The Old Testament strictly maintains the distinction between Jew and Gentile, distinguishes their hope, their promises, and God's dealing with them. That is the main point of the Old Testament. The idea that Jews and Gentiles might be united in one entity without any distinction whatever, with equal privileges, rights, and fellowship is foreign to the Old Testament.

Relation to premillennialism. Of importance to premillennialism is the obvious conclusion that if God's present dealings with the body of Christ do not fulfill His promises concerning the kingdom age then a future fulfillment is demanded. The central concept of the church as the body of Christ including Jew and Gentile on an equal basis is described as a mystery in this passage. As such, it is described as "not made known" and "hid in God" until the time of the New Testament. This one passage certainly constitutes a stumbling block to any interpretation which attempts to find millennial kingdom promises fulfilled in the present age.

III. THE CHURCH AS AN ORGANISM

Of the mysteries relating to the church, the revelation in Colossians of the church as an organism is most important. In the mystery of the one body, the equality of Jew and Gentile is stressed. In this mystery the church as an organism is presented with the distinctive feature of being indwelt by Christ Himself.

---

[14]*Ibid.*, p. 99.

Christ in you. In Colossians 1:26-27 the central feature of this mystery is described as the fact of the indwelling Christ: "The mystery which hath been hid for ages and generations: but now hath it been manifested to his saints, to whom God was pleased to make known what is the riches of the glory of this mystery among the Gentiles, which is Christ in you, the hope of glory." The passage begins by affirming in most absolute terms that the truth here revealed was "hid for ages and generations." The truth is then defined as "Christ in you." It is significant that Allis in his argument attempting to show that truth concerning the church as the body of Christ was partially revealed in the Old Testament does not so much as mention this verse of Scripture. The truth is that the Old Testament, while speaking of the coming Messiah both in suffering and in glory, never once anticipates such a situation as "Christ in you." While some passages picture the Holy Spirit as indwelling the believer in the coming kingdom, the Second Person is never so presented.

In the preceding context (Col. 1:24) the entity thus indwelt by Christ is identified as the body and the church. The enlarging revelation comprehends the church as the body of both Jew and Gentile believers in this age indwelt by Christ Himself. This, of course, has been predicted by Christ in the Upper Room in John 14:20, and was a part of His prayer in John 17:23. Here is amazing condescension—the Lord of glory dwelling in vessels of clay. The truth is described as "the riches of the glory of this mystery" and the fact of the indwelling Christ is called "the hope of glory."

Everything in this passage stands in contrast to the Old Testament doctrine of the millennial kingdom. There the glory of the Lord will be manifest to all the earth and His dwelling is with men. Here His glory is veiled, but His presence is the hope of future glory. It is difficult to imagine a greater contrast between the position of Christ in the believer in this age and the position of Christ in the millennial kingdom.

Christ the fullness of the Godhead bodily. The significance of this tremendous revelation is subject to enlargement in later portions of Colossians. In Colossians 2:9-19 Christ is presented as possessing "all the fulness of the Godhead bodily" with the result that those who are indwelt by Christ are also "made full," or complete. On this ground they are warned against fleshly observance of ordinances or worshiping of angels. By contrast, Christ is the "Head, from whom all the body, being supplied and knit together through the joints and bands, increaseth with the increase of God" (Col. 2:19). Here again, as the theme of the mystery is enlarged, there is truth utterly foreign to Israel's covenants. Israel is regarded as a nation, a theocracy, and people, among whom God dwells. The church is regarded as a living organism in whom Christ dwells, united by vital life and growing by inner spiritual supply. Again it may be seen that, while the church itself is not described by the term *mystery,* the central features of the church are. In other words, if the qualities observed here which are the very essence of the church in the present age are described as mysteries, it is not too much to regard the church itself as unheralded in the Old Testament.

The indwelling Christ the hope of glory. As far as the Old Testament foreview is concerned, Israel's hope of glory was the glorious return of Christ in His second advent. They were promised a share in His glorious government of the earth during the kingdom. By contrast, for the believer now the indwelling Christ is declared to be the "hope of glory" (Col. 1:27). This thought is enlarged in Colossians 3.

In Colossians 3:4 it is revealed, "When Christ, who is our life, shall be manifested, then shall ye also with him be manifested in glory." The indwelling Christ is integral with the believer's hope. He is equated with our present existence as "our life" and with our future as the promise of fully manifested glory when He is glorified. The ultimate goal of spiritual experience is reached in Colossians 3:11 when the believer enters into the truth that "Christ is all, and in all."

The revelation given in Colossians is in sharp contrast to the Old Testament revelation. Allis misses the point when he identifies the mystery as "Christ" or the "gospel" or the "will" of God, or "the faith."[15] The mystery is not in the general truths relating to Christ or the gospel, but in the particular detail which is revealed in this context. The mystery is Christ indwelling. Allis is partly right that the person involved or general subject is not entirely unknown in a mystery.[16] It is the particular truth revealed for the first time that is the mystery. An examination of these particular truths reveal that they are the distinctive qualities relating to the church in contrast to Israel's promises.

The two great mysteries which have been discussed thus far constitute the essential and distinctive qualities of the church. The mysteries considered are in sharp contrast to anything known to Israel in either history or prophecy. The church is composed of Jew and Gentile on exactly the same terms and the same fellowship, united in the one body of Christ in such a way that both are cut off from their distinctive national program and introduced into vitally different order. In this new relationship, they enjoy individually the indwelling presence of Christ as the ground of present experience and hope of future glory. The church historically has lost much by the blurring of these distinctive truths in the attempt to combine the spiritual destinies of Israel and the church. While in themselves they are sufficient to label the church as a mystery on the ground that its essential qualities are mysteries, these truths are supported by two other great mysteries which point to the same conclusion, namely, the mystery of the translation of the saints and the mystery of the bride.

IV. THE MYSTERY OF THE TRANSLATION OF THE SAINTS

The doctrine of the translation of the saints has been often neglected in the discussion of the millennial question. It has been assumed that the Scriptural revelation of the translation of the saints has no vital bearing on the debate concerning the millennium. Allis for instance does not discuss the main passage of 1 Corinthians 15:51-52 at all in his attack on premillen-

---

[15]*Ibid.*, p. 90.
[16]*Ibid.*

nialism.[17] Premillenarians have not always been aware of the strategic force of this revelation in support of the premillennial position either. Much of this neglect has accompanied a failure to realize the tremendous significance of this and other truths designated as mysteries in the New Testament.

V. THE CONTENT OF THE MYSTERY OF THE TRANSLATION

In the fifteenth chapter of 1 Corinthians the general subject of the resurrection of the human body is discussed. The resurrection of Christ and its certainty is presented first and the whole structure of Christian doctrine is seen to depend upon the resurrection of Christ. The necessity of resurrection of all men is then discussed in full concluding in 1 Corinthians 15:50: "Now this I say brethren that flesh and blood cannot inherit the kingdom of God; neither doth corruption inherit incorruption."

The necessity having been shown for a change from a corruptible body to an incorruptible, normally accomplished by resurrection, a dramatic new revelation is introduced: "Behold, I tell you a mystery: We all shall not sleep, but we shall all be changed in a moment, in the twinkling of an eye, at the last trump; for the trumpet shall sound, and the dead shall be raised incorruptible, and we shall be changed (1 Cor. 15:51-52).

This passage reveals that there are two possible ways by which a corruptible body can be transformed into an incorruptible: one way is by resurrection; the other is by translation. This latter truth is introduced as a "mystery." It should be clear to all careful students of the Word of God that it is not a mystery that saints who die will be raised again. The doctrine of resurrection is taught in both the Old and New Testaments and is not a hidden truth. Nor is it a mystery that there will be living saints on the earth at the time of the coming of the Lord. All passages dealing with the second advent as well as passages which speak of Christ coming for His church assume or state that saints will be on earth awaiting His coming. The precise mystery is the added revelation of the fact of translation without dying in connection with the coming of the Lord.

---

[17]Allis, *Prophecy and the Church.*

A common assumption of amillennialism is that living saints will be translated at the time of the second advent. There is seldom any facing of the significant fact that none of the Old Testament passages dealing with the second advent teach anything on the subject of the translation of the saints. In fact, the idea of a general translation is foreign to the Old Testament. The viewpoint of Old Testament prophecies is that saints on earth at the time of the second advent will enter the millennial kingdom *in the flesh,* an obvious contradiction of the idea of translation. This is clearly taught by the fact that saints will till the ground, raise crops, and have children born to them, all of which would be quite incredible for translated saints. It is safe to say that no passage in the Old or New Testament which is accepted by all parties as relating to the second advent of Christ at the end of the tribulation period ever speaks of translation of the saints. All passages dealing with translation concern the coming of Christ for His church which is distinguished from the second coming proper.

VI. Significance of the Revelation

It is surprising that the tremendous significance of the 1 Corinthians passage has been overlooked by so many scholars. As it relates to amillennialism, its main point is its contradiction of the amillennial interpretation of the second advent. Never in Scripture are the Old Testament saints or the saints of the future tribulation promised translation. The thought of translation is in fact a pure mystery, a truth not revealed at all in the Old Testament. It is peculiarly the hope of saints in the present age and is not extended anywhere in the Scripture to the saints who will live in the tribulation period.

The chief force of the passage, however, relates to the controversy between pretribulationists and posttribulationists who accept premillennialism in general. While this will be discussed later in relating premillennialism to the tribulation, it should be pointed out that any literal interpretation of this passage makes posttribulationism an impossibility. The normal premillennial position is that saints on earth at the second advent will enter the millennium and will be in the flesh, produce children, and have normal earthly experiences in contrast to resurrected or translated saints who will have spiritual bodies. It is obviously impossible to incorporate a translation of all saints at the end of the tribulation and the beginning of the millennium as it would result in all saints receiving a spiritual body, leaving none to populate the earth in the millennium. The fumbling of Scriptural revelation on this point by both amillenarians and premillenarians has only served to obscure the real issues in the millennial controversy.

A clear understanding of the mystery of the translation of the saints will serve, therefore, to support the premillennial position in general and the pretribulation interpretation in particular. It also substantiates the interpretation of a mystery as a truth revealed in the New Testament but hidden in the Old.

VII. THE TRANSLATION OF THE SAINTS AS A COMFORTING HOPE

In 1 Thessalonians 4:13-18 a further revelation is given concerning the translation of the church. From a doctrinal standpoint, the main teaching of the passage is the truth that the translation of the church living on earth will take place at the same moment as the resurrection of "the dead in Christ." A definite order is established, however: "the dead in Christ shall rise first; then we that are alive, that are left, shall together with them be caught up in the clouds, to meet the Lord in the air, and so shall we ever be with the Lord" (1 Thess. 4:16-17).

Another tremendous truth is implicit in the passage: the translation and resurrection take place *before* Christ actually returns to the earth. From a doctrinal standpoint both the order of these events and the time they occur distinguish them from the second coming. In passages concerning the second coming to the earth the separation of saints from the unsaved takes place uniformly *after* the return of Christ. Matthew 25:31-46 pictures this in regard to the Gentiles as taking place after a throne is established on earth subsequent to the Lord's return. Ezekiel 20:33-38 portrays the judgment of Israel and separation of the saved of Israel from the rebels as taking place after the regathering is completed, a time-consuming process and occurring after the second advent. The event pictured in 1 Thessalonians, therefore, cannot be identified as the second coming of Christ pictured in Matthew and in the Old Testament.

The fact of translation of saints, if occurring at the second advent, would be in contradiction of the teaching of Matthew and Ezekiel that the separation of saints from the lost at the time of the second advent deals with those still in the flesh upon the earth. In neither Matthew nor Ezekiel is any translation involved—in fact, it is foreign to the passages. The righteous in both cases enter the kingdom and the land of Palestine as their immediate reward.

From the standpoint of exhortation, the revelation of translation is connected with a message of comfort. The Thessalonians were to be comforted or encouraged by the hope of their reunion with their loved ones at the coming of the Lord, which they regarded as imminent. The nature of this comfort is also most illuminating. It is not simply the *fact* of resurrection, but the *time* of resurrection. They apparently knew that a period of trouble was predicted for the earth. They expected the Lord to return at any time before this trouble would begin. Their comfort was that their loved ones would be resurrected at the same time as their translation, not at some later resurrection such as might precede the establishment of the kingdom on earth. Their comfort was based, then, on the hope of the imminency of the coming of the Lord and the expectation that this would also result in reunion with loved ones who had fallen asleep in Christ. The nature of their expectation distinguishes it from the second coming of Christ to the earth and supports the distinction between the translation of the church and the events related to the second advent.

VIII. The Mystery of the Bride

In connection with a series of exhortations in Ephesians 5, the proper relationship of husbands to wives is illustrated by the relationship of Christ to the church. It is revealed that Christ "loved the church, and gave himself up for it" (Eph.

5:25). The purpose of His sacrifice is "that he might sanctify it, having cleansed it by the washing of water with the word, that he might present the church to himself a glorious church, not having spot or wrinkle or any such thing; but that it should be holy and without blemish" (Eph. 5:26-27). Upon the ground of this illustration, husbands are exhorted to love their wives. The statement is made: "Even so ought husbands also to love their own wives as their own bodies" (Eph. 5:28). It is declared to be a most natural thing to love one's own body as further illustrated in the love of Christ for the church, "because we are members of his body" (Eph. 5:30). The marriage union results in man and wife becoming "one flesh" (Eph. 5:31). As applied to the church, it is then affirmed: "This mystery is great: but I speak in regard of Christ and of the church" (Eph. 5:32).

In this passage the church is not explicitly called either a "wife" or a "bride," but the obvious figure of the passage is that the church at present is a bride and in heaven will become the wife of Christ when she is presented a glorious church (Eph. 5:27). The church is expressly called "his body" in this passage. It is natural to conclude that the present bride, the future wife, and the church which is the body of Christ are all one and the same entity. On the one hand, this identifies the passage as relating to truth previously considered about the church as the body of Christ and, on the other hand, defines the bride of Christ as the believers of this age.

The attempt of E. W. Bullinger[18] to distinguish the bride from the body by making the bride consist of Jewish Christians in the early apostolic age only and the body to consist of Gentile Christians in the later apostolic period is made impossible by this passage. It has been previously shown that the body of Christ began at Pentecost by the work of the baptism of the Spirit and is therefore inclusive of all believers since Pentecost. The Ephesian passage obviously considers the body and the bride one and the same. The list of inhabitants of the heavenly

---

[15]E. W. Bullinger, *How to Enjoy the Bible*, pp. 94-96; 145-49; *The Companion Bible*, Part VI, 1769, 1912; also Appendix 197:4.

Jerusalem in Hebrews 12:22-24, while distinguishing between the "church of the first-born" and "the spirits of just men made perfect"—the latter reference apparently to Old Testament saints—does not divide the church into two groups. Even the Gentile church is referred to as a "pure virgin" to be presented to Christ (2 Cor. 11:2), a passage Bullinger slides over hurriedly.[19] The church in heaven returning with Christ is one wife, not two (Rev. 19:7-9). The body and the bride are different figures but referring to the same entity, the church.

The relationship of Christ to the church is declared to be a mystery. The idea of God related to man under the figure of marriage is by no means new. In the Old Testament Israel is declared to be the wife of Jehovah, and the entire Book of Hosea is devoted to a historical allegory of this relationship. Israel is pictured as an untrue wife to be restored in millennial days. It should be borne in mind that this is a figure and not an actual marriage. By contrast the church in figure is described as a pure virgin being prepared for future marriage. In view of the Old Testament relationship, in what sense is the relationship of Christ to the church a mystery?

The mystery is not explained in Ephesians 5. The mystery is certainly not the sacrament of marriage—the Roman Church translates the verse: "This is a great sacrament" (Eph. 5:32, Douay Version), an obvious error carried over from the Vulgate.[20] It is rather the concept of mystery as elsewhere in the New Testament—a truth hitherto not revealed but now made known. The reference in this passage is to the union between Christ and the church composed of Gentile and Jewish believers in the present age. Such a union is never contemplated in the Old Testament. The thought of the body of Christ as the church is a New Testament revelation as well as a New Testament work of God. While Israel as a nation was joined to God in a spiritual union, the new entity of the body of Christ in this age is never contemplated in such a relationship. It is

---

[19]E. W. Bullinger, *The Companion Bible*, VI, 1743.

[20]Even Catholic writers admit this. Cf. Jamieson, Fausset, Brown, *A Commentary, Critical, Experimental, and Practical, on the Old and New Testaments*, VI, 419.

therefore a revelation of the union of love binding Christ and the church in addition to the union of life indicated in the figure of the one body.

The various mystery aspects of the church combine to form a united testimony. The features therein revealed are foreign to divine revelation given in the Old Testament. They are related to the church as a distinct entity in the present age. They mark out the church as a separate purpose of God to be consummated before the resumption of the divine program for Israel.

Premillennialism is therefore related to the church primarily in maintaining the distinctions between the church and Israel which are so confused by the amillenarians and at the same time distinguishing the purpose of God for the present age from other ages past or future. This form of interpretation provides a literal and natural exegesis of the key passages which is honoring to the Word of God and furnishing an intelligent understanding of the program of God in past, present, and future ages.

Chapter XXI

PREMILLENNIALISM AND THE RAPTURE

I. Four Concepts of the Rapture

Within premillennial interpretation of the Scriptures four different concepts of the rapture have been advanced. The fact that these have existed among premillenarians has demonstrated both that premillennialism does not necessarily dictate a viewpoint on the rapture, and, that vice versa, a particular view of the rapture does not necessarily determine the millennial question. However, certain tendencies and logical relationships can be established. Some views on the rapture are difficult to harmonize with the premillennial interpretation.

Posttribulationism. One of the leading views regarding the rapture of the church is that this event will occur in connection with Christ's return to establish His millennial kingdom. As this follows rather than precedes the time of the tribulation predicted in Scripture, it is commonly known as the posttribulation view. The term *rapture* itself is derived from the Latin Vulgate version of 1 Thessalonians 4:17 where the expression "caught up" is translated by the Latin *rapturo.* The English word *rapture,* though it does not occur in Scripture, is therefore synonymous with the idea that living Christians at the time of the coming of Christ for them will be translated and caught up to meet the Lord in the air.

Posttribulationists rely upon a number of arguments to sustain their point of view.[1] Among the more important posttribulation arguments are the following: (1) the historical argu-

---

[1] For more extensive treatment of posttribulationism see John F. Walvoord, *The Rapture Question,* pp. 127-70; J. Dwight Pentecost, *Things to Come,* pp. 164-78; Gerald B. Stanton, *Kept From the Hour,* pp. 209-50. For works advocating posttribulationism cf. George E. Ladd, *The Blessed Hope;* Alexander Reese, *The Approaching Advent of Christ.*

ment based on the supposition that the early church fathers were posttribulational; (2) argument that the tribulation is not explicitly a time of wrath and that the church will be preserved through it; (3) argument based on references to saints in the tribulation which is taken as proving that the church is in the tribulation; (4) argument that certain events must be fulfilled first, thereby denying the imminency of Christ's coming for His church; (5) argument based on prophecies that a resurrection will occur at the beginning of the millennium. If this resurrection is the same as that occurring at the translation, it would prove the translation of the church took place at the same time, that is, after the tribulation. (6) the argument based on the terminology for the Lord's return, that is, that the same expressions are used for the rapture and for His return to establish His millennial kingdom; (7) argument from the parable of the wheat and tares in Matthew 13, especially that the tares are gathered out "first"; (8) argument based on use of the expression "the day" and "day of the Lord" holding that it is a technical expression always referring to the same event; (9) argument from the chronology of 2 Thessalonians 2:1-12 and the posttribulational contention that two signs must be fulfilled before Christ's return, viz., the apostasy, and the appearance of the man of sin, which they identify as events in the tribulation period; (10) argument based on the use of the term "the end" which they take as a technical expression always referring to the same period, viz., the end of the interadvent age; (11) argument based on certain Scriptures such as Matthew 24:31 as identified with the rapture, thereby making it posttribulational. All of these arguments have a sufficient rebuttal in pretribulation writings.

Generally speaking, posttribulationists are content to attack other points of view rather than setting forth their own arguments. Actually the church is never found in any portion of Scripture dealing with the time of the tribulation, and the translation of the church is never mentioned in any passage picturing the return of Christ to set up His millennial kingdom. Posttribulationism is built principally upon the identification of the church with tribulation saints, a conclusion which is without substantiation in Scripture. Posttribulationists cannot cite a single passage where this confusion is justified, and their arguments as a whole have been often refuted. For this reason most thorough-going premillenarians have abandoned the posttribulation position as not being the hope for the rapture of the church taught in the Scriptures.

Midtribulation rapture. A compromise position between pretribulationism and posttribulationism has attracted some scholars who have held that the church will be raptured before the great tribulation, but not before some of the preceding events. Adopting the position that the last seven years of Israel's program outlined in Daniel 9:27 is still future and depicts a seven-year period, midtribulationists believe that the church will be on earth during the first half of the seven-year period, but will be raptured before the last half described in Scripture as the great tribulation.

Arguments offered in favor of the midtribulation position are: (1) the church is raptured at the seventh trumpet of Revelation 11 which they identify with the last trump for the church and as the signal for the beginning of the great tribulation; (2) the church may expect rapture soon, but must await the fulfillment of the first three and one half years of Daniel's seventieth week. The midtribulation point of view has not produced a large amount of literature, and has attracted only a few adherents. Its refutation consists in demonstrating that the seventh trumpet of Revelation is not the trumpet connected with the rapture; that the seventh trumpet is near the end of the great tribulation rather than at its beginning; and that no rapture or translation of the saints is mentioned in connection with the seventh trumpet.[2]

Partial-rapture theory. Some interpreters of Scripture have advanced the theory that only especially qualified saints will be raptured before the tribulation, and that others will be

---

[2]Principal argument for the midtribulation position is found in Norman B. Harrison's book *The End.* For refutation and discussion see Walvoord, *op. cit.*, pp. 171-89; Pentecost, *op. cit.*. pp. 179-92; Stanton, *op. cit.*, pp. 178-208.

raptured during the tribulation or at its close when they qualify spiritually. The theory originated in the works of Robert
Govett a century ago.[3] Leading contender for the view in the
twentieth century is G. H. Lang.[4]

This viewpoint is based on passages of Scripture in which
believers are warned to be ready for the Lord's return. Among
the passages cited are Matthew 24:40-51; 25:13; Mark 13:33-37;
Luke 20:34-36; 21:36; Philippians 3:10-12; I Thessalonians 5:6; 2
Timothy 4:8; Titus 2:13; Hebrews 9:24-28; Revelation 3:3; 12:1-6.
The theory is based on the idea that good works are necessary
to qualify for the rapture, a theory which becomes almost immediately untenable when the question is asked: "How much
works?" The partial-rapture theory is also objectionable because it divides the body of Christ and ignores plain teaching
of Scripture which indicates that all true believers will be
translated at the same time as indicated in the phrase "we all"
in 1 Corinthians 15:51. The partial-rapture theory is probably
the least popular of all the rapture viewpoints.[5]

Pretribulation rapture. The most widely held viewpoint of
Bible expositors who specialize in premillennial eschatology is
the pretribulation rapture position. This point of view holds
that the rapture of the church occurs before the entire seven-
year period of Daniel's seventieth week and can be expected at
any moment of any day, and therefore emphasizes the imminency
of the Lord's return. In view of the extended treatment of this
concept by the author in a separate volume,[6] only a summary
is presented here.

II. ARGUMENTS FOR PRETRIBULATIONISM

Many arguments have been advanced in support of the
pretribulation rapture viewpoint and as many as fifty can be

---

[3]Cf. Robert Govett, *Entrance into the Kingdom.*
[4]Cf. G. H. Lang, *The Revelation of Jesus Christ; Firstborn Sons; Their
Rights and Risks.*
[5]For further discussion see Walvoord, *op. cit.* pp. 105-25; Pentecost, *op. cit.*
pp. 156-63; Stanton, *op. cit.* 165-77.
[6]*The Rapture Question,* 204 pp.

itemized.[7] Two important presuppositions, however, are essential to the pretribulation position: (1) the definition of the church as a separate body of saints distinct from saints of other ages; (2) the doctrine of a future tribulation of unprecedented severity. This involves usually the concept that the seventieth week of Daniel's prophecy for Israel is also future in its entirety. Most discussions in support of posttribulationism seriously beg the question by failing to recognize the importance of these two premises. Obviously if the word *church* includes saints of all ages and saints are mentioned in the tribulation time, it is futile to debate the question of pretribulationism. Likewise, if the tribulation of which the Scriptures speak is already past or present, it is also illogical to discuss whether the church will go through the tribulation because under this approach the church is already in that period.

If the two premises for pretribulationism can be sustained, other important arguments may be itemized in support of the pretribulation position as follows: (1) The same literal form of interpretation of millennial passages which leads to premillennialism, if applied to passages on the tribulation, tends to demonstrate that the church could not be in this time of wrath. (2) There is no evidence that the church is in the tribulation period as no distinctive term is ever used connecting saints in the period with the church. (3) Further, the tribulation concerns Israel and the Gentiles, not the church, and the church is promised deliverance from the time of tribulation (1 Thess. 5:9, cf. Rev. 6:17; 1 Thess. 1:9-10; Rev. 3:10). (4) The rapture is presented as an imminent event with no intervening prophecies and as such is offered as a ground of comfort (1 Thess. 4:18) and a basis of exhortation (1 Thess. 5:6; Titus 2:13; 1 John 3:1-3). (5) The work of the Holy Spirit as the restrainer of sin cannot be terminated until the Holy Spirit is taken out of the way (2 Thess. 2:7). This would be impossible unless the church was also raptured, and requires a pretribulational chronology. (6) Important events must occur between the rapture of the church and the establishment of the millennial kingdom such

---

[7]Cf. *ibid.*, pp. 191-99.

as the judgment seat of Christ (2 Cor. 5:10), the union of Christ and the church in the marriage relationship (Eph. 5:27), and the necessity of a program of salvation over a period of time to provide saints to dwell on the earth during the millennium who are not raptured but enter the millennium in their natural bodies (Isa. 65:20-25). This is further confirmed by the fact that the separation of the saved from the unsaved of those living on the earth at the time of the millennial return of Christ is accomplished in a judgment of God upon Israel (Ezek. 20:34-38) and a judgment of the Gentiles (Matt. 25:31-46), judgments which would be unnecessary and out of chronological order if the rapture had already separated all the saved from the unsaved at the end of the tribulation. A posttribulational rapture would leave no saints in their natural bodies to dwell upon the earth and fulfill millennial predictions. (7) The translation of the church and the events connected with the return of Christ to establish His kingdom are contrasted in Scripture. At the rapture the church will meet Christ in the air, living saints will be translated and will return with Christ to heaven. At the rapture the earth is not judged, for the translation is before the day of wrath and concerns only those who are in Christ. By contrast, the second coming of Christ will involve Christ returning to the Mount of Olives, the establishment of His kingdom, and His remaining in the earthly sphere and reigning as King. Sin will be judged, and righteousness will characterize the earth. The second coming will follow the great tribulation, and will be preceded by definite prophesied signs. It will affect the entire population of those living on the earth at that time. These and many other contrasts make clear that the events related to the rapture and those related to Christ's return to establish His kingdom cannot be harmonized without denying many of the details given in Scripture.[8]

---

[8]For further discussion on contrasts cf. *ibid.*, pp. 101-3. For treatment of pretribulationism as a whole cf. *ibid.*, pp. 7-103; Pentecost *op. cit.*, pp. 193-218; Stanton, *op. cit.*, pp. 25-164; 251-75; L. S. Chafer, *Systematic Theology*, IV, 364-73; E. Schuyler English, *Rethinking the Rapture;* J. F. Strombeck, *First the Rapture.*

III. Pretribulationism the Logical Outcome of Premillennial Interpretation

Taken as a whole, the same approach to the Scriptures and the same arguments which lead to the conclusion that Christ will return to the earth to reign for one thousand years also point to the conclusion that He will come for His church before the fulfillment of Daniel's seventieth week. The same literalness of interpretation and the same distinctions between Israel's program and that for the church, both of which are contrasted with God's dealings with the Gentiles, support both points of view. Further, the premillenarian who puts the rapture at the close of the tribulation is left without an explanation concerning the saints who live on the earth in their natural bodies. Posttribulationists who are also premillenarian seldom offer a detailed chronology of events in connection with the second advent for the obvious reason that such a chronology would contradict their posttribulationism. Even leading exponents of posttribulationism such as Alexander Reese and more recently George E. Ladd do not even discuss this problem, much less offer a solution for it. It is not sufficient for posttribulationists to offer arguments against pretribulationism if they cannot establish their own point of view and offer a reasoned exegesis of the order of events portrayed in Scripture in connection with the second advent. Though amillenarians are not embarrassed by a lack of saints still in their natural bodies at the second advent as they have already eliminated the millennium, premillenarians are obligated to offer some solution to this problem. It is rather significant that premillenarians who are specialists in the field of prophecy and who characteristically have labored over a period of years in this field are predominately pretribulationists. Often an abandonment of the pretribulation position by its former adherents is the first step to abandoning premillennialism as well. The logical alternatives which face a reverent scholar seem to be on the one hand the pretribulational and premillennial position resulting from a literal interpretation of prophecy or the amillennial and posttribulational position built upon a spiritualization or figurative interpretation of prophecy on the other hand. Those who attempt to establish a mediate position by borrowing arguments from both conflicting millennial positions are to that extent in an untenable compromise between two opposing principles of interpretation.

CHAPTER XXII

THE GREAT TRIBULATION

Though premillenarians have been in essential agreement on the central fact of the coming of Christ as preceding the thousand-year reign, a variety of detail is found in the exposition of the millennium itself. This is also true of the prophetic context of the millennium, that sequence of important events which anticipate and prepare the way for the coming of Christ and His reign upon the earth. Much of the existing confusion, however, is immediately dissipated if the view is followed that the rapture of the church occurs first and is followed by the fulfillment of the prophesied seventieth week of Israel. Under this interpretation, a tremendous succession of events unfolds as preparing the way for the coming of the millennial kingdom. If the church is removed before this period of trouble, it becomes immediately clear that the tribulation is a divine preparation and prophetic sign of the approaching second coming of Christ. Though many details of the tribulation have already been discussed in connection with the rapture question, the same area of prophetic revelation may now be examined as a prelude to the millennium.

I. THE NATURE OF THE TRIBULATION

The Old Testament as well as the New constantly warns that there will be a time of trouble preceding the millennial kingdom of Christ. This period of trial is in sharp contrast to tribulations which characterize the experience of saints in all ages. The future period is described as having certain specific characteristics which have never been fulfilled and cannot be fulfilled until the church is raptured. In general, this future time of trouble will concern three divisions of humanity:

(1) The nation Israel; (2) the nations or the pagan Gentile world; (3) the elect saints who will live in that time of trouble. Divine dealing with each of these three groups differs widely.

Place of Israel in the tribulation. For the nation Israel the tribulation will be a time of discipline and purging in preparation for the coming millennial kingdom. It stands in contrast to all previous times of trial and discipline and is repeatedly declared to be unprecedented in its character and severity. It is predicted that Israel's trials will bring spiritual revival to a portion of the nation and a godly remnant will emerge. Passages which deal with the tribulation reveal that when this has been realized the tribulation will close with Israel's deliverance accomplished by the return of Christ as the Messiah of Israel. Israel will then be regathered from all over the earth, restored as a nation, and given a place of honor safety, and prominence in the millennial kingdom.

Place of Gentiles in the tribulation. For the Gentiles, the tribulation marks the close of the extended period of the "times of the Gentiles" (Luke 21:24), that period marked by Gentile control of Jerusalem since 600 B. C. During the tribulation frightful judgments will be poured out upon the Gentiles, resulting in utter destruction of their cities and civilization and leading to their complete doom at the time of the return of Christ. During the tribulation, a world government will come into being headed by a dictator of unprecedented evil and guilty of utter blasphemy against the true God. For a time he will hold the entire world in his power, a satanic imitation of the true reign of Christ in the millennial kingdom. His attempt to deify himself begins the "great tribulation" (Matt. 24:21), with its terrible persecution of Jew and Christian. The great tribulation is brought to its close by the second advent of Christ and destruction of the world power of Gentiles as predicted by Daniel and many prophetic portions of the Old and New Testaments.

The elect in the tribulation. The elect or the saved of the tribulation period are composed of both Jews and Gentiles who turn to Christ for salvation. During the early part of the period between the rapture and the second coming of Christ, there is some religious freedom as indicated by the restoration of Jewish sacrifices. With the beginning of the great tribulation, however, this freedom is abruptly ended, and Jewish sacrifices cease. All who oppose the deification and worship of the world dictator are subject to persecution. Both Jew and Christian become the objects of this satanic oppression, and many are martyred. The elect are delivered by the return of Christ at the close of the tribulation period.

The Scriptures which present the revelation of this coming tribulation constantly reiterate that it will be a time of trouble without precedent in the history of the world. It will be a climactic period, expressly designed by a sovereign God to bring the forces of evil to a crescendo before the millennial reign of Christ which will be characterized by peace and righteousness. The millennial kingdom is therefore set off from preceding dispensations by this unmistakable future period of trial, which serves to make evident that both the tribulation and the millennium which follows are as yet unfulfilled.

II. The Tribulation in the Old Testament

The first reference to the tribulation as such is found in Deuteronomy 4:29-30: "But from thence ye shall seek Jehovah thy God, and thou shalt find him, when thou searchest after him with all thy heart and with all thy soul. When thou art in tribulation, and all these things are come upon thee, in the latter days thou shalt return to Jehovah thy God, and hearken unto his voice." According to this first reference, the tribulation is the occasion for some in Israel turning to the Lord and constitutes a divine preparation for the kingdom which will follow.

The prophet Jeremiah contributes one of the most important Old Testament revelations as recorded in Jeremiah 30:4-11. The coming tribulation is described as inducing terror on the part of those who will be living at that time. The period itself is described: "Alas! for that day is great, so that none is like it: it is even the time of Jacob's trouble; but he shall be saved out of it" (Jer. 30:7). The prophecy continues with a prediction of the millennial scene when Jews will no longer be under the yoke of Gentile bondage (v. 8) and instead will be under the rule of Jehovah and David, their king (v. 9). On the basis of this glorious prospect, Israel is encouraged not to fear but instead to look forward to the deliverance which will come when they return from their captivities and are brought back to their land to enjoy peace and quiet where "none shall make him afraid" (v. 10).

This passage from the prophecy of Jeremiah makes clear that this time of trouble is distinct from any preceding trial of Israel. It states flatly "that none is like it" (v. 7). It also indicates that the time of trouble will be followed immediately not by the eternal state but by Israel restored to the land and delivered from Gentile political domination. Jeremiah therefore includes all the major elements of the tribulation and sets it in a millennial context as a necessary antecedent to the glory of the kingdom.

One of the most important Old Testament predictions comes from the pen of the Prophet Daniel and is contained in Daniel 9:27. If the futuristic interpretation of this passage be accepted, it yields an important chronology for the context of the millennium. The sixty-nine "weeks" of Daniel (9:24-26) have demonstrated by their fulfillment that the time unit is a year —each "week" being a period of seven years. By this token the seventieth week described in Daniel 9:27 must also represent a period of seven years. As no such period followed immediately the fulfillment of the sixty-ninth week, the futuristic interpretation of the passage looks for fulfillment in the last seven years preceding the second advent of Christ to establish His millennial kingdom. The one making the covenant mentioned in Daniel 9:27 is identified with "the prince that shall come" of verse 26 and is the same individual who becomes the dictator of the whole world during the tribulation time. The arguments for and against this interpretation have been stated in an abundance of scholarly literature and need not be debated again here.[1]

---

[1]Cf. Sir Robert Anderson, *The Coming Prince*, pp. 51-129; Robert Culver,

According to Daniel's prophecy, the last seven years before the second advent will begin with a covenant between the prince and the people of Israel. It is evidently a covenant of protection and of religious liberty under which Israel is free to re-establish their ancient system of sacrifices. In the middle of the seven years, the covenant is broken and the sacrifices cease. This may be done in connection with the effort to deify the world ruler of that day which would make the worship of Israel as well as the true faith of believers in Christ illegal. Thus begins the great tribulation, the period of trial never before experienced for all who would worship the true God. This time of tribulation must run its course, "even unto the full end" (Dan. 9:27), but it is constantly reiterated in Scripture that deliverance will come with the second advent of Christ. According to Daniel's prophecy, this will occur seven years after the covenant is made, and three and one half years after the beginning of the great tribulation.

In Daniel's prophecy, as in Jeremiah, the period of trouble is followed by deliverance and restoration of Israel as a nation. According to Daniel 12:1, the consummation of the period of trouble in blessing is assured: "There shall be a time of trouble, such as never was since there was a nation even to that same time: and at that time thy people shall be delivered, every one that shall be found written in the book." In other portions of Daniel, further information is given concerning the tribulation, and though Daniel does not occupy himself preeminently with the millennial kingdom itself, it is evident that the consummation of the tribulation ushers in a time of victory and peace. Details of the tribulation itself are given in Daniel 7:7-8, 19-27; 11:36-45; 12:11-13.

Not only are Daniel and Jeremiah clear on this important truth but confirmation is found in most of the Minor Prophets in which the dominant theme is the future time of trouble for Israel and the ultimate deliverance and restoration of Israel nevertheless. Important passages on the theme in the

------

Daniel and the Latter Days, pp. 135-60; H. A. Ironside, *Lectures on Daniel*, pp. 155-71; A. C. Gaebelein. *Daniel*, pp. 119-50.

Minor Prophets are Joel 2:1-11, 28-32; Zephaniah 1:14-18; Zechariah 13:8—14:2. The Old Testament revelation of the tribulation as a whole is therefore amazingly complete and confirms in general the premillennial concept of the millennial kingdom to follow the tribulation.

III. The New Testament Doctrine of the Tribulation

In the prophetic ministry of Christ a notable confirmation of this Old Testament teaching is found in the New Testament as contained in the Olivet Discourse dealing with signs and exhortations relative to the coming of the Lord. According to Matthew 24:15-30, the specific details of the tribulation are presented as signs of the coming of the Lord. Matthew 24:15 refers to the abomination of desolation of which Daniel spoke (Dan. 9:27; 12:11). Like Jeremiah and Daniel, Christ declares that this coming time of trouble will be unprecedented: "For then shall be great tribulation, such as was not since the beginning of the world until now, no, nor ever shall be" (Matt. 24:21). As in the Old Testament, the tribulation is primarily a divine dealing with Israel, but is also the consummation and final display of Gentile world domination. Like the Old Testament prophecies, Christ also teaches that the second advent will "immediately" follow the tribulation (Matt. 24:29-30).

The theme of divine revelation concerning the tribulation is found occasionally in the Pauline epistles and in 1 Thessalonians 5:1-11 under the terminology of "day of the Lord." The period is revealed to be one in which unbelievers will experience sudden destruction as those who walk in darkness in contrast to "the children of light" who will be delivered. A particular comfort to the church is the fact that "God appointed us not unto wrath, but unto the obtaining of salvation through our Lord Jesus Christ" (1 Thess. 5:9). In 2 Thessalonians 2:1-12, attention is directed to the fact that the tribulation will be dominated by "the man of sin" (v. 3) "whose coming is according to the working of Satan with all power and signs and lying wonders" (v. 9). The tribulation period is therefore described as that specific future time when the man of sin will reign.

Though other Scriptures allude to the period, the major New Testament revelation is found in the last book of the Bible, Revelation, chapters 4-19. Approximately fifteen chapters of the book are used to describe this time of trouble. Even a casual reading of these stupendous events will disclose a period exceeding in importance all other periods in human history, presenting the final throes of the forces of evil prior to the second advent of Christ. Only by following an allegorical or spiritualized interpretation of the tremendous events predicted can these great prophetic Scriptures be robbed of their intended meaning. In the book of Revelation, however, as in other passages dealing with the tribulation, the time of trouble is revealed as temporary and Israel, even though in great distress, will be ultimately delivered. It is made plain in chapter 19 that the second advent of Christ is the occasion for the destruction of Gentile power in the world and at the same time introduces the thousand years of Christ's reign upon the earth.

As has been indicated in previous discussions, nowhere does the church appear in these tremendous scenes. The events of the tribulation have their major significance as the consummation of "the times of the Gentiles" and a divine preparation of the nation Israel for their role of restoration and blessing in the millennium. The tribulation is therefore a major aspect of the prophetic context of the millennium.

CHAPTER XXIII

THE SECOND COMING OF CHRIST

The Biblical doctrine of the coming millennial kingdom of Christ is one of the greatest themes of divine revelation. In its simple definition, the millennium is the reign of Christ for one thousand years on the earth following His second coming. As such it is the consummating dispensation of human history on earth. Though millennial truth is essentially eschatological, it is integral to the entire volume of Scripture and its proper understanding is an important essential to theology as a whole. Millennialism cannot therefore be brushed aside as a dispute on the interpretation of Revelation 20, but is rather the product of a system of Biblical interpretation established as the positive teaching of both Testaments. It constitutes a refutation of both amillennialism and postmillennialism.

In discussing the great theme of the kingdom and prophecy, Nathaniel West summarized the importance of millennial truth in these words; "From first to last, the Kingdom of God on earth, its inception, progress, conduct, and consummation in glory, is the one theme of Old Testament · prophecy. To this end were the covenants with Christ, Adam, Noah, Abraham, Israel, and David. To this end was the choice of the one national 'Israel,' the 'choice forever,' as a prophetic, priestly, kingly nation, a messianic and mediatorial nation, the one national 'Servant of Jehovah,' and national Son of God, standing between God and mankind, and bringing salvation to a lost world; a people from whom should come the one personal 'Israel,' Prophet, Priest, and King, the one Mediator and true Messiah, Seed of the Woman, Seed of Abraham, Seed of David, Son of Man and Son of God, in whom all nations should bless themselves—*Jesus Christ*. Identified with Him, individually, and called by His name, stands Israel collectively, in His whole Mes-

sianic work and kingdom. Neither acts without the other. The
Pentateuch prophecies refer chiefly to the people. The Messianic Psalms emphasize the King, the Kingdom, and the Priest.
Isaiah dwells upon the prophetic character of Israel; Ezekiel
displays the priestly; Daniel reveals the kingly; Zechariah blends
all in one. *Old Testament prophecy knows no other subjects of
discourse than these, Israel, Messiah, and the nations.* As to the
kingdom, Israel had it, under the Old Testament, in its outward form; the Gentiles have it under the New Testament in
its inward form; in the age to come, Jews and Gentiles together,
shall have it, both forms in one, one kingdom of Messiah, spiritual, visible and glorious, with Israel still the central people,
the prelude of the New Jerusalem and the nations walking in
its light forever."[1]

The most important aspect of the prophetic context of
the millennium is the personal return of Jesus Christ to the
earth. The tribulation which precedes it is a dramatic preparation for that coming and is climaxed by the glorious appearance of the Lord in the heavens accompanied by the saints and
the holy angels. Though the second coming may not be as
important to the total program of God as the first coming, it
certainly is without precedent in manifestation of the glory and
power of the Triune God. It constitutes the most tremendous
intervention of divine power in the entire course of human history.

On every hand one discovers that the Scripture dealing
with the second coming is the key to the prophetic future. The
important place given the premillennial second coming of
Christ in Scripture justifies using the term *premillennial* to
describe the whole system of Biblical interpretation which is
involved. Just as Scripture concerning the rapture of the church
is climactic and determinative in truth revealed about the church,
so the second coming is determinative in tracing the future
course of Gentiles and Israel in the world, the resurrection of
the righteous, and the fulfillment of prophecies concerning the
kingdom of God on earth.

---

[1]Nathaniel West, *The Thousand Years in Both Testaments.* pp. 4-5.

I. OLD TESTAMENT PROPHECIES OF THE SECOND COMING

Though the Old Testament never mentions the rapture of the church, many prophecies are recorded about the second coming of Christ to the earth. The blindness of amillenarians to this witness of Scripture is illustrated by Berkhof's statement: "I do not know of a single passage in the Bible which teaches that Christ will come again in order to establish a temporal Jewish kingdom. If there is one, I should like to know where it can be found. The Old Testament contains no explicit statement respecting the second coming of Christ."[2] The Old Testament indeed does not use the phrase "second coming," but neither does the New Testament. The Scriptures to be considered will speak for themselves as evidence for the second coming of the Old Testament.

The first of these prophecies of the second coming is recorded in Deuteronomy 30:3: ". . . then Jehovah thy God will turn thy captivity, and have compassion upon thee, and will return and gather thee from all the peoples whither Jehovah thy God hath scattered thee." In this first prophecy of the "return" of the Lord, the event is linked with the final regathering of Israel promised in verse 2 and enlarged in verses 4-6; Israel is promised spiritual revival so that they will "love Jehovah thy God with all thy heart, and with all thy soul" (v. 6) ; their enemies will be judged; Israel will be blessed abundantly with full harvests, much cattle, and many offspring (v. 9). Here, in brief, is the essence of all prophetic Scripture relative to the second coming of Christ. Though references to the second coming are few in the Pentateuch and historical books of the Old Testament, this passage established the doctrine as a major prophetic truth from the very beginning of written revelation.

The Psalms contribute a great deal to the prophetic foreview of Christ. Psalm 2 pictures Christ as enthroned in Zion as God's answer to the rebellion of the nations. In Psalm 24 the gates of Jerusalem are exhorted to welcome the King of glory. Psalm 50 speaks of God shining forth from Zion: "Out of

---

[2]L. Berkhof, *The Second Coming of Christ*, p. 61.

Zion, the perfection of beauty, God hath shined forth" (v. 2),
and declares, "Our God cometh, and doth not keep silence"
(v. 3). Psalm 72 is an unusually complete picture of the millennial reign of Christ. In this psalm it is stated: "He will come
down like rain upon the mown grass, as showers that water
the earth" (v. 6). The psalm as a whole pictures the peace
and righteousness and universal rule of the King of whom it
is predicted: "Yea, all kings shall fall down before him; all
nations shall serve him" (v. 11).

Psalm 96 exhorts the whole world to praise and worship
Jehovah: "For he cometh to judge the earth: he will judge
the world with righteousness, and the peoples with his truth"
(v. 13). Psalm 110 contrasts the present position of the King
at "my right hand" (v. 1) with His rule "in the midst of thine
enemies" (v. 2). His judgment upon the wicked in the future
kingdom described in the words "in the day of thy power" (v.
3) is given in verses 5-7. Taken as a whole, these representative psalms give another complete picture of the coming of the
King of Kings to reign over and subdue a wicked earth.

The Major and Minor Prophets abound in references to
the King and His millennial reign. Isaiah 9:6-7 declares ma-
jestically of Christ: "For unto us a child is born, unto us a son
is given; and the government shall be upon his shoulder: and
his name shall be called Wonderful, Counsellor, Mighty God,
Everlasting Father, Prince of Peace. Of the increase of his government and of peace there shall be no end, upon the throne
of David, and upon his kingdom, to establish it, and to uphold it with justice and with righteousness from henceforth even
for ever. The zeal of Jehovah of hosts will perform this." In
this and similar passages the second coming is implied in what
the Son of God accomplishes upon the earth. A full picture of
the millennial reign following the second advent is given in
Isaiah 11:1—12:6. Christ is described as coming from Edom to
judge the wicked in the day of vengeance (Isa. 63:1-6). As the
prophet contemplates the wickedness of his day, he cries out:
"Oh that thou wouldest rend the heavens, that thou wouldest
come down, that the mountains might quake at thy presence"

(Isa. 64:1). This great book closes with two chapters devoted largely to the time of millennial blessings (65-66).

The second coming itself is in view in Daniel 7:13-14, where Daniel records a prophetic vision: "I saw in the night-visions, and, behold, there came with the clouds of heaven one like unto a son of man, and he came even to the ancient of days, and they brought him near before him. And there was given him dominion, and glory, and a kingdom, that all peoples, nations, and languages should serve him: his dominion is an everlasting dominion, which shall not pass away, and his kingdom that which shall not be destroyed." This same event was predicted early in Daniel 2:44: "And in the days of those kings shall the God of heaven set up a kingdom which shall never be destroyed, nor shall the sovereignty thereof be left to another people; but it shall break in pieces and consume all these kingdoms, and it shall stand for ever."

The Prophet Zechariah spoke of the second coming and the presence of Jehovah in the millennial earth: "Sing and rejoice, O daughter of Zion; for, lo, I come, and I will dwell in the midst of thee, saith Jehovah. And many nations shall join themselves to Jehovah in that day, and shall be my people; and I will dwell in the midst of thee, and thou shalt know that Jehovah of hosts hath sent me unto thee" (Zech. 2:10-11). According to Zechariah 14:3-11, the coming of the King shall be timed to put down the wicked just as they are conquering Jerusalem: "Then shall Jehovah go forth, and fight against those nations, as when he fought in the day of battle. And his feet shall stand in that day upon the mount of Olives, which is before Jerusalem on the east; and the mount of Olives shall be cleft in the midst thereof toward the east and toward the west, and there shall be a very great valley; and half of the mountain shall remove toward the north, and half of it toward the south" (vv. 3-4). The coming of the Lord, according to this Old Testament prophecy, shall be a specific event, a return to the very place from which our Lord ascended, and it shall be marked by the dividing asunder of the Mount of Olives.

II. THE SECOND COMING OF CHRIST IN THE NEW TESTAMENT

The revelation of the second coming of Christ is one of the most important and most frequently mentioned doctrines of the New Testament. One out of every twenty-five verses in the New Testament refers either to the rapture of the church or to Christ's coming to reign over the world.[3] Though it is not always possible to distinguish references to Christ's coming for the church from references to His coming to establish His earthly kingdom, there are many passages which clearly present a premillennial coming at the close of the great tribulation to judge the world and to bring in the righteous reign of the King. Approximately twenty major references are found in the New Testament alone (Matt. 19:28; 23:39; 24:3—25:46; Mark 13:24-37; Luke 12:35-48; 17:22-37; 18:8; 21:25-28; Acts 1:10-11; 15:16-18; Rom. 11:25-27; 1 Cor. 11:26; 2 Thess. 1:7-10; 2 Pet. 3:3-4; Jude 1:14-15; Rev. 1:7-8; 2:25-28; 16:15; 19:11-21; 22:20).

His return to reign is posttribulational. Though many premillenarians believe that the Lord will come for His church before the tribulation and that the rapture is pretribulational, they agree that the second coming to the earth to reign is a posttribulational event. Exceptions to the rule would include the old school of postmillenarians who place the return of Christ after the millennium instead of before it.[4] Those who completely spiritualize the second coming and find it fulfilled at Pentecost in the advent of the Spirit, or at the destruction of Jerusalem in A.D. 70, or those who find the second coming fulfilled in any spiritual crisis are of course exceptions to the rule. Most conservative amillenarians as well as premillenarians, however, consider the return of Christ to reign as a posttribulational event. This is so clearly taught in Scripture that only extensive spiritualization can escape such a conclusion.

In Matthew 24:21-29 the period preceding the second advent is described as the great tribulation (v. 21), in which there will appear many false Christs (vv. 23-25), and false reports of

---

[3] Jesse Forrest Silver, *The Lord's Return*, p. 29.
[4] Cf. Charles Hodge, *Systematic Theology*, III, 792.

the coming of Christ (v. 26). The second coming is described as following these events. In verse 29 it is declared: "But immediately after the tribulation of those days the sun shall be darkened, and the moon shall not give her light, and the stars shall fall from heaven, and the powers of the heavens shall be shaken." In the next verse it is stated: "And then shall appear the sign of the Son of man in heaven: and then shall all the tribes of the earth mourn, and they shall see the Son of man coming on the clouds of heaven with power and great glory." Mark 13:24-26 gives precisely the same order and so does Luke 21:25-27. In the book of Revelation, likewise, the second coming of Christ is given as the climax to the tremendous scenes of the tribulation described in the earlier chapters and scholars even of differing schools of interpretation usually agree that Revelation 19 is climactic. Unless the Scriptures bearing on this subject are robbed of all literal meaning, they teach unmistakably that Christ will come to reign after the predicted tribulation.

A personal return. The graphic description of the second coming in its principal passages should leave no doubt that the coming of Christ is a personal event in which Christ comes from heaven to the earth. Support to this idea is given in the words of the angels in Acts 1:11 where His second coming is compared to His ascension and it is declared: "This Jesus, who was received up from you into heaven, shall so come in like manner as ye beheld him going into heaven." That His second coming is a personal return is borne out by all the details revealed in the many passages bearing on this subject.

A bodily return. The Scriptures also indicate that the return of Christ, like the ascension, is a bodily return in the same sense that His ascension was a bodily ascension into heaven. There is no evidence that the second coming can be explained as merely a change of state as some Lutheran theologians have seemed to teach.[5] The resurrection body of Christ never becomes omnipresent. His body does not "fill all things"

---

[5]Cf. H. E. Jacobs, *A Summary of the Christian Faith*, pp. 156-57.

(Eph. 4:10),[6] but always has a local characteristic even though it may be granted that Christ in His divine nature is always omnipresent. Zechariah 14:4 refers to the fact that "his feet shall stand in that day upon the mount of Olives, which is before Jerusalem on the east." This would certainly confirm a bodily return.

A visible and glorious return. The Scriptures leave no doubt that when Christ returns in power and glory it will be visible and is compared to lightning shining from the east even unto the west (Matt. 24:27). That it will be visible is implied by Acts 1:11 in that the ascension was visible. Revelation 1:7 states explicitly: "Behold, he cometh with the clouds; and every eye shall see him, and they that pierced him; and all the tribes of the earth shall mourn over him." In contrast to His first coming in which His glory was hidden, it is clear that in His second coming Christ appears in all the full glory of His deity. The description given in Revelation 19:11-12 coupled with the earlier description of Revelation 1:12-17 should leave no doubt as to the extent of His glory. His glory is magnified by the fact that He cometh with clouds as the Scriptures indicate (Matt. 24:30; Rev. 1:7) even as He ascended: "And the cloud received him out of their sight" (Acts 1:9). Every description of the second coming would indicate that it is the most spectacular and glorious event ever to take place on the earth.

A geographical event. The specific character of the second coming is further indicated by its relation to a return to the earth in the vicinity of Jerusalem. This is plainly noted in the Old Testament prophecies of Zechariah (14:1-4) and in the fact that in Romans 11:26 He is said to fulfill the prediction that "there shall come out of Zion the Deliverer." In the frequent mention of Christ in His second coming in relation to Zion as revealed in the Old Testament, the prophets predict both that Christ will come to Zion and that thereafter He will come out of Zion (cf. Ps. 14:7; 20:2; 53:6; 110:2; 128:5; 134:3; 135:21; Isa. 2:3; Joel 3:16; Amos 1:2). Further confir-

---

[6]Cf. *ibid.*, p. 157.

mation of the geographical return of Christ is found in the book of Revelation where He comes to judge the armies gathered in Palestine in rebellion against Him (Rev. 19:11-21). The geographical nature of Christ's return serves to confirm His coming as a specific future prophetic event.

Accompanied by the holy angels and the saints. In keeping with the pretribulational rapture of the church, the second coming of Christ to the earth is pictured as an event in which He is accompanied by the holy angels and the saints. Specific mention is made of this fact in Matthew 25:31: "When the Son of man shall come in his glory, and all the angels with him. . . ." According to the prophecy of Jude, quoting Enoch, the second coming is described in the words: "Behold, the Lord came with ten thousands of his holy ones." Some have taken the statement in 1 Thessalonians 3:13, "the coming of our Lord Jesus with all his saints," as a similar reference though the passage itself is not conclusive. In the description of the second coming in Revelation 19:11-21 it is further stated: "The armies which are in heaven followed him upon white horses, clothed in fine linen, white and pure" (v. 14). The armies here mentioned may be angelic beings, if so, are in contrast to the church which is described earlier in the passage as the wife of the Lamb (v. 7). In view of the fact that the event pictured in Revelation 19:7 is the marriage feast of the Lamb, it would follow in the oriental custom of marriage that the bridegroom had previously gone to receive the bride to himself. Then, the event in view is the final step, that is, the marriage feast. In this case, the wife would accompany the bridegroom.

To judge the earth. One of the most prominent features of the second coming mentioned in most of the passages is the prediction that Christ in His second coming returns to judge the earth. This is introduced in Matthew 19:28 where Christ predicts that the Twelve Apostles will judge the twelve tribes of Israel "when the Son of man shall sit on the throne of his glory." The major portion of Matthew 24:29—25:46 bears out that Christ will judge both Jew and Gentile living in the world at the time of His second advent. The various parables and illustrations found in the Gospels in connection with the second advent are all to the same point (cf. Luke 12:37, 45-47). Likewise in Luke 17:29-30 the judgment of Christ at the second advent is compared to the judgment upon Sodom when fire and brimstone destroyed them. Second Thessalonians 1:7-9 describes "the revelation of the Lord Jesus from heaven with the angels of his power in flaming fire, rendering vengeance to them that know not God, and to them that obey not the gospel of our Lord Jesus: who shall suffer punishment, even eternal destruction from the face of the Lord and from the glory of his might."

The time of this event is plainly stated in 2 Thessalonians 1:10 as the time "when he shall come to be glorified in his saints." According to 2 Thessalonians 2:8, the second advent will also be the occasion when the lawless one shall be judged, "whom the Lord Jesus shall slay with the breath of his mouth, and bring to nought by the manifestation of his coming." According to Jude 1:15, the Lord's coming is with the divine purpose "to execute judgment upon all, and to convict all the ungodly of all their works of ungodliness which they have ungodly wrought, and of all the hard things which ungodly sinners have spoken against him." Revelation 2:27 pictures the reign of Christ as being shared by the faithful saints who in Christ's name "shall rule them with a rod of iron, as the vessels of the potter are broken to shivers." The final description is given in Revelation 19:11-21 where Christ is described as being "arrayed in a garment sprinkled with blood." It is further revealed: "And out of his mouth proceedeth a sharp sword, that with it he should smite the nations: and he shall rule them with a rod of iron: and he treadeth the winepress of the fierceness of the wrath of God, the Almighty." The passage also describes the utter destruction of men and horses, and the false prophet and the beast will be cast alive into the lake of fire. Satan himself is cast into the abyss where he is chained until the end of the thousand-year reign of Christ after which he too is cast into the lake of fire.

A problem exists in some of the descriptive passages of

the second advent relative to the use of fire as a divine judgment in connection with the establishment of the millennial reign of Christ. According to 2 Peter 3:7 the earth eventually is to be destroyed by fire and in verse 10 it is stated: "The day of the Lord will come as a thief; in the which the heavens shall pass away with a great noise, and the elements shall be dissolved with fervent heat, and the earth and the works that are therein shall be burned up." The idea of complete destruction of the earth at the beginning of the millennium is contradicted, however, by numerous passages where the present characteristics of the earth are carried over into the millennium, such as the location of the city of Jerusalem and the geographic identification of certain areas according to their present occupants by the nations involved. If the earth is destroyed by fire at the beginning of the millennium, it would also be difficult to explain the continuity of men in natural bodies and the continued existence of plant and animal life. The best solution to the problem is that the expression "the day of the Lord" is an extensive time period which includes not only the tribulation and the judgments taking place at the second advent, but which includes also the entire millennial reign of Christ as a time period in which the Lord deals directly with human sin. The destruction of the earth described, therefore, in 2 Peter 3:10 is at the close of the Day of the Lord, rather than at the second coming, and is properly located at the end of the millennium when all wickedness in the earth will be judged in a final way.

To deliver the elect. The second advent of Christ to the earth not only brings judgment upon the wicked, but it is an event which brings deliverance to the elect, the saved of both Jews and Gentiles, and to the nation Israel as such. In Matthew 24:22 it is revealed that the second advent cuts short the great tribulation which would otherwise have eventually brought death to all flesh upon the earth. The judgment is limited to the time indicated in Scripture "for the elect's sake" (Matt. 24:22). The same idea is indicated in Romans 11:26-27 where it is predicted: "And so all Israel shall be saved: even as it is written, There shall come out of Zion the Deliverer; he shall turn away ungodliness from Jacob." Luke 21:28 indicates that when they shall see the second advent of Christ they are exhorted to "look up, and lift up your heads; because your redemption draweth nigh." This is in keeping with many passages in the Old Testament which likewise describe deliverance that will take place at the time of the second advent (cf. Zech. 14:1-4).

To bring spiritual revival to Israel. Along with the deliverance of the godly, the Scriptures predict that at the second coming Israel will experience spiritual revival. This is intimated in Romans 11:26-27 and is involved in the fulfillment of numerous Old Testament passages of which Jeremiah 31:31-34 may be taken as representative.

To re-establish the Davidic kingdom. In the discussion of the relation of Israel to Gentiles in the present age in the council at Jerusalem, it was brought out by James in his quotation from Amos 9:11-12, and other Old Testament predictions, that a future day was coming in which Israel would once again be restored. According to Amos, God has promised: "In that day will I raise up the tabernacle of David that is fallen, and close up the breaches thereof; and I will raise up its ruins, and I will build it as in the days of old" (Amos 9:11). According to Ezekiel 37:24, after Israel is regathered to their ancient land, David is going to be raised from the dead to be king over Israel, and God will make a covenant of peace with His people (Ezek. 37:26). To be fulfilled also is the prediction of the angel to Mary in Luke 1:31-33 in regard to Jesus: "He shall be great, and shall be called the Son of the Most High: and the Lord God shall give unto him the throne of his father David: and he shall reign over the house of Jacob for ever; and of his kingdom there shall be no end."

It should be clear from the many Scriptures dealing with the second coming and their graphic revelation of this glorious event that the future climax to the interadvent age is one of the most important events of all time, taking its place with the incarnation itself and the death and resurrection of Christ. The precise nature of the judgments in connection with the second advent and the resurrection of saints such as the tribulation martyrs gives the event tremendous significance.

Chapter XXIV

THE RESURRECTION AND JUDGMENTS
AT THE SECOND ADVENT

I. Seven Future Judgments

Practically all classes of conservative Bible expositors agree that there will be judgments at the time of the second coming of Christ. Postmillenarians and amillenarians usually subscribe to a general resurrection and a general judgment at this time in which all the righteous and the wicked dead are brought before the divine tribunal. Premillenarians of course postpone the judgment of the wicked dead until after the millennium, but find in the Scriptures ample evidence that the wicked living on the earth will be judged at the time of the second coming.

Seven judgments are distinguished in Scriptures as being related in some sense to end-time events. The first of these is the judgment of the church, the body of Christ, at the judgment seat of Christ, usually considered by pretribulationists to have taken place in heaven immediately after the rapture and prior to the return of Christ to the earth. A second divine judgment has to do with the resurrection and reward of tribulation saints as indicated in Revelation 20:4. Closely associated with this apparently is a third judgment of the resurrection and judgment of Old Testament saints as prophesied in the Old Testament in connection with the second advent. The fourth judgment has to do with Gentiles living in the world at the time of the second advent at which time the righteous are separated from the wicked living on the earth. A fifth judgment has to do with living Israel in the world at the time of the second advent who are regathered and judged relative to their place in the millennial reign of Christ. Two final judgments mark the close of the millennium—the judgment of the angels and Satan, and the judgment of the wicked dead at the great white throne. Though not mentioned in the Bible, it is apparent that there will be need for a judgment of millennial saints at the close of the millennium in addition to these that are revealed. The time and place of all these judgments, the character of the judgments, and the character of those being judged require that these judgments be distinguished. To affirm that all of these judgments take place in one great judgment, at the time of the second coming of Christ, requires extensive spiritualization of many of the details of the predictions involved and makes impossible a literal fulfillment. Without attempting a formal refutation of conflicting views, an outline of the premillennial interpretation of the judgments taking place at the beginning of the millennium can now be presented.

II. THE JUDGMENT OF THE CHURCH

Many references in the New Testament present the truth that the church will be judged by Christ Himself (Rom. 14:10-12; 1 Cor. 3:11-16; 4:1-5; 9:24-27; 2 Cor. 5:10-11; 2 Tim. 4:8). Inasmuch as the translation of the church, according to the pretribulational point of view, has already separated the righteous from the unrighteous, only saved people will be involved in the judgment of Christ in connection with the church. The judgment will have as its supreme question the matter of reward. According to 1 Corinthians 3:14, that which abides the fire of judgment will constitute a basis for reward. Those, however, who do not have ground for rewards shall nevertheless be saved, as stated in 1 Corinthians 3:15. It is intimated, however, in 1 Corinthians 4:5 that ". . . then shall each man have his praise from God." The reward is pictured in 1 Corinthians 9:24-27 like the prize awarded a runner, and Christians are exhorted so to live or run the race that they may obtain the prize: "Know ye not that they that run in a race run all, but one receiveth the prize? Even so run that ye may attain. And every man that striveth in the games exerciseth self-control in all things. Now they do it to receive a corruptible crown; but we an incorruptible. I therefore so run, as not uncertainly; so fight I, as not beating the air: but I buffet my body, and bring it into bondage: lest by any means, after that I have preached to others, I myself should be rejected." The original word, *adokimos*, translated "rejected," means *to be disapproved*, that is, disqualified for reward. It does not indicate a loss of salvation, as is made clear in 1 Corinthians 3:15. The "fear of the Lord" of which Paul speaks in 2 Corinthians 5:11 is the dread of standing before the judgment seat of Christ with a wasted life that is not due a reward. The judgment, distinguishing as it does that which is good and bad, again is primarily occupied with the question of reward, not of punishment. As Romans 8:1 states: "There is therefore now no condemnation to them that are in Christ Jesus." As creatures of grace, sins are forgiven, but rewards are distributed on the basis of effective testimony for Christ.

III. The Resurrection and Judgment of Tribulation Saints

One of the major revelations concerning the second coming of Christ is the prediction of the resurrections which will take place at that time. According to Revelation 20:4-6, the event described as the "first resurrection" takes place immediately after the second coming. The Apostle John records the vision in the following words: "And I saw thrones, and they sat upon them, and judgment was given unto them: and I saw the souls of them that had been beheaded for the testimony of Jesus, and for the word of God, and such as worshipped not the beast, neither his image, and received not the mark upon their forehead and upon their hand; and they lived, and reigned with Christ a thousand years" (Rev. 20:4-6).

The expression "first resurrection" has constituted an exegetical problem for all interpreters. Posttribulationists cite this reference as evidence that the rapture could not occur until after the tribulation. Pretribulationists have rightly held that the first resurrection is not an event, but an order of resurrection. It is evident that our Lord rose from the dead as the first one to receive a resurrection body—others previously raised from the dead had merely been restored to their former natural bodies. His resurrection, though widely separated from resurrections which follow, is included in the first resurrection, otherwise the event described in Revelation would not be "first." According to 1 Corinthians 15:20, Christ is "the firstfruits of them that are asleep," i.e., the first part of the resurrection of all saints. Likewise, the evidence that the translation of the church takes place before the tribulation would point to a large segment of the righteous dead being raised before the tribulation. These also would qualify as taking part in the first resurrection.

In contrast to the first resurrection of Revelation 20 is the resurrection of the wicked dead portrayed in the latter part of the chapter. The first resurrection therefore becomes the resurrection of all the righteous in contrast to the final resurrection which is the resurrection of the wicked. The question remains, however, concerning the identity of these who take part in the first resurrection at this time.

According to the description given in Revelation 20:4, those who are included in the first resurrection are those who have "been beheaded for the testimony of Jesus, and for the word of God, and such as worshipped not the beast, neither his image, and received not the mark upon their forehead and upon their hand." This is a description of those who were martyred for their faith in Christ during the time of the great tribulation, as predicted in Revelation 13:7-18. In Revelation 20:4, their resurrection is described in the words "they lived." All doubt is removed as to the meaning of the words "they lived" by their identification as those who have been partakers of the "first resurrection" (vv. 5-6). They are raised to reign with Christ a thousand years, or throughout the millennium, as priests of God and of Christ. Practically all conservative expositors agree that the tribulation saints are raised at this time, though some see it as the beginning phase of a general resurrection of all the righteous.

IV. The Resurrection and Judgment of Old Testament Saints

The chief problem relative to the resurrections at the second coming of Christ among premillenarians is the question of whether righteous Israel and Old Testament saints in general are raised at this time. A popular interpretation originating in

Darby and his associates is that resurrection of Old Testament saints takes place at the same time as the rapture of the church, that is, before the tribulation. This interpretation has been followed by such worthy expositors as William Kelly, A. C. Gaebelein, C. I. Scofield, and a host of others. Support for this interpretation is provided by three general arguments: (1) Christ died for Old Testament saints as well as for the church and therefore they are entitled to resurrection at the same time as the church. (2) According to 1 Thessalonians 4:16, the voice of the archangel is heard at the time of the rapture. Inasmuch as Michael, the archangel, is the special protector of Israel, his presence at the rapture would indicate Israel's resurrection. (3) The twenty-four elders of Revelation 4 are composed of both Old and New Testament saints and, inasmuch as these are pictured in heaven crowned and therefore rewarded in Revelation 4 before the tribulation, it would indicate that Old Testament saints as well as the church have already been raised from the dead.

Though the foregoing interpretation has had widespread recognition among premillenarians of the Brethren school of interpretation, there are good reasons for reconsideration. The reference to "the dead in Christ" (1 Thess. 4:16) by no means clearly includes all saints. The expression "in Christ" is uniformly used in the New Testament, wherever it has theological meaning, as a reference to those who have been baptized by the Spirit into the body of Christ, and is never used in reference to saints before the Day of Pentecost. It is significant that the word *saints,* a more general designation of the righteous, is not used but that a technical expression, "the dead in Christ," is used instead. It would seem to indicate a limitation of the prediction to those who die in the present dispensation.

The second argument relative to Michael, the archangel and special protector of Israel, is not based on explicit statement of the text. It is true that Michael is the special protector of Israel, but he is also the archangel, that is, the head of all the angels. In view of the spiritual conflict which has been raging ever since sin entered the universe, the presence of Michael at so tremendous an event as the rapture can hardly be taken *ipso facto* as evidence ʈhat his voice is directed to Israel only. It could conceivably be a shout of triumph in view of the tremendous accomplishment and victory over Satan and death which the rapture represents.

Of the three general arguments usually offered, that based on Revelation 4 is probably the most uncertain. It is by no means clear that the four and twenty elders represent both Old and New Testament saints. Some believe that the four and twenty elders represent only the church. Others believe that they are not redeemed men at all, but holy angels. The revised text of Revelation 5:9 opens the possibility of this latter interpretation. In view of the disagreement on the identification of the twenty-four elders even among premillenarians, the argument based upon this section becomes one of dubious value. It should be evident to an impartial observer that none of the arguments are explicit, and one is left without clear revelation concerning the time of Israel's resurrection as far as these passages are concerned.

Over against the obscurity in the New Testament, however, is the fact that the Old Testament seems to place the resurrection of Israel after the tribulation. In Daniel 12 immediately after the description of the great tribulation in the preceding chapter, a deliverance is promised Israel at the close of the tribulation in the following words: "And at that time shall Michael stand up, the great prince who standeth for the children of thy people; and there shall be a time of trouble, such as never was since there was a nation even to that same time: and at that time thy people shall be delivered, every one that shall be found written in the book. And many of them that sleep in the dust of the earth shall awake, some to everlasting life, and some to shame and everlasting contempt" (Dan. 12:1-2).

According to Daniel, the deliverance occurs after the "time of trouble," an obvious reference to the great tribulation, and it is predicted: "At that time thy people shall be delivered, every one that shall be found written in the book." In other words, a general deliverance for the righteous among Israel is promised. In this connection, in verse 2 it is stated: "And many of them that sleep in the dust of the earth shall awake, some to everlasting life, and some to shame and everlasting contempt." A problem arises within premillennial interpretation because there is brought together in one verse the resurrection of the righteous which according to premillenarians occurs before the millennium, and the resurrection of the wicked, which according to Revelation 20 occurs after the millennium. Some have tried to solve this difficulty by spiritualizing the resurrection of Daniel 12:2. A. C. Gaebelein, for instance, writes: "The physical resurrection is not taught in the second verse of this chapter, if it were the passage would be in clash with the revelation concerning resurrection in the New Testament. There is no general resurrection. . . . We repeat the passage has nothing to do with physical resurrection. Physical resurrection is however used as a figure of the national revival of Israel in that day. They have been sleeping nationally in the dust of the earth, buried among the Gentiles. But at that time there will take place a national restoration, a bringing together of the house of Judah and the house of Israel."[1]

Most premillenarians would agree with the point of view that there is a future restoration of the nation Israel and that this is sometimes portrayed in terms of resurrection as, for instance, in Ezekiel 37:1-14. The only reason, however, for assigning such an interpretation to Daniel 12 is Gaebelein's statement that to do so would "clash with the revelation concerning resurrection in the New Testament." Such a "clash," however, is by no means a necessary conclusion, as the distinction between resurrection before and after the millennium is not contradicted. Daniel places the resurrection of both after the tribulation. The only real contradiction is with the idea that Israel is not raised after the tribulation. Inasmuch as Revelation 20:4-6 clearly places the resurrection of tribulation saints after the tribulation there is no real problem in placing . the resurrection of Old Testament saints at the same time. Spiritualizing the resurrection of Daniel 12 would leave unsolved the resurrection of tribulation saints.

Tregelles translates Daniel 12:2 as follows. "And many from

---

[1]A. C. Gaebelein, *The Prophet Daniel*, p. 200.

among the sleepers of the dust of the earth shall awake; these shall be unto everlasting life; but those [the rest of the sleepers] shall be unto shame and everlasting contempt."[2] By this translation Tregelles solves easily and with proper reason the distinction between the resurrection of the righteous before the millennium and the resurrection of the wicked after the millennium. It also makes clear that this is a literal resurrection, not merely a restoration of the nation Israel.

Nathaniel West supplies a similar translation as follows: "The true rendering of Dan. xii. 1-3, in connection with the context, is 'And (at that time) *Many* (of thy people) shall awake (or be separated) *out from among* the sleepers in the earth-dust. *These* (who awake) shall be unto life everlasting, but *those* (who do not awake at that time) shall be unto shame and contempt everlasting.' So, the most renowned Hebrew Doctors render it, and the best Christian exegetes."[3]

As these translations bring out, there is really no justification in the text for spiritualizing the resurrection of the righteous dead in the Daniel passage. The principal reason offered by those who follow this interpretation is that this is necessary to conform to the New Testament, but the New Testament teaching does not require this interpretation.

A similar difficulty is found in another important Old Testament passage on the resurrection of Israel, namely, Isaiah 26:19 which is as follows: "Thy dead shall live; my dead bodies shall arise. Awake and sing, ye that dwell in the dust; for thy dew is as the dew of herbs, and the earth shall cast forth the dead." In the passage, as in Daniel, writers such as William Kelly insist that literal resurrection is not in view. Supposed support for this is found in the context in Isaiah 26:14 where, according to Kelly, a literal interpretation would mean that the expression, "they shall not live; they are deceased, they shall not rise," would teach that the unsaved are not raised at all.[4] This is by no means necessary, however, as the passage could

---

[2] S. P. Tregelles, *Remarks on the Prophetic Visions in the Book of Daniel*, p. 159; words in brackets supplied by Tregelles.
[3] Nathaniel West, *The Thousand Years in Both Testaments*, p. 266.
[4] Cf. William Kelly, *Exposition of Isaiah*, p. 265.

be interpreted as meaning that the unsaved in view here will die and therefore not be able to rise, that is, stand up. The issue of resurrection, then, is not involved in verse 14. By contrast, verse 19 is a very clear reference to resurrection where the expression, "Thy dead shall live; my dead bodies shall arise," seems to be a clear reference to resurrection. Again, one suspects that Kelly and those who follow this interpretation are being guided by their preconceived ideas that Israel must be raised at the time the church is translated.

While this point in doctrine is not one of major moment, those who insist that Israel is raised at the rapture are required thereby to spiritualize both the Daniel and Isaiah passages, which are the principal references to the resurrection of Israel in the Old Testament. In fact, it is difficult to find any passage which clearly teaches the general resurrection of righteous Israel in the Old Testament if the Daniel and Isaiah passages are disqualified from literal interpretation. It furthermore puts an unnecessary burden upon those who would follow the pretribulation view to link the resurrection of Israel with the rapture of the church, as the Daniel passage puts the resurrection of Israel after the tribulation and not before. It may be concluded, therefore, that the preferable view is that the resurrection of righteous Israel takes place when Christ comes to establish His millennial kingdom. This in no way complicates the pretribulation rapture and in fact strengthens this point of view, solving as it does many of the problems raised by posttribulationists against the idea that Israel is raised before the tribulation.

V. The Judgment of the Living Gentiles

One of the important truths related to the second coming of Christ is that "the times of the Gentiles" ends upon Christ's return to the earth. At that point it is fitting that a judgment of the Gentiles should take place as a preparation for the millennial kingdom. A number of important Old Testament Scriptures give the details of this judgment. Psalm 2 anticipates a judgment upon the Gentiles as a prelude to Israel's restoration as a nation. According to Isaiah 63:1-6, the Gentiles will be put down in that day and many of them put to death. A specific reference to this future judgment is found in Joel 3:1-2, 12 as follows: "For, behold, in those days, and in that time, when I shall bring back the captivity of Judah and Jerusalem, I will gather all nations, and will bring them down into the valley of Jehoshaphat; and I will execute judgment upon them there for my people and for my heritage Israel, whom they have scattered among the nations: and they have parted my land. . . . Let the nations bestir themselves, and come up to the valley of Jehoshaphat; for there will I sit to judge all the nations round about." Other important references are found in Zephaniah 3:8 and Zechariah 14:1-19.

The principal New Testament passage is found in Matthew 25:31-46. The context indicates that this judgment will occur immediately after the second coming of Christ as verse 31 states. Some have inferred that prior to this judgment Israel has already been regathered (cf. Matt. 24:31) and judged (Matt. 24:34—25:30). The time specified for the judgment of the Gentiles is simply stated as being "when the Son of man shall come in his glory."

The place of the judgment is clearly in the earth, rather than heaven. The coming of the Son of Man is from heaven to the earth and those who are gathered before Him are gathered from all parts of the earth. Neither the righteous nor the unrighteous who are gathered before Him are resurrected, but they are still in their natural bodies. This judgment, therefore, must be distinguished both by place and time from the judgment of the translated church which is in heaven and the judgment of the resurrected wicked dead at the great white throne which takes place in space after the present heaven and earth have been destroyed.

A matter of major significance is the question of the subjects of this judgment in Matthew 25. This is described as being "all the nations." The Greek word translated the *nations* is *ta ethne*. This word is used principally for races and peoples who are not Jewish with possibly the best translation being *the people.* It does not connote, as the English word *nation* does, a political entity, or a people from a specific geographic area. Because the word *nation* has been used, however, as an equivalent to *ta ethne,* some have thought that the representatives of the various nations of the world are here gathered and judged. A. C. Gaebelein teaches, for instance, that some of the nations will receive the testimony of those who preach during the tribulation time. These nations will enter into the kingdom and inherit it on their basis of the reception of the messengers.[5] A number of difficulties in this point of view, however, are immediately apparent. The natural question is, Which are the nations who will welcome the gospel during the tribulation? It seems clear that practically the entire world will go into apostasy and that all nations of the world will be affiliated with the blasphemous beast of Revelaton 13. Gaebelein recognizes this issue when he states: "The question may arise who these nations are, who will receive the Gospel of the Kingdom. This can hardly be answered now."[6] The fact is that in no age do entire nations accept a message and thereby justify eternal salvation.

A preferable view is that the nations here mentioned are not political entities, but simply Gentiles, as the word *ta ethne* is commonly translated in other passages (cf. Matt. 6:31-32; 12:21; 20:19; 28:19; Acts 11:18; 26:20). H. A. Ironside takes the position that the nations are individual Gentiles.[7] William Kelly has a similar point of view when he writes: "It follows that the persons meant by 'the sheep' and 'the goats' are respectively the righteous and the ungodly among the nations then living on the earth, when our Lord comes to judge in His quality of Son of Man."[8] The idea that the Gentiles in view here are individuals rather than national entities is made clear by reference to their works. Nations as such do not visit people in prison, nor are they as a corporate entity subject to promises of salvation or eternal judgment.

More important, however, than this distinction is the fact

---

[5]Cf. A. C. Gaebelein, *Gospel of Matthew,* II, 247.
[6]*Ibid.,* II, 248.
[7]H. A. Ironside, *Expository Notes on the Gospel of Matthew,* p. 338.
[8]William Kelly, *Lectures on the Gospel of Matthew,* p. 481.

that the Gentiles referred to in this judgment are living on the earth at the time of Christ's return and do not include the living Jews, the translated church, or resurrected saints in general. They are in the words of the Scripture "all the nations." As William Kelly points out: "Those gathered before Him here are 'all the nations'—a term never used about the dead or the risen, but only applied to men here below, and indeed applied only to the Gentiles as distinct from the Jews."[9]

George N. H. Peters in his Proposition 134 supports the same conclusion.[10] On the point of the meaning of "all nations," he states the following: "The question before us is this: Does the 'all nations' include *'the dead,'* or only *living nations?* In deciding this point we have the following: (1) Nothing is said of 'the dead.' To say that they are denoted is inferred from the fact that this passage is made—wrongfully—to synchronize with Rev. 20:11-15. (2) The word translated 'nations' is *never,* according to the uniform testimony of critics and scholars, used to designate *'the dead,'* unless this be a solitary exception. . . . (3) The word is employed to denote living, existing nations, and almost exclusively 'Gentile' nations. (4) The Spirit gives us abundant testimony that precisely *such a gathering of living nations* shall take place *just before* the Mill. age commences, and that there shall be *both* an Advent and judging [Peters cites Rev. 19:17-20; 16:13-16; Isa. 66:15-21; Zeph. 3:8-20; and Joel 3:9-21]."[11] Peters goes on to list other arguments such as the fact that the dead are not referred to as nations and that the passage is absolutely devoid of any reference to resurrection or that any of the righteous descended from heaven to be judged.[12] It seems a natural and normal conclusion that the reference to *ta ethne* in this passage refers to living Gentiles who are on the earth at the time of the second coming who are judged as a preliminary to the inauguration of the whole millennial reign of Christ.

The basis of their judgment is declared in the passage to

[9]*Ibid.,* p. 478.
[10]George N. H. Peters, *The Theocratic Kingdom*, II, 372-84.
[11]*Ibid.,* II, 374.
[12]*Ibid.,* II, 374-75.

be the treatment of the "brethren." Reference is made to the fact that the "sheep" have befriended the brethren and that the "goats" have failed to do so. The question arises as to the identity of the brethren. It will follow, however, that if the Gentiles are those who are non-Jews, those referred to as "my brethren" (Matt. 25:40) would be the Jews, specifically the Jews of the tribulation time who were the objects of fearful persecution. Under such circumstances, befriending a Jew by clothing him or visiting him in prison, when according to governmental edict they were to be hounded to the death, would inevitably reveal a confidence in the Scriptures and in God. While the appeal is to the "works," it seems clear that their works as such reveal faith in Christ and in the Word of God and are therefore the fruit or evidence of salvation. This is the basic reason why they are ushered into the millennial kingdom and called "the righteous."

The outcome of the judgment is that the righteous or the sheep enter the millennial kingdom, but obviously they are also admitted to the eternal kingdom of God. In contrast, the goats are cast into everlasting fire because their lack of works indicates that they do not belong to the redeemed. The judgment as here described is fully in keeping with premillennial truth. Such a judgment would in fact be absolutely necessary before the righteous kingdom of Christ could be inaugurated. It had formerly been indicated in Matthew 13 in the parable of the wheat and tares as well as the parable of the good and bad fish that the end of the age would have a judgment resulting in only the saved entering the kingdom. This, then, is confirmed by the specific revelation of Matthew 25. Though the outcome of the judgment may not be in the character of an eternal one, some have considered the judgment of the wicked here a final one and making unnecessary further judgment for this group at the great white throne. No revelation is given in Scripture concerning a future judgment of those who enter the millennial kingdom as the righteous.

VI. The Judgment of Living Israel

The Scriptures record many tremendous judgments of Israel

which have been already historically fulfilled and predict a future purging during the time of the great tribulation when only one third of the living Jews in the land will survive (Zech. 13:8-9). The remnant of Israel, however, surviving the tribulation and who are on earth at the time of the return of Christ, are the specific objects of a judgment described in Ezekiel 20:33-38. This passage, given in a context of predictions of judgment upon Israel, is obviously the climactic judgment of God upon that nation. As stated by Ezekiel, the event is described as follows: "As I live, saith the Lord Jehovah, surely with a mighty hand, and with an outstretched arm, and with wrath poured out, will I be king over you. And I will bring you out from the peoples and will gather you out of the countries wherein ye are scattered, with a mighty hand, and with an outstretched arm, and with wrath poured out; and I will bring you into the wilderness of the peoples, and there will I enter into judgment with you face to face. Like as I entered into judgment with your fathers in the wilderness of the land of Egypt, so will I enter into judgment with you, saith the Lord Jehovah. And I will cause you to pass under the rod, and I will bring you into the bond of the covenant; and I will purge out from among you the rebels, and them that transgress against me; I will bring them forth out of the land where they sojourn, but they shall not enter into the land of Israel: and ye shall know that I am Jehovah."

Like the predictions of judgment upon the Gentiles, this future event has its special characteristics which distinguish it from all past judgments upon the nation. It is described as a part of a work of God in declaring Himself to be "king over you" (v. 33). The judgment itself follows the final regathering of Israel predicted in verses 34-35. The judgment will take place in the specific geographic location described as "the wilderness of the peoples" (v. 35). Though this is not clearly to be identified with any locality, the comparison with the dealings of God with Israel on the way from Egypt to the promised land seems to indicate that the judgment takes place just outside the area given to Israel for perpetual possession. Just as Israel because of failure at Kadesh-Barnea was condemned to wander in the wilderness until all the adults except the few faithful ones died, and only then the nation could enter the promised land, so the rebels will be purged out at the future time when the millennial kingdom is established. Only those who are not rebels, that is, those who are true believers in Christ as their Messiah and Savior, will be allowed to participate in the blessing of the millennial kingdom.

The description given does not mention any resurrection from the dead and it may be assumed in view of the fact that regathering is a prerequisite to the judgment that this applies only to the living Israelites in the world at the time of the second coming. Those who are resurrected have a different judgment entirely. Like other judgments at the second coming of Christ, the judgment of works will be prominent, but as in the case of the Gentiles it will be what the works indicate rather than their intrinsic moral character. In the prophecies of Malachi a refining of the sons of Levi is predicted at the time of His coming and their particular sins are dealt with at that judgment (cf. Mal. 3:2-5). This conclusion is confirmed by the statements and parables of Matthew 24 and 25 which seem, with the exception of Matthew 25:31-46, to deal primarily with God's judgments upon Israel. In each case, the works brought into view demonstrate whether the person is saved or not.

The result of the Ezekiel judgment is that the rebels are cut off and therefore do not enter the land. This is to be interpreted as a judgment of physical death, and they will be raised from the dead at the judgment of the great white throne after the millennium to participate in the destiny of all the wicked. Those who remain alive, however, are counted righteous and enter into the millennial blessing provided for them. In the words of Ezekiel, God says to them: "I will bring you into the bond of the covenant" (v. 37). The covenant herein mentioned is no doubt the same as that revealed in Jeremiah 31:31-34. The blessings of that entrance into the promised land are summarized in Jeremiah 31:10-13 as follows: "Hear the word of Jehovah, O ye nations, and declare it in the isles afar off; and say, He that scattered Israel will gather him, and keep him as a shepherd doth his flock. For Jehovah hath ransomed Jacob, and redeemed him from the hand of him that was stronger than he. And they shall come and sing in the height of Zion, and shall flow unto the goodness of Jehovah, to the grain, and to the new wine, and to the oil, and to the young of the flock and of the herd: and their soul shall be as a watered garden; and they shall not sorrow any more at all. Then shall the virgin rejoice in the dance, and the young men and the old together; for I will turn their mourning into joy, and will comfort them, and make them rejoice from their sorrow."

Taking in view all the divine judgments that pertain to this sequence of events, it may be concluded that as the millennium begins all the righteous are judged in one way or another and that the wicked are put to death and declared unworthy to enter the millennial kingdom. The church has previously been judged and rewarded in heaven. Living Gentiles and living Jews are judged in their respective judgments and those who are righteous are permitted to enter the millennial kingdom. The Old Testament saints and resurrected Israel are also raised from the dead and given their places of honor and privilege and are associated with Christ in His millennial government.

VII. The Binding of Satan and His Later Final Judgment

An important judgment attending the others is the divine dealing of God with Satan as recorded in Revelation 20. The account as given in the Scriptures has been one of the major stumbling blocks to both postmillennialism and amillennialism. As stated in Scripture, the Apostle John describes his vision as follows: "And I saw an angel coming down out of heaven, having the keys of the abyss and a great chain in his hand. And he laid hold on the dragon, the old serpent, which is the Devil and Satan, and bound him for a thousand years, and cast him into the abyss, and shut it, and sealed it over him, that he should deceive the nations no more, until the thousand years

should be finished: after this he must be loosed for a little time"
(Rev. 20:1-3).

Anyone who attempts an exegesis of this passage is faced
with the obvious question as to whether Satan has been bound
already or whether this is a future event. On this question
also hangs the decision as to whether the millennium has already begun. Postmillennialists who are willing to postpone the
millennium until some distant time accommodate their interpretation to this passage by stating that Satan's binding is yet
future. The amillenarian, however, who believes that the millennium has already begun either on earth or in heaven, is
faced with the defense of the idea that Satan is now bound.

B. B. Warfield, whose eschatology seems to embrace some of
the elements of both amillennialism and postmillennialism, attempts to support the idea that Satan is bound in respect to
heaven. He writes: "The 'binding of Satan' is therefore in
reality not for a season but with reference to a sphere; and
his 'loosing' again is not after a period but in another sphere:
it is not subsequence but exteriority that is suggested. There
is, indeed, no literal 'binding of Satan' to be thought of at
all: what happens, happens not to Satan but to the saints,
and is only represented as happening to Satan for the purposes of the symbolical picture. What actually happens is that
the saints described are removed from the sphere of Satan's
assaults. The saints described are free from all access of Satan
—he is bound with respect to them: outside of their charmed
circle his horrid work goes on. This is indicated, indeed, in
the very employment of the two symbols 'a thousand years'
and 'a little time.' A 'thousand years' is the symbol of heavenly
completeness and blessedness; the 'little time' of earthly tur-
moil and evil. Those in the 'thousand years' are safe from
enduring his attacks."[18]

According to Warfield, therefore, there is no chronological
system whatever to the twentieth chapter of Revelation. The
millennium is not a millennium. The loosing of Satan is not
an event. Actually Satan is not bound at all, but saints are

---

[18]B. B. Warfield, *Biblical Doctrines*, p. 651.

really removed from his power by being taken to heaven. The nations mentioned in Revelation 20:3 are not nations upon earth but glorified saints in heaven. In a word, Revelation 20:1-3 is a picture of the intermediate state.

It is obvious that an interpretation such as Warfield's involves the complete spiritualization of all essential terms in this revelation. It is true, of course, that what is here recorded in the Scripture is a vision and as such is given in symbolic terms. What is ignored by Warfield and others, however, is the distinction between what John saw and the interpretation which was revealed. John saw the angel having the key of the abyss, binding Satan and casting him into the abyss, shutting it, and sealing it over him. The interpretation is given by inspired Scripture that this binding was for a period of time—one thousand years—and that the purpose of this binding was that Satan should no longer deceive the nations. It is further revealed that after the thousand years Satan will be loosed again for a short period of time. If we were left without an explanation of the binding of Satan, it might justify some spiritualization of the terms, but, inasmuch as the Scriptures explicitly tell us what the meaning is, there is no justification for denying a literal interpretation.

It should be noted also that the binding of Satan as represented in this passage is not the total of what God did. He was not only bound but cast into the abyss and shut up and sealed. Even a symbolic picture as here given would indicate total inactivity, not simply a limiting of the power of Satan. It is of course true that Satan has always been limited by the power of God as witnessed by the restraint of God in the case of Satan's dealing with Job. It has never been true up to the present time, however, that Satan has been shut up in the abyss and not permitted to deceive the nations. The popular idea advanced by such amillenarians as William Masselink and Floyd E. Hamilton, who espouse the Augustinian type of amillennialism, that Satan is partially bound in the present age, is not an adequate explanation of the text."[14]

---

[14]Cf. William Masselink, *Why a Thousand Years?* p. 202; Floyd E. Hamilton, *The Basis of Millennial Faith,* p. 130.

In contrast to these amillennial suggestions of a partial binding of Satan, what is the testimony of Scripture? Can Satan deceive the nations now? Is he actually bound in the abyss or is he free to deceive the nations? According to Acts 5:3, Satan is the one who filled the heart of Ananias and caused him to lie to the Holy Spirit. In 1 Corinthians 7:5 it is stated that Satan tempts believers. 2 Corinthians 4:3-4 reveals that Satan blinds the minds of the unbelieving lest they believe the gospel. The statement is made in 2 Corinthians 11:14 that Satan masquerades as an angel of light. Paul bears witness in 2 Corinthians 12:7 that his thorn in the flesh was a "messenger of Satan." Paul further declares in 1 Thessalonians 2:18 that Satan hindered him from coming back to the Thessalonian church. It is predicted in 2 Thessalonians 2:8-9 that the power of the future lawless one will be after "the working of Satan with all power and signs and lying wonders." Other passages such as 1 Timothy 1:20, 1 John 3:8, 10, likewise bear witness to the power of Satan. Peter exhorts us in 1 Peter 5:8: "Be sober, be watchful: your adversary the devil, as a roaring lion, walketh about, seeking whom he may devour." If one accepts these Scriptures testifying to the fact that Satan has power to tempt, to deceive, to blind, to buffet, to hinder, to work signs and lying wonders, and who is free like a raging lion to walk about seeking whom he may devour, how then can one hold that Satan is now bound? The only reasonable explanation of the revelation given to John is to assign this future event to the time of the second coming of Christ and the thousand years mentioned as the reign of Christ to follow His second advent. As Revelation 20 makes plain, Satan is to be loosed at the conclusion of the millennium at which time he will be cast into the lake of fire and brimstone into which the beast and the false prophet had been previously cast at the beginning of the millennium (Rev. 20:10). The final judgment of the wicked angels apparently occurs at the same time as Satan's final judgment when he is cast into the lake of fire and brimstone.

From the fact that God deals thus in judgment with all

wicked men living in the world as well as Satan, the way is open for the fulfillment of the prophecies of the millennial reign of Christ. The stage is set in this way for the extended period of righteousness and peace which shall cover the earth as the waters cover the sea.

Chapter XXV

THE RIGHTEOUS GOVERNMENT OF THE MILLENNIUM

I. Views of the Kingdom of God

The cumulative evidence for the millennial reign of Christ presented in preceding discussion serves as a logical introduction to the prophecies of the Old ＿and New Testaments fulfilled in the millennial reign of Christ. The doctrine of the millennial kingdom of God is one of the major revelations of Scripture pertaining to God's program. As a theme for theological investigation, it has attracted a host of writers who have developed the kingdom theme from various standpoints.

J. Dwight Pentecost has summarized the various viewpoints on the kingdom of God as follows: "To some the kingdom of God is synonymous with the eternal state, or heaven, into which one comes after death, so that it has no relationship to the earth whatsoever. To others it is a non-material or 'spiritual' kingdom in which God rules over the hearts of men, so that, while it is related to the present age, it is unrelated to the earth. To still others the kingdom is purely earthly without spiritual realities attached to it, so that it is a political and social structure to be achieved by the efforts of men and thus becomes the goal of the social and economic evolution to which men press. To others with the same general concept, it has to do with a nationalistic movement on the part of Israel that will reconstitute that nation as an independent nation in the political realm. Then there are those who view the kingdom as synonymous with the visible organized church, so that the church becomes the kingdom, thus making the kingdom both spiritual and political. In addition there are those that view the kingdom as manifestation, in the earthly realm, of the universal sovereignty of

God, in which He rules in the affairs of men, so that the kingdom is conceived as being both spiritual and material in its concept."[1]

Premillenarians of course recognize the validity of more than one aspect of the kingdom. They insist, however, that the millennial form of the kingdom of God is not fulfilled by the eternal state, nor a present rule of God in the hearts of men. The doctrine of the millennial kingdom as held by premillenarians contradicts the amillennial concept, which identifies to a large extent the kingdom of God with the soteriological divine program and denies thereby any future earthly political kingdom of the Messiah subsequent to His second advent. It should be obvious, however, that the millennial kingdom, though in some respects the consummation of much kingdom truth in Scripture, is not the sum total of God's kingdom purpose. There is, of course, a validity to the concept of an eternal kingdom to be identified with God's government of the universe. In contrast, however, to this universal aspect, the millennial kingdom is the culmination of the prophetic program of God relative to the theocratic kingdom or rule of the earth. This in one sense began in the creation of Adam in the Garden of Eden, continued through human government, was manifested in the kingly line which ruled Israel, and has its consummation in the millennial kingdom which in turn is superseded by the timeless eternity which follows. Though there is a rule of God in the present age which can properly be described by the word *kingdom*, it is not the fulfillment of those prophecies that pertain to the millennial reign of Christ upon the earth.

II. THE MILLENNIAL GOVERNMENT AN EARTHLY KINGDOM

One of the most significant facts relating to the millennial doctrine distinguishing it from the amillennial point of view is the teaching that the millennial kingdom is a rule of God on earth, thereby distinguishing it from a purely spiritual reign in the hearts of men through centuries of human history

---

[1] J. Dwight Pentecost, *Things to Come*, p. 427.

and distinguishing it from the will of God as expressed in heaven or in eternity future. The evidence for this is so abundant that it is strange that learned men have been able to deny this plain teaching of the Word of God. Psalm 2:8 records the invitation of the Father to His blessed Son: "Ask of me, and I will give thee the nations for thine inheritance, and the uttermost parts of the earth for thy possession."

Isaiah 11 paints the graphic picture of the reign of Christ on earth, a scene which cannot be confused with the present age, the intermediate state, or the eternal state if interpreted in any normal literal sense. As presented it describes the millennial earth. The righteous government of Christ is depicted in Isaiah 11: 4: "But with righteousness shall he judge the poor, and decide with equity for the meek of the earth; and he shall smite the earth with the rod of his mouth; and with the breath of his lips shall he slay the wicked." The description which follows describes animals such as wolves, lambs, leopards, kids, calves, young lions, all of which are creatures of earth and not of heaven, and further pictures them in a time of tranquillity such as only can apply to the millennial earth. The sweeping statement of Isaiah 11:9 confirms this judgment: "They shall not hurt nor destroy in all my holy mountain; for the earth shall be full of the knowledge of Jehovah, as the waters cover the sea." In the verses following, various countries of the earth are mentioned as having some part in the dealings of God at that time and therefore confirm that the earth is in view, not heaven. For similar passages see Isaiah 42:4; Jeremiah 23:3-6; Daniel 2:35-45; Zechariah 14:1-9.

By no theological alchemy should these and countless other references to earth as the sphere of Christ's millennial reign be spiritualized to become the equivalent of heaven, the eternal state, or the church as amillenarians have done. A righteous reign of Christ on earth is of course precisely what one would have expected from previous study of the Abrahamic covenant with its promises to the earth, the Davidic covenant relative to the Son of David reigning on the throne forever, and the many promises pertaining to Israel's regathering and re-establishment in their ancient land. The theocratic kingdom, therefore, of which the prophets spoke is an earthly kingdom which can find its fulfillment only in a literal reign of Christ upon the earth.

III. Jesus Christ the Supreme King of the Millennial Kingdom

In Psalm 2:6, in spite of the opposition of the kings of the earth, God declares His purpose: "Yet I have set my king upon my holy hill of Zion." This purpose will be fulfilled in the millennial kingdom in the reign of Jesus Christ as the Son of David. As Lewis Sperry Chafer has succinctly stated: "Every Old Testament prophecy on the kingdom anticipates His kingly office: (a) Christ will yet sit on the throne as David's heir (2 Sam. 7:16; Ps. 89:20-37; Isa. 11:1-16; Jer. 33:19-21). (b) He came as a King (Luke 1:32-33). (c) He was rejected as a King (Mark 15:12-13; Luke 19:14; cf. Gen. 37:8; Ex. 2:14). (d) He died as a King (Matt. 27:37). (e) When He comes again, it is as a King (Rev. 19:16; cf. Luke 1:32-33)."[2]

The fact that Christ will reign over the earth is of course imbedded in practically every prophecy concerning the millennial kingdom. The absolute character of His reign is indicated in Isaiah 11:3-5. This central prophecy is confirmed by the angel to Mary in announcing the coming birth of Christ in these words: "He shall be great, and shall be called the Son of the Most High: and the Lord God shall give unto him the throne of his father David: and he shall reign over the house of Jacob for ever; and of his kingdom there shall be no end" (Luke 1:32-33). It should be clear from the details surrounding these predictions that these prophecies are not being fulfilled in the present age, nor are they a description of the sovereignty of God in the heavenly sphere. Many other Scriptures can be cited to substantiate the reign of Christ as King in the millennium of which the following are representative: Isaiah 2:1-4; 9:6-7; 11:1-10; 16:5; 24:23; 32:2; 40:1-11; 42:3-4; 52:7-15; 55:4; Daniel 2:44; 7:27; Micah 4:1-8; 5:2-5; Zechariah 9:9; 14:16-17. These pas-

---

[2]L. S. Chafer, *Systematic Theology*, VII, 233.

sages if interpreted in the ordinary literal meaning lead to the conclusion that Christ is the King who will reign over the earth in the millennial period.

A legitimate problem has arisen in the interpretation of the reign of Christ concerning how this relates to various prophecies which speak of David as King in the millennial kingdom. References to this concept are found in Jeremiah 30:9; 33:15-17; Ezekiel 34:23-24; 37:24-25; Hosea 3:5, with more indirect references in Isaiah 55:3-4, and Amos 9:11. Several solutions have been offered to resolve this problem. One of the most common is to take references to David as indicating Christ Himself as the greater David. Keil and Peters, as well as Ironside, support this view.[3] There are obvious difficulties, however, in this point of view in that Christ is never referred to as David elsewhere in the Bible though He is frequently called the Son of David, Seed of David, etc. A second view held by some interpreters is that the reference in some passages is to a future literal son of David who will sit on the Davidic throne, but who is not to be identified as Christ. Passages such as Jeremiah 33:15-21 are cited in support of this view. From many standpoints, however, this is less desirable than the first view. As many have indicated, no one today aside from Christ could prove His kingly lineage among the people of Israel. It is most unlikely that there should be another person closely related to Christ who is a descendent of David other than David himself.

A third solution of the problem is more simple and seemingly in keeping with the prophetic references throughout Scripture, namely, that by David is meant the resurrected David who shares with Christ as prince some of the government duties of the millennial kingdom. It should be clear from many Scriptures that the reign of Christ is shared with others. As Newell has written: "David is not the son of David. Christ, as Son of David, will be King; and David, His father after the flesh, will be *prince*, during the Millennium."[4] In the light of many

---

[3]Cf. Karl Friedrich Keil, *The Twelve Minor Prophets*, I, 72; Peters, *The Theocratic Kingdom*, III, 572; Ironside, *Ezekiel the Prophet*, p. 262.
[4]William R. Newell, *The Revelation*, p. 323.

prophecies which promise saints the privilege of reigning with Christ, it would seem most logical that David the king raised from the dead should be given a place of prominence in the Davidic kingdom of the millennial reign of Christ. As indicated in Revelation 19:16, Christ is "KING OF KINGS AND LORD OF LORDS." This would certainly imply other rulers (cf. Isa. 32:1; Ezek. 45:8-9; Matt. 19:28; Luke 19:12-27).

IV. CHARACTERISTICS OF DIVINE GOVERNMENT IN THE MILLENNIUM

From a governmental standpoint, the reign of Christ in the millennium will have three important characteristics. First, it will be a rule over the entire earth. It was God's intent from the beginning of the creation of man that the earth should be ruled over by man. Adam sacrificed his right to rule when sin entered the human race. God's purpose, however, is fulfilled in Jesus Christ. In Psalm 2:6-9 God declares His purpose to set His king in Zion who will have as His possession "the uttermost parts of the earth." In Daniel 2:35 a stone which fills the whole earth is an anticipation of the universal rule of Christ. Daniel 7:14 is explicit: "And there was given him dominion, and glory, and a kingdom, that all the peoples, nations, and languages should serve him: his dominion is an everlasting dominion, which shall not pass away, and his kingdom that which shall not be destroyed." This idea is repeated in Daniel 7:27 and becomes a frequent theme of prophecy (cf. Ps. 72:8; Mic. 4:1-2; Zech. 9:10). The title of Christ given in Revelation 19:16, "KING OF KINGS AND LORD OF LORDS," makes it plain that He is supreme ruler over the entire earth.

The second important characteristic of the millennial rule of Christ is that His government will be absolute in its authority and power. This is demonstrated in His destruction of all who oppose Him (cf. Ps. 2:9; 72:9-11; Isa. 11:4). Such an absolute rule, of course, is in keeping with the person and majesty of the King in whom is all the power and sovereignty of God.

The third important aspect of the government of Christ in the millennium will be that of righteousness and justice. Most of the millennial passages emphasize this as the outstanding feature of the millennium. Isaiah 11:3-5 assures the poor and the meek that their cause will be dealt with righteously in that day. The wicked are warned to serve the Lord lest they feel His wrath (Ps. 2:10-12). It seems evident from many passages that no open sin will go unpunished.

The subjects of the millennial rule of Christ at the beginning of the millennium will consist in those who survive the searching judgments of both Israel and Gentiles as the millennial reign of Christ begins. From many Scriptures it may be gathered that all the wicked will be put to death after the second coming of Christ, and only saints who have lived through the preceding time of trouble will be eligible for entrance into the millennial kingdom. This is demonstrated in the judgment of the Gentiles in Matthew 25:31-46, where only the righteous are permitted to enter the millennium. According to Ezekiel 20:33-38, God will also deal with Israel and purge out all rebels, that is, unbelievers, permitting only the saints among Israel to enter the millennial kingdom. The parables of the wheat and the tares (Matt. 13:30-31) and of the good and bad fish (Matt. 13:49-50) teach likewise that only the wheat and the good fish, representing the righteous, will survive the judgment. Confirmation is also found in Isaiah 65:11—66:16; Jeremiah 25:30-33. As the millennium continues, however, children will be born to those who are thus ushered into the millennial reign of Christ. Before many generations the children born to these tribulation saints will far outnumber their parents. They too will be subject to Christ's reign and if openly rebellious will be put to death (Isa. 66:20, 24; Zech. 14:16-19). While it is obvious that even under the rule of Christ there will arise from children born in the millennium those who merely profess to follow the King without actually being saints, the true character of these is manifested at the end of the millennium in the final revolt. Meanwhile they are forced to obey the King or be subject to the penalty of death or other chastisement.

V. The Place of Israel in the Government of Christ

In contrast to the present church age in which Jew and Gentiles are on an equal plane of privilege, the millennium is clearly a period of time in which Israel is in prominence and blessing. Though many passages speak of Gentile blessing as well, Christ will reign as the Son of David, and Israel as a nation will be exalted.

Passages of the Old Testament which have been studied previously anticipating a future day of glory for Israel find their fulfillment in the millennial reign of Christ. The regathering of Israel, a prominent theme of most of the prophets, has its purpose realized in the re-establishment of Israel in their ancient land. Israel as a nation is delivered from her persecutors in the time of tribulation and brought into the place of blessing and restoration.

J. Dwight Pentecost gives an excellent summary of the important place of Israel in the millennium in the following statement: "Israel will become the subject of the King's reign (Isa. 9:6-7; 33:17, 22; 44:6; Jer. 23:5; Mic. 2:13; 4:7; Dan. 4:3; 7:14, 22, 27). In order to be subjects, Israel, first, will have been converted and restored to the land, as has already been shown. Second, Israel will be reunited as a nation (Jer. 3:18; 33:14; Ezek. 20:40; 37:15-22; 39:25; Hos. 1:11). Third, the nation will again be related to Jehovah by marriage (Isa. 54:1-17; 62:2-5; Hos. 2:14-23). Fourth, she will be exalted above the Gentiles (Isa. 14:1-2; 49:22-23; 60:14-17; 61:6-7). Fifth, Israel will be made righteous (Isa. 1:25; 2:4; 44:22-24; 45:17-25; 48:17; 55:7; 57:18-19; 63:16; Jer. 31:11; 33:8; 50:20, 34; Ezek. 36:25-26; Hos. 14:4; Joel 3:21; Mic. 7:18-19; Zech. 13:9; Mal. 3:2-3). Sixth, the nation will become God's witnesses during the millennium (Isa. 44:8, 21; 61:6; 66:21; Jer. 16:19-21; Mic. 5:7; Zeph. 3:20; Zech. 4:1-7; 4:11-14; 8:23). Seventh, Israel will be beautified to bring glory to Jehovah (Isa. 62:3; Jer. 32:41; Hos. 14:5-6; Zeph. 3:16-17; Zech. 9:16-17)."[5]

The lesser role of Gentiles in the millennium is the subject of many Old Testament Scriptures such as the following: Isaiah 2:4; 11:12; 16:1-5; 18:1-7; 19:16-25; 23:18; 42:1; 45:14; 49:6, 22; 59:6-8; 60:1-14; 61:8-9; 62:2; 66:18-19; Jeremiah 3:17; 16:19-21; 49:6; 49:39; Ezekiel 38:23; Amos 9:12; Micah 7:16-17; Zepha-

---

niah 2:11; 3:9; Zechariah 8:20-22; 9:10; 10:11-12; 14:16-19.[6] Outstanding in these Scriptures is the fact that, first, the Gentiles will share many of the spiritual and economic blessings of the millennial reign of Christ. Second, they will, however, occupy a subordinate role to Israel (Isa. 14:1-2; 49:22-23; 61:5-9). Third, as indicated previously, only Gentiles who are declared righteous by the King will be allowed entrance into the millennial kingdom at it beginning.

---

[6]Cf. *ibid.*, p. 508.

CHAPTER XXVI

SPIRITUAL LIFE IN THE MILLENNIUM

One of the objections frequently raised against the doctrine of the millennium is that it substitutes a materialistic and earthly kingdom for one which is primarily spiritual. Augustine, for instance, is cited as one who forsook millennialism because of its alleged carnal and sensuous character. Amillenarians frequently attempt to refute premillennial doctrine by evidence that the kingdom introduced by Jesus was a spiritual kingdom. Oswald T. Allis, for instance, writes: "The Kingdom announced by John and by Jesus was primarily and essentially a moral and spiritual kingdom."[1] He goes on to say: ". . . from the very outset Jesus not merely gave no encouragement to, but quite definitely opposed, the expectation of the Jews that an earthly, Jewish kingdom of glory, such as David had established centuries before, was about to be set up."[2]

In answer to this common objection, premillenarians first of all concede that there is a present spiritual kingdom, a rule of God existing now in the hearts of men who are willingly obedient to God. To this kingdom every Christian in the present dispensation belongs. This kingdom, however, is to be contrasted to the future millennial kingdom, not by the demonstration that the future kingdom is devoid of spirituality, but rather by the fact that its spirituality is expressed in a special way, namely, the rule of Christ on earth with many accompanying special features of spiritual life and activity. Instead of a carnal and materialistic concept of the kingdom, the Scriptural description of the millennium presents a rule of God fulfilling the highest standards of spirituality.

---

[1] Oswald T. Allis, *Prophecy and the Church*, p. 70.
[2] *Ibid.*, p. 71.

I. THE GLORIOUS PRESENCE OF CHRIST IN THE MILLENNIUM

Of central importance in the spiritual life of the millennial kingdom is the fact that Christ in His glorious person will be present and visible in the world during this period. This was the burden of Old Testament prophecy according to Peter: ". . . who prophesied of the grace that should come unto you: searching what time or what manner of time the Spirit of Christ which was in them did point unto, when it testified beforehand the sufferings of Christ, and the glories that should follow them" (1 Pet. 1:10-11). The glories that were predicted to follow are not only that glory which is Christ's in heaven but that which is manifested to the earth at His second advent. It is stated also in Matthew: ". . . then shall all the tribes of the earth mourn, and they shall see the Son of man coming on the clouds of heaven with power and great glory" (Matt. 22:30).

Imbedded in countless prophecies of the millennium are predictions of the manifested glory which will feature the millennial earth. Isaiah writes: "Every valley shall be exalted, and every mountain and hill shall be made low; and the uneven shall be made level, and the rough places a plain: and the glory of Jehovah shall be revealed, and all flesh shall see it together; for the mouth of Jehovah hath spoken it" (Isa. 40:4-5).

It was a prayer of Solomon relative to the future kingdom: "And blessed be his glorious name for ever; and let the whole earth be filled with his glory" (Ps. 72:19). The glory of the God of Israel will truly be manifested in Christ in abundant measure. It is indicated in so many Scriptures that one wonders how amillenarians can equate the millennium with the inglorious present age.

H. C. Woodring has provided an analytical summary of the glory of Christ in the millennium.[3] The glory of the humanity of Christ is manifested in His glorious dominion (Heb. 2:8-9); a glorious government (Ps. 2:8-9; 72:19; Isa. 9:6-7; 11:4); a glorious inheritance of the promised land (Gen. 15:7; 17:8;

---

[3]For extensive discussion of the glory of Christ in the millennium see Hoyt Chester Woodring, Jr., "The Millennial Glory of Christ," unpublished master's thesis, Dallas Theological Seminary, pp. 62-134.

Dan. 8:9; 11:16, 41); a glorious prophet and lawgiver (Deut. 18:18-19; Isa. 2:2-4; 33:21-22; 42:4; Acts 3:22); a glorious house and throne fulfilling the Davidic covenant (2 Sam. 7:12-16; Isa. 9:6-7; Matt. 25:31; Lk. 1:31-33); and the glory of the kingdom itself (Ps. 72; Isa. 9:7; 11:10; Jer. 23:6).

In like manner Woodring cites the glory of Christ as it pertains to His deity in the millennium. Divine attributes such as omniscience (Isa. 66:15-18), and omnipotence (Ps. 46:1-5; Isa. 41:10, 17-18) are revealed in the millennium. As God He receives worship (Ps. 46:6-11; 86:9; Isa. 66:23; Zech. 14:16-19). Other attributes and divine qualities manifested in the millennial reign of Christ are righteousness (Ps. 45:4, 7; 98:2; Isa. 1:27; 10:22; 28:17; 60:21; 63:1; Dan. 9:24; Mal. 4:2); divine mercy (Ps. 89:2-3; Isa. 54:7-10; 63:7-19; Hos. 2:23); divine goodness (Isa. 52:7; Jer. 33:9-15; Zech. 9:17); and holiness (Isa. 4:3-4; 6:1-3; Ezek. 36:20-23; 45:1-5; Joel 3:17; Zech 2:12; Rev. 15:4); divine truth (Isa. 25:1; 61:8; Mic. 7:20).

The glorious presence of Christ in the millennial scene is of course the center of worship and spirituality. The many Scriptures bearing on this theme which cannot in any reasonable sense be applied to the present age nor limited to heaven point to the millennial kingdom of Christ on earth. The glory of Christ is further revealed in all aspects of the millennium and affects the spiritual life of the human race to an extent never realized in previous dispensations.

II. GENERAL CHARACTERISTICS OF SPIRITUALITY IN THE MILLENNIUM

Because of the fact that Christ is in the world and ruling over all nations, the millennium is characterized as a time in which the truth of God is widespread. Isaiah writes, for instance: "The earth shall be full of the knowledge of Jehovah as the waters cover the sea" (Isa. 11:9). Jeremiah in connection with the fulfillment of the new covenant records the prediction of God: "I will put my law in their inward parts, and in their heart will I write it; and I will be their God, and they shall be my people. And they shall teach no more every man his neighbor, and every man his brother, saying, Know Jehovah; for they shall all know me, from the least of them unto the greatest of them, saith Jehovah: for I will forgive their iniquity, and their sin will I remember no more" (Jer. 31:33-34). The present age obviously does not fulfill the prediction, "They shall all know me," but it will be true in the millennium.

Righteousness is another outstanding feature of the millennial earth. Solomon predicts: "In his days shall the righteous flourish" (Ps. 72:7) and Isaiah predicts concerning Christ: "And his delight shall be in the fear of Jehovah; and he shall not judge after the sight of his eyes, neither decide after the hearing of his ears; but with righteousness shall he judge the poor, and decide with equity for the meek of the earth; and he shall smite the earth with the rod of his mouth; and with the breath of his lips shall he slay the wicked. And righteousness shall be the girdle of his waist, and faithfulness the girdle of his loins (Isa. 11:3-5).

Coupled with righteousness is universal peace. Famous is the prediction of Isaiah: "And he will judge between the nations, and will decide concerning many peoples; and they shall beat their swords into plowshares, and their spears into pruning-hooks; nation shall not lift up sword against nation, neither shall they learn war any more" (Isa. 2:4). Solomon speaks of abundance of peace (Ps. 72:7). The agelong desire for peace among nations is an outstanding feature of the millennium.

Coupled with frequent references to righteousness and peace is a joy which will characterize the millennial earth. Isaiah speaking of millennial times predicts: "Therefore with joy shall ye draw water out of the wells of salvation. And in that day shall ye say, Give thanks unto Jehovah, call upon his name, declare his doings among peoples, make mention that his name is exalted" (Isa. 12:3-4). Picturing that future millennial day, Isaiah declares God's purpose: "to appoint unto them that mourn in Zion, to give unto them a garland for ashes, the oil of joy for mourning, the garment of praise for the spirit of heaviness. . . . Instead of your shame ye shall have double; and instead of dishonor they shall rejoice in their portion: therefore in their land

they shall possess double; everlasting joy shall be unto them"
(Isa. 61:3, 7).

Attending these tokens of divine grace is unusual manifestation of the power of the Holy Spirit in the millennial scene. Frequent mention of the power of the Spirit in the millennium is found in millennial passages (Isa. 32:15; 44:3; Ezek. 39:29; Joel 2:28-29). While the power of the Spirit has been manifested in some saints in previous generations, it will be common and abundant in the millennial period.

Taken as a whole, the spiritual life of the millennium as manifested in these particulars fully justifies the concept that the millennial kingdom is not the materialistic carnal picture sometimes ascribed to premillennialism. While different in many major respects from any preceding dispensation and embodying theocratic and political aspects, the kingdom is essentially spiritual in its principal characteristics. This is further illustrated in the worship of God which is predicted for the millennial age.

III. The Millennial Temple and Worship of God

A debated point and occasion for much criticism of premillennialism is the picture given of the millennial temple and the worship of God in the Old Testament predictions of the period. A major section of Ezekiel (40:1—46:24) describes a temple in detail as well as the ritual and priesthood connected with it. The explanation of the meaning of this prophecy has been a major problem in the premillennial interpretation of Scripture.

Five possible explanations have been given. Some have explained the Ezekiel description as either the specifications for the temple of Solomon or plans for the later temple built after the return of the Babylonian captivity. The Scriptures, however, give detailed specifications for both temples (1 Kings 6:2—7:51; 2 Chron. 3:3—4:22; Ezra 6:3-4), and a comparison of these with the Ezekiel passage will demonstrate beyond question that the Ezekiel temple is different in its structure than either of the other temples built by Israel in the Old Testament. Some have offered a third view in an attempt to explain these variations by considering Ezekiel's temple as an ideal which the returning pilgrims should have observed but did not. There is no Scripture, however, to substantiate that the returning captives knew anything of Ezekiel's temple. Still another concept is that the picture of Ezekiel's temple was intended to be a typical presentation only to be fulfilled by the church in the present age. This of course provides no exegesis of the passages and raises innumerable problems

The fifth view, and the only one which provides any intelligent explanation of this portion of Scripture is that which assigns Ezekiel's temple to the future millennial period. Inasmuch as no fulfillment of this passage has ever taken place in history, if a literal interpretation of prophecy be followed, it would be most reasonable to assume that a future temple would be built in the millennium as the center of worship. Premillenarians such as Merrill F. Unger, Arno C. Gaebelein, and James M. Gray have written cogently in support of a future temple to be built in the millennium in fulfillment of Ezekiel's prophecy.[4] Other premillenarians such as H. A. Ironside feel uncertain whether Ezekiel's temple will be built.[5] Some have been troubled by the dimensions of Ezekiel's temple. Though it is true that the dimensions of the future temple would not fit the temple site as used historically in previous temples, a changed topography of Palestine in the millennium predicted in many passages would permit a rearrangement of the amount of space assigned to the temple. Actually, other views do not provide any legitimate explanation of the size of the temple either, except to deny literal fulfillment.

The only real problem in connection with a future literal temple is not the question as to whether such a temple could be built in the millennium, but the fact that this would indicate also a literal interpretation of the temple ritual and sacrifices.

---

[4]Cf. Merrill F. Unger, *Great Neglected Bible Prophecies*, pp. 55-95; A. C. Gaebelein, *The Prophet Ezekiel*, pp. 271-73; James M. Gray, *Christian Workers' Commentary*, pp. 265-66.
[5]Cf. H. A. Ironside, *Ezekiel*, pp. 284-85.

This introduces some real problems.[6] Allusions are made to these sacrifices in the details of the construction of the temple (Ezek. 40:39-42) with further details on the sacrifices themselves (Ezek. 43:18—46:24). Ezekiel is not alone in his testimony to millennial sacrifices as Isaiah refers to it (Isa. 56:7) and implies the institution of a sacrificial system and observance of the Sabbath (Isa. 66:20-23). Jeremiah refers to the same thing (Jer. 33:18). Zechariah has similar references (Zech. 14:16-21). The details such as are offered for these sacrifices make it clear that it is a distinct system from the Mosaic, but that it involves animal sacrifices as well as other forms of worship similar to that provided in the Mosaic law. The suggestion that there would be literal sacrifices in the millennium is a focal point of opposition from amillenarians and is not necessarily embraced by all premillenarians.

Objections to sacrifices in the millennium stem mostly from New Testament affirmations concerning the one sacrifice of Christ. According to Hebrews 7:27, Christ "needeth not daily, like those high priests, to offer up sacrifices, first for his own sins, and then for the sins of the people: for this he did once for all, when he offered up himself." According to Hebrews 9:12 Christ "through his own blood, entered in once for all into the holy place, having obtained eternal redemption." A similar expression is found in Hebrews 9:26 where it affirms: "Now once at the end of the ages hath he been manifested to put away sin by the sacrifice of himself." Similar expressions are found elsewhere. The question is naturally raised why the sacrifices should be observed in the millennium if the sacrifice of Christ once for all fulfilled the typical expectation of the Old Testament sacrificial system. While other objections are also made of a lesser character, it is obvious that this constitutes the major obstacle, not only to accepting the sacrificial system but the possibility of the future temple in the millennium as well.

Those who consider the millennial sacrifices as a ritual

---

[6]For a full discussion see John L. Mitchell "The Question of Millennial Sacrifices," *Bibliotheca Sacra*, July 1953, pp. 248-67; October 1953, pp. 342-61.

which will be literally observed in the millennium invest the sacrifices with the central meaning of a memorial looking back to the one offering of Christ. The millennial sacrifices are no more expiatory than were the Mosaic sacrifices which preceded the cross. If it has been fitting for the church in the present age to have a memorial of the death of Christ in the Lord's Supper, it is suggested that it would be suitable also to have a memorial of possibly a different character in the millennium in keeping with the Jewish characteristics of the period.

A. C. Gaebelein writes in support of this view: "But what is the meaning and the purpose of these animal sacrifices? The answer is quite simple. While the sacrifices Israel brought once had a prospective meaning, the sacrifices brought in the millennial temple have a retrospective meaning. When during this age God's people worship in the appointed way at His table, with the bread and wine as the memorial of His love, it is a retrospect. We look back to the Cross. We show forth His death. It is 'till He comes.' Then this memorial feast ends forever. Never again will the Lord's Supper be kept after the Saints of God have left the earth to be with the Lord in glory. The resumed sacrifices will be the memorial of the Cross and the whole wonderful story of the redemption for Israel and the nations of the earth, during the kingdom reign of Christ. And what a memorial it will be! What a meaning these sacrifices will have! They will bring to a living remembrance everything these sacrifices will have! They will bring to a living remembrance everything of the past. The retrospect will produce the greatest scene of worship, of praise and adoration this earth has even seen. All the Cross meant and the Cross has accomplished will be recalled and a mighty 'Hallelujah Chorus' will fill the earth and the heavens. The sacrifices will constantly remind the peoples of the earth of Him who died for Israel, who paid the redemption price for all creation and whose glory now covers the earth as the waters cover the deep.[7]

Other writers such as William Kelly, Adolph Saphir, and Nathaniel West subscribe to the same point of view. Though

---

[7]A. C. Gaebelein, *The Prophet Ezekiel*, pp. 312-13.

West is not as sure that all of the details of Ezekiel's prophecy will be fulfilled literally, he does say this of Ezekiel's predictions: "But to return to Chapters xl-xlviii,—so long perplexing to so many,—the favorite retreat of postmillennialists, and the ready refuge when pressed by Chiliastic argument. Intrenched here, they deem themselves secure. How interpret these Chapters? Do they belong to the 1000 years of John? Are these also a Millennial picture? We answer, Yes. They cannot be literalized into the times of the Restoration under Zerubbabel, nor spiritualized into the times of the New Testament Church, nor celestialized into the heavenly state, nor allegorized into the final New Heaven and Earth, nor idealized into an oriental phantasmagorial abstraction. Whatever difficulties attend the interpretation which regards them simply as the expansion of Chapter xxxviith, a picture of Israel's dwelling safely in their own land glorified, with the temple shining on exalted Zion, as the prophets have predicted it, more and greater difficulties attend any other exposition. . . . That *bloody sacrifices* seem a stumbling block, never can avail to dislodge the section from its place in prophecy or history. The picture is a picture of *restored Israel* from an Exile-point of view, when the Temple was destroyed, the City laid waste by the king of Babylon, Israel's instituted worship wrecked, and the prophet-priest, Ezekiel, was moved by 'the hand of God' to comfort the exiles of the Gola! It covers, perspectively, the *whole temporal future* of the people, and blends the Restoration, the Non-Restoration, the Abolition, the future Restitution, all in one. Isaiah had chiefly dwelt upon the *prophetic* side of the kingdom, in thrilling terms, Daniel dwells upon the *kingly* side and, to Ezekiel it is given to paint the *priestly* side of it."[8] Though West elsewhere refers to Israel "offering perpetual spiritual sacrifice to God through Jesus Christ" (p. 239), he cannot resist the literal character of Ezekiel's prophecy.

H. Bonar likewise writes in support of the literal view as follows: "The temple, the worship, the rites, the sacrifices, have all their centre in the Lamb that was slain. To Him they point,

---

[8]Nathaniel West, *The Thousand Years in Both Testaments*, pp. 424-26.

and of Him they speak. Why should they not be allowed to do so in the millennial age, if such be the purpose of the Father? They are commemorative not typical. They are retrospective then, not prospective, as of old. And how needful will retrospection be then, especially to Israel? How needful, when dwelling in the blaze of a triumphant Messiah's glory, to have ever before them some memorial of the cross, some palpable record of the humbled Jesus, some visible exposition of his sin-bearing work, in virtue of which they have been forgiven, and saved, and loved,—to which they owe all their blessedness and honour, —and by means of which, God is teaching them the way in which the exceeding riches of His grace can flow down to them in righteousness. And if God should have yet a wider circle of truth to open up to us out of His word concerning his Son, why should he not construct a new apparatus for the illustration of that truth?"[9]

Opponents of literal sacrifices, such as Oswald Allis, Keil, Lange, etc., have no real exegesis to offer for the Ezekiel passage and other references to millennial sacrifices. Other than to suggest that they are not to be interpreted literally, their principal argument against the literal sacrifices is the seeming incongruity of such sacrifices as properly representing the work of Christ now fully revealed historically and exegetically in the New Testament.

Floyd E. Hamilton in his discussion of the question of whether Old Testament prophecy should be interpreted literally, loses little time in plunging into the question of millennial sacrifices as a demonstration of the impossibility of interpreting prophecy literally. He dwells upon "the blood and filth" and "the stench of the slaughterhouse" as being unfit for a future temple as a center of worship.[10] It would seem that Hamilton and others have temporarily forgotten that the entire sacrificial system of the Old Testament, while perhaps incongruous with western civilization aesthetics, was nevertheless commanded by God Himself as a proper typical presentation of the coming work of

---

[9]H. Bonar, *Coming and Kingdom of the Lord Jesus Christ*, 1849, pp. 222-23.
[10]Floyd E. Hamilton, *The Basis of Millennial Faith*, p. 41.

Christ. If such sacrifices were fitting in the mind of God to be the shadows of the cross of Christ, what more fitting memorial could be chosen if a memorial is desired for that same sacrifice. Obviously, a memorial is not intended to equal or to be a substitute of the real sacrifice, but as a ritual it is to point to the reality which is Christ.

The literalness of the future temple and its sacrificial system, however, is not inseparable from the premillennial concept of the millennium and, though in keeping with the general principle of literal interpretation, is not the *sine qua non* of millennialism. It is significant, however, that most thoroughgoing students of premillennialism who evince understanding of the relation of literal interpretation to premillennial doctrine usually embrace the concept of a literal temple and literal sacrifices.

If a literal view of the temple and the sacrifices be allowed, it provides a more intimate view of worship in the millennium than might otherwise be afforded and, though the system as revealed is different from the Mosaic in many particulars, it obviously has as its center the redemptive and sacrificial system.

Spiritual life in the millennium will be characterized by holiness and righteousness, joy and peace, the fullness of the Spirit, and the worship of the glorious Christ. The fact that Satan will be bound and demons will be inactive will provide a world scene in which spiritual life can abound. Premillennialism instead of denying the spiritual character of the millennium affirms its high standard of spiritual life which in many respects is far above any previous dispensation.

Chapter XXVII

SOCIAL, ECONOMIC, AND PHYSICAL ASPECTS OF THE MILLENNIUM

The reign of Christ on earth during the millennium, featuring as it does His righteous and universal government over all nations and characterized by spiritual blessing, obviously will affect all phases of life on the earth. Though the principal effects of the reign of Christ will be manifested in righteous government and in the spiritual realm, the rule of Christ will have extensive impact on the economic and social aspects of life on the earth.

I. Universal Justice and Peace

The fact that wars will cease during the millennium will have a beneficial effect upon both the social and economic life of the world. Instead of large expenditure for armaments, attention no doubt will be directed to improving the world in various ways. Even under present world conditions, a relief from taxation due to military expenditure would have a great effect upon the economy. This coupled with absolute justice, assuring minority people of government protection and greatly reduced crime, will establish a social and economic order far different from anything the world had ever experienced prior to the millennium. Many of the prophetic Scriptures such as Psalm 72 and Isaiah 11 testify to these unusual millennial conditions.

II. Salvation of the Majority of Men

Due to the unusual conditions in the world where all will know the great truths concerning Christ and redemption (Isa. 11:9), it is safe to assume that the majority of the earth's population will be saved in contrast to all previous generations where only a comparatively few ever came to know the Lord. The testimony of Scripture is to the effect that at the beginning of the millennium all unsaved people are put to death. In the parable of the wheat and the tares (Matt. 13:24-30, 36-43) and in the parable of the good and bad fish (Matt. 13:47-50) it seems clear that only the righteous survive. This is also confirmed by the judgment of Matthew 25:31-46. What is here pictured for the Gentile nations seems also indicated in the judgment of Israel where all rebels or unbelievers are purged out (Ezek. 20:33-39). The enemies of Christ are thereby eliminated (cf. Rev. 19:11-21). The millennial period therefore begins with a society in which both Jews and Gentiles are saved. As children are born into their homes, however, even though they are in the favorable circumstances of the millennial scene, it seems obvious that some of these will not actually be born again, and of these the company of those who rebel against Christ in Revelation 20:8-9 is formed. Though it is impossible to prove that the majority of the earth's population are saved in the latter stages of the millennium, it is safe to assume that a large percentage in any case will really know the Lord. This will automatically set up a world situation quite different from that known in any previous dispensation.

III. The Curse on the Earth Lifted

Another important factor in the millennium is the fact that the curse which descended upon the physical world because of Adam's sin apparently is lifted during the millennium. According to the prophet Isaiah: "The wilderness and the dry land shall be glad; and the desert shall rejoice, and blossom as the rose. It shall blossom abundantly, and rejoice even with joy and singing; the glory of Lebanon shall be given unto it, the excellency of Carmel and Sharon: they shall see the glory of Jehovah, the excellency of our God" (Isa. 35:1-2). The rest of the thirty-fifth chapter of Isaiah continues in the same theme. Abundant rainfall characterizes the period (Isa. 30:23; 35:7) and abundance of food and cattle are pictured (Isa. 30:23-24). Though the curse on the earth is only partly lifted as indicated by the continuance of death, and will remain in some measure until the new heaven and the new earth are brought in (Rev. 22:3), the land of Palestine will once again be a garden. The world in general will be delivered from the unproductiveness which characterized great portions of the globe in prior dispensations.

IV. General Prosperity

Widespread peace and justice, spiritual blessing, and abundance of food will result in a general era of prosperity such as the world has never known (Jer. 31:12; Ezek. 34:25-27; Joel 2:21-27; Amos 9:13-14). The many factors which produce poverty, distress, and unequal distribution of goods will to a great extent be nonexistent in the millennium. Labor problems which now characterize the world will be solved, and everyone will receive just compensation for his labors (Isa. 65:21-25; Jer. 31:5). Thus the curse which creation has endured since Adam's sin (Gen. 3:17-19) will be in part suspended as even animal creation will be changed (Isa. 11:6-9; 65:25).

V. Health and Healing

One of the predictions regarding the coming of the Messiah was that healing from sickness would characterize His reign. Though Christ healed many in His first advent, most of the prophecies seem to point to the millennial situation. Thus Isaiah writes: "And the inhabitant shall not say, I am sick: the people that dwell therein shall be forgiven their iniquity" (Isa. 33:24). Those who have physical disability shall be healed of blindness and deafness (Isa. 29:18) and healing will be experienced in a similar way by others. Again Isaiah states: "Then the eyes of the blind shall be opened, and the ears of the deaf shall be unstopped. Then shall the lame man leap as a hart, and the tongue of the dumb shall sing: for in the wilderness shall water break out, and streams in the desert" (Isa. 35:5-6). The brokenhearted will be comforted and joy will replace mourning (Isa. 61:1-3). Longevity will apparently characterize the human race for Isaiah speaks of the death of a person one hundred years old as the death of a child (Isa. 65:20). The freedom from these human ills so common in the present world is in keeping with the lifting of many other aspects of the curse upon nature. Not only will people live much longer, but there will be also a tremendous increase in birth rate as children are born to those who survive the tribulation. Of this Jeremiah says: "I will multiply them, and they shall not be a few; I will also glorify them, and they shall not be small. Their children also shall be as aforetime, and their congregation shall be established before me" (30:19-20). This blessing will not only characterize Israel, but also the Gentile in the millennial kingdom (Ezek. 47:22).

Taken as a whole, the social and economic conditions of the millennium indicate a golden age in which the dreams of social reformists through the centuries will be realized, not through human effort but by the immediate presence and power of God and the righteous government of Christ. That mankind should again fail under such ideal circumstances and be ready to rebel against Christ at the close of the millennium is the final answer to those who would put faith in the inherent goodness of man.

VI. Cleavage of the Mount of Olives

According to millennial prophecies, many topographical changes will take place in the land of Palestine in connection with the establishment of the millennial reign of Christ. While some of these may be due to the lifting of the curse upon the earth, the alterations seem to be more extensive than this.

In connection with the return of Christ to the earth, Zechariah 14 pictures the battle for the possession of Jerusalem which in its early stages seems to be in favor of the Gentiles. This is reversed, however, by the return of Christ described in the following words: "Then shall Jehovah go forth, and fight against those nations, as when he fought in the day of battle. And his feet shall stand in that day upon the mount of Olives, which is before Jerusalem on the east; and the mount of Olives shall be cleft in the midst thereof toward the east and toward the west, and there shall be a very great valley; and half of the mountain shall remove toward the north, and half of it toward the south" (Zech. 14:3-4). In view of the fact that the Mount of Olives nowhere in Scripture is given a spiritualized interpretation, it seems clear that this refers to the physical Mount of Olives to the east of Jerusalem. When Christ returns, there will be where the Mount of Olives now stands a great valley extending toward the east with the Mount of Olives split in two.

The purpose of this cleavage seems to be indicated in the context as providing a temporary route for flight for those who are caught in the warfare about Jerusalem. Zechariah pictures it: "And ye shall flee by the valley of my mountains; for the valley of the mountains shall reach until Azel; yea, ye shall flee, like as ye fled from before the earthquake in the day of Uzziah king of Judah; and Jehovah my God shall come, and all the holy ones with thee" (Zech. 14:5). Other phenomenal things will occur at the same time. In the succeeding context a long day is described when "at evening time there shall be light" (Zech. 14:7). Subsequent description pictures the "living waters" which "shall go out from Jerusalem; half of them toward the eastern sea, and half of them toward the western sea: in summer and in winter shall it be" (Zech. 14:8). It should be clear from this description that the character of the land to the east of Jerusalem shall be much different than it is now and that the changes mentioned will be a preparation for other features of the millennial kingdom. Ezekiel adds more details concerning the river with special attention to the eastward flow of the river into the Dead Sea (cf. Ezek. 47:1-12). The river like the cleavage is miraculous as to its source and brings life and fruitfulness to the land through which it goes (cf. Ezek. 47:7-12). The effect on the Dead Sea is to bring healing to it and not only cause fruitfulness of trees and vegetation, but also to permit fish to thrive in its waters.

Though scholars who are not premillennial have tended to give this a figurative rather than a literal meaning, the details are such that a literal meaning makes sense in the millennial context. James M. Gray writes for instance: "The whole thing is literal in fact, and yet supernatural in origin."[1]

VII. The Exaltation of the City of Jerusalem

More important than the changes concerning the Mount of Olives are those in which the entire land of Palestine is involved. According to Zechariah 14:10: "All the land shall be made like the Arabah, from Geba to Rimmon south of Jerusalem; and she shall be lifted up, and shall dwell in her place, from Benjamin's gate unto the place of the first gate, unto the corner gate, and from the tower of Hananel unto the king's wine-presses." The effect of all the changes will be to elevate Jerusalem above the surrounding territory and to change the topography of Palestine to suit millennial conditions. This will accommodate therefore the temple of Ezekiel which would not fit Palestine in its present form.

Nathaniel West describes the changes as follows: "Jerusalem and Mount Zion, by means of physical convulsion and geological changes suddenly effected through disruption, depression, fissure, and elevation, at the Lord's appearing, shall be 'exalted' or 'lifted high,' above the surrounding hills, and the adjacent region be reduced 'to a plain,' like the Arabah, or Ghor, that runs from the slopes of Hermon to the Red Sea. *'All the land will change itself,'* and the geographic center of the reconstruction will be determined by the boundaries of the ancient territory of Judah."[2]

Charles L. Feinberg summarizes these topographical changes as follows: "All the land will be depressed in order that Jerusalem might be elevated. See Isaiah 2:2 and Micah 4:1. The directions given cannot be determined with certainty, but they prove two things: (1) the description must be taken literally (else why the abundance of detail?) and (2) the city will be rebuilt in its former extent. Compare Jeremiah 31:37, 38. Geba was on the northern frontier of Judah, probably Gibeah of

[1]James M. Gray, *Christian Workers' Commentary*, p. 268.
[2]Nathaniel West, *The Thousand Years in Both Testaments*, p. 289.

Saul (II Kings 23:8). Rimmon south of Jerusalem is to be distinguished from the Rimmon of Galilee (Josh. 19:13) and that in Benjamin (Judg. 20:45-47). The city here designated was on the border of Edom given to Simeon by Judah. The subject of *wera' amah* is Jerusalem. The verb is probably an expanded form of *weramah* from *rum*, like *qa'm* in Hosea 10:14.

"The city will be inhabited on its ancient site (for the same use of the preposition see 12:6) ; it will possess its old boundaries. The gate of Benjamin was on the north wall, facing the territory of Benjamin (Jer. 37:13; 38:7). The first gate is probably the old gate (Neh. 3:6). The corner gate was westward of the old gate. Compare II Kings 14:13. The winepresses of the king were probably in the royal gardens in the valley southeast of Jerusalem. See II Kings 25:4; Jeremiah 39:4; 52:7; and Nehemiah 3:15. Not only will the city have its former bounds but its population will live therein, not to go out as captives or fugitives. They will need to fear no further hostile attacks. There will be no more curse, that complete devoting to destruction when given up by God to a curse. . . . The description is literal and conveys the interrelation of outward fact with inward condition, as Genesis 3 (thorns and thistles resulting from the sin of man) and Romans 8."[3]

VIII. Resulting Changes in the Land of Palestine

The topographical changes seem to be the preparation for the new division of the enlarged land of Palestine now embracing the total area promised to Abraham (Gen. 15:18-21). Palestine is going to be divided into three parts. The northern part will be divided into areas for Dan, Asher, Naphtali, Manasseh, Ephraim, Reuben, and Judah (cf. Ezek. 48:1-7). The southern portion in like manner is devoted to the tribes of Benjamin, Simeon, Issachar, Zebulun, and Gad (Ezek. 48:23-27). In between the northern and southern parts of the land is placed the "holy oblation" of Ezekiel 48:8-20, set apart in a special way as holy to the Lord. The extent of this portion of the land

---

[3]Charles L. Feinberg, *God Remembers*, pp. 257-58.

is described as a square twenty-five thousand reeds on each side which is further subdivided into two fifths of the area for the Levites (Ezek. 45:5; 48:13-14), another two fifths for the temple and priests (Ezek. 45:4; 48:10-12), and the remaining one fifth of the city (Ezek. 45:6; 48:15-19). According to Merrill F. Unger, it is probable that of the three different cubits used in ancient Babylon the one intended in Ezekiel's prophecy was equivalent to 7.2 feet.[4] If so, the holy oblation would be thirty-four miles square and would contain 1,156 square miles. Though this would not fit in the present topography of Palestine, it seems that the changes in the land at the beginning of the millennium are in preparation for this. It would be almost impossible to ascertain any figurative meaning of these specific dimensions, and in keeping with the literal interpretation of other features of the millennial kingdom, description of changes in the land seem likewise to point to changes corresponding to the literal interpretation.

---

[4] Cf. Merrill F. Unger, "The Temple Vision of Ezekiel," Bibliotheca Sacra, 105:427-28, October, 1948).

CHAPTER XXVIII

THE HEAVENLY JERUSALEM

One of the theological problems in relation to the doctrine of the millennium is the Scriptural teaching concerning the heavenly Jerusalem. This has not only confused opponents of premillennialism, but often has not been understood by those who hold to a millennial reign of Christ. Bound up in the problem also is the question of the relation of resurrected saints to the inhabitants of the millennial kingdom who are still in their natural bodies. Opponents of premillennialism have frequently heaped ridicule upon the teaching on the ground that it is impossible for resurrected beings and nonresurrected beings to mingle freely in the millennial scene. George L. Murray, for instance, refers to this when he states: ". . . pre-millennialism makes no provision for the reconciliation of such irreconcilables as resurrected saints and mortal sinners in the same society."[1]

Solution to this entire problem, however, is afforded by a proper understanding of the Scriptural doctrine of the heavenly Jerusalem.[2] It may be demonstrated from Scripture that (1) the heavenly Jerusalem is the eternal habitation of all resurrected and translated saints; (2) the heavenly Jerusalem is in existence in the millennium; (3) the Scriptures teach that there is some participation of these resurrected saints in the government of the millennium; (4) objections to comingling of resurrected with nonresurrected beings are unjustified.

I. THE ETERNAL HOME OF ALL THE SAINTS

Much of the confusion that exists in regard to the millen-

---

[1] George L. Murray, *Millennial Studies*, p. 91.
[2] Cf. J. Dwight Pentecost, *Things to Come*, pp. 563-83.

nium and the eternal state stems from a failure to distinguish between the promises that are given to the last generation of saints who are on the earth at the time of the second advent and the promises that are given resurrected or translated saints in both the Old and New Testaments. The prophecies of the Old Testament give adequate basis for the doctrine that Israel has an earthly hope. The prophets in Israel's darkest hours painted the most glowing picture of the coming earthly kingdom in which Israel would participate as a favored nation and possess their promised land under the reign of the Son of David. The promises as given, however, clearly refer to those who were not resurrected and are directed to the nation of Israel as it is to be constituted at the time of the second advent, that is, the Israelites who will survive the great tribulation. They and their seed will inherit the promised land and fulfill the hundreds of prophecies that have to do with Israel's hope in the millennial kingdom. These promises are delineated in the Abrahamic, Davidic, Palestinian, and new covenants.

The Old Testament, however, also records promises to saints which are individual in their character. They, for instance, are promised resurrection (Job 19:25-27; Isa. 26:19-20; Dan. 12:2-3). Along with the promise of their resurrection is the promise of reward such as characterizes God's dealings with the saints in eternity (Dan. 12:3; Mal. 3:16-17). In a few instances these promises specifically are related to the new heaven and the new earth and constitute a description of the eternal state which follows the millennium (Isa. 65:17-18; 66:22). From these passages it is evident that the millennial reign of Christ on earth as such is not the ultimate hope of the resurrected saints, but rather of the saints who enter the millennium in their natural bodies and who are fitted for the earthly scene.

This conclusion seems to be confirmed by the New Testament revelation concerning the heavenly city. In stating the faith of Abraham in Hebrews 11 it is stated: "For he looked for the city which hath foundations, whose builder and maker is God" (Heb. 11:10). It is further stated of Abraham and his descendants who died in the Old Testament that they did not receive the promises, and in fact were seeking a heavenly city: "These all died in faith, not having received the promises, but having seen them and greeted them from afar, and having confessed that they were strangers and pilgrims on the earth. For they that say such things make it manifest that they are seeking after a country of their own. And if indeed they had been mindful of that country from which they went out, they would have had opportunity to return. But now they desire a better country, that is, a heavenly: wherefore God is not ashamed of them, to be called their God; for he hath prepared for them a city" (Heb. 11:13-16). It is evident from these verses that the hope which was Abraham's in resurrection had to do with a heavenly city rather than an earthly kingdom.

This is confirmed also by another passage in Hebrews 12:22-24 where Christians of the present age are related to the heavenly city: "But ye are come unto mount Zion, and unto the city of the living God, the heavenly Jerusalem, and to innumerable hosts of angels, to the general assembly and church of the firstborn who are enrolled in heaven, and to God the Judge of all, and to the spirits of just men made perfect, and to Jesus the mediator of a new covenant, and to the blood of sprinkling that speaketh better than that of Abel." This important passage teaches that saints of all ages will be in the heavenly Jerusalem. The inhabitants of the heavenly city are itemized as an innumerable company of angels, the church, God, Jesus, the Mediator, and the spirits of just men made perfect, the latter designation seemingly referring to all Old Testament saints.

It should be noted, however, that while the saints of all ages are included in the New Jerusalem their separate identity is maintained, that is, Old Testament saints are still classified as such. Those who are members of the church, the body of Christ, are so described, angels are still angels, and God also retains His identity. This at once provides for the unity and diversity of God's program, the unity in the common salvation experienced by all the saints, the diversity in their peculiar character and dispensational background.

II. INTERPRETATIONS OF REVELATION 21:9—22:5

The heavenly city of Jerusalem is described in detail in Revelation 21:1—22:5. Most conservative expositors agree that Revelation 21:1-8 has reference to the eternal state, the new heaven and the new earth which will be created after the millennium, and the holy city, the New Jerusalem as it will exist in eternity. Difference of opinion, however, has risen regarding the express application of Revelation 21:9—22:5. Three principal interpretations have been advanced. Some believe that this portion of Scripture is a retrospect, like certain other portions of the book of Revelation, and is in fact a description of the millennial scene in figurative language.[3] In support of this position it is noted in Revelation 21:24 that nations and kings of the earth are mentioned which some think would be incongruous with the eternal state. Further, in Revelation 22:2 reference is made to the leaves of the tree of life which are for the healing of the nations, and from this it is inferred that the reference is to the millennial scene because no healing will be necessary in the eternal state.

A second view is advanced that Revelation 21:9 and following is a description of the eternal state introduced in the first eight verses of the chapter.[4] Inasmuch as there is in the context a new heaven and a new earth to which the holy city is coming down, it would imply that the description of the city is contemporary with the eternal state. According to this view, the city is proceeding from heaven to the earth as seen in Revelation 21:10 and is established with its foundations on the new earth. It is evident from any careful study of the millennial scene that the heavenly Jerusalem does not correspond to the earthly Jerusalem of the millennium. It would be impossible for such a city in the size that is given, 1500 miles square, to be situated on the earth in the Holy Land. Adherents of both views therefore hold that if the heavenly Jerusalem is in existence during the millennium that it is located above the earth and not on the earth. Exponents of this position point out that there is

---

[3] Cf. William Kelly, *Lectures on the Book of Revelation,* pp. 459-90.
[4] L. S. Chafer, *Systematic Theology,* IV, 418-20, 427, V, 365-68.

nothing incongruous with the racial background of the saints continuing in the eternal state. The word *nations* actually is the word *Gentiles* and is no more out of place than reference to Israel or angels or the church as separate entities in the eternal scene. Further, the problem of the healing of the nations in Revelation 22:2 is dissolved when it is recalled that the tree of life originally existed in the Garden of Eden before sin came into being and therefore is a normal part of eternity as well. The word translated "healing" can just as well be translated *health* or *benefit* which would not necessarily mean more than that the leaves of the tree were beneficial in some way. Though scholars argue at length on both sides of this question, there does not seem to be any solid reason for denying the possibility that the New Jerusalem as pictured in Revelation 21:9 ff. is viewed from the standpoint of its descent to the earth at the beginning of the eternal state.

A third view, however, is sometimes offered which is a mediate view between the first two mentioned. This view contemplates the heavenly Jerusalem as in existence during the millennium over the earth as the habitation of the resurrected saints, and is in contrast to the city of Jerusalem located on the earth. The heavenly Jerusalem apparently is withdrawn at the time of the destruction of the present earth and heaven. Then as pictured in Revelation 21:2 it returns to the new heaven and the new earth when the scene is ready for its descent. This interpretation regards Revelation 21:9 ff. as the heavenly city in the eternal state though recognizing its existence in the millennium. This seems to solve most of the exegetical problems that are involved and, in fact, answers many objections to the premillennial interpretation of Scripture as a whole. It provides a clear distinction between resurrected saints who inhabit the New Jerusalem and the millennial saints on the earth who will inhabit the millennial earth. It is assumed, though the Scriptures do not state it, that the millennial saints at the end of the millennium will be translated prior to their entrance into the eternal state and thus will qualify for entrance into the heavenly Jerusalem.

III. RELATION OF RESURRECTED SAINTS TO THE MILLENNIAL EARTH

Though the major difficulty of the relationship of resurrected saints to those who are still in their natural bodies in the millennium is explained by the residence of the resurrected saints in the heavenly Jerusalem, Scriptures afford several instances in which there will be some relation of resurrected saints to those in the millennial earth. Christ promised His followers that they would participate with Him in His judgment upon the twelve tribes of Israel in His kingdom. Christ declared: "Verily I say unto you, that ye who have followed me, in the regeneration when the Son of man shall sit on the throne of his glory, ye also shall sit upon twelve thrones, judging the twelve tribes of Israel" (Matt. 19:28). A larger promise is given by reminder to the Corinthians when Paul wrote them: "Know ye not that the saints shall judge the world? and if the world is judged by you, are ye unworthy to judge the smallest matters?" (1 Cor. 6:2). It is further promised believers who participate in the first resurrection that they "shall reign with him a thousand years" (Rev. 20:6). Further reference to reigning on the earth is found in Revelation 5:10 and 2 Timothy 2:12. If resurrected saints are to reign with Christ over the millennial earth, it would seem evident that there must be at least a limited amount of communication and association between resurrected saints and those in their natural bodies. If the reference in Ezekiel 37:24 to David as king over Israel is a reference to resurrected David as ruler over the promised land in the role of a subruler of Christ, then further evidence is given for this comingling. As far as Scripture revelation is concerned, however, it seems to be limited to a few specific functions, and the primary activity of the resurrected saints will be in the new and heavenly city.

IV. SCRIPTURAL GROUND FOR COMINGLING OF RESURRECTED AND NONRESURRECTED SAINTS

The objection frequently raised that any comingling of resurrected with nonresurrected being is impossible is of course denied by the simple fact that our Lord in His resurrection body was able to mingle freely with His disciples. Though there evidently was some change in their relationship, he could still talk with them, eat with them, and be subject to physical contact with them. Further, it is clear that even at the present time there is a ministry of angels to human beings even though angels are of an entirely different order of beings than men and are invisible in their earthly activities under ordinary circumstances. Though the free mingling of resurrected and nonresurrected beings is contrary to our present experience, there is no valid reason why there should not be a limited amount of such association in the millennial earth.

Undoubtedly the millennial kingdom will be a dispensation graphically different from any previous one and involving many unique features which can only partially be understood now from the Scriptures. As a dispensation it is fitted to be climactic in its character and a divine preparation for the eternal state which will follow. The prospect for such a kingdom, however, is the answer to the world's longing for peace, righteousness, and equity which will never be achieved until Christ Himself returns to reign.

CHAPTER **XXIX**

THE CLOSE OF THE MILLENNIUM AND THE ETERNAL STATE

I. THE FINAL REVOLT

According to Revelation 20:7-9, at the conclusion of the thousand-year reign of Christ, Satan, who has been bound, will be loosed again and be permitted to deceive the nations as he has done through the ages.[1] Those who will be deceived evidently are those who will be born in the millennial kingdom whose parents previously entered the millennium in their natural bodies. Some of the children born no doubt will become true children of God, whereas others will merely profess to follow Christ under the compulsion of the absolute reign of the Lord. With the renewed activity of Satan these will be encouraged to rebel against God and according to Revelation 20:8 will gather themselves to battle against the Lord and surround the earthly city of Jerusalem. In this connection it is stated that Satan will go out "to deceive the nations which are in the four corners of the earth, Gog and Magog. . . ." This should not be confused with a similar reference to Gog and Magog in Ezekiel 38:2 which is an event referring to a battle which probably precedes the millennium. The similarity of terms is best explained by defining Gog as the prince and Magog as the people of the prince, or the land over which he rules. So interpreted, the passage states that Satan will deceive the nations which are in all parts of the earth, both prince and people, that is, both rulers and those under them. Apparently the defection against Christ will extend even to some of the subrulers involved in the political government of the world at the close of the millennium.

The revolt will be summarily judged and the Scriptures re-

---

[1] Cf. L. S. Chafer, *Systematic Theology*, V, 360-1.

cord that "fire came down out of heaven, and devoured them" (Rev. 20:9). Further, it is declared that the devil will be cast into the lake of fire, the final destiny of all unsaved. Into this place of punishment the beast and the false prophet—the political and religious rulers of the world during the great tribulation preceding the millennium—were cast to begin their endless torment (Rev. 20:10).

II. The Judgment of the Great White Throne

In Revelation 20:11-15 one of the saddest passages of Scripture is found. It is recorded that subsequent to the conclusion of the millennium a great white throne is established, apparently in space, as both earth and the starry heavens flee away from it in the destruction of the present earth and heaven. Before this throne are assembled the dead, small and great. Though the Scriptures do not state so directly, it is implied that this is a judgment of the wicked dead who have not previously been raised from the grave. They are judged according to their works as written in "the books" which are the divine record of human activity. It is stated that the dead are brought back to this judgment, their bodies being delivered from the grave, whether in the sea or on the land, and their soul and spirit is brought up from hades. The summary judgment is given: "If any was not found written in the book of life, he was cast into the lake of fire" (Rev. 20:15). This is defined as "the second death" (Rev. 20:14). Just as physical death is separation of the immaterial part of man from his physical body, so the second death is eternal separation of the wicked from God. There has been some debate as to the exact character of the book of life, but whatever construction is placed upon this expression as it is found in Scripture the conclusion is evident that the book of life records at this time the names of those who are saved. Though the wicked will be judged according to their works as to degree of punishment, the fact that their names are not in the book of life is the ground for their final judgment.

III. The New Heaven and the New Earth

According to Revelation 21:10, following the judgment of the great white throne a new heaven and a new earth is revealed to John apparently created to replace the present earth and heaven. Very little description is given of this in Scripture though it is mentioned in Isaiah 65:17 where it is stated that when the new heavens and the new earth are created the former would not be remembered. The new heaven and the new earth differ greatly from the present situation. It is declared that there is no more sea (Rev. 21:1). The physical characteristics of it differ widely from the present earth as well. It may be gathered from the fact that the New Jerusalem does not need sun or moon, that the glory of the Lord will be the light of the new creation, and that there will be no night. It is a scene of release from earth's sorrows. God "shall wipe away every tear from their eyes; and death shall be no more; neither shall there be mourning, nor crying, nor pain, any more: the first things are passed away" (Rev. 21:4). Excluded from the new earth are all the unsaved described in Revelation 21:8.

A principal feature of the new earth will be the New Jerusalem pictured as a bride adorned for her husband and a city which comes down from God out of heaven to the new earth (Rev. 21: 2, 9-10). The city is described as having twelve foundations on which are the names of the twelve apostles. It is square in shape and has three gates on each of the four sides bearing the names of the twelve tribes of Israel. The Scriptures give a graphic description of its beauty in which pure gold, which is compared to clear glass, is a principal ingredient. The walls and the foundations are garnished with precious stones, twelve of which are mentioned, apparently representing the twelve tribes of Israel. Each of the gates is a large pearl. The streets of the city are paved with pure gold transparent like glass. Other features of the city include the fact that there is no temple in it, for the Lord Himself dwells in the city. Access to the city will be given to the saved, both Jew and Gentile. The gates shall not be shut, but no one will be permitted to enter who would in any way defile the city, entrance being reserved to

those "that are written in the Lamb's book of life" (Rev. 21:27).
A major feature of the city is a pure river which proceeds
from the throne of God and winds its way through the city.
The tree of life originally mentioned as being in the Garden
of Eden is here seen again bearing fruits each month. It is
stated that in this new earth there will be no more curse, but
instead abundant blessing from God.

A most astounding feature is the dimension of the city
which is given as 1500 miles square and also 1500 miles high.
Such a dimension quite unfamiliar even to a modern world with
its high buildings would provide a city of impressive and spa-
cious dimension as the seat of God's eternal government and
dwelling place for the saints. Expositors differ as to whether the
city is in the form of a cube or a pyramid though the latter
seems more likely. If in the form of a pyramid, it is possible
that the throne of God will be at the top and the river of life
will wend its way from the throne down the various levels of
the city. In these brief terms is given a description of the ultimate resting place of the saints beyond which Scripture revelation does not go in its unfolding of the endless ages of eternity.
How pale in comparison are the monuments of men! How satis-
fying is the revelation of the divine purpose of the grace of God
in bestowing these benefits on those who have put their trust
in His blessed Son. How blessed is the hope of the imminent
coming of Christ which will begin that grand sequence of future events which have their goal in eternity in the glorious presence of the Triune God.

> The sands of time are sinking,
> The dawn of heaven breaks;
> The summer morn I've sighed for,
> The fair, sweet morn awakes
> Dark, dark hath been the midnight,
> But dayspring is at hand,
> And glory, glory dwelleth
> In Immanuel's land.

BIBLIOGRAPHY

ABBOTT-SMITH, G. *A Manual Greek Lexicon of the New Testament.* Edinburgh: T. and T. Clark Co., 1937.

ADAM, M. T. *The Millennium.* New York: Robert Carter, 1887.

ALFORD, HENRY. *The New Testament.* 4 vols. New York: Harper and Brothers, 1859.

ALLIS, OSWALD T. *Prophecy and the Church.* Philadelphia: The Presbyterian and Reformed Publishing Co., 1945.

ANDERSON, SIR RORERT. *The Coming Prince.* London: Hodder and Stoughton, 1909.

ARMERDING, CARL. *The Last Trump and the Seventh Trumpet.* New York: Loizeaux Brothers [n. d.].

AUGUSTINE, A. *City of God.* Translated by Marcus Dods. Vol. II of *The Nicene and Post-Nicene Fathers of the Christian Church.* New York: The Christian Literature Co., 1887.

BARON, DAVID. *Israel's Inalienable Possessions.* London: Morgan and Scott [n. d.].

BAUMAN, LOUIS. *Russian Events in the Light of Biblical Prohecy.* Philadelphia: The Balkiston Co., 1942.

BEECHER, WILLIS JUDSON. *The Prophets and the Promise.* New York: Crowell, 1905.

BERKHOF, LOUIS. *The Kingdom of God.* Grand Rapids: William B. Eerdmans Publishing Co., 1951.

———. *Principles of Biblical Interpretation.* Grand Rapids: Baker Book House, 1950.

———. *The Second Coming of Christ.* Grand Rapids: William B. Eerdmans Publishing Co., 1953.

———. *Systematic Theology.* Grand Rapids: William B. Eerdmans Publishing Co., 1941.

BIEDERWOLF, W. E. *The Millennium Bible.* Chicago: The W. T. Blessing Co., 1924.

BLACKSTONE, W. E. *Jesus is Coming.* New York: Fleming H. Revell Co., 1908.

———. *The Millennium.* New York: Fleming H. Revell Co., 1918.

BONAR, HORATIUS. *The Coming and Kingdom of the Lord Jesus Christ.* London: J. Nisbet and Co., 1889.

BRADBURY, JOHN W. (ed.). *Hastening the Day of God.* Wheaton: Van Kampen Press, 1953.

———. (ed.). *A Sure Word of Prophecy.* New York: Fleming H. Revell Co., 1943.

BRIGGS, CHARLES AUGUSTUS. *Messianic Prophecy.* New York: Charles Scribner's Sons, 1886.

BRIGHT, JOHN. *The Kingdom of God.* New York: Abingdon-Cokesbury Press, 1953.

BROCK, A. CLUTTON. *What is the Kingdom of Heaven?* New York: Charles Scribner's Sons, 1920.

BROOKES, JAMES H. "Kept Out of the Hour," *Our Hope,* 6:153-57, November, 1899.

———. *Maranatha.* New York: Fleming H. Revell Co., 1889.

———. *Till He Come.* Chicago: Gospel Publishing Co., 1891.

BROOKS, KEITH L. *Prophetic Questions Answered.* Grand Rapids: Zondervan Publishing House, 1941.

———. *The Rapture.* Los Angeles: American Prophetic League, Inc., 1940.

BROWN, DAVID. *Christ's Second Coming: Will It Be Pre-Millennial?* New York: Robert Carter and Brothers, 1851.

BRUCE, ALEXANDER BALMAIN. *The Kingdom of God*. Edinburgh: T. and T. Clark, 1904.

BRUNNER, EMIL. *Eternal Hope*. Translated by Harold Knight. Philadelphia: Westminster Press, 1954.

BULLINGER, E. W. *The Apocalypse*. London: Eyre and Spottiswoode [n. d.].

———. *The Companion Bible*. 6 vols. New York: Oxford University Press [n. d.].

———. *How to Enjoy the Bible*. London: Eyre and Spottiswoode, 1907.

———. *Ten Sermons on the Second Advent*. Fifth edition. London: Eyre and Spottiswoode, 1888.

BURROWS, MILLAR. *An Outline of Biblical Theology*. Philadelphia: Westminster Press, 1946.

BURTON, ALFRED H. *Russia's Destiny in the Light of Prophecy*. New York: Gospel Publishing House, 1917.

CALVIN, JOHN. *Commentary on Romans*. Translated and edited by John Owen. Edinburgh: Calvin Translation Society, 1849.

———. *Institutes of the Christian Religion*. 2 vols. Philadelphia: Presbyterian Board of Christian Education, 1936.

CAMERON, ROBERT. *Scripture Truth about the Lord's Return*. New York: Fleming H. Revell Co., 1922.

CAMP, NORMAN H. *The Resurrection of the Human Body*. Chicago: Bible Institute Colportage Association Press, 1937.

CAMPBELL, RODERICK. *Israel and the New Covenant*. Philadelphia: Presbyterian and Reformed Publishing Co., 1954.

CARTLEDGE, SAMUEL A. *Fact and Fancy about the Future Life*. Richmond, Virginia: John Knox Press, 1943.

CASE, SHIRLEY JACKSON. *The Millennial Hope*. Chicago: The University of Chicago Press, 1918.

CHAFER, LEWIS SPERRY. *The Kingdom in History and Prophecy.* Philadelphia: Sunday School Times, 1919.

————. *Must We Dismiss the Millennium?* Crescent City, Florida: Biblical Testimony League, 1921.

————. *Systematic Theology.* 8 Vols. Dallas: Dallas Seminary Press, 1947.

CHAFER, ROLLIN T. *The Science of Biblical Hermeneutics.* Dallas: Bibliotheca Sacra, 1939.

CHALMERS, THOMAS M. *Israel and Covenant History.* New York: author, 1926.

CHARLES, R. H. *Critical and Exegetical Commentary on the Revelation of St. John.* 2 vols. New York: Charles Scribner's Sons, 1920.

CLARKE, WILLIAM N. *An Outline of Christian Theology.* Fifth edition. New York: Charles Scribner's Sons, 1899.

COHN, JOSEPH H. *Will the Church Escape the Tribulation?* Findlay, Ohio: Fundamental Truth Publishers [n. d.].

CONRADI, L. R. *The Impelling Force of Prophetic Truth.* London: Thynne and Co., Ltd., 1935.

COOPER, DAVID L. *Future Events Revealed.* Los Angeles: author, 1935.

————. *The God of Israel.* Los Angeles: The Biblical Research Society, 1945.

————. "Will the Church Go Through the Tribulation?" *Biblical Research Monthly,* 13:10, 16-17, January-June 1948.

CULBERTSON, WILLIAM, and HERMAN B. CENTZ (ed.). *Understanding the Times.* Grand Rapids: Zondervan Publishing House, 1956.

CULVER, ROBERT D. *Daniel and the Latter Days.* Westwood, New Jersey: Fleming H. Revell Co., 1954.

DARBY, J. N. *Notes on the Apocalypse.* London: G. Morrish [n. d.].

——. *Synopsis of the Books of the Bible.* 5 vols. London: G. Morrish [n. d.].

——. *Will the Saints Be in the Tribulation?* New York: Loizeaux Brothers [n. d.].

DAVID, IRA E. "Translation: When Does It Occur?" *The Dawn,* 12:358-59, November 15, 1935.

DAVIDSON, A. B. *Old Testament Prophecy.* Edinburgh: T. and T. Clark, 1903.

DEAN, I. R. *The Coming Kingdom, the Goal of Prophecy.* Philadelphia: Philadelphia School of the Bible, 1928.

DEHAAN, M. R. *The Jew and Palestine in Prophecy.* Grand Rapids: Zondervan Publishing House, 1950.

DELITZSCH, FRANZ. *Messianic Prophecies in Historical Succession.* Edinburgh: T. and T. Clark, 1891.

DOUTY, NORMAN F. *Has Christ's Return Two Stages?* New York: Pageant Press, Inc., 1956.

DUNHAM, T. RICHARD. *The Great Tribulation.* Hoytville, Ohio: Fundamental Truth Publishers, 1933.

EDWARDS, D. MIALL. "Mystery," *International Standard Bible Encyclopaedia,* Grand Rapids: William B. Eerdmans Publishing Co. [n. d.].

EERDMAN, CHARLES R. "Parousia," *International Standard Bible Encyclopaedia.* Grand Rapids: William B. Eerdmans Publishing Co. [n. d.].

ELLICOTT, CHARLES J. *St. Paul's First Epistle to the Corinthians.* London: Longmans, Green, and Co., 1887.

ELLIOTT, E. B. *Horae Apocalypticae.* 4 vols. London: Seeley, Burnside, and Seeley, 1846.

ENGELDER, T. H. *Scripture Cannot Be Broken.* St. Louis, Missouri: Concordia Publishing House, 1944.

ENGLISH, E. SCHUYLER. *Re-Thinking the Rapture.* Traveler's Rest, South Carolina: Southern Bible Book House, 1954.

EVANS, ROBERT L. *The Jew and the Plan of God.* New York: Loizeaux Brothers, Inc., 1950.

EVANS, WILLIAM. *The Coming King.* New York: Fleming H. Revell Co., 1923.

FAIRBAIRN, PATRICK. *Hermeneutical Manual.* Edinburgh: T. and T. Clark, 1858.

————. *Prophecy Viewed in Respect to Its Distinctive Nature, Its Special Function, and Proper Interpretation.* Second edition. Edinburgh: T. and T. Clark, 1865.

————. *The Prophetic Prospects of the Jews.* Grand Rapids: Willian B. Eerdmans Publishing Co., 1930.

FARRAR, F. W. *History of Interpretation.* London: Macmillan and Co., 1886.

FEINBERG, CHARLES L. *God Remembers.* Wheaton: Van Kampen Press, 1950.

————. *Premillennialism or Amillennialism?* Second edition. Wheaton: Van Kampen Press, 1954.

FROST, HENRY W. *The Second Coming of Christ.* Grand Rapids: William B. Eerdmans Publishing Co., 1934.

FOWLER, C. L. *Building the Dispensations.* Denver: Maranatha Publishers, 1940.

FRASER, ALEXANDER. *The Any Moment Return of Christ: A Critique.* Pittsburgh: Evangelical Fellowship, Inc., 1946.

————. *Is There But One Return of Christ?* Pittsburgh: Evangelical Fellowship, Inc., 1943.

FROMOW, GEORGE H. *Will the Church Pass Through the Great Tribulation?* London: The Sovereign Grace Advent Testimony [n. d.].

FROOM, LEROY EDWIN. *The Prophetic Faith of Our Fathers.* 4 vols. Washington, D. C.: Review and Herald, 1945.

GAEBELEIN, ARNO C. *The Gospel of Matthew.* 2 vols. New York: Publication Office, *Our Hope,* 1910.

———. *The Harmony of the Prophetic Word.* New York: Publication Office, *Our Hope,* 1907.

———. *Hath God Cast Away His People?* New York: Gospel Publishing House, 1905.

———. *The Prophet Daniel.* New York: Publication Office, *Our Hope,* 1911.

———. *The Prophet Ezekiel.* New York: Publication Office, *Our Hope,* 1918.

———. *Revelation.* New York: Publication Office, *Our Hope,* 1915.

———. *Studies in Prophecy.* New York: Publication Office, *Our Hope,* 1918.

GIBBON, EDWARD. *The Decline and Fall of the Roman Empire.* London: J. Bale, Sons, and Danielsson, Ltd., 1934.

GIRDLESTONE, R. B. *The Grammar of Prophecy.* London: Eyre and Spottiswoode, 1901.

GORDON, A. J. *Ecce Venit, Behold He Cometh.* New York: Hodder, 1899.

GOVETT, RICHARD. *Entrance Into the Kingdom.* London: Thynne, 1922.

GRANT, F. W. *Facts and Theories as to a Future State.* New York: Loizeaux Brothers, 1889.

———. *The Numerical Bible.* 7 vols. New York: Loizeaux Brothers, 1891.

————. *The Revelation of Christ.* New York: Loizeaux Brothers [n. d.].

GRAY, JAMES M. *Christian Workers' Commentary.* New York: Fleming H. Revell Co., 1915.

————. *Prophecy and the Lord's Return.* New York: Fleming H. Revell Co., 1917.

————. *A Textbook of Prophecy.* New York: Fleming H. Revell Co., 1918.

GUINNESS, GRATTON H. *The Approaching End of the Age.* New York: A. C. Armstrong, 1884.

————. *Light for the Last Days.* London: Hodder and Stoughton, 1886.

HALDEMAN, I. M. *The Coming of Christ: Both Pre-millennial and Imminent.* Philadelphia: Philadelphia School of the Bible, 1906.

————. *The History of the Doctrine of Our Lord's Return.* New York: First Baptist Church [n. d.].

————. *The Kingdom of God.* A review of Phillip Mauro's book "The Gospel of the Kingdom." New York: Francis Emory Fitch, Inc., 1931.

————. *The Secret and Imminent Coming of Christ.* New York: Charles C. Cook, 1917.

HAMILTON, F. E. *The Basis of Millennial Faith.* Grand Rapids: William B. Eerdmans Publishing Co., 1942.

HAMILTON, GAVIN. *Will the Church Escape the Great Tribulation?* New York: Loizeaux Brothers, 1944.

HARNACK, ADOLF. "Millennium," *Encyclopaedia Britannica.* Chicago: Encyclopaedia Britannica, Inc., 1950.

HARNER, NEVIN C. *I Believe.* Philadelphia: Christian Education Press [n. d.].

HARRISON, NORMAN B. *The End: Re-Thinking the Revelation.* Minneapolis: The Harrison Service, 1941.

——— *His Coming.* Minneapolis: The Harrison Service, 1946.

———. *His Sure Return.* Chicago: Bible Institute Colportage Association, 1926.

HARRISON, NORMAN, JR. "The Partial Rapture Theory." Unpublished Master's thesis, Dallas Theological Seminary, Dallas, 1940.

HENDRIKSEN, WILLIAM. *And So All Isreal Shall Be Saved.* Grand Rapids: Baker Book Store, 1945.

HENGSTENBERG, E. W. *Revelation of St. John Expounded for Those Who Search the Scriptures.* New York: Carter and Brothers, 1852.

HODGE, A. A. *Popular Lectures on Theological Themes.* Philadelphia: Presbyterian Board of Publication, 1887.

HODGE, CHARLES. *Commentary on Romans.* Philadelphia: H. B. Garder, 1883.

———. *An Exposition of the First Epistle to the Corinthians.* London: James Nisbet and Co., 1868.

———. *Systematic Theology.* 3 vols. New York: Charles Scribner's Sons, 1887.

HODGES, JESSE W. *Christ's Kingdom and Coming.* Grand Rapids: William B. Eerdmans Publishing Co., 1957.

HOGG, C. F. and W. E. VINE. *The Church and the Tribulation.* London: Pickering and Inglis, Ltd., 1938.

———. *The Epistles of Paul the Apostle to the Thessalonians.* Glasgow: Pickering and Inglis, Ltd., 1914.

HOSPERS, GERRIT H. *The Principle of Spiritualization in Hermeneutics.* East Williamson, New York: author, 1935.

HOSTE, W. *The Great Tribulation Theory*. Glasgow: Pickering and Inglis [n. d.].

HUBBARD, W. R. *Does the Church Go Through the Great Tribulation?* St. Petersburg, Florida: author [n. d.].

IRONSIDE, H. A. *Expository Notes on the Gospel of Matthew*. New York: Loizeaux Brothers, 1948.

―――. *Ezekiel the Prophet*. New York: Loizeaux Brothers, 1949.

―――. *The Great Parenthesis*. Grand Rapids: Zondervan Publishing House, 1943.

―――. *The Lamp of Prophecy*. Grand Rapids: Zondervan Publishing House, 1940.

―――. *Lectures on the Book of Revelation*. New York: Loizeaux Brothers, 1919.

―――. *Lectures on Daniel the Prophet*. New York: Loizeaux Brothers [n. d.].

―――. *The Mysteries of God*. New York: Loizeaux Brothers, 1946.

―――. *Not Wrath, but Rapture*. New York: Loizeaux [n. d.].

JACOBS, H. E. *A Summary of the Christian Faith*. Philadelphia: United Lutheran Publishing House, 1905.

JAMIESON, FAUSSET, and BROWN. *A Commentary, Critical, Experimental, and Practical on the Old and the New Testaments*. 6 vols. Philadelphia: Lippincott, 1868.

JENNINGS, F. C. *Studies in Revelation*. New York: Loizeaux Brothers, 1937.

JOHNSON, ANDREW and L. L. PICKETT. *Post-millennialism and Higher Critics*. Chicago: Glad Tidings Publishing Co., 1923.

KELLOGG, S. H. *Are Premillennialists Right?* New York: Fleming H. Revell, 1923.

―――. *The Jews, or Prediction and Fulfillment*. New York: James Nisbet Co., 1883.

KEIL, K. F. *The Book of the Prophet Daniel*. Edinburgh: T. and T. Clark, 1872.

————. *The Twelve Minor Prophets*. 2 vols. Translated by James Martin. Edinburgh: T. and T. Clark, 1878.

KELLY, WILLIAM. *Exposition of Isaiah*. London: Robert L. Allen, 1916.

————. "The Future Tribulation," *The Bible Treasury*, 4:206-8, December, 1902; 4:222-23, January, 1903.

————. *Lectures on the Book of Daniel*. London: James Carter, 1897.

————. *Lectures on the Book of Revelation*. London: G. Morrish [n. d.].

————. *Lectures on the Gospel of Matthew*. New York: Loizeaux Brothers [n. d.].

KEPLER, THOMAS. *The Book of Revelation*. New York: Oxford University Press, 1957.

————. *Contemporary Thinking about Jesus*. New York: Abingdon-Cokesbury, 1944.

KING, WILLIAM P. *Adventism: The Second Coming of Christ*. New York: Abingdon-Cokesbury Press, 1941.

KIRSH, J. P. "Millennium," *The Catholic Encyclopedia*. New York: The Encyclopedia Press, Inc., 1913.

KLAUSNER, JOSEPH. *The Messianic Idea in Israel*. New York: The Macmillan Co., 1955.

KLINGERMAN, AARON JUDAH. *Messianic Prophecy in the Old Testament*. Grand Rapids: Zondervan Publishing House, 1957.

KNAPP, C. *Does Scripture Teach a Partial Rapture?* New York: Loizeaux Brothers [n. d.].

KROMMINGA, D. H. *The Millennium*. Grand Rapids: William B. Eerdmans Publishing Co., 1948.

————. *Millennium in the Church*. Grand Rapids: William B. Eerdmans Publishing Co., 1956.

LADD, GEORGE E. *The Blessed Hope*. Grand Rapids: William B. Eerdmans Publishing Co., 1956.

————. *Crucial Questions about the Kingdom of God*. Grand Rapids: William B. Eerdmans Publishing Co., 1952.

LAIDLAW, ROBERT A. *Will the Church Go Through the Great Tribulation?* New York: Loizeaux Brothers [n. d.].

LANDIS, IRA D. *The Faith of Our Fathers and Eschatology*. Lititz, Pennsylvania: author, 1946.

LANG, G. H. *Firstborn Sons: Their Rights and Risks.* London: Oliphants, 1943.

————. *Firstfruits and Harvest*. Dorset, England: author, 1946.

————. *Gospel of the Kingdom*. London: Oliphants, Ltd., 1944.

————. *The Histories and Prophecies of Daniel*. London: Oliphants, Ltd., 1942.

————. *The Revelation of Jesus Christ*. London: Oliphants, Ltd., 1945.

LANGE, JOHN PETER. *The Revelation of John*. New York: Scribner, Armstrong, and Co., 1874.

LARKIN, CLARENCE. *The Book of Revelation*. Philadelphia: Rev. Clarence Larkin Estate, 1919.

————. *The Second Coming of Christ*. Philadelphia: Rev. Clarence Larkin Estate, 1918.

LENSKI, R. C. H. *The Interpretation of St. John's Revelation*. Columbus: Lutheran Book Concern, 1935.

LINCOLN, CHARLES FRED. "The Covenants." Unpublished Doctor's dissertation, Dallas Theological Seminary, Dallas, 1942.

LINDBERG, MILTON B. *Gog All Agog in the Latter Days*. Findlay, Ohio: Fundamental Truth Publishers, 1939.

Ludwigson, R. *Simplified Classroom Notes on Prophecy.* Wheaton, Illinois: author, 1951.

MacCorkle, Douglas B. "A Study of Amillennial Eschatology." Unpublished Master's thesis, Dallas Theological Seminary, Dallas, 1947.

MacIntosh, Douglas C. *Personal Religion.* New York: Charles Scribner's Sons, 1942.

Mackintosh, C. H. *Papers on the Lord's Coming.* New York: Loizeaux Brothers [n. d.].

MacMillan, George Whitfield. *The Coming Millennium, or the Reign of Christ.* Steubenville, Ohio: Herald Publishing Co. [n. d.].

MacRae, Allan A. "The Millennial Kingdom of Christ," *Our Hope,* 53:463-80, February, 1947.

Mains, G. P. *Premillennialism.* New York: The Abingdon Press, 1920.

Marsh, F. E. *Will the Church or Any Part of It Go Through the Great Tribulation?* Glasgow: Pickering and Inglis [n. d.].

Masselink, William. *Why a Thousand Years?* Grand Rapids: William B. Eerdmans Publishing Co., 1930.

Mauro, Philip. *Looking for the Saviour.* New York: Fleming H. Revell Co., 1913.

———. *The Seventy Weeks and the Great Tribulation.* Boston: Hamilton Brothers, 1923.

McClain, Alva J. "The Greatness of the Kingdom," *Bibliotheca Sacra,* 114:11-27, January, 1955; 112:107-24, April, 1955; 112:209-24, July, 1955; 112:304-10, October, 1955.

———. *Daniel's Prophecy of the Seventy Weeks.* Grand Rapids: Zondervan Publishing House, 1940.

McPherson, Norman S. *Triumph Through Tribulation.* Otego, New York, author, 1944.

MILES, F. J. *Prophecy, Past, Present, and Prospective.* Grand Rapids: Zondervan Publishing House, 1943.

————. *Understandest Thou? Principles of Biblical Interpretation.* London: Marshall, Morgan, and Scott, 1946.

MILLER, EARL. *The Kingdom of God and the Kingdom of Heaven.* Meadville, Pennsylvania: author, 1950.

MILLIGAN, E. M. *Is the Kingdom Age at Hand?* New York: George H. Doran Co., 1924.

MILLIGAN, GEORGE. *St. Paul's Epistles to the Thessalonians.* London: Macmillan and Co., 1908.

MILLIGAN, WILLIAM. *The Revelation of St. John.* London: Macmillan and Co., 1887.

MINEAR, PAUL A. *Christian Hope and the Second Coming.* Philadelphia: Westminster Press, 1954.

MITCHELL, JOHN L. "The Question of Millennial Sacrifices," *Bibliotheca Sacra,* 110:248-67, July, 1953; 110:342-61, October, 1953.

MUNHALL, L. W. *The Lord's Return.* Philadelphia: author, 1895. Harper and Brothers Publishers, 1930.

MURRAY, G. L. *Millennial Studies.* Grand Rapids: Baker Book House, 1948.

NEEDHAM, MRS. GEORGE C. *The Antichrist.* New York: Charles C. Cook [n. d.].

NEWELL, WILLIAM R. *The Book of Revelation.* Chicago: Moody Press, 1935.

————. *The Church and the Great Tribulation.* Chicago: Scripture Press, 1923.

NEWTON, B. W. *The Millennium and Israel's Future.* London: Lucas Collins, 1913.

OEHLER, GUSTAV FRIEDRICH. *Theology of the Old Testament.* New York: Funk and Wagnalls, 1883.

OLSHAUSEN, HERMANN. *Biblical Commentary on the New Testament.* 6 vols. New York: Sheldon, Blakeman, and Co., 1857.

OTTMAN, FORD C. *God's Oath.* New York: Publication Office, *Our Hope,* 1911.

————. *Imperialism and Christ.* New York: Publication Office, *Our Hope,* 1912.

————. *The Unfolding of the Ages.* New York: Publication Office, *Our Hope,* 1905.

PACHE, RENE. *The Return of Jesus Christ.* Translated by William S. LaSor. Chicago: Moody Press, 1955.

PANTON, D. M. "The Removal of the Church from the Earth," *The Dawn,* 4:387-94, December 15, 1927.

PAYNE, HOMER L. "Amillennial Theology as a System." Unpublished Doctor's dissertation, Dallas Theological Seminary, Dallas. 1948.

PEMBER, G. H. *The Great Prophecies of the Centuries.* London: Oliphants, Ltd., 1942.

PENTECOST, J. DWIGHT. *Things to Come.* Findlay, Ohio: Dunham Publishing Co., 1958.

PETERS, GEORGE N. H. *The Theocratic Kingdom.* 3 vols. Grand Rapids: Kregel Publications, 1952.

PETRY, RAY C. *Christian Eschatology and Social Thought.* New York: Abingdon Press, 1956.

PETTINGILL, WILLIAM L. *God's Prophecies for Plain People.* Findlay, Ohio: Fundamental Truth Publishers, 1923.

————. *Israel—Jehovah's Covenant People.* Harrisburg, Pennsylvania: Fred Kelker, 1915.

PIERSON, ARTHUR T. *The Coming of the Lord.* New York: Fleming H. Revell Co., 1896.

PIETERS, ALBERTUS. *The Seed of Abraham.* Grand Rapids: William B. Eerdmans, 1941.

————. "Darbyism Vs. the Historic Christian Faith," *The Christian Forum*, 2:225-28, May, 1936.

PINK, ARTHUR W. *The Millennium.* Swengel, Pennsylvania: Bible Truth Depot [n. d.].

————. *The Redeemer's Return.* Swengel, Pennsylvania: Bible Truth Depot, 1918.

POHLE, JOSEPH. *Eschatology, the Doctrine of the Last Things.* St. Louis, Missouri: B. Herder Book Co., 1942.

POLLOCK, WALLACE. "Chiliasm in the First Five Centuries." Unpublished Master's thesis, Dallas Theological Seminary, Dallas, 1945.

RALL, HARRIS F. *Modern Premillennialism and the Christian Hope.* New York: The Abingdon Press, 1920.

RAMM, BERNARD. *Protestant Biblical Interpretation.* Boston: W. A. Wilde Co., 1950.

REESE, ALEXANDER. *The Approaching Advent of Christ.* London: Marshall, Morgan, and Scott Co. [n. d.].

RILEY, W. B. *The Evolution of the Kingdom.* New York: Charles C. Cook, 1913.

RIMMER, HARRY. *The Coming King.* Grand Rapids: William B. Eerdmans Publishing Co., 1941.

————. *The Coming War and the Rise of Russia.* Grand Rapids: William B. Eerdmans Publishing Co., 1940.

ROBERTS, ALEXANDER, and JAMES DONALDSON. *The Ante-Nicene Fathers.* 10 vols. New York: Charles Scribner's Sons, 1899.

Robertson, A. T. *A Grammar of the Greek New Testament*. New York: Hodder, 1919.

————. *Word Pictures in the New Testament*. 6 vols. New York: Harpers, 1930.

Robinson, J. A. T. *Jesus and His Coming*. New York: Abingdon Press, 1957.

Robinson, William C. *Christ the Hope of Glory*. Grand Rapids: William B. Eerdmans Publishing Co., 1949.

Rogers, W. H. *Things That Differ*. New York: Loizeaux Brothers, 1940.

Rose, George L. *Tribulation till Translation*. Glendale, California: Rose Publishing Co., 1943.

Rowley, H. H. *The Relevance of the Apocalyptic*. New York: Harper and Brothers, 1946.

Rutgers, W. H. *Premillennialism in America*. Goes, Holland: Oosterbaan and Le Cointre, 1930.

Rutledge, David D. *Christ, Anti-christ, and the Millennium*. London, Marshall Brothers, 1903.

Ryrie, Charles C. *The Basis of the Premillennial Faith*. New York: Loizeaux Brothers, 1953.

Sale-Harrison, L. *The Coming Great Northern Confederacy*. New York: Sale-Harrison Publications, 1918.

————. *Palestine, God's Monument of Prophecy*. New York: Sale-Harrison Publications, 1933.

————. *The Remarkable Jew*. London: Pickering and Inglis [n. d.].

————. *The Resurrection of the Old Roman Empire*. Harrisburg, Pennsylvania: The Evangelical Press [n. d.].

Saphir, Adolph. *Christ and Israel*. London: Morgan and Scott, 1911.

SAUER, ERIC. *From Eternity to Eternity*. Grand Rapids: William B. Eerdmans Publishing Co., 1954.

The New Schaff-Herzog Encyclopedia of Religious Knowledge. Grand Rapids: Baker Book House, 1950.

SCHAFF, PHILIP. *History of the Christian Church*. 8 vols. Grand Rapids: William B. Eerdmans Publishing Co., 1950.

SCOFIELD, C. I. *Addresses on Prophecy*. New York: A. C. Gaebelein, 1910.

————. (ed.). *Scofield Reference Bible*. New York: Oxford University Press, 1917.

————. *Will the Church Pass Through the Great Tribulation?* Philadelphia: Philadelphia School of the Bible, Inc., 1917.

————. *What Do the Prophets Say?* Philadelphia: Philadelphia School of the Bible, 1918.

SCOTT, WALTER. *Exposition of the Revelation*. London: Alfred Holness, 1914.

SCROGGIE, W. GRAHAM. *A Guide to the Gospels*. London: Pickering and Inglis, 1948.

————. *The Lord's Return*. London: Pickering and Inglis [n. d.].

SCRUBY, JOHN J. *The Great Tribulation: The Church's Supreme Test*. Dayton: author, 1933.

SEISS, JOSEPH A. *Lectures on the Apocalypse*. 3 vols. Philadelphia: General Council Publication Board, 1911.

SHIMMEALL, R. C. *The Second Coming of Christ*. New York: Henry S. Goodspeed and Co., 1873.

SHODDE, GEORGE H. *Outlines of Biblical Hermeneutics*. Columbus: Lutheran Book Concern, 1917.

SILVER, JESSE FORREST. *The Lord's Return*. New York: Fleming H. Revell, Co., 1914.

SMITH, OSWALD, J. *The Book of Revelation.* Grand Rapids: Zondervan Publishing House, [n. d.].

———. *Daniel's Seventieth Week.* Grand Rapids: Zondervan Publishing House, 1932.

SMITH, WILBUR M. *A Preliminary Bibliography for the Study of Biblical Prophecy.* Boston: W. A. Wilde Co., 1952.

———. *Egypt in Biblical Prophecy.* Boston: W. A. Wilde Co., 1957.

———. "The Prophetic Literature of Colonial America," *Bibliotheca Sacra,* 100:67-82, January, 1943; 100:273-88, April, 1943.

———. *This Atomic Age and the Word of God.* Boston: W. A. Wilde, Co. 1948.

———. *World Crisis in the Light of Prophetic Scriptures.* Chicago: Moody Press, 1951.

SNOWDEN, JAMES H. *The Coming of the Lord.* New York: The Macmillan Co., 1919.

STANTON, GERALD B. *Kept from the Hour.* Grand Rapids: Zondervan Publishing House, 1956.

STEVENS, GEORGE B. *The Theology of the New Testament.* New York: Charles Scribner's Sons, 1914.

STIFLER, JAMES M. *The Epistle to the Romans, a Commentary Logical and Historical.* New York: Fleming H. Revell, 1897.

STROMBECK, J. F. *First the Rapture.* Moline, Illinois: Strombeck Agency, Inc., 1950.

STRONG, A. H. *Systematic Theology.* 3 vols. Philadelphia: American Baptist Publication Society, 1907.

SWETE, H. B. *The Apocalypse of St. John.* New York: The Macmillan Co. 1906.

TALBOT, LOUIS T. *The Prophecies of Daniel.* Wheaton, Illinois: Van Kampen Press, 1954.

TERRY, MILTON S. *Biblical Hermeneutics*. New York: The Methodist Book Concern, 1883.

THAYER, JOSEPH H. *A Greek-English Lexicon of the New Testament*. New York: American Book Co., 1886.

THIESSEN, HENRY C. *Introductory Lectures in Systematic Theology*. Grand Rapids: William B. Eerdmans Publishing Co., 1949.

———. *Will the Church Pass Through the Tribulation?* New York: Loizeaux Brothers, 1941.

TODD, JAMES H. *Principles of Interpretation*. Chicago: The Bible Institute Colportage Association, 1932.

TREGELLES, S. P. *The Hope of Christ's Second Coming*. London: Samuel Bagster and Sons, 1886.

———. *Remarks on the Prophetic Visions in the Book of Daniel*. Sixth edition. London: Bagster, 1883.

TRUMBULL, CHARLES G. "The Rapture and the Tribulation," *Sunday School Times*, 80:329-34, May 7, 1938.

UNGER, MERRILL F. *Great Neglected Bible Prophecies*. Chicago: Scripture Press, 1955.

———. "The Temple Vision of Ezekiel," *Bibliotheca Sacra*, 105:427-28, October, 1948.

URQUHART, JOHN. *Wonders of Prophecy*. Sixth edition. New York: Christian Alliance Publishers, 1925.

VAN OOSTERZEE, JAN JACOB. *Christian Dogmatics*. New York: Charles Scribner's Sons, [n. d.].

VOS, GEERHARDUS. *The Kingdom of God and the Church*. New York: American Tract Society, 1903.

———. *The Pauline Eschatology*. Grand Rapids: William B. Eerdmans Publishing Co., 1952

WALVOORD, JOHN F. *The Rapture Question*. Findlay, Ohio: Dunham Publishing Co., 1957.

————. *The Return of the Lord.* Findlay, Ohio: Dunham Publishing Co., 1955.

WARFIELD, B. B. *Biblical Doctrines.* New York: Oxford University Press, 1929.

————. *Studies in Tertullian and Augustine.* New York: Oxford University Press, 1930.

WAUGH, T. *When Jesus Comes.* London: Charles H. Kelly, 1901.

Webster's New International Dictionary. Second edition. Springfield, Massachusetts: G. and C. Merriam Co., 1941.

WEST, NATHANIEL. *Daniel's Great Prophecy.* New York: The Hope of Israel Movement, 1898.

————. *The Thousand Years in Both Testaments.* New York: Fleming H. Revell, 1880.

WHITING, ARTHUR B., "The Rapture of the Church," *Bibliotheca Sacra,* 102:360-72, July, 1945; 490-99, December, 1945.

WILKINSON, SAMUEL H. *The Israel Promises and Their Fulfillment.* London: John Bale, Sons and Danielsson, Ltd. 1936.

WOODRING, CHESTER. "The Millennial Glory of Christ." Unpublished Master's thesis, Dallas Theological Seminary, Dallas, 1950.

WUEST, KENNETH S. *Prophetic Light in the Present Darkness.* Grand Rapids: William B. Eerdmans Publishing Co., 1955.

WYNGAARDEN, MARTIN J. *The Future of the Kingdom in Prophecy and Fulfillment.* Grand Rapids: Zondervan Publishing House, 1934.

————. "The New Covenant in Biblical Theology," *The Calvin Forum,* 11:208-12, May, 1946.

YOUNG, EDWARD J. *The Prophecy of Daniel.* Grand Rapids: William B. Eerdmans Publishing Co., 1949.

TOPICAL INDEX

INDEX TO SCRIPTURES